THE COMMENTATORS' ROSH CHODESH

THE COMMENTATORS' ROSH CHODESH

Halachic and aggadic interpretations, laws and customs regarding the celebration of the new month

by

RAV YITZCHAK SENDER

DESIGN EDITOR
DAVID C. ZARETSKY

FIRST EDITION

FELDHEIM PUBLISHERS
Jerusalem / New York

THE COMMENTATORS' ROSH CHODESH

First Edition
March 2002

ISBN 1-58330-521-1

Copyright © 2002
by Rabbi Yitzchak Sender

All rights reserved. No part of this book may be translated, reproduced, stored in a retrieval system or transmitted in any form or by any means, electronic, mechanical, photocopying, recording or otherwise, without prior permission in writing from the publisher.

Address of the Author:
Rabbi Yitzchak Sender
6620 North Whipple
Chicago, IL 60645

Feldheim Publishers, POB 35002 / Jerusalem, Israel
Feldheim Publishers, 200 Airport Executive Park, Nanuet, NY 10954

www.feldheim.com

Printed in Israel

ברכה
מהגאון הגדול, פאר הדור,
מרן ר' שלמה זלמן אויערבאך זצוק"ל
ראש הישיבה "קול תורה" בירושלים
ומחבר ספר "מעדני ארץ" ב"ח ועוד

ב"ה

כבר איתמחי האי גברא יקירא ידידי הרה"ג המופלא והמהולל מוה"ר יצחק אייזיק סנדר שליט"א ונודע לתהלה בספריו היקרים שזכה לחבר על הרבה ענינים חשובים וגדולי תורה נתנו עליהם עדותם ויהללו אותם. אשר על כן גם יקרתו של ספר חשוב זה תעיד על ערכו החשוב וכל מכתב תהלה אך למותר הוא. רק מברך אני את ידידי הרה"ג המחבר שנותן התורה יהא בעזרו וימלא משאלות לבו להיות שבתו כל הימים באהלה של תורה ולהרביץ תורה לרבים מתוך הרחבה ושמחה וגם יפוצו מעינותיו חוצה להג-דיל תורה ולהאדירה כאות נפשו ונפש ידידו ומוקירו.

שלמה זלמן אויערבאך

In memory of my dear friend,

HaRav Victor Segal, ז"ל

CONTENTS

PREFACE 1

CHAPTER ONE: BIRCAS HACHODESH — THE BLESSING OF THE NEW MONTH 7

   I.   THE UNIQUENESS OF THE HEBREW CALENDAR MONTH 8
        THE TUR AND THE SHULCHAN ARUCH DO NOT MENTION THIS CUSTOM 9
        "הכרזת החודש" OR "ברכת החודש" 9
   II. THE PURPOSE OF THIS PRAYER 11
   III. THE RATIONALE BEHIND THE ASHKENAZI PRACTICE 14
   IV. UNDERSTANDING THE TUR AND THE SHULCHAN ARUCH 18
   V.   REINFORCING OUR PREVIOUS THEORY 18
   VI. RECONCILING FURTHER QUESTIONS 22
   VII. FOUR QUESTIONS ON THE BIRCAS HACHODESH CEREMONY 25
   VIII. RESOLVING OUR QUESTIONS 27
   IX. THE MITZVOS OF KIDDUSH HACHODESH 28
   X.   THE PRAYERS OF THE BIRCAS HACHODESH 30
   XI. "אהבת תורה ויראת שמים" – WHY THE REDUNDANCY? 33
   XII. "מי שעשה נסים" — ITS RELEVANCE TO BIRCAS HACHODESH 35
   XIII. "ALL YISRAEL ARE COMRADES" — "חברים כל ישראל" 39
   XIV. ALIYAS HAREGEL AND BUILDING THE BAIS HAMIKDASH 41
   XV. THE PRAYER OF "יחדשהו" 44

CHAPTER TWO: THE PRAYER OF יעלה ויבוא 49

   I.   WHERE DOES THIS PRAYER BELONG? 50
   II. THE DIFFERENCE BETWEEN "ואומר" AND "ומוסיף" 52
        REINFORCING THIS CONCEPT 53
        OTHER CASES OF "ואומר" AND "ומוסיף" 54
        UNDERSTANDING ANOTHER HALACHA 56
        AN APPARENT CONTRADICTION 57
        RESOLVING THIS APPARENT CONTRADICTION 59
   III. יעלה ויבוא AND ITS VARIOUS PRAYERS 60
        EXPLAINING THE DIFFERENCE 64
   IV. קדושת היום OR מעין המאורע 66
   V.   TWO DIFFERENT TEXTS 67
        RECONCILING DIFFERENCES 69
   VI. TWO VIEWS: WHERE TO INSERT יעלה ויבוא 71

VII.	Explaining R' Eliezer's View	73
VIII.	Justifying R' Eliezer's View	76
IX.	A Different Approach	79
X.	Explaining R' Eliezer – Homiletically	81
XI.	If one forgot to say יעלה ויבוא — Two Opinions	83
	Questioning the decision of the Rema	85
XII.	Another way to view this difference of opinion	86
	Another possible explanation	87
	Suggesting a resolution	89
	Defending the Magen Avraham	90
XIII.	If one mentioned Rosh Chodesh in the שמע קולנו	92
XIV.	The מאמר מרדכי disagrees	95
	Refuting both proofs	98

Chapter Three: The Half Hallel of Rosh Chodesh 101

I.	Half-Hallel on Rosh Chodesh – A minhag	102
II.	Various explanations of why Half-Hallel	103
	As a memorial to the Kiddush HaChodesh ceremony	103
	To publicize that today is Rosh Chodesh	104
	Questioning the Meiri's rationale	105
III.	A memorial to the Bais HaMikdash	107
	Hallel of Rosh Chodesh – song of the future	107
IV.	Two forms of Hallel	109
V.	Hallel commemorates extraordinary miracles	111
VI.	Rashi: Hallel recited only for something new	113
	A possible answer	114
	The three components of Hallel	116
VII.	Two types of Hallel	118
	Hallel of Shirah	118
	Hallel of Kriyah	118
	Another reason for half Hallel	120
	Justifying the abridged version	121
VIII.	The sources for the sequence of Hallel	122
IX.	Why do we need this source?	123
X.	The manner of how to say Hallel	126
XI.	Reciting Hallel in poetic fashion	129
XII.	The Exodus: A miracle outside the Land of Yisrael	130
	The question of the טורי אבן	133
	Other questions	135
XIII.	Answering these questions	136
	Answering our other questions	138
XIV.	The Halachic Status of Half-Hallel	139
	Answering these questions	140

	THE RATIONALE OF THE MEIRI AND THE MAHARASHA	140
	THE RATIONALE OF THE YERUSHALMI	142
	THE RATIONALE OF RABBENU YONA	142
XV.	IS HALF-HALLEL A LEGITIMATE HALLEL	143
	THE LEGITIMACY OF HALF-HALLEL	146

CHAPTER FOUR: THE PROHIBITION AGAINST WORKING ON ROSH CHODESH 151

I.	CONTRARY INDICATIONS IN THE GEMARA	152
II.	QUESTIONS ARISING FROM THE GEMARA	154
III.	RASHI: AN APPARENT CONTRADICTION	157
IV.	THE APPROACH OF THE טורי אבן	159
	THE VIEW OF HARAV YOSEF DOV SOLOVEITCHIK	161
	OTHER EXPLANATIONS OF PROHIBITING WORK ON ROSH CHODESH	163
V.	PUBLICIZING ROSH CHODESH WITH VARIOUS MITZVOS	161
	ANSWERING OUR PREVIOUS QUESTIONS	169
VI.	ROSH CHODESH: A SPECIAL GIFT TO THE WOMEN	170

CHAPTER FIVE: THE MITZVA OF KIDDUSH LEVANAH 173

I.	THE MESSAGE OF KIDDUSH LEVANAH	174
II.	THE SOURCE FOR THIS MITZVAH	175
III.	ANSWERING THESE QUESTIONS	177
IV.	UNTIL WHEN MAY WE BLESS THE NEW MOON?	181
	RASHI'S OPINION	182
	THE VIEW OF THE MAHARSHAL (מהרש"ל)	182
	THE OBJECTION OF THE MAHARSHA (מהרש"א)	184
V.	WHAT KIND OF BLESSING IS KIDDUSH LEVANA?	185
	THE GEMARA'S SOLUTION	188
VI.	THE CONCLUDING BERACHA — "מחדש" OR "מקדש"	190
	THE OPINION OF THE תניא רבתי	191
	THE TEXT OF THE MIDRASH RABBAH	192
	ANSWERING THE COMMENTATORS	193
VII.	IS KIDDUSH LEVANA A TIME-BOUND MITZVAH?	195
VIII.	MAN'S ROLE IN RESTORING THE MOON TO ITS ORIGINAL SIZE	198

CHAPTER SIX: THE PRAYERS AND CUSTOMS OF ROSH CHODESH 201

I.	THE PSALM OF THE DAY RECITED ON WEEKDAYS	202
II.	THE PSALM OF THE MUSSAF SACRIFICE	204

	On Shabbos Day	204
	On Rosh Chodesh	205
	On Yom Tov	205
III.	Various problems	206
	A possible solution	208
IV.	Answering all our previous questions	209
V.	Raising other questions	212
VI.	Reciting the Prayer of "וראשי חדשיכם"	215
	Answering the objections of the "המנהיג"	217
VII.	The Laws of the Mussaf Prayers	219
	The question of the צל"ח	220
VIII.	Answering the צל"ח	222
	Taking issues with this view	225
IX.	The Nusach of the Mussaf Rosh Chodesh Prayer	226
	The Shabbos Rosh Chodesh prayer of "אתה יצרת"	227
X.	"תמידים כסדרם ומוספים כהלכתם"	229
XI.	The structure of the concluding beracha	232
XII.	The Haftarah of Rosh Chodesh	235
XIII.	Justifying the Haftarah of "מחר חדש"	237
XIV.	When do we read "מחר חדש"?	238

Chapter Seven: The Mitzva of Kiddush HaChodesh 243

I.	Sefer Bereishis and Kiddush HaChodesh	244
	Answering the question of the Griz HaLevi	246
II.	Explaining Rashi	247
III.	Not the first but the foremost mitzva	249
IV.	The purpose of this mitzva	251
	Man's natural tendency to be fascinated by the heavenly bodies	251
V.	The approach of the "Akeidas Yitzchak"	255
VI.	The view of Abarbanel	257
VII.	The view of the הר"ן דרשות	259
VIII.	Other explanations of this matter: Rashi	263
	The insight of the Ritba	264
IX.	It is a mitzva to count the months	266
X.	Various interpretations of the Ramban	268
	The position of the מהר"ץ חיות	269
	The Opinions of the ר"י בן חביב and the מהר"ל	270
XI.	Clarifying the position of the Ramban	272
	According to the "מהר"ץ חיות"	272
	According to the מהר"ל	274
XII.	Applying the insight of the חתם סופר	274

XIII.	Bais Din determines the month, year and seasons	277
	The opinion of the Rambam	279
XIV.	The Rambam's position according to the גרי"ז הלוי	282
XV.	The opinion of the Ramban	285
XVI.	HaRav Perlow's objection to the Ramban's proofs	288
	Defending the Ramban	290
	The insight of the sefer "אגן הסהר"	291

Chapter Eight: How the Month is Determined 295

I.	Various methods of determining the "new moon"	296
	Rashi's comments here	297
II.	Not all agree	299
	The Sages differ on this issue	300
III.	Exactly when can the moon be sighted?	302
	The Maharal reconciles Torah and science	304
IV.	Do Eyewitnesses Determine or only Indicate?	305
	The opinion of the ראב"ח	306
	The opinion of the "כפתור ופרח"	307
	Explaining the views of the Rishonim	308
	Expanding on the view of the "כפתור ופרח"	308
V.	Did Moshe Rabbenu receive prophecy at night?	312
	The opinion of the Ibn Ezra	313
	The view of the Ramban	313
	The Abarbanel defends the Ibn Ezra	314
	Questioning the Ramban	314
	A new insight regarding Moshe's prophecies	315
VI.	Is Rosh Chodesh one day or two?	317
	The Rambam's explanation	318
	Rosh Chodesh in the era of eyewitnesses	319
	The opinion that Rosh Chodesh was only one day	320
	Rashi's view	320
	The opinion that Rosh Chodesh was two days	321
	Another proof that two days were always observed	322
	Why two days of Rosh Chodesh?	323
	The opinion of the "בנין אריאל"	324
	The opinion of the צל"ח	325
	The insight of the "אור גדול"	326
VII.	The Bais Din Determines the New Month	326
	The opinion of the ריטב"א	328
VIII.	Sanctifying the day of Rosh Chodesh	329
IX.	What is meant by "?קידשוהו שמים"	332
	Rashi's opinion	332

	THE OPINION OF TOSAFOS	333
	ANSWERING THE QUESTION OF THE "כלי חמדה"	333
X.	THE OPINIONS OF THE MEIRI, RABBENU YONA AND THE	
	CHIDDUSHEI HARAN	335
	THE CONSEQUENCES OF THESE DIFFERENT OPINIONS	336
XI.	WHICH TAKES PRECEDENCE: EYEWITNESSES OR CALCULATION?	337
	THE OPINION OF RABBENU SAADIA GAON, THE "רס"ג	338
	THE RAMBAM'S OPINION	341
	THE OPINION OF THE RAMBAN	342
XII.	QUESTIONING THE POSITION OF RAV SAADIA GAON	343
	CHALLENGING THE RAMBAM'S POSITION	344
	DEFENDING THE RAMBAM	347
XIII.	A SOURCE FOR THE RAMBAM'S POSITION	348
	THE GRIZ HALEVI: NOT BY MERE CALCULATION ALONE	349

CHAPTER NINE: KIDDUSH HACHODESH ONLY IN ERETZ YISRAEL **353**

I.	THE SOURCE FOR THIS HALACHA	354
	THE POSITION OF THE מהרש"א	355
II.	THE VIEW OF THE צל"ח	357
	EXPLAINING THE THINKING OF THE צל"ח	358
III.	THE INSIGHT OF THE "דורות הראשונים"	360
IV.	WHERE IS KIDDUSH HACHODESH ALLUDED TO?	361
V.	THE SECOND APPROACH OF THE מהרש"א	363
	THE INSIGHT OF HARAV BEZALEL HAKOHEN OF VILNA	363
	TWO POSSIBLE WAYS OF UNDERSTANDING "כי מציון"	364
	RAMBAM'S POSITION QUESTIONED	366
	DEFENDING THE RAMBAM	368
VI.	EXPLORING THE RAMBAM'S POSITION	370
VII.	CALCULATION IN THE DIASPORA	372
	THE RAMBAM'S POSITION	374
VIII.	THE LAW OF "לא הניח כמותו"	376
	THE OPINION OF THE PIRKEI D'REBBE ELIEZER	377
	RECONCILING THE ISSUES	378
	THE CHASAM SOFER AGREES	378
	A SECOND DISTINCTION	381
IX.	THE QUESTION OF תוספות חדשים	382
X.	WHO WAS GREATER: R' AKIVA OR R' ELAZAR BEN AZARIA?	383
	WHO IS GREATER IN TORAH OR IN ASTRONOMY?	384
XI.	THE QUESTION OF THE "דורות הראשונים"	385
	THE אבני נזר ADDRESSES THESE QUESTIONS	387
XII.	WHAT IF THE GADOL HADOR IN ERETZ YISRAEL CANNOT ACT?	388

Chapter Ten: The Role of Sanhedrin in Sanctifying the Month 391

I. Bais Din HaGadol or Semicha 392
   The opinion of the Rambam 393
   The Ramban's objections 394
   Defending the Rambam 396
   Clarifying this rationale 397
II. Other objections cited by the Ramban 398
   The "מגילת אסתר" dismisses these proofs 400
   The Ramban's view: three סמוכים suffice 400
   Defending the Rambam 401
III. The Semichah Controversy 402
   The objection of the RalBach 404
   Rav Yaacov Berav's Response 405
   The Ralbach answers Rav Berav 405
IV. The Rambam's view in Sefer HaMitzvos 406
   Rav Yaacov Berav's explanation 408
   The Ralbach answers the Ramban 409
   The Acharonim and the questions of the Ramban 410
   The insight of the "שו״ת נפש חיה" 410
V. Justifying the legality of our calendar 412
   Answering the second question 413
VI. The insight of the "אוצר התפלות" 416
   Reinforcing the approach of the אוצר התפלות 417

Chapter Eleven: The Rosh Chodesh Witnesses 419

I. Three categories of witnesses 420
   Explaining the order of Mishnayos Rosh Hashanah 420
   Eyewitnesses 423
   The Rishonim present the sources 424
   Refuting Rav Saadia Gaon 426
II. Time allotted for travel on Shabbos 427
   The question of the Yerushalmi 428
III. Desecrating the Shabbos to provide eyewitnesses 430
   The question of the טורי אבן 431
   Answering the טורי אבן 432
   Travelling more than twenty-four hours on the Shabbos 433
   Two possible solutions 435
IV. Can character witnesses desecrate the Shabbos 436
   Trying to fool the Bais Din 438
   Desecrating the Shabbos even when in doubt 439
V. Messengers sent to proclaim Rosh Chodesh 440

	Why didn't the torch-lighting system precede the sending of messengers	446
VI.	Shabbos must not be desecrated	447
	No difference between Nissan, Tishrei and any other month	449
	One witness is enough	451
	The messengers sent other messengers	454
VII.	The "six months" when messengers were sent forth	455
VIII.	Kislev on account of Chanukah	457
	The unique position of the "מנחת חינוך"	458
IX.	Ineligible witnesses disqualify eligible witnesses	461
	Resolving the question of the "מנחת חינוך"	464
	The insight of the "קהלת יעקב"	464

Chapter 12: The Unique Laws of Kiddush HaChodesh 467

I.	The law of "אתם"	468
	Answering the above questions	473
	There is an "order" to the Mishna	474
II.	When to apply the law of "אתם"	478
	All agree to the application of "אתם"	480
III.	"אתם" said only "בזמנו"	482
IV.	The law of "אתם" in determining a leap year	484
	Dismissing these proofs — מנ"ח	485
	Defending the צל"ח	487
	The Yerushalmi and Tosefta dispute this matter	488
V.	"אתם" only relates to Bais Din of Eretz Yisroel	489
	The טורי אבן questions these views	492
	The insight of the "יסוד עולם"	492
	The ריטב"א disagrees with Tosafos	493
VI.	The difference between אתם and לא תסור	494
	The opinion of the רמב"ן	495
	Questioning the Ramban	496
VII.	Sanctifying the month retroactively	497
	The objections of the ריטב"א and רשב"א	499
	Defending the Rambam	500
	The opinion of the הגרי"ז הלוי	501
	The insight of the "נתיבות חיים"	501
	The answer of the "תרועת המלך"	502
	"Four or Five Days" is to be understood literally	504
VIII.	Preserving the rituals of Rosh Hashanah	506

PREFACE

Rashi begins his commentary on the Torah with the following question. Since the Torah is a book of laws, it should have begun with the very first mitzva that Bnai Yisrael were commanded to observe, namely the mitzva of Kiddush HaChodesh. Why, then, does the Torah begin with the story of Creation in Sefer Bereishis? Rashi answers that if the nations of the world were to claim that Bnai Yisrael were robbers, for they seized the land of Canaan and occupied it, the Torah proves that the whole world belongs to Hashem, for He created it by His will and He gave it to whomever He pleased. Rashi states that Yisrael can convincingly reply to the nations: "When He willed, He gave it to them, and when He willed, He took it from them and gave it to us."

Yet one might still ask, even though it is true that Hashem is the Master of the world, and He can give Eretz Yisrael to whomever He wishes, how do we know that He wished to give Eretz Yisrael to Bnai Yisrael? The answer is obvious — the Torah tells us that Hashem promised our forefathers (the Avos) that their children would inherit the land. But, once again, we might contend, as do the nations of the world, that Hashem fulfilled His promise by giving their descendants the land of Yisrael once in the distant past. But *now* He desires to give it to someone else. What proof do we have that Eretz Yisrael is ours even today?

We might suggest an answer here which gives a deeper meaning to Rashi's words. The Rambam, in his commentary on the Mishna in *Mesechtas Chullin 7:6* writes: "Be aware of the fundamental principle...that all the mitzvos which are observed today are observed only because Hashem commanded them to Moshe and not because He commanded the prophets who preceded him."

The "משך חכמה", in *Parashas VeZos Haberacha* asks, what difference does it make whether we observe the commandments because they were given by Moshe Rabbenu or because they were given to the Avos and the earlier prophets? Isn't the end result the same? Hashem commanded us to perform these mitzvos and we must do so, no matter who presented them to us? Why then is it a fundamental principle that we observe the mitzvos only because they were given to us by Moshe Rabbenu?

The answer to this question, maintains the "משך חכמה", is that Moshe Rabbenu's words are binding on us forever, because his prophecy was on the highest possible level — "באספקלריה המאירה" — as if looking into a transparent mirror. Thus it is impossible for any future miracle or sign by any future prophet to contradict or overturn any of Moshe Rabbenu's prophetic statements. It is on this level that the Torah was written, and this demonstrates that it is eternal. And indeed, if a future prophet were to attempt to nullify any of the commandments which were given to us through Moshe Rabbenu, the Torah cautions us to consider such a person a false prophet and a charlatan. This means that if we were to observe the mitzvos because we were enjoined to do so by the Avos, whose prophetic vision was not on as high a level as that of Moshe Rabbenu, the danger would exist that in the future another so-called "prophet" might arise who would claim that Hashem "told" him to nullify these mitzvos of the Avos.

Thus we might say that this is what Rashi had in mind here in his comments on the beginning of Sefer Bereishis. The story of Creation and the whole of Sefer Bereishis had to be written by Moshe Rabbenu and included as part of the Torah, in order to underscore the fact that the promise given to the Avos regarding Eretz Yisrael was eternal and no one can claim that Hashem changed His mind and now desires to give the land to someone other than Bnai Yisrael. Thus, because we received the Torah through Moshe Rabbenu, we know that the Torah and its mitzvos retain the status of eternity — נצחיות — and Hashem's promise of Eretz Yisrael to the Jewish people is a promise for all time.

We might explain homiletically Rashi's question why the Torah began with the mitzva of Kiddush HaChodesh by pointing out that the Torah was meant to teach Klal Yisrael throughout the generations how to live, and therefore the lives of the Avos and the life of Yosef HaTzaddik also served as examples of how one must conduct oneself with righteousness.

In every generation the Jew is confronted with numerous tests of faith, נסיונות. Sometimes we are faced with overpowering coercion from the nations of the world to forsake our religious observance and our faith in Hashem. Sometimes we have no other choice but to live as a "lonely man of faith", out of step with the rest of the modern world and surrounded by an environment hostile to the ethical and moral values of the Torah. It is for this reason that the Torah teaches us about the lives of our forefathers, in order to remind us of the values they represented in their lives and to inspire us to emulate these same values in our own lives. Thus we are told of Avraham Aveinu that he was called "אברהם העברי" to allude to the fact that the entire world was on one side and Avraham was on the other. Avraham's lifestyle was completely different from that of the rest of society. And if we can imagine the daily life of Avraham Aveinu we will realize that he did not wake up in the morning and go to attend a daily minyan in a synagogue packed with other Jews. On Shabbos day he did not sit at a *tisch,* a festive table filled with Jews all singing zemiros. Rather he was a solitary Jew, all alone in a hostile world, and yet he served Hashem with perfect faith. So, too, were the other Avos challenged in the same way, and in addition they tasted the bitter pill of antisemitism. Yosef and his children lived alone in a world steeped in idolatry and immorality and yet they stood their ground and were true to their beliefs and acted righteously.

Throughout the generations, when faced with these challenges, Jews have called upon the Avos for inspiration and as role models to help them through whatever circumstances they might find themselves in. Thus we can see the vital importance of Sefer Bereishis, for it serves to give us hope and teach us how to survive as a Jew.

This led Rashi to ask, if the purpose of presenting the lives of our forefathers was to give us hope and inspiration to survive as a nation, then isn't this lesson also alluded to in the first mitzva, that of Kiddush HaChodesh?

As our midrashim and classic commentators tell us, Kiddush HaChodesh is a particularly appropriate mitzva with which to begin the Torah, because the life of the Jew waxes and wanes very much like the cycle of the moon. There are times when the moon shines brightly, yet at other times it almost disappears from view. However, it then returns and shines once again. This reflects the history of the Jewish people. We lived through a golden age and then descended into a dark era, when it seemed as though the Jew would vanish from the face of the earth. But then we reappeared, to shine even more brightly then ever. And we were given the assurance that with the coming of Moshiach we would shine more brightly still. And yet we might ask, if the mitzva of Kiddush HaChodesh teaches us the same lesson we can learn from the lives of our forefathers, why did the Torah expound for us the story of their lives and their deeds?

A possible answer might be that that even though it is true that the mitzva of Kiddush HaChodesh teaches us the lesson of hope, yet this only extends to the existence of the Jewish people as a whole. However, it is the lives of our Avos in all their details which offers us hope and inspires us as individuals. This is the reason why the entire book of Bereishis was committed to writing.

In light of this, we can explain the goal and structure of this sefer which details the laws and customs of Rosh Chodesh and the mitzva of Kiddush HaChodesh. For the prayers and the practice of Rosh Chodesh serve as an inspiration to us, a beacon of hope for each individual Jew to live with anticipation and renewed vigor to serve Hashem in the new month. The mitzva of Kiddush HaChodesh offers us hope and belief in the Ultimate Redemption of the Jewish nation and with it the re-emergence of the mitzva of Kiddush HaChodesh as it was practiced in the Bais HaMikdash, which we pray will be rebuilt speedily in our days.

Once again, I wish to express my sincere and heartfelt gratitude to all those contributors who made this present publication possible. I am grateful not only for their generosity in material terms, but also for the generosity of spirit evident in the gracious manner in which their contributions were given.

A special debt of gratitude to Harvey Klineman, who designed the cover of this sefer. His artistic abilities and expertise have greatly enhanced the appearance of this sefer and many others in this series.

I also offer my heartfelt thanks to my editor and friend Mrs. Wendy Dickstein, who has as always given of herself above and beyond the call of duty. Her talents and dedication have made this volume what it is.

A special thanks to my friend David Zaretsky for his talented contribution to the final layout and an acknowledgement of his technical abilities.

Finally, and most important, my gratitude to my dear wife, הרבנית נחמה תחי׳, for all of her encouragement and for affording me the time and opportunity to work on this sefer. May Hashem bless her and our children and grandchildren with the strength, health and dedication to continue the teachings of the Torah and mitzvos to His people.

Chapter One
Bircas HaChodesh: The Blessing of the New Month

I

The Uniqueness of the Hebrew Calendar Month

The Zultzbach Machzor presents a remarkable insight into the reason we recite Bircas HaChodesh, the blessing of the new month. In modern times we have a fixed calendar, which was established by Hillel II, the son of Rav Yehudah N'siah II. This might lead us to believe that our calendar is nothing more than a tool with which we mark the number of days in a month, and that the first day of the month is simply "day one" of a particular division of time into thirty day intervals, with no particular spiritual significance.

To dispel this illusion, the religious ceremony of Bircas HaChodesh was instituted, accompanied by special prayers to be recited at this time. This ceremony signifies that a new spiritual entity was coming into being with the beginning of the next calendar month. Thus, this unique day was designated by the great Sage, Hillel II and sanctioned and sanctified in heaven. And because this day has religious significance, we recite the Bircas HaChodesh prayer before the actual day of Rosh Chodesh, on the Shabbos directly preceding it, in order to create an atmosphere of anticipation for the Rosh Chodesh which is soon to come.

Thus Rosh Chodesh is not simply another day being marked off on the calendar but has special significance, and it is fitting to celebrate it with dignity and honor. In addition, the ceremony of Bircas HaChodesh serves as a reminder of the days of old, when Yisrael had an active Sanhedrin, which declared this day holy, מקודש. Thus, the day of Rosh Chodesh did not come into being on its own but was rather intentionally and deliberately designated and sanctified, after examination and testimony, as the first day of the new month.

We can take a wider view, and reflect upon the following. Every new month should inspire us to be cognizant of the Hand of Hashem at work in the world, in time and in all of creation.

And this day of Rosh Chodesh should be treated with awe as a day of special significance, and not like any other day of the month.

THE TUR AND THE SHULCHAN ARUCH DO NOT MENTION THIS CUSTOM

On the Shabbos preceding Rosh Chodesh, a special prayer is recited, whose purpose is to *bless* the congregation and *announce* to them the exact day(s) and hour when the new month will come into being. This practice has been accepted universally by all Jewish congregations, both Ashkenazi and Sephardi, and it is to be found in every siddur in every *nusach*, dating back to the days of Rav Amram Gaon. And yet, strangely enough, this ceremony of Bircas HaChodesh, blessing the new month, is mentioned neither by the Tur nor the Shulchan Aruch, even though the Shulchan Aruch does discuss שבת מברכים, the ceremony of "Welcoming of the New Month" during the synagogue service on the Shabbos preceding Rosh Chodesh. However, the reference to this ceremony is not directly connected with the laws of Rosh Chodesh, but is rather to be found in ש"ע אור"ח סימן רפ"ד, where the Rema cites the custom of not reciting the prayer of "Av HaRachamim" on the Shabbos when we bless the new month. Despite this reference, we are left with the larger question as to why neither the Tur nor the Shulchan Aruch saw fit to mention the universally accepted practice of blessing the new month on the Shabbos preceding Rosh Chodesh.

"הכרזת החודש" OR "ברכת החודש"

Just as we find a difference in custom between the Ashkenazi and the Sephardi communities in other prayers and rituals, so too do we find a number of differences between them here in regard to this ceremony of welcoming the new month. These differences can be summarized as follows:

According to the Sephardim, this prayer is referred to as "הכרזת החודש" — "Announcing the Festival of the New Month". *The chazzan alone* announces on which day(s) Rosh Chodesh will fall, and the congregation does not repeat this announcement. Furthermore, the traditional blessing of "יהי רצון מלפניך", the prayer for a blessed month, is not recited. Instead, the following short prayer is offered, which includes a petition for the welfare of Torah scholars:

יהי רצון מלפני אל-הי השמים לקים לנו את כל חכמי ישראל, הם, ונשיהם, ובניהם, ותלמידיהם, בכל מקומות מושבותיהם, ואמרו אמן.

May it be the will of the Lord of the Heavens to preserve for us all the scholars of Yisrael; them, their wives, their children and their students, in all the places they reside, and let us say, Amen.

In contrast, the prayer service of the Ashkenazim includes the following elements: the prayer for the new month is referred to as "ברכת החודש" — "Blessing the New Month", with the intention that it should be ushered in as a good and blessed month. The prayer of "יהי רצון מלפניך" expands on the blessings that constitute a "good and blessed month". The special prayer on behalf of Torah scholars which is recited by the Sephardim is not recited by Ashkenazi congregations. And finally, everyone repeats the announcement, made first by the chazzan, of what day(s) Rosh Chodesh will be.

It is important to explore these differences in custom and practice between the two communities. There are other issues which need clarification regarding how these two traditions inaugurate the new month. For example, why is the blessing for the new month — either "ברכת החודש" or "הכרזת החודש" — recited on the *Shabbos before* Rosh Chodesh rather than on Rosh Chodesh itself? Indeed, according to Rav Amran Gaon, it is recited on the day of Rosh Chodesh. Why, then, do we not follow this practice? In fact, the Aruch HaShulchan (in סימן תי"ז, ט) vehemently rejects this practice of reciting "יהי רצון מלפניך", for he contends that it violates the law that prohibits making petitions in our prayers on the Shabbos. He therefore concludes that if it were in his power, he would abolish the practice of reciting this prayer on Shabbos. The Aruch HaShulchan writes as follows:

אך מה שאומרים ה"יהי רצון" מקודם, תמיהני האיך מותר להתפלל בשבת תפלה חדשה מה שאינה בטופס ברכות אלא תפלה בפני עצמה, ומבקשים על פרנסה ושארי צרכים **ואיך מותר בשבת** ותפלה זו הוא תפלת רב בכל השנה (ברכות ט״ז) והתחלתה "שתתן לנו חיים ארוכים" ובכאן הוסיפו בתחלתו "שתחדש עלינו החדש הזה לטובה ולברכה"...

II

THE PURPOSE OF THIS PRAYER

In order to fully understand the importance of these issues, we must clarify the purpose of this prayer. All the commentators agree that it alone was never intended to sanctify the month. The "ספר יראים" (סימן ק״ג), emphasizes that it was only the Sanhedrin and the Nasi that had the authority to do that. He writes:

ומה שנהגו העולם להגיד ראש חודש בשבת **אין זה קידוש**, כי ראש בית דין אינו ביננו והמצוה הזאת אינה תלויה אלא בראש בית דין...

Neither was this prayer intended to serve as a memorial to the mitzva of sanctifying the new month, Kiddush HaChodesh, by means of witnesses, who saw the new moon and testified to this effect before the Sanhedrin — "קידוש על פי הראייה".

Proof of this can be established by the following considerations: the mitzva of Kiddush HaChodesh is fulfilled only on the day(s) of Rosh Chodesh; whereas we offer this prayer before Rosh Chodesh. This is explained in the sefer "שבלי הלקט" (סימן קע) where we read:

מה שמברכין אותו בשבת שלפני ראש חודש **אינו זכר לקידוש החודש**, שהרי, אין מקדשין ראש חודש אלא בזמנו...

The commentator, "תקון תפלה", cited in the siddur, "אוצר התפלות" offers the following proof that this prayer does not serve as a memorial, a זכר. A memorial is established only for a mitzva which was once practiced in the past but is no longer in existence, according to Torah law. For example, the mitzva of *maror*, bitter herbs, eaten at the Passover seder, was intended, according to Torah law, to accompany the Korban Pesach at the time of the Bais HaMikdash, as the Torah commands: "על מצות ומרורים יאכלוהו".

Today, however, when we no longer have a Bais HaMikdash in which to offer a Korban Pesach, we eat the bitter herbs as a rabbinic decree, מרור מדרבנן, to serve as a memorial to that maror which was once eaten according to the dictates of the Torah.

The mitzva of Kiddush HaChodesh, on the other hand, can not be a *memorial,* in the same sense, since the mitzva is still in effect today, based on the fact that Hillel II instituted a fixed calendar. We will expand upon this point later in our discussion.

And so we can say that the purpose here is to *announce* on which day(s) Rosh Chodesh will occur, so that we will be able to fulfill our obligations regarding this day as set down in the halacha.

These requirements and obligations include adding "יעלה ויבוא" to our three Amidah prayers of the day, reciting half-Hallel at Shacharis, etc. This is set forth in detail by the "ספר יראים" (ibid.):

אבל המצוה הזו **תקנת ראשונים להגיד לעולם** ראש חודש להזהיר בו ובתלוי בו...

And a similar justification for this practice is offered by the "אור זרוע", הל' ר"ח, סימן תנג:

שתקנו רבותינו להכריז בצבור...שידעו מתי יהא ראש חודש, **ויזהרו** בכל הלכות החודש.

This explains the rationale behind the Sephardic tradition and helps us to understand why they refer to this day as "הכרזת החודש" — "*Announcing* the festival of the new month". And this explains the purpose of the special prayer recited on this day. Furthermore, we can understand why no special blessing of the month accompanies this announcement, for the sole purpose here is to announce when the new month will occur, and not to offer any petitionary prayers. We can also understand why a prayer was recited in honor of Torah scholars, since they were the ones who proclaimed this day as Rosh Chodesh, both in the past and in the present; and therefore we honor them for their endeavors on behalf of Klal Yisrael. This is articulated by the Avudraham, in "הכרזת ר"ח", where we find the following:

והטעם שמבקשין רחמים על החחכמים **בהכרזת** ר"ח מה שלא מצינו כן בכל מקום בעולם, מפני **שהם** היו מקדשין החודש בזמנו על פי הראייה, כי להם נמסר קדושו, שנאמר "אלה מועדי ה' מקראי קדש אשר תקראו אתם", "אתם" כתיב...ולולי הם לא היינו יודעים מתי יבא החדש. ולכן אנו מזכירין אותם לטובה, שיקיים אותם הבורא ויחזיר עטרה ליושנה ויקדשו החודש כבראשונה...

And we can now appreciate why it is only the chazzan who announces when Rosh Chodesh will be, and this declaration need not be repeated by the congregation, for, as we have seen, the purpose of this prayer is simply to make an announcement, which can be done by a single individual-in this case, the chazzan-and everyone else need do nothing more than just listen to what is being announced.

III

THE RATIONALE BEHIND THE ASHKENAZI PRACTICE

Some commentators maintain that the Ashkenazi practice of ברכת החודש should also be viewed as an act of fulfilling the requirement of announcing the new month. However, since a blessing for the new month was recited as well, in time people came to refer to this ritual as "blessing the new month" rather than "announcing the new month".

This explanation, though, does not answer the basic question as to why a prayer was attached to this required announcement. To answer this question, we must examine the Mishna in Succah 3/12, which tells us that originally, when the Bais HaMikdash was in existence, the lulav was taken for seven days. Anywhere other than the Bais HaMikdash, it was taken for only one day. This is based on the pasuk "ושמחתם לפני ה' אל-היכם שבעת ימים" — "And you shall rejoice before Hashem, your God, for seven days." *(Vayikra 23:40)*. The Torah here does not tell us explicitly that we are to take the lulav in the Bais HaMikdash; it says merely, "לפני ה'" — "before Hashem'. From here we understand that this alludes to the place where the Divine Presence, the *Shechinah*, rests; that is, the Bais HaMikdash, Hashem's Holy Temple.

The Rambam, however, in his commentary on the fourth chapter of Mesechtas Rosh HaShanah, contends that the holy city of Yerushalayim in its entirety is to be considered a place where the Divine Presence dwells, "לפני ה'". Based on this consideration, the ערוך לנר in his classic sefer (סימן תר"נ ח"א) "בכורי יעקב" maintains that even today the lulav is to be taken in Yerushalayim all seven days of the festival of Succos, as dictated by the Torah. And this means that all the stringencies attached to the requirements of lulav are to be applied. On the other hand, if we were to take the lulav all seven days only as a זכר, a memorial to the time the Bais HaMikdash stood, this practice would have Rabbinic sanction alone, and thus we would be able to waive many of the laws relating to the mitzva of lulav.

This raises another question. We are taught that Rabban Yochanan ben Zakkai instituted that the lulav be taken in the provinces for seven days "in remembrance of the Temple" — זכר למקדש. However, if it is as the Rambam contends, and the stipulation that we are to take the lulav for seven days in Yerushalayim is based on the pasuk of "ושמחתם לפני ה' אל-היכם" then why do we need a memorial in the provinces, for isn't a memorial applicable only when a mitzva no longer exists? Yet the mitzva dictated by the Torah, to take the lulav for seven days, has not ceased to exist.

To explain this, we might suggest the following rationale. According to the Aruch LaNer, what we have here is not a memorial to the mitzva of lulav being taken for seven days, for, as we have pointed out, this needs no memorial. But rather the memorial is to what once transpired in the Holy Temple, a "זכר למקדש". We commemorate that a lulav was taken there for seven days, and because this is no longer done, only a memorial of this practice remains.

Similarly, in regard to our ritual of Bircas HaChodesh, we do not actually sanctify the new month in the way they did at the time of the Sanhedrin, and furthermore, we do not need a memorial of this mitzva, for, as we have said, the mitzva is still intact because of the enactment of Hillel II. And yet we make a memorial to the *ceremony*, the celebration at the time the new month was determined by eye-witnesses and the Sanhedrin was seated in the "Chamber of Hewn Stone" — לשכת הגזית. Thus when we recite the Bircas HaChodesh today, we are commemorating that inspiring ceremony as a זכר.

This leads to a further question. Why should we make a זכר, a memorial, to a mere ceremony, when it is usually made for a mitzva? The answer to this question is that the ceremony signifies much more than a mere ritual. The essence of declaring a new month based on the sighting of the moon is a celebration of the re-emergence of the Jewish people in all their former glory, and it looks forward to the time in the future when they will regain that status. Thus we not only make a זכר for the realization of past glory, but offer a prayer in anticipation of our ultimate redemption and restoration in the future to the rebuilt Yerushalayim and the Land of Yisrael.

In *Mesechtas Sofrim 9:9,* we are told that when the month was sanctified by the Bais Din, a prayer was offered to bless both the new month and the Jewish people. Since our Bircas HaChodesh today is based on that ceremony, we accompany our זכר here with the blessing offered then. In other words, the prayer we offer today is part of the ancient ceremony of Kiddush HaChodesh.

This helps answer the question asked by the Aruch HaShulchan, of how we are justified in making petitions on the Shabbos day, when this is normally forbidden. We can answer this with the words of the Aruch HaShulchan himself. He maintains that the recitation of the prayer "יחדשהו הקב״ה" and "מי שעשה נסים" even though they can be viewed as petitionary prayers, should be seen primarily as expressions of hope for the ultimate redemption of the Jewish people. Thus, when we pray that the new month be blessed, we pour out our hearts to express our deepest aspirations that Yisrael too will be renewed and restored to its former glory.

ונהגו לומר "מי שעשה נסים" ו"יחדשהו" ואין זה תפלה בשבת אלא לסימן טוב **ותקות הגאולה**, דכשם שהחדש מתחדש כמו כן יחדשהו ישראל...

Consequently, in the light of this explanation, we might suggest that the prayer of "יהי רצון מלפניך" also alludes to the hope for the restoration of the ceremony of Kiddush HaChodesh as in days of old, and therefore there is no infraction of the prohibition against offering petitions in the prayers of the Shabbos day.

With this explanation, we can now understand and appreciate the following points. We refer to this prayer as "Bircas HaChodesh", for indeed we offer a prayer as they did in days of old, when the sanctification of the new month was made by eye-witnesses.

Furthermore, we need not offer a prayer here for the scholars, for we have already done so in the Yekum Purkan, and also in the "יהי רצון", which was offered after the Kriyas HaTorah on Monday and Thursday. In addition, the Bircas HaChodesh is not intended to actually sanctify the month, rather this was done by the scholars of old. The Bircas HaChodesh of today is intended as a memorial to that elaborate ceremony which characterized the inauguration of the new month in ancient times.

Finally, we repeat the chazzan's words announcing when Rosh Chodesh will be. The reason for this is that in days of old after the Nasi proclaimed "מקודש" — that the month be sanctified — the people repeated "מקודש, מקודש", the month is to be sanctified! Thus today we follow this practice and call out the exact day of Rosh Chodesh after the chazzan has done so; thereby emulating the Kiddush HaChodesh ceremony of ancient times.

IV

UNDERSTANDING THE TUR AND THE SHULCHAN ARUCH

With this explanation in mind, we can perhaps answer our original question, which was why neither of these classic commentators mention the preliminary ceremony which takes place on the Shabbos preceding Rosh Chodesh. In Hilchos Rosh Chodesh both commentators focus their discussion on the particular laws and customs which pertain to the *day* of Rosh Chodesh itself and do not deal with the ceremony of "announcing" or "blessing" the new month. The reason they did not mention this preliminary ceremony was because it did not constitute a *law* pertaining to Rosh Chodesh itself, but rather it served as a *memorial* to the days when eye-witnesses proclaimed the new month before the Sanhedrin. Thus it was a commemoration of an ancient ritual, rather than a halacha, which was the subject of Hilchos Rosh Chodesh.

V

REINFORCING OUR PREVIOUS THEORY

We can cite further evidence to reinforce the theory that our recitation of Bircas HaChodesh today is based on the ceremony that took place at the time when the Sanhedrin proclaimed the month sanctified as a result of the testimony of eye-witnesses, "קידוש על פי הראייה". This process is described in *Mesechtas Sofrim* 19:9.

We also follow the custom of announcing the *molad*, the precise moment when the new moon makes its first appearance in Yerushalayim. Many reasons are given for this custom. The Aruch HaShulchan, for example, writes in סימן תי"ז:

המנהג לידע המולד בעת שמברכין החודש, דהבית דין כשקידשו פשיטא שבלא ידיעת המולד לא היו מקדשין.

It is the custom to announce the *molad* when we bless the new month, for it is quite obvious that the *Bais Din* were well aware when the *molad* would take place; otherwise they would not have sanctified the month.

At least one authority does indicate that a reason for calling out the coming Rosh Chodesh in advance, on the preceding Shabbos, is that the public should know and understand that Rosh Chodesh is based, in our days, not on observation, but on calculation of the Molad.

Other than this, the announcement of the Molad is related to another law connected with the Molad – that of Kiddush Levana. There is an earliest and latest time for Kiddush Levana; both times are dependent on the Molad. Thus, it is important to know when the Molad occurs, hence, the announcement.

In addition, we also spell out on which day(s) of the week Rosh Chodesh will occur. All this is done so that everyone should be aware when Rosh Chodesh will occur, and thereby act accordingly. Yet perhaps there are other reasons for these practices as well.

The Gemara in *Mesechtas Succah 54b* tells us that when Rosh Chodesh was on Shabbos, two indications were made to signify that this day was Shabbos Rosh Chodesh. First, the Psalm for Rosh Chodesh day preceded the Psalm for the Shabbos day.

ראש חודש שחל להיות בשבת, שיר של ראש חודש דוחה שיר של שבת... אמר רב ספרא מאי "דוחה", דוחה לקדם.

The Gemarah then asks:

> ואמאי, תדיר ושאינו תדיר, תדיר קודם? אמר ר' יוחנן לידע
> שהוקבע ראש חודש **בזמנו**. והא האי היכרא עבדינן? הא
> היכר אחרינא עבדינן, דתניא: חלבי תמיד של שחר ניתנין
> מחצי כבש ולמטה...ושל מוספין ניתנין מחצי כבש
> ולמטה...ושל ראש חדש ניתנין תחת כרכוב המזבח ולמטה
> [דהיינו בחצי העליון של כבש –רש"י].

According to the Gemara, this was done "in order to publicize the fact that Rosh Chodesh was established by the Court in its proper time" — "לידע שהוקבע ראש חודש בזמנו".

Rashi elaborates on this point:

> האי חשיבותא עבדינן ליה להיכרא, שיכירו דפשיטא להו
> לב"ד שקידשוהו כהלכתו ולא יגמגם לב אדם עליו, דרוב בני
> אדם לא ראו חידוש הלבנה.

Since not everyone sighted the new moon, it was necessary to publicize, as much as possible, the fact that the court had declared that day as Rosh Chodesh. Therefore, the Levites would recite the Psalm for Rosh Chodesh first, despite it being the less frequent mitzva (אינו תדיר) in order to emphasize that the day had definitely been declared Rosh Chodesh.

Although the limbs of the *Korban Tamid,* the daily sacrifice which was to be burned on the Altar and the limbs of the Mussaf sacrifice, the additional offering, were always placed on the *lower* half of the ramp, the limbs of the special Rosh Chodesh sacrifice were placed on the *upper* half of the ramp.

And the Gemara concludes as follows:

> תרי היכרא עבדינן, דחזי האי חזי, וחזי בהאי חזי.

We make two indications (one is reciting the psalm of Rosh Chodesh first, and the second is placing the Rosh Chodesh limbs on the higher part of the ramp), so that one who saw one indication saw it, while those who saw the other indication saw it, and now each one is now aware (even though he did not see *both* indications), that Rosh Chodesh had been declared properly.

Consequently, we see that there are two separate reasons for making indications to show when Rosh Chodesh occurs. The first reason is in order that Jews will be able to fulfill the specific obligations incumbent upon them on the day(s) of Rosh Chodesh. The second reason is to assure the people that the day "declared' by the Bais Din was chosen according to the halacha and is to be viewed as the legitimate day of Rosh Chodesh.

When tracing the source for this practice of assuring the people that the Bais Din correctly declared this day as Rosh Chodesh, we turn once again to the *Mesechtas Sofrim 19:9.* In the blessing recited in honor of this occasion of the Bais Din declaring this day as Rosh Chodesh, the following expressions were used:

החודש מקודש, בראש חודש מקודש, בזמנו מקודש, בעיבורו מקודש, בתורה מקודש. בהלכה מקודש, בעליונים מקודש, בתחתונים מקודש, בארץ ישראל מקודש, בציון מקודש, בכל מקומות ישראל מקודש, בפי רבותינו מקודש, בבית הועד מקודש...

Consecrated is the new moon, consecrated at the beginning of the month, consecrated in its *proper time,* consecrated at its intercalation, consecrated *according to the Torah,* consecrated *according to the halacha,* consecrated in the celestial regions, consecrated in the terrestrial regions, consecrated in the Land of Yisrael, consecrated in Zion, consecrated in Yerushalayim, consecrated in the habitations of Yisrael, consecrated *by the order of our Rabbis*, consecrated in the assembly…

Thus we see that the Bais Din was deeply concerned with assuring the people that Rosh Chodesh was properly established according to the halacha. Consequently, we might say that the present-day ceremony of Bircas HaChodesh is intended not only to specify when Rosh Chodesh occurs, so that we will be sure to abide by its laws and fulfill our particular obligations to Rosh Chodesh on that day, but also to declare that Rosh Chodesh has been duly declared according to the halacha and is to take effect in all places. Thus our celebration of Bircas HaChodesh essentially follows the prescription set down in Mesechtas Sofrim to assure the people that today is indeed Rosh Chodesh and our offering of prayers commemorates the ceremony which took place at the time of the Sanhedrin when the eye witnesses confirmed the appearance of the new moon and the people were informed that a particular day was designated as Rosh Chodesh for the observance of all the proper rituals.

VI

Reconciling Further Questions

In light of what we have presented above, we can suggest an answer to the question raised by the eminent gaon HaRav Yosef Engel, in his classic sefer "גליוני הש"ס". He explains that it is well known that when Rosh Chodesh was declared, the shofar was sounded to announce that the Bais Din had sanctified the new month. This is also explained to us by Rashi in his commentary to *Mesechtas Sanhedrin, 41b*. There the Gemara states that at the beginning of each month, a shofar was sounded, regardless of whether it was a full month (of 30 days) or a short one (of only 29 days).

ובשיפורא ידע
ופרש"י: שופר היו תוקעין בקידוש החדש ביום שהוא
מתחיל הן מלא הן חסר, וזה לא שמע את **השופר**.

    Thus, if the shofar announced the declaration of this day as Rosh Chodesh, asks Rav Engel, why did the Gemara in Mesechtas Succah (ibid.) not also include this as an additional indication? Why were there only two indications — that of reciting the psalm of Rosh Chodesh before that of the Shabbos day, and the unique placing of the limbs of the Rosh Chodesh sacrifice— why not also list the sounding of the shofar, which indeed indicated that it was Rosh Chodesh?

    Rav Engel answers that here in Mesechtas Succah the subject being addressed is when Rosh Chodesh coincides with Shabbos; and because we are not allowed to sound the shofar on Shabbos, משום שבות, this is exactly the reason why the sounding of the shofar was not included in the list of indications.

    However, we might simply say that the Gemara in Mesechtas Succah concerns itself only with those kinds of indications whose purpose was to signify that Rosh Chodesh was *duly declared* in its proper time. By changing the position of the limbs of the Rosh Chodesh sacrifice and reciting the Rosh Chodesh psalm first, this indicated that this day was indeed Rosh Chodesh. However, the purpose of sounding the shofar was simply to *announce* that today was Rosh Chodesh and to draw attention to the prescribed practices of the day.

    Following this line of thought, we can suggest an answer to the question why the Gemara did not emphasize the mere fact that a Korban Mussaf was offered on this day as being the definitive indication that this day was Rosh Chodesh. In addition, we find that the Torah demands that trumpets were to be sounded on the day of Rosh Chodesh. Why was this fact not included in the list of indications? In light of what we have explained above, the answer is simply that the trumpet, like the shofar, was sounded only to indicate that today was Rosh Chodesh. It was only the other indications which were to ensure that Rosh Chodesh would be properly designated. (See the sefer עלה החדש", עמ' מ, או"ק טז".)

Furthermore, we might suggest that when we emphasize the matter of "indications" to point out that today is Rosh Chodesh, our primary purpose is to ensure that the mitzvas of the day will be observed. For example, we wish to emphasize that the prayer of "יעלה ויבוא" must be added in the Shacharis Amidah, that half-Hallel must be recited, etc. The תשב"ץ, in his responsa "שו"ת תשב"ץ" (סימן קסא), points out that even when the Bais HaMikdash was in existence and sacrifices were offered, these additional prayers were still recited as a voluntary practice. They only became obligatory after the destruction of the Bais HaMikdash, when our Sages instituted prayer in place of the sacrifices, which could no longer be offered.

אבל התפילות בפירוש אמרו בגמרא שהיו מתפללין בזמן הבית ממה שאמרו בגמרא סוכה (נג, א): אמר רב יהושע בן חנניה כשהיינו שמחים בשמחת בית השואבה לא ראינו שינה בעינינו. כיצד שעה ראשונה היינו מקריבין תמיד של שחר משם **לתפלת שחר**. משם לקרבן מוסף משם **לתפלת מוספין**...משם **לתפלת מנחה**, משם לתמיד של בין הערבים. והרי זה מפורש שאף על פי שהיו מקריבין תמידים ותפלות כנגד תמידים תקנום, עם כל זה היו **מתפללין**.

The Gemara explicitly states that the daily order of prayers were recited during the period of the Second Temple. This is apparent from the description given in *Succah 53a* by Rav Yehoshua concerning the water-drawing ceremony. "When we used to rejoice at the place of the water drawing, our eyes saw no sleep. How was this? The first hour was occupied with the daily Morning Sacrifices, from there we proceeded to the *Morning Prayers*. From there we proceeded to the additional sacrifices, then to the prayers which accompanied the additional sacrifices [*the Mussaf prayers*] ...From there to the minchah prayers and from there to the afternoon Tamid offering..." Thus we clearly see that prayers were recited even during the period when sacrifices were offered.

If this is so, then only those indications that would affect the proper recitation of the prayers before the Shacharis prayer could be considered as acts performed for the purpose of indicating "our obligations to the prayers". However, the Rosh Chodesh Mussaf prayer, which was offered *after* the recitation of the Shacharis Amidah, could not serve as an indication that today is Rosh Chodesh. However, the placing of the limbs and the singing of the psalms were not for the purpose of indicating that today was Rosh Chodesh. Rather, as we explained earlier, the purpose of these practices was to ensure that Rosh Chodesh was duly declared. Thus they could certainly serve as indications of the day, even after the Shacharis Amidah prayer had already been said.

VII

Four Questions on the Bircas HaChodesh Ceremony

As we have discussed, some commentators contend that the purpose of announcing the day(s) of the forthcoming month was to make everyone aware of exactly when Rosh Chodesh would occur and thus ensure that the mitzvas of the day would be properly fulfilled. Yet one may ask, why do we not find anywhere else that we are commanded to go out of our way to make the public aware of a forthcoming occasion on which mitzvas will have to be observed? Why was Rosh Chodesh singled out for this purpose?

To answer this, we might suggest a source for this practice based on the following insights.

The Bircas HaChodesh, the prayer which blesses the new month, raises several questions. Why is this prayer recited prior to the Mussaf prayer, *after* the reading of the Torah, rather than *before* the Torah is read, right after Shacharis? It must be noted here that in fact in many Sefardi communities the "הכרזת החודש", the "announcing of the new month", is said *before* the reading of the Torah. Why do the Ashkenazi communities not follow the same practice?

It is customary for the chazzan to hold a Sefer Torah while reciting this prayer. Where is the source of this custom, and what relevance does it have to Rosh Chodesh?

The Magen Avraham writes in אור"ח (סימן תי"ז ס"ק א') as follows:

נהגו **לעמוד** בשעת אמירת ראש חודש פלוני, דוגמת קידוש החודש שהי' מעומד...

> It was customary to stand when the chazzan announced on which day(s) Rosh Chodesh would occur, just as we find that the Sanhedrin would stand when it sanctified the month.

HaRav Akiva Eiger, in his commentary to the Shulchan Aruch *(ibid.)* asks the following question. In the Mishna in *Mesechtas Rosh HaShanah 25b,* there is a description of the procedure which took place when the Bais Din declared the month sanctified, מקודש; and in that ceremony the Bais Din *remained seated.* How then, can the Magen Avraham tell us that *we stand as they did* when they sanctified the month?

Finally, why do we recite this prayer on the Shabbos before Rosh Chodesh rather than on Rosh Chodesh itself?

VIII

Resolving our Questions

Before we attempt to answer these questions, we must first address the issue of how we determine Rosh Chodesh today, when we no longer have a functioning Sanhedrin, since the law requires that they alone are authorized to designate the months. There are several solutions to this problem.

According to the strict reading of the Torah, it is Klal Yisrael who determines when to celebrate the new month. Based on the pasuk from *Shemos 12:2-3,* which states: "This month shall be unto you…speak unto all the congregation of Yisrael." — "החודש הזה לכם...דברו אל כל בני ישראל".

The Mechilta points out that initially it was Klal Yisrael who had the authority to determine the day of Rosh Chodesh. However, they relinquished that right in favor of the Sanhedrin. Thus it was the Sanhedrin which now acted as the representative body of Klal Yisrael (See *The Commentators' Gift of Torah, p. 250).* Thus, after the decline of this institution, the right to determine Rosh Chodesh reverted back to Klal Yisrael. However, it is the Jews who reside in Eretz Yisrael who constitute Klal Yisrael. The source for this law is based on the following considerations.

Chazal finds the source for Kiddush HaChodesh being determined by the Bais Din of Eretz Yisrael, in the pasuk which says: "כי מציון תצא תורה ודבר ה' מירושלים" — "From Zion shall go forth the Torah, and the Word of Hashem from Yerushalayim". Thus, it follows that the declaration of a new month must emanate from Zion and from Yerushalayim.

The *tzibur* (Klal Yisrael) is made up of those who live in Eretz Yisrael, as determined by the parasha of "פר העלם דבר של צבור". If the community errs by following the decision of the Bais Din HaGadol, then if a majority of the people follow that decision, only one sacrifice is offered as atonement. If, however, a minority sinned, each individual must bring his own sacrifice. To determine how many people accidentally transgressed, a census is taken of those Jews who live in Eretz Yisrael, for they constitute the *tzibur*, the community of Jews.

The sefer "אוצר התפלות" discusses the opinion of Rav Amram Gaon, who maintains in his siddur that Bircas Rosh Chodesh should be announced on the day of Rosh Chodesh itself, for this recitation of "הכרזת החודש" by Klal Yisrael designates this day as Rosh Chodesh. However, this is not our custom. In modern times, we announce the new month on the Shabbos preceding Rosh Chodesh, and this is based on other solutions of how we determine Rosh Chodesh.

The Ramban, in his commentary on the Sefer HaMitzvos of the Rambam, as well as in his commentary to Gemara Gittin, cites the historical fact that Hillel the Second foresaw the dispersal of the Jews from the Land of Yisrael, and therefore he calculated the months, years and holidays in order to determine all the future days of Rosh Chodesh. But if this was done, what is the purpose of the Blessing the Month, which we recite on שבת מברכין, the Shabbos before Rosh Chodesh?

IX

The Mitzvos of Kiddush HaChodesh

The mitzva of Kiddush HaChodesh involves witnesses who serve three different functions. The first function is eye-witnesses, עידי הראייה, who see the new moon and testify to that effect before the Bais Din, which then determines and declares which day will be Rosh Chodesh. The second function is character witnesses, עידי הכרה, who appear before the Bais Din to verify the reliability of the eye-witnesses. Finally, the third function is messengers, עידי הודעה, despatched by the Bais Din, who travel as far as time allows to inform the people which day was designated by the Bais Din as Rosh Chodesh, שלוחי בית-דין.

In modern times, the first two kinds of witnesses are no longer applicable, because the Bais HaMikdash has been destroyed and the Sanhedrin annulled. However, the third role of the witnesses, that of informing the people on which day Rosh Chodesh will occur, is applicable even in our day. And therefore, we can say that this is the function of our recitation of "הכרזת החודש"; whereas in ancient times, it was the messengers of the Bais Din — "שלוחי בית-דין"— who informed the masses when Rosh Chodesh day would occur, today it is the "הכרזת החודש" — the official announcing of the day of Rosh Chodesh on the preceding Shabbos, which fulfills that function.

With this view in mind, we can now answer the questions we raised previously. We recite הכרזת-ברכת החודש *after* the Kriyas HaTorah, because by then all those who intend to be present for the Shabbos services have already arrived at the synagogue. If we were to recite the Bircas HaChodesh *before* the Kriyas HaTorah, not everyone would have yet arrived, since we know that people are often late to synagogue. Consequently, since the Bircas HaChodesh serves as the fulfillment of the function of the messengers of the Bais Din— which was to inform the people when it would be Rosh Chodesh— therefore we delay this prayer as much as possible, so that all will hear the announcement of when the new month will be.

The reason the chazzan holds a Sefer Torah while he recites the Bircas HaChodesh is to ensure that the congregants will be standing and will therefore pay respectful attention to his announcement of the day of Rosh Chodesh., At other times as well, when we wish to capture the attention of the congregation, we hold a Sefer Torah. And on this occasion, when the time of the new month is to be declared, it is crucial to have the undivided attention of the entire congregation. We can now also answer the question posed by Rav Akiva Eiger regarding the contention of the Magen Avraham, that the reason we stand when we recite the Bircas HaChodesh is to emulate the Sanhedrin, who stood when they decreed the sanctity of the new month. As Rav Akiva Eiger pointed out, the Sanhedrin actually remained seated when it proclaimed Rosh Chodesh, yet when the messengers, שלוחים, were sent they stood, for they were preparing to leave as soon as possible. It is for this reason that we too stand when we announce Rosh Chodesh, for, as we have explained, this prayer fulfills the same role as did the messengers of the Bais Din, and therefore we must also stand and show our eagerness to do the mitzva with alacrity.

Now we have a source and a valid reason to announce when Rosh Chodesh will occur, even though we do not do this in relation to other mitzvos, for, as explained, this prayer takes the place of this function of "announcing" that was done in ancient times by the שלוחי בית דין, the messengers of the Bais Din.

X

THE PRAYERS OF THE BIRCAS HACHODESH

In many texts of the Bircas HaChodesh, the concluding words are: "In the merit of this prayer of Rav" — "בזכות תפלת רב". The allusion here to "Rav" refers to the fact that it was he who formulated this prayer. This is stated in the Gemara *Berachos, 16b*. However, many are perplexed as to why at the end of his prayer, we add the phrase, "in the merit of this prayer of Rav" (See the Aruch HaShulchan previously cited.) This phrase is problematic for several reasons.

When we recite the Bircas HaChodesh as a petition that

Hashem accept our prayer and answer us, what is gained by mentioning, "in the merit of this prayer of Rav"?

Furthermore, in the Gemara *Berachos* (ibid.) we find references to many prayers which were formulated by various Tanaim and Amoraim and included among our daily prayers. Yet nowhere at the conclusion of these prayers do we beseech Hashem to answer us "in the merit of" the author of that particular prayer. For example, each morning we recite "שתצילני מעזי פנים וכו'" after the *Bircas HaShachar*. This prayer was formulated by Rav Yehudah HaNasi, yet we do not conclude this prayer by mentioning the author or with a plea that we be answered in its merit. The same can be said regarding the prayer "אלוקי נצור לשוני", recited at the end of the Amidah. This prayer was formulated by מר בריה דרבינא. But we neither mention its author nor invoke his merit. Why, then, do we follow this unusual practice in the case of the Bircas HaChodesh?

Some commentators suggest an interesting possibility. (See the sefer "ברוך שאמר", על תפלות השנה, עמ' רסט-ע and the commentary of the "תקון תפלה" cited in the "אוצר התפלות".) It was customary to print the source and the name of the author in the siddur at the end of each prayer. For example, at the conclusion of the *Bircas HaChodesh*, we find the words, "ברכות תפלת רב". This practice easily could have led to a misunderstanding. The publishers may have made one of the following errors: They might have misread the word "ברכות", and substituted a "ז" in place of the "ר". Thus, instead of the word "ברכות", what was printed was the word "בזכות", "in the merit of..." Afterwards, subsequent editions may have continued to reproduce the erroneous spelling and thus perpetuate the misreading.

Other later publishers may have made their own corrections. Instead of writing "בזכות תפלת רב", which troubled them, they tried to amend this "error" by writing "בזכות תפלת **רבים**" — "in the merit of the prayers of the many". This also does not manage to solve the problem of justifying the alteration of the text as we have it. The common element in these two possible ways of correcting the text was that neither of them realized that all that was being indicated here was simply the source of this prayer — "ברכות, תפלת רב".

After all our speculation, to justify this phrase, we might suggest the following. The צל"ח, in his classic commentary on Mesechtas Berachos, points out that all the prayers mentioned here in the Gemara were composed by different Tanaim and Amoraim. And they were all intended to be recited after the daily Amidah. Their purpose was to add a dimension of personal intensity to the experience of prayer. They feared that because the Amidah had a set text and one was obligated to recite it three times a day, it might come to be recited by rote and without the proper intention which is required in prayer. Therefore, the Sages composed personal prayers to inspire and motivate themselves and others, so that they would be able to sustain the appropriate concentration required of prayer.

דהנה כל הני תנאי ואמוראי שהיו רגילים להיות אומרים בקשות ותחנונים אחר התפלה היה כוונתן למה שהזהירו שלא יעשה האדם תפלתו קבע אלא רחמים ותחנונים, וכל תפלות י"ח כיון שכבר קבעו לנו אנשי כנסת הגדולה הרי הם חובה עלינו ואין היכר בזה שאנחנו מתכוונים לרחמים ותחנונים אלא כמו פורע חוב. ולכן קיימו דבר זה ברחמים ותחנונים שביקשו אחר סיום התפלה שסדרו לנו אנשי כנסת הגדולה הוסיפו כל אחד משלהם...

In light of this view, we might suggest that the phrase "בזכות תפלת רב" alludes neither to the author of this prayer nor to the merit of its composition, but rather to the manner in which it was intended to be recited—with proper concentration. This leads to a further question. Why do we not also conclude those other prayers listed here in the Gemara (and formulated by the Sages for the same reason as the prayer of Rav), with the words: "in the merit of..." The answer might be that many of the prayers mentioned in the Gemara are now recited every day in our prayers either before or after the Amidah. Therefore, these prayers themselves, which were added in order to sustain our fervor and concentration in prayer, have become so habitual that they, too, are in danger of being recited by rote. And so, because they may not be recited with the intensity and inspiration envisioned by their authors, it would not be appropriate to conclude these prayers with the words, "in the merit of..." However, since the prayer of "יהי רצון" in the Bircas HaChodesh is not recited every day, but rather only once a month, it could certainly be assumed to be said with the proper concentration. And thus we conclude with the words, "בזכות תפלת רב", as if to say, "answer us in the merit of the heart-felt fervor with which this prayer was just said, in the same manner as its author, Rav, recited it. And in his merit may we be blessed with a good and productive month."

XI

"אהבת תורה ויראת שמים" – WHY THE REDUNDANCY?

Before we make this petition, that we be granted "love of Torah and fear of heaven", we have asked for "a life in which there is fear of heaven and fear of sin" — "חיים שיש בהם יראת שמים ויראת חטא". Why do we repeat this plea for "fear of heaven" here?

The commentators give several answers to this question. Some contend that we actually have two separate petitions that make different requests. The first is a personal petition that *our life* be filled with fear of heaven. The second, in another vein, is that *all Jews* be granted the same precious gift, fear of heaven, so that we may rejoice in the knowledge that others have attained love and understanding of the Torah, even if this means that they possess a greater measure of these blessings than we do.

Another answer as to why we repeat "יראת שמים" is that between the two requests for fear of heaven is a request for *"wealth and honor"* — "עושר וכבוד". If one succeeds in attaining these blessings, there is a danger than one's exalted station in life might lead to arrogance and diminish one's fear of heaven. Thus we repeat our request for "יראת שמים" *after* we have prayed for wealth and honor, to make sure that even after we may have attained those gifts, the overriding value of fear of heaven is stressed. For this repetition reminds us that there is One who is wealthier and more powerful, and that we must fear Him always. This point can be illustrated by the following story.

Rav Chaim Brisker once invited a notorious thief into his home for a frank discussion. He promised not to disclose details of their conversation to anyone. How, then, do we know what was said at their meeting? The answer must be that Rav Chaim promised not to reveal the thief's *identity*; even though the story was repeated in order to teach a moral lesson. Or perhaps it was the thief himself who later told the story, after he had learned his lesson from it.

In any case, Rav Chaim opened their conversation by asking, "Do you really steal from others?"

"Yes, Rabbi, I do," the thief replied, matter-of-factly.

The rabbi then asked, "If you had to break into a house and destroy property, would you do so in order to steal?"

"Of course I would," the thief answered, without a moment's hesitation.

"And if it were Shabbos, would you steal even then?"

"Yes, that would not stop me", replied the thief proudly.

"And if there was a slab of treif meat in the house, would you steal that too?"

Again, the answer was "Yes".

"Would you eat the treif meat", inquired the Rav.

"Of course not," insisted the thief with a shudder of horror.

"Do you hear what you are saying?" Rav Chaim remarked. "You are willing to transgress all the serious sins detailed in the Torah — stealing, destroying property, desecrating the Shabbos; yet you would not eat a piece of treif meat, which is a lighter sin. Does this make any sense?" challenged the Rav.

The thief was eager to explain himself. He said to the Rav, "What do you think, Rabbi? Am I not מזרע ישראל, a Jew by birth, descended from the Avos? All the other things I am willing to do is for the sake of earning my livelihood. But to eat treif? That has nothing to do with making a living, so why should I sin?"

Similarly, we might say that after our prayer for wealth and honor, "עושר וכבוד", has been answered, perhaps our perspective has become distorted, and we are no longer capable of attaining the fear of heaven. For if we lack that sense, we will easily be led astray, and we will never know what is true wealth and true honor. And therefore, we ask once again for the insight to distinguish what is most important in life —namely, serving Hashem— and the wisdom to understand that this takes precedence over any amount of wealth and honor that we could possibly acquire.

XII

"מי שעשה נסים" — Its relevance to Bircas HaChodesh

Several questions emerge here regarding this prayer of "מי שעשה נסים". What does it have to do with the blessing of the new month? Certainly, a prayer for the Ultimate Redemption is most commendable, but we do not attach this prayer to any of the other mitzvas. Why do we do it here in Bircas HaChodesh?

The order regarding our return to Eretz Yisrael and being freed from slavery is reversed here from that of Pesach, when we deal with the same themes. In the "מי שעשה נסים", the sequence is as follows: First we say "וגאל אותם מעבדות לחרות" — "And redeemed them from slavery to freedom." And then we say: "ויקבץ נדחינו מארבע כנפות הארץ" — "And gather in our dispersed from the four corners of the earth."

This is a petition that the Jewish people be returned to Eretz Yisrael, the land of their forefathers. Yet in the Pesach Haggadah the order appears to be reversed. In the section of "הא לחמא עניא", we read the following: "השתא הכא לשנה הבאה בארעא דישראל" — "Now we are here [in exile]; next year may we be restored to the land of Yisrael." And then we say: "השתא עבדי לשנה הבא בני חורין" — "Now we are slaves in bondage; next year may we be free men." First, we speak of returning to our homeland and only then do we speak of being free men.

All the commentators ask what this phrase of "חברים כל ישראל" — "all Yisrael are comrades" has to do with either the Bircas HaChodesh portion here or the prayer of "מי שעשה נסים", the petition for the Ultimate Redemption.

Several answers are offered as to why we specifically pray here for the Ultimate Redemption. The first mitzva in which Bnai Yisrael were commanded after their liberation from Egypt was Kiddush HaChodesh. This is why the petition for redemption in the Bircas HaChodesh serves as a memorial to that redemption from Egypt, זכר ליציאת מצרים, and the hope that we be redeemed as well in the near future.

We extend a petition for redemption, that we may merit to see the ingathering of all Jews to Eretz Yisrael and with it the restoration of sanctifying the month by means of eyewitnesses,

"קידוש על פי הראייה", as was done in the days of the Sanhedrin. Based on these reasons, we can perhaps now understand the difference between the prayer said here by the Sefardi and the Ashkenazi communities. The Sefardi *nusach* reads:

מי שעשה נסים לאבותינו וממצרים גאלם, הוא יגאל אותנו, וישיב בנים לגבולם...

> He who performed miracles for our forefathers and delivered them from Egypt — may He deliver us and return the children to their territory...

The Ashkenazi *nusach* reads differently:

מי שעשה נסים לאבותינו וגאל אותם מעבדות לחרות, הוא יגאל אותנו בקרוב, ויקבץ נדחינו מארבע כנפות הארץ...

> He Who performed miracles for our forefathers and redeemed them from slavery to freedom, may He redeem us soon and gather in our dispersed from the four corners of the earth...

We might ask, why doesn't the Sefaradi nusach stress this element of redemption from slavery to freedom — "מעבדות לחרות" — as does the Ashkenazi nusach? Perhaps we can answer this by saying that the Sefardim are of the opinion that this prayer for redemption is based on the concept of offering a memorial to that redemption from Egypt, "זכר ליציאת מצרים", and thus the focus here is exclusively on the concept of "וממצרים גאלם" — "and from Egypt they were redeemed". On the other hand, the Ashkenazim focus on the fact that prayer is offered as a petition for the restoration of the "קידוש על פי הראייה", the process of eyewitnesses, which will be reinstated when all Jews are gathered together in Eretz Yisrael, as the phrase "חברים כל ישראל" suggests.

This is the reason why we stress the transition from slavery to freedom, "מעבדות לחירות", for then we will be able to return to the land of Yisrael.

In light of this, we can now answer our second question, namely, why we begin by mentioning the petition that we be taken "from slavery to freedom" and only then do we mention the petition that we be restored to the land of our forefathers, Eretz Yisrael. For here we stress the *process* of freedom, as our commentators point out (see the commentary of the "דובר שלום", cited in the אוצר התפלות) that the Ultimate Redemption will follow a specific process, consisting of these elements: redemption from the yoke of oppression of foreign powers, return to the land of Yisrael, and the ingathering of all Jews from the four corners of the earth.

This is the order followed in this prayer: from slavery to freedom — "מעבדות לחירות", the ingathering of Jews to Eretz Yisrael — "ויקבץ נדחינו", which results in the unity of all Jewry — "חברים כל ישראל". This completes the process of redemption.

זהו בתחלה יגאל מעול השעבוד, ואחר זה יקבץ הנדחים מארבע כנפות הארץ למקום אחד, ואחר זה כשיהיו חברים כל ישראל, תושלם הגאולה.

However, in the Passover Haggadah the stress is on the renewal of the mitzva of bringing a *Korban Pesach*, the Passover sacrifice. This is why we first petition for the return of the Jewish people to Eretz Yisrael, for only there can we offer a Pesach sacrifice. Consequently, we pray to return to our land, that we will no longer be ruled by other nations. Thus the order in the Haggadah is: return to Eretz Yisrael — "השתא הכא לשנה הבאה בארעא דארץ ישראל", and autonomy — "השתא עבדי לשנה הבאה בני חורין".

This sequence is different from the one we find in the prayer of "מי שעשה נסים", and this helps us understand the relevance of the statement here of "חברים כל ישראל", which is an important aspect in the process of ultimate redemption.

In addition, as we have explained, we pray that the original practice of sanctifying the new month by means of eyewitnesses be reinstated so that all of Klal Yisrael will have the opportunity to take part in the process of Kiddush HaChodesh. At present, it is only the Jews who find themselves in Eretz Yisrael who can take part in this process; whereas the Jews in the Diaspora have no portion in designating the day(s) of Rosh Chodesh.

XIII

"All Yisrael are Comrades" — "חברים כל ישראל"

We have seen that the commentators question the relevance here of the phrase "חברים כל ישראל" in our petition for redemption. An insight of HaRav Shmuel Yaacov Borenstein, *shlita*, Rosh Yeshiva of Yeshivas Chevron – Geula, enables us to understand this problem in a wider context and suggest a possible answer.

The Gemara in *Ta'anis 26b* tells us:

אמר רבן שמעון בן גמליאל: לא היו ימים טובים לישראל כחמשה עשר באב וכיום כפור, שבהן בנות ירושלים יוצאות... וחולות בכרמים.

Rabban Shimon ben Gamliel said: Yisrael had no days as festive as the fifteenth of Av and Yom Kippur, when the maidens would go out...and dance in the vineyards.

וכן הוא אומר: ,צאינה וראינה בנות ציון במלך שלמה בעטרה שעטרה לו אמו ביום חתונתו וביום שמחת לבו. "ביום חתונתו" זה מתן תורה. "וביום שמחת לבו" זה בנין בית המקדש שיבנה במהרה בימינו.

Similarly, it says elsewhere (in *Shir HaShirim 3:11*) "Go forth and gaze, O daughters of Zion, upon King Solomon, adorned with the crown his mother made for him on the day of his wedding and on the day of his heart's joy". The phrase "on the day of his wedding", refers to the day of the giving of the Torah (i.e., the day of Yom Kippur when we received the second set of Tablets – Rashi). The phrase "and the days of his heart's joy" refers to the building of Bais HaMikdash.

According to Rashi, the reference to the building of the Bais HaMikdash also alludes to the day of Yom Kippur. The dedication ceremonies of the first Bais HaMikdash lasted from the seventh to the twenty-first of Tishrei. Thus, Yom Kippur, which is the tenth of Tishrei, is described here as a day of Hashem's gladness, for it too was included in this joyous period. However, the Maharsha contends that this allusion to "the day of his heart's joy", which is related to the building of the Bais HaMikdash, refers to the Fifteenth of Av.

פרש"י יום הכפורים שנתנו בו לוחות אחרונות ע"ש והוסיף הרע"ב וביום שמחת לבו זה בנין בית המקדש שנתחנך ביום הכפורים. ולפני עניינו נראה דאחמשה עשר באב קאי, **שטעמי שמחתו** אמרינן בגמ' תלויה בבנין המקדש.

The concluding statement here of the Maharsha seems very difficult to understand. His contention is that since the reason given in the Gemara for the celebration of Tu B'Av is related to the building of the Bais HaMikdash. Therefore, the joy of the building of the Bais Hamikdash must refer to the Fifteenth of Av. However, when one examines the reasons given here in the Gemara *30b – 31a*, for the celebration of Tu B'Av, we are puzzled as to how these reasons have any relevance to the building of the Bais HaMikdash.

Since we are only concerned with showing why "חברים כל ישראל" is said here, we will limit ourselves to those issues that will help us understand the connection of this phrase to the petition for the Ultimate Redemption. HaRav Borenstein, however, manages to beautifully explain how all the reasons cited in the Gemara are related to the Bais HaMikdash.

XIV

ALIYAS HAREGEL AND BUILDING THE BAIS HAMIKDASH

One of the reasons given for celebrating Tu B'Av as a festive occasion was that on that day Hoshea ben Elah, the last king of Yisrael, removed the sentries that Yerovam ben Nevat had stationed on the roads leading to Yerushalayim to prevent the Jews from ascending to the Bais HaMikdash on the three pilgrimage festivals. (See *The Commentators' Gift of Torah*, pp. 314-315.)

The mitzva of Aliyas HaRegel certainly has relevance to the building of the Bais HaMikdash. The Rambam points this out in the first chapter of Hilchos Bais Habechirah, the first halacha, where he writes:

מצות עשה לעשות בית לה' להיות מקריבין בו הקרבנות
וחוגגין אליו שלש פעמים בשנה...

The purpose of building a Bais HaMikdash was twofold, to have a place to offer sacrifices, and to have a place for pilgrimage on the three festivals of Shavous, Succos and Pesach.

Now we can understand why this reason given in the Gemara *Ta'anis 30b* for the celebration of Tu B'Av does indeed have relevance to the building of the Bais HaMikdash. However, for two of the other reasons given for the celebration of Tu B'Av, it seems difficult to see their connection to the matter of the building of the Bais HaMikdash.

יום שהותרו שבטים לבוא זה בזה.

One of these was that on this day the tribes were permitted to intermarry. Until that time a maiden was prohibited to marry outside her own tribe. (See *Bamidbar 36:8-9.*)

יום שהותר שבט בנימין לבוא בקהל.

The second was that this day was the day that the tribe of Binyomin was permitted to marry into the congregation of Yisrael. After the incident involving the concubine of Givah (*Shoftim* 19-20) the tribes took an oath not to give their daughters in marriage to the tribe of Binyomin, and it was only on the Fifteenth of Av that this ban was lifted.

These two incidents would certainly seem to have no connection with the building of the Bais Hamikdash. How then can the Maharsha say that *all* of the reasons given here in the Gemara relate to the Bais HaMikdash?

HaRav Borenstein contends that the answer to this question is based on the commentary of the Sages on the words of *Psalm 122:3*:

ירושלים הבנויה כעיר שחוברה לה יחדיו.

Yerushalayim is built like a city which is entirely concentrated within itself.

Chazal tell us in *Mesechtas Chagigah 26a* that during the pilgrimage festivals all of Yisrael was united, as the pasuk states in *Shoftim 2:11*:

> ויאסף כל איש ישראל אל העיר כאיש אחד חברים.

And all the men of the city congregated to the city like one man, as comrades.

We see from this that when Jews gather in one place, Scripture considers them as comrades, even those who have the status of being unlearned, *"am ha'aretz"*. The Yerushalmi Chagigah bases this concept on the above-mentioned verse of "ירושלים הבנויה כעיר שחוברה לה יחדיו", which suggests that Yerushalayim unites all Jews.

The Rambam further writes, in his *Sefer HaMitzvos* (20) that the purpose of building the Bais Hamikdash is the same as the purpose he states in Hilchos Bais HaBechirah. However, he adds one word here: "והקבוץ", which means "joining together". This is to be understood not simply as a description of Jews gathered together, but rather to make the point that as a prerequisite for this mitzva of building the Bais HaMikdash to be fulfilled, all Jews must first gather together in unity.

> ואליו תהי' ההליכה והעליה **והקבוץ** בכל שנה...

Thus we can see the connection here. A prerequisite to building the Bais HaMikdash—whose purpose is to serve as a place of pilgrimage—is the gathering together of all of Yisrael in unity as comrades, חברים.

With this in mind, we can now perhaps explain the following Midrash. When Elkanah made his annual pilgrimage to Shiloh in order to fulfill the mitzva of Aliyas HaRegel, he would knock on the doors of his fellow Jews and urge them to join him in this mitzva. This might lead us to ask, did he also knock on their doors to urge them to fulfill other mitzvos? Why was he so concerned about this particular mitzva of Aliyas HaRegel? Based on our previous discussion, we can understand that his concern was partially a personal one; for the fulfillment of the mitzva of Aliyas HaRegel depends on everyone joining together. Thus he tried to encourage everyone to participate, for only then was he able to fulfill his own mitzva.

And this is why when we petition the Almighty to bring about the Ultimate Redemption, we add the words which call for unity among the Jewish people "חברים כל ישראל". For included in the redemption process is the building of the Bais HaMikdash, and, as we have seen, in order to fulfill the mitzva of Aliyas HaRegel— the purpose for which the Temple was built—all Jews must join together in unity — "חברים כל ישראל, ונאמר אמן".

XV

THE PRAYER OF "יחדשהו"

In the sefer "רוקח" we read the following:

מן יחדשהו עד אמן י"ב תיבות, כנגד י"ב חדשים.

In this prayer, there are only twelve words, which correspond to the twelve months of the year. Thus, the Rokeach's reading of this prayer is:

יחדשהו הקדוש ברוך הוא לששון ולשמחה עלינו ועל כל ישראל ונאמר אמן.

This prayer also contains only twelve words in the "מחזור ויטרי":

יחדשהו הקב"ה עלינו לששון ולשמחה לרויח ולהצלה ולהצלחה, ולחיים ולשלום ונאמר אמן.

Here הקב"ה is counted as one word; whereas in the prayer of the Rokeach it is counted as three. However, in the siddur of Rav Amram Gaon, the reading is slightly different:

הקדוש ברוך הוא יחדשהו עלינו ועל כל עמו ישראל בכל מקום שהם, לטובה ולברכה, לששון ולשמחה, לישועה ולנחמה, ופרנסה ולכלכלה, לחיים ולשבוע, לשמועות טובות ולבשורות טובות ולגשמים בעתם, ואמרו אמן.

Nusach Ashkenaz is somewhat like the nusach of the מחזור ויטרי. It reads:

יחדשהו הקב"ה עלינו ועל כל עמו בית ישראל לחיים ולשלום, לששון ולשמחה, לישועה ולנחמה, ונאמר אמן.

Nusach Sefarad has an expanded version of this prayer, similar to that in the siddur of Rav Amram Gaon, with slight variations.

יחדשהו הקב"ה עלינו ועל כל עמו בית ישראל לטובה ולברכה, לששון ולשמחה, לישועה ולנחמה, לפרנסה טובה ולכלכלה, לחיים טובים ולשלום, לשמועות טובות ולבשורות טובות, ולגשמים בעתם, ולרפואה שלמה, ולגאלה קרובה, ונאמר אמן.

In this version, "לחיים ולשבוע" is deleted; whereas the phrase "רפואה שלמה ולגאלה קרובה" is added. According to the Chassidic master, HaRav Shimon Yarislover, we are meant to understand that the words "ונאמר אמן" recited at the end of the petition of "יחדשהו" are an integral part of the blessings for which we are entreating the Almighty. Essentially we are praying that in addition to all the blessings, we also pray for the merit to celebrate other occasions of blessings. In essence, we are saying, let us be able to enjoy each other's simchas and answer "אמן" to each other's wishes for continued blessings and happiness. It is clear that the words

"ונאמר אמן" are considered an important component of these blessings. In fact, we can count eleven blessings, which corresponds to the eleven months of the year when we offer this prayer — except for the month of Tishrei, when this blessing is not said.

This leads us to ask, what about the previous prayer of "מי שעשה נסים"? We also conclude that prayer with the words "ונאמר אמן". Are we then to understand that there too this concluding phrase is to be taken as a petition for an additional blessing?

We might suggest the following answer to this question. In "מי שעשה נסים", the central theme is the Ultimate Redemption, גאולה, which we yearn for in our prayers. We can list the process of this redemption, which includes the ingathering of all Jewry from the four corners of the earth, the return of all Jews to Eretz Yisrael, and finally, the uniting of all Jews as one, "חברים כל ישראל", as we have previously discussed, is the prerequisite to the redemption process.

We say "Amen", as we appeal to the Almighty to expedite this process. Thus the phrase here is really a petition that all this will speedily come to pass. On the other hand, in the prayer of "יחדשהו", we outline our request that He bestow His blessings upon us. When we conclude the list of blessings with the words, "ונאמר אמן", it is clear that this phrase too can be viewed as a blessing.

Our problem, though, is the previously mentioned law which prohibits requests and petitions in our prayers on Shabbos. How are we to justify what seem to be explicit petitions in these Rosh Chodesh prayers, both in the "יחדשהו" and in "מי שעשה נסים"?

The Aruch HaShulchan, in סימן תיז, אות ט' answered this question as follows:

ונהגו לומר מי שעשה נסים ויחדשהו, ואין זה תפלה בשבת
אלא לסימן טוב ותקוה הגאולה, דכשם שהחחדש מתחדש כן
יתחדש ישראל.

He explains that indeed these two prayers are not to be viewed as petitions said on the Shabbos day, but rather as expressions of hope and symbolic of the impending Ultimate Redemption. For just as the month is renewed, so too shall the glory of Yisrael be renewed.

In light of this insight, we might attempt to explain the following phenomenon. There is a custom that when we mention these blessings, we "sing" them rather than simply recite them. In fact, there are special melodies when this prayer is offered in a particular month. For example, when blessing the month of Kislev, the words of "לששון ולשמחה" should be sung to the melody of "מעוז צור" — the familiar hymn that accompanies the lighting of the Chanukah candles. In the month of Adar, it should be sung to the melody of the beracha of the Megillah. In Nissan, it should be sung to the melody of *Adir Hu*, one of the traditional songs found at the end of the Haggadah of Pesach night. In Av, it should be sung to the sad tune of the Tisha B'Av prayers.

Based on our previous discussion, we can now understand the reason for singing rather than simply reciting these blessings. For, as we have pointed out, they all express hope and anticipation of the Ultimate Redemption. This is articulated in the verse:

ואני ברוב חסדך בטחתי, אשירה לה' כי גמל עלי.

> As for me, I trust in Your kindness; my heart will rejoice in Your salvation. I will sing to Hashem for He has dealt kindly with me.

Therefore, when we express hope, King David directs us to articulate this with melody and song.

Chapter Two
The Prayer of יעלה ויבוא

I

WHERE DOES THIS PRAYER BELONG?

In the second chapter of *Hilchos Tefillah, Halacha 10,* the Rambam writes:

בראשי חדשים ובחולו של מועד מתפלל ערבית שחרית ומנחה תשע עשרה ברכות כשאר הימים. **ואומר** בעבודה אלקינו ואלוקי אבותינו יעלה ויבוא.

> On Rosh Chodesh and the intermediate days of a festival, one *recites* nineteen blessings in the Evening, Morning and Afternoon prayers, as on other days. In the *Avodah,* one *adds,* "Our God, and God of our fathers, let our remembrance rise and come...before You."

The question arises, why did the Rambam feel it necessary to tell us that on Rosh Chodesh the "Eighteen (actually, nineteen) Benedictions" are recited and the יעלה ויבוא is said in the Avodah section of the Shemoneh Esrei? This fact, that the eighteen benedictions must be said, seems obvious. All that was really necessary was to inform us that the יעלה ויבוא is to be added in the Avodah section of the Shemoneh Esrei. Indeed, later on in *Halacha 13,* when he discusses the addition of the Al HaNissim prayer, the Rambam writes: "בחנוכה ובפורים מוסיפין בהודאה על הנסים" — "On Chanukah and Purim the Al HaNissim is added to the thanksgiving section."

There he does not mention the requirement of reciting the Eighteen Benedictions, but simply informs us that we are obligated to add "Al HaNissim" in our prayers. Here, too, it would seem as if all that was needed to be said was that on Rosh Chodesh the יעלה ויבוא must be recited. Why then did he mention the obvious fact that the Eighteen Benedictions must be recited on Rosh Chodesh, since they are required every day of the year?

We know from the Kessef Mishna that the source for the Rambam here is the Gemara in *Shabbos 24a:*

> דתני ר' אושעיא: ימים שיש בהן קרבן מוסף כגון ראש חודש וחולו של מועד, ערבית ושחרית ומנחה, מתפלל שמונה עשרה **ואומר** מעין המאורע בעבודה...

> For Rav Oshaya taught in a baraisa: On those days when there is an obligation to bring a Mussaf offering, such as on Rosh Chodesh and the intermediate days of a festival, in the evening, morning and afternoon, one prays the eighteen blessings of the Shemoneh Esrei and recites a prayer that reflects the occasion...

And the Kessef Mishna concludes by saying that this statement of "a prayer that reflects the occasion", alludes to the יעלה ויבוא. Thus, since the Rambam's source is the Gemara, he quotes the exact words of this Gemara, which includes an explicit reference to the Eighteen Benedictions — "One prays the *Eighteen Benedictions* and recites a prayer that reflects the occasion of the day, i.e., יעלה ויבוא." This could very well be the reason why they are mentioned here-simply because they appear in the Gemara.

Of course, one might ask why the Gemara found it necessary to emphasize this requirement "to recite the Eighteen Benedictions on Rosh Chodesh", when this seems to be so obvious. Why did the Gemara not simply state that יעלה ויבוא is to be added in the Amidah prayer, as the Rambam does when he refers to the prayer of Al HaNissim recited on Purim and Chanukah?

The simple explanation would seem to be that on Rosh Chodesh and Chol HaMoed there is a special sanctity of the day

קדושת היום — which derives from the additional sacrifice, the Korban Mussaf, which is offered on these days. One might think that this would affect the Amidah prayer in some significant way, as it does on the days of a festival, when only seven blessings are recited in the Amidah prayer, and יעלה ויבוא. is added. Thus it is important for us to be informed that this is not the case, and in fact it is the regular weekday Shemoneh Esrei which we must recite, כשאר הימים, just as we do on every other day of the year that is not a festival day or a Shabbos.

II

The difference between "ואומר" and "ומוסיף"

When the Rambam speaks about the requirement to recite יעלה ויבוא, he uses the phrase "ואומר".

ואומר בעבודה אלקינו ואלוקי אבותינו יעלה ויבוא.

However, in relation to the recitation of Al HaNissim on Chanukah and Purim, the Rambam states:

בחנוכה ובפורים **מוסיפין** בהודאה על הנסים.

On Chanukah and Purim Al HaNissim is *added* to the thanksgiving section.7

How do we account for this change in terminology? Why didn't the Rambam also say here, "ואומר" — and one should "recite" the Al HaNissim- instead of using the phrase "מוסיפין", — "add"?

To answer this question, we might suggest that there is a vast difference between Rosh Chodesh as compared to Purim and Chanukah. On Purim and Chanukah we do not merely "say" or "add" a new prayer, but rather we *extend* the thanksgiving prayer. Our everyday thanksgiving prayer requires us to give thanks for Hashem's beneficence to us.

But on Purim and Chanukah, when an additional kindness was done for us, we are obligated to express our gratitude in an even greater measure. That expression of gratitude is included in the הודאה, the thanksgiving section of the Amidah. This, then, is to be viewed as an integral part of the general prayer of thanksgiving. That is why the Rambam describes this as "ומוסיפין" — we add or extend our usual thanksgiving prayer to include Al HaNissim. On Rosh Chodesh and Chol HaMoed, however, we do not add to or extend the content of the Avodah prayer, but rather we are required to "recite" — ואומר — a separate prayer that calls our attention to the uniqueness of the day. However, this prayer which expresses the uniqueness of the day cannot be recited independently, but must be included within the context of the blessings of the daily Amidah prayer. Thus we are given permission to "insert" within the Avodah section, the portion of יעלה ויבוא.

This explains why the Rambam uses the word "ומוסיפין" — "extended" — in relation to Chanukah and Purim; whereas in relation to Rosh Chodesh he used the word "ואומר", indicating that we are obligated to "state" or *make a declaration* regarding the uniqueness of this day.

Reinforcing this concept

With this difference in mind between the use of "ואומר" and "ומוסיפין", we can explain why, if one forgets to recite יעלה ויבוא in the Amidah prayer, one is required to repeat the Amidah. The reason for this is that one is *obligated* to mention the uniqueness of the day, and failure to do this requires that one repeat the Amidah, because one can only fulfill one's obligation to recite יעלה ויבוא within the context of the blessings of the Amidah. On the other hand, if one fails to say Al HaNissim on Purim or Chanukah, one need not repeat the Amidah, for, as we have explained, Al HaNissim is not to be viewed as a separate prayer, but rather it is to be considered an integral part of the Thanksgiving section — the "הודאה" — of the daily prayers.

Therefore, since the thanksgiving prayer was said when reciting "מודים אנחנו לך" the failure to mention Al HaNissim does not mean that we did not express our gratitude to Hashem. We did indeed express it there, and by forgetting Al HaNissim we merely "skipped' a fragment of that prayer. And for that, we are not obligated to repeat the entire Amidah prayer.

Other cases of "ואומר" and "ומוסיף"

There are several halachos which reinforce this theory. For example, the Rambam in *Hilchos Tefillah, 2:14* states:

בימי התענית, אפילו יחיד שהתענה, **מוסיף** בשומע תפלה: "עננו..."

On fast days, even an individual who fasts [by his own volition] adds: "Answer us" in the section of "the One Who hears prayer".

And in the same place he adds:

בתשעה באב מוסיפין ב"בונה ירושלים", "רחם...ועל ירושלים עירך ועל העיר האבילה, וכו'..."

On the Ninth of Av one adds to the blessing of "One who rebuilds Yerushalayim", "Have mercy on us...and on Yerushalayim, Your city, the mourning city"...

In these two instances the Rambam emphasizes the word "ומוסיפין" — "adds". Yet in *Halacha 15*, he writes:

כל ימות הגשמים **אומר** בברכה שניה "מוריד הגשם", ובימות החמה — "מוריד הטל".

During the rainy season the phrase "the One Who causes the rain to fall" is *recited* in the second blessing.

Here the word "ואומר" is used. But why not "מוסיפין", as in "עננו"? Based on the above explanations, we can easily understand the difference. On a fast day and on Tisha B'Av, the prayers which are added become part of the main prayer. They blend with the theme of the Amidah prayer. Such prayers include, for example, "עננו" — "Answer us", in the prayer of "שמע קולנו" — "One Who hears prayer", and "רחם" — "Have mercy", in the prayer of "Have mercy on Yerushalayim" — "ירושלים...ברחמים". These prayers can be viewed as an *extension* of the main prayers — "מוסיפין".

Correspondingly, the halacha concerning these prayers reads that if one failed to recite them, no repetition of the Amidah is necessary. In addition to the rationale already given for this, we can understand that these prayers of "עננו" and "רחם" are not separate prayers, but rather an *extension* of existing prayers, and thus failure to mention them does not mean that the central theme was not addressed.

However, in relation to "מוריד הגשם", this phrase is not to be viewed as an integral part of an existing prayer, but is rather a separate prayer which is inserted here. Thus the Rambam uses the term "ואומר" — "one should *recite*", and failure to do this obligates one to repeat the entire Amidah.

UNDERSTANDING ANOTHER HALACHA

We might further explain yet another halacha to be found in *Hilchos Tefillah 2:19:*

יש מקומות שנהגו **להוסיף** בעשרת ימים אלו בברכה ראשונה זכרנו לחיים...
וכן יש מקומות שנהגו **להוסיף** בעשרת ימים אלו בברכה שלישית, ובכן תן פחדך...אבל בראש השנה וביום הכפורים מנהג פשוט הוא **להוסיף** בשלישית: ובכן תן פחדך וכו'.

> There are places in which it is customary during these ten days (the ten days of repentance between Rosh Hashanah and Yom Kippur) to add in the first blessing, "Remember us for life".

During these ten days, there is also the custom among some to *add* in the third blessing, "Now, Lord our God, put Your awe upon all whom You have made, Your dread upon all whom You have created..." On Rosh Hashanah and Yom Kippur it is the commonly accepted practice to *add* these prayers in the third blessing."

Here, too, the Rambam employs the term "ומוסיף" rather than "ואומר". For here these additions become an integral part of the actual prayers in which they are included. And, as we have pointed out, failure to recite them does not require that we repeat the entire Amidah prayer.

There is a difference of opinion among the Rishonim as to whether or not a repetition is required. The Ba'alei Tosafos maintain that a repetition is indeed called for; whereas the רא"ש is of the opinion that no repetition is required. Most poskim subscribe to the opinion of the רא"ש.

In light of what we have presented above, we can answer a classic question posed by the commentators. The law stipulates that we are not allowed to insert petitions in either the first or the third sections of the Amidah. How, then, can we justify adding "זכרנו לחיים" in the first section of the Amidah (See *The Commentators' Machzor Companion*, pages 116-125.) Based on our previous contention that "ומוסיף" is to be understood not merely as "to add", but rather as "to extend", we can say that "זכרנו לחיים" is not an additional prayer, but rather an integral part of the first section of the Amidah, the section which contains praises, שבחות. Thus we praise Hashem, for He holds our lives in His hand. This explains how we can justifiably make this addition here.

An Apparent Contradiction

The following statements of the Rambam appear to contradict our previous theory. However, we shall endeavor to show that not only is there no real contradiction based on these sources, but they will actually serve to reinforce this approach.

In *Hilchos Berachos 2:5*, the Rambam states:

בשבתות ובימים טובים מתחיל בנחמה ומסיים בנחמה, ואומר קדושת היום באמצע. כיצד? מתחיל...רחם ה' אלוקינו על ישראל עמך ועל ירושלים עירך...ואומר באמצע בשבת: או"א, רצה והחליצנו...

ובימים טובים **אומר** "יעלה ויבוא", וכן בראשי חדשים ובחולו של מועד **מוסיף** באמצע ברכה שלישית...יעלה ויבוא.

> On Shabbos and on the Festivals, one should begin with the concept of comfort and conclude with the concept of comfort and in the midst of the blessing mention the sacred quality of the day. How should one begin? Either with "Have mercy upon us, Hashem, our Lord, and on Yisrael, Your people, on Yerushalayim, Your city..."
>
> On Shabbos, in the midst of the blessing one should say: "Hashem, the Lord of our fathers, may it please You to strengthen us through Your mitzvos..." On the festivals, one should say the prayer of יעלה ויבוא in this blessing. Similarly, on Rosh Chodesh and Chol HaMoed, one should *add* the prayer of יעלה ויבוא in the third blessing.

Here we see that in regard to Rosh Chodesh the Rambam uses the term "ומוסיף". This might appear to contradict our earlier contention that in relation to Rosh Chodesh the proper term is "ואומר", which implies an obligation to make a special declaration concerning the sanctity of the day. Yet here the Rambam uses the other term, "ומוסיף".

In addition to this, we see that regarding the festivals, he does use this term, "ואומר", when he mentions the requirement to recite the יעלה ויבוא. Why then does he insist on using the terminology "ומוסיף" when it comes to Rosh Chodesh?

There is similarly an apparent contradiction to our previous theory in another statement of the Rambam's, in "תפלות לכל השנה (בנוסח ברכות התפלה וסידורן)". Here we find the following statement:

> בראשי חדשים ובחולו של מועד **מוסיף** בברכת יז, בערבית ושחרית ומנחה... יעלה ויבוא.

> On Rosh Chodesh and Chol HaMoed one *adds* in

the seventeenth Amidah blessing in the Evening, Morning and Afternoon prayers... "Our God, and God of our fathers, let our remembrance rise and come...before You."

Thus here too the Rambam uses the term "ומוסיף" in relation to the, יעלה ויבא which contradicts our theory that "ואומר" is the appropriate term to be used when dealing with the prayer of יעלה ויבא.

Resolving this apparent contradiction

Before we can give a satisfactory answer to this question, we must first establish the following rules pertaining to the requirement of when יעלה ויבא is to be recited.

There are generally two reasons for us to add יעלה ויבא to our Rosh Chodesh prayers. The first is to emphasize the sanctity of the day, קדושת היום, marked by the offering of the special Mussaf sacrifice, we are required to explicitly mention that this particular day is Rosh Chodesh: "ביום ראש החודש הזה". The second reason is to mention that Rosh Chodesh is the beginning of a new month, we are required to mention the "occasion of the day" — "מעין המאורע".

There is a practical difference between these two reasons. First of all, if the reason for reciting יעלה ויבא is because of the aspect of "מעין המאורע", the occasion of the day, then the failure to mention יעלה ויבא in the Amidah would not require one to repeat the entire Amidah prayer. However, if the recitation of יעלה ויבא is due to the sanctity of the day, then the failure to recite יעלה ויבא would indeed require a full repetition of the Amidah.

We must also point out that if it is the Mussaf sacrifice which causes us to view this day as a day of sanctity, and therefore to recite the יעלה ויבוא, then this would only affect the Amidah prayer but not the Grace after Meals, ברכת המזון.

With these insights in mind, we can now explain the seemingly contradictory statements of the Rambam in a way that reconciles them with our previous theory.

In *Hilchos Berachos 2:5* the Rambam uses the term "ואומר" in relation to the festivals, stating that we are required to recite יעלה ויבוא in the middle of the blessing. This then would mean that failure to recite יעלה ויבוא would require that the entire prayer be repeated. Thus, apart from the requirement on Shabbos and Yom Tov to eat a festive meal, and consequently to recite the Grace after Meals (which includes יעלה ויבוא), we can see that the failure to recite the יעלה ויבוא in the Grace after Meals would require us to repeat that prayer in its entirety. And since on Shabbos and Yom Tov there is the aspect of קדושת היום, the sanctity of the day, based on the fact that work is forbidden on this day, this is the consideration which requires us to recite יעלה ויבוא and consequently to repeat the prayer which contains it if we forget to include it. Thus we can see that the Rambam was justified in using the term "ואומר", to indicate that one must recite יעלה ויבוא on these occasions.

On Rosh Chodesh, however, there is no קדושת היום, since there is no prohibition against work on this day and thus the only aspect of the day which is sanctified is the fact that the special Mussaf sacrifice is offered on Rosh Chodesh. As we have discussed, the requirement to recite יעלה ויבוא because of the Mussaf offering affects only the Amidah and not the Grace after Meals.

Therefore, the Rambam does not say "ואומר", that one must "recite" the יעלה ויבוא, but rather he uses the term "ומוסיף", because of the aspect of מעין המאורע, which is the reason we "add" יעלה ויבוא.

However, as we have previously explained, this does not require repetition if one failed to recite it.

And finally, we can explain why the Rambam used the term "מוסיף" in "תפלות לכל השנה" in relation to the addition of יעלה ויבוא. This is because the sanctity of the day, קדושת היום, dependent on the Mussaf offering, relates only to the prayers during the day. The reason for this is that only during the day can a sacrifice be offered; never at night. Thus the only reason יעלה ויבוא is said at night is because of the aspect of מעין המאורע, and, as we have explained, failure to mention this aspect does not require one to repeat the Amidah prayer. Thus the Rambam here, since he refers to the evening prayers, uses the term "ומוסיף", rather than "ואומר", in order to emphasize this fact.

In summary, we now no longer have a contradiction between these laws. On the contrary, this serves to prove our theory that "ואומר" refers to an absolute obligation to recite the prayer; whereas "ומוסיף" is only a requirement at the outset but is not decisive.

III

יעלה ויבוא AND ITS VARIOUS PRAYERS

There are various occasions on which this prayer is recited. These include: Rosh Chodesh and Chol HaMoed, festivals, and Rosh Hashanah.

On Rosh Chodesh, יעלה ויבוא is inserted in the Avodah section of the Amidah, in the prayer of רצה; whereas on Yom Tov it is inserted in the middle section of the Amidah, in the קדושת היום, which begins with "אתה בחרתנו". How can we account for this difference? Why on Yom Tov do we not insert יעלה ויבוא in the Avodah, as we do on Rosh Chodesh?

In the Rosh Hashanah prayers, it is our custom to insert "יעלה ויבוא" in the section of קדושת היום, (in the prayer which begins with the words "אתה בחרתנו"). The Tur tells us (in סימן תקצ"א) that it was the custom of the Jews of Toledano, Spain, to include it in the section of Remembrances, זכרונות. The Tur commended them for doing this. What, then, is the basis for their disagreement? And why was it not added in the Avodah section, as it is on Rosh Chodesh?

We might suggest a possible answer based on the following insights. There are three major themes included in the יעלה ויבוא: The first theme is Remembrances — זכרונות:

ויפקד, ויזכר זכרוננו ובפקדוננו, וזכרון אבותינו וזכרון משיח בן דוד עבדך, וזכרון ירושלים עיר קדשיך, וזכרון כל עמך בית ישראל לפניך וכו'.

The second theme is Divine help — ישועות:

ובדבר ישועה ורחמים...והושיענו...

Finally, the last theme is a reference to the uniqueness of the day:

ראש חודש הזה...חג המצות הזה...חג הסוכות הזה.

The source for the first two themes here, זכרונות and ישועות, is based on the verse in *Bamidbar 10:9*:

וכי-תבאו מלחמה בארצכם על הצר הצרר אתכם. והרעתם בחצצרת **ונזכרתם לפני ה' אלוקיכם ונושעתם מאויביכם**.

And if you go to war in your land against the adversary that oppresses you, then you shall blow an alarm with the trumpets; and you shall be remembered before the Eternal your God and you shall be saved from your enemies.

From this verse we learn that whenever we petition Hashem, whether by sounding the trumpet or by prayer, His mindfulness is stirred and He will bring about our salvation.

In *verse 10 (ibid.)* we read:

וביום שמחתכם ובמועדיכם ובראשי חדשיכם ותקעתם בחצצרת על עלתיכם ועל זבחי שלמיכם, והיו לכם לזכרון לפני אלוקיכם, אני ה' אלוקיכם.

On your days of rejoicing and your holy days and at the beginning of your months, you shall sound the trumpets over your offerings and they shall be for you a remembrance for you before Hashem. I am Hashem, your God.

On these days we are commanded to make sure that Hashem's memory is stirred, so that He will grant us salvation. We do this by reciting יעלה ויבוא. All the phrases of remembrance mentioned in the יעלה ויבוא are based on the verse, "ויהיו לכם לזכרון לפני אלוקיכם".

The "והושיענו" phrases we articulate here are based on the above-mentioned verse of "ונושעתם" *(Bamidbar 10:9)*. With this in mind, we can understand and appreciate the structure and source of the beginning and ending sections of the "יעלה ויבוא" prayer.

The requirement to mention the uniqueness of the day is based on two distinct factors: We are obligated to articulate the occasion of the day — מעין המאורע. The sanctity of the day, קדושת היום, requires us to mention the name of this unique day. Thus, for example, on Yom Tov, the קדושת היום is based on the fact that there is a prohibition against doing any work on this day, איסור מלאכה. And on Rosh Chodesh, even though work is not forbidden, the holiness of the day derives from the Mussaf sacrifice which is offered on this day. This in turn obligates us to mention the unique nature of this day in our prayers.

(Later in our discussion, we will attempt to explain why we need two separate reasons.)

Explaining the difference

If Rosh Chodesh occurs on a weekday, when there is no קדושת היום section in the Amidah, we insert יעלה ויבוא in the Avodah section of the weekday Amidah. The rationale for this is explained by *Tosafos* in *Mesechtas Shabbos 24a*.

ובי"ח [ובשמונה עשרה] תיקנוה בעבודה שהיא תפלה להשב ישראל לירושלים.

On Rosh Chodesh, יעלה ויבוא is inserted in the Avodah section of רצה, because in this prayer we pray for the service in the Bais HaMikdash to be restored, and similarly, in the יעלה ויבוא we also pray for Hashem to remember Yerushalayim.

If Rosh Chodesh occurs on Shabbos, even though the Shabbos Amidah prayer does contain a section of קדושת היום — this is the section which begins with the words "ישמח משה" — yet we still insert the יעלה ויבוא in the Avodah section. The reason for this is that the קדושת היום of the Shabbos prayers relates exclusively to the theme of Shabbos and not that of Rosh Chodesh. Proof of this is that the concluding beracha of the Shabbos section of קדושת היום, even when Rosh Chodesh falls on a Shabbos, reads "מקדש השבת"

and not "מקדש השבת וראשי חדשים". Furthermore, Shabbos itself is never mentioned in the יעלה ויבוא prayer. The reason for this is that the mention of Rosh Chodesh in the יעלה ויבוא is based on the consideration of remembrance, זכרון, which is articulated in the pasuk of "וביום שמחתכם וכו' ובראשי חדשיכם". Shabbos is not mentioned in this verse at all. This is explained by the לבוש, who writes as follows:

> עיקר יעלה ויבוא לא נתיסד אלא על הזכירה והפקידה, ואין שייך זכרון אלא בראש חודש וביום טוב דכתיב וביום שמחתכם ובמועדיכם ובראשי חדשיכם וכו' והיו לכם לזכרון, לפיכך אין צריכין להזכיר שבת במקום שעיקרו משום זכרון שהוא משום ר"ח וי"ט...

On the holidays, יעלה ויבוא is recited *within* the section of the קדושת היום, for it is this aspect of קדושת היום that requires us to mention the uniqueness of this day. Therefore, it is more appropriate to include יעלה ויבוא in the section of קדושת היום rather than in the Avodah section.

On Rosh Hashanah we also insert יעלה ויבוא in the section of קדושת היום. The reason for this is that in the Rosh Hashanah Mussaf prayer we join the מלכיות section with the קדושת היום section. The rationale behind this practice is that the essential nature of the sanctity of this day, קדושת היום, is מלכיות, to proclaim Hashem our King. Here the קדושת היום and מלכיות are synonymous. Consequently, the prayer of יעלה ויבוא which expresses קדושת היום, belongs here in the section of מלכיות — קדושת היום.

The rationale behind the custom of the Jews of Toledano was that since the essence of Rosh Hashanah day is remembrance — זכרונות, therefore, יעלה ויבוא which alludes to the essence of the day, rightfully belongs in the זכרונות section. (See *The Commentators' Machzor Companion*, pp.292-3.)

IV

קדושת היום OR מעין המאורע

In *Mesechtas Shabbos 24a* we read:

דתני ר' אושעיא: ימים שיש בהן קרבן מוסף כגון ראש חדש וחולו של מועד, ערבית ושחרית ומנחה מתפלל שמונה עשרה ואומר **מעין המאורע** בעבודה, ואם לא אמר מחזירין אותו...

On those days when there is an obligation to bring a Mussaf offering, such as on Rosh Chodesh and the intermediate days of a festival, in the *evening*, morning and afternoon, one prays the eighteen blessings of the Shemoneh Esrei prayer and recites a prayer that reflects the occasion of the day in the blessing for the return of the Temple Service. And if one did not recite this extra prayer, we require him to return and rectify the omission…

From this we can see that the prayer of יעלה ויבוא here is alluded to by the phrase "מעין המאורע" — the "occasion of the day". Yet in the *Tosefta Berachos 3:14*, we find the following:

כל שאין בו מוסף כגון חנוכה ופורים ערבית שחרית ומנחה מתפלל שמונה עשרה ואומר מעין המאורע בהודאה. ואם לא אמר מעין המאורע אין מחזירין אותו. וכל שיש בו מוסף כגון ר"ח וחולו של מועד שחרית ומנחה מתפלל שמונה עשרה ואומר **קדושת היום** בעבודה...ואם לא אמר מחזירין אותו.

On those days when there is *no* obligation to bring a Mussaf offering, such as Chanukah and Purim, in the evening, morning and afternoon one prays the eighteen blessings of the Shemoneh Esrei prayer and recites a prayer that reflects the occasion of the day in the Thanksgiving section of the service. And if one did not recite the extra prayer, we do not require him to return and rectify the omission.

On those days when *there is an obligation to bring a Mussaf offering*, such as on Rosh Chodesh and the intermediate days of the festival, morning and afternoon, one prays eighteen blessings of the Shemoneh Esreh prayer and recites a prayer that reflects *the sanctity of the day*, in the blessings for the return of the Temple service. And if he did not recite the extra prayer, we require him to return and rectify the omission.

Here in the Tosefta we see two differences between what is said here and what is said in *Mesechtas Shabbos 24a*. Here we refer to the יעלה ויבוא prayer as "the sanctity of the day" — קדושת היום, whereas in *Mesechtas Shabbos* we refer to it as מעין המאורע — "the occasion of the day".

Furthermore, whereas in *Mesechtas Shabbos* all the prayers of the day are listed, including the evening, morning and afternoon, where one is required to mention the occasion of the day. Yet in the *Tosefta Berachos*, only the morning and evening prayers are mentioned in relation to the sanctity of the day. To account for these differences, the standard answer given is that we have here two different versions of the text, which has been corrupted over time. However, we can suggest that the texts are as they should be and we can account for the differences by employing a remarkable insight.

V

Two Different Texts

The obligation to recite יעלה ויבוא in our prayers on Rosh Chodesh depends on the following two factors. First of all, מעין המאורע —

one is obligated to mention the occasion of the day in one's prayers. This is based on a statement in the Gemara Berachos (מ, א):

אמר קרא, [תהלים סח] ברוך ה' יום יום, וכי ביום מברכין אותו ובלילה אין מברכין אותו, אלא לומר לך, כל יום ויום תן לו מעין ברכותיו.

> For the verse states: "Blessed is Hashem day by day". Is it possible to say that this means that we bless Him *by day*, but by night we do not bless Him? Rather on every single day, give Him praise reflective of its particular blessing.

And Rashi explains: "בשבת מעין שבת, ביום טוב מעין יום טוב" — "On Shabbos one should recite a special blessing reflecting the nature of the Shabbos and on Yom Tov a special blessing reflecting the nature of the Yom Tov."

And secondly, קדושת היום — due to the holiness of the day, it is incumbent on us to articulate what day it is today. For example, on Rosh Chodesh one *must* say "יום ראש חודש הזה"; on Pesach, "יום חג המצות הזה", etc.

The requirement to spell out the occasion of the particular day is due to the Mussaf sacrifice which is offered on this day. Thus we say here, "ימים שיש בו מוסף אומר קדושת היום". And it is this Mussaf offering that not only requires us to mention the uniqueness of the day, but also obligates us that if we omit mentioning the uniqueness of the particular day we must repeat the Amidah prayer. However, if the obligation is the result of the consideration of "מעין המאורע" mentioning the particular occasion of the day, then one would not be required to repeat the Amidah.

Thus it is only when we are able to offer a Mussaf sacrifice — that is, during the day-would we be obligated to repeat the

Amidah if we failed to mention the קדושת היום, the particular sanctity of the day. In the evening, however, when we are not allowed to offer sacrifices, the only obligation we have to mention Rosh Chodesh would be due to the aspect of מעין המאורע, the occasion of the day. And therefore, as we pointed out, the failure to mention the מעין המאורע does not call for us to repeat the Amidah. Proof of this is that on Chanukah and Purim we are only obligated to mention the מעין המאורע, and failure to recite Al HaNissim does not require us to repeat the entire Amidah.

Reconciling differences

Equipped with this strategy, we can suggest an answer to the question why different terms are used in the *Tosefta Berachos* and *Mesechtas Shabbos*. The issue in *Mesechtas Shabbos 24a* is whether to include the occasion of the day, מעין המאורע, in other words, יעלה ויבוא, in the Bircas HaMazon, the Grace after Meals. As we have discussed, the requirement to mention the unique sanctity of the day, קדושת היום, applies only to the Amidah prayers. However, in the Bircas HaMazon, it is only the aspect of מעין המאורע that needs to be considered. Consequently, if we are to prove that יעלה ויבוא should be included in the Bircas HaMazon because it is mentioned in the Amidah prayers, then we must understand this to mean that we consider יעלה ויבוא to be integral to the aspect of mentioning the occasion of the day, מעין המאורע. This explains the statement of Rav Oshiah, that יעלה ויבוא relates to the consideration of מעין המאורע and not that of קדושת היום.

With this in mind, we can understand why in the *Mesechtas Shabbos*, Maariv, the evening prayer, is included in the list of occasions when יעלה ויבוא is to be recited. Although the Maariv prayer does not call for the recitation of יעלה ויבוא based on the consideration of קדושת היום, as we have explained, yet because of the consideration of the aspect of מעין המאורע, it should be recited even at night. Thus if the evening prayer is to be included in the obligation to recite יעלה ויבוא, this accounts for the reason that the Gemara in Shabbos uses the term "מעין המאורע".

This leaves us with the following problem. Why does the Gemara conclude with the statement that failure to recite יעלה ויבוא requires a repetition of the Amidah, when we have already established that יעלה ויבוא is said only out of consideration for the aspect of מעין המאורע, which in itself does not require repetition. We will address this problem later in this discussion.

In the *Tosefta Berachos*, on the other hand, the issue concerns the fact that יעלה ויבוא is recited due to the consideration of קדושת היום. This is clearly stated: "כל שיש בו מוסף". It is because of the Mussaf sacrifice offered on this day of Rosh Chodesh that the day contains a special holiness, קדושת היום. Consequently, Maariv, the evening prayer, is not included here, for, as we have explained, the קדושת היום of Rosh Chodesh applies only when a Mussaf sacrifice is offered, that is, during the day, but not at night. Therefore, failure to mention יעלה ויבוא in the daytime requires that the Amidah be repeated. This is the reason why only the morning and afternoon prayers, Shacharis and Mincha, are mentioned in the Tosefta; whereas the evening prayer, Maariv, has no place here.

To summarize: the Tosefta refers to יעלה ויבוא as dependent on קדושת היום, for it refers to the prayers said during the day, which is the only acceptable time for the Mussaf Sacrifice to be offered. The Gemara in Shabbos, however, refers to יעלה ויבוא as dependent on מעין המאורע, and thus it involves even the evening prayer, Maariv, for this is said also in consideration of the aspect of מעין המאורע.

VI

TWO VIEWS: WHERE TO INSERT יעלה ויבוא

The *Tosefta Berachos 3:14* states:

וכל שיש בו מוסף כגון ראש חודש וחולו של מועד, שחרית ומנחה מתפלל שמונה עשרה ואומר קדושת היום בעבודה. רבי אליעזר אומר **בהודאה**...

> On those days when there is an obligation to bring a Mussaf offering, such as on Rosh Chodesh and on the intermediate days of the festivals, morning and afternoon, one prays the eighteen blessings of the Shemoneh Esrei prayer and recites a prayer that reflects the sanctity of the day in the blessings for the return of the Temple service, in the Avodah. R' Eliezer disagrees and maintains that יעלה ויבוא should be said in the *blessings of thanksgiving*...

There is an interesting question raised here in relation to this view of R' Eliezer. As we know, the Shemoneh Esrei prayer is made up of three sections: Praise — שבחות, Petitions — צרכיו, Thanksgiving — הודאה. The halacha stipulates that petitions are only to be made in the section designated for petitions, and it is therefore forbidden to offer petitions in the first section, the praise section of the Amidah — שבחות — or in the last, thanksgiving, section — הודאה. This is stated in *Mesechtas Berachos 34a:*

> אמר רב יהודה: לעולם אל ישאל אדם צרכיו לא בשלש ראשונות ולא בשלש אחרונות אלא באמצעיות.

> Said Rav Yehudah: A person should never ask for his needs, neither in the first three berachos of the

Amidah prayer nor in the last three, but only in the middle section.

Given this explicit statement, we might ask the following question. Since the prayer of יעלה ויבוא is viewed as a petition, how did R' Eliezer justify its insertion in the thanksgiving, הודאה section? This question is touched upon in the sefer "ברכת אברהם" (על מסכת ביצה (יז,א):

ר' אליעזר אומר בהודאה: תמוה, מה זה שייך להודאה הלא כולו תפילה היא. ורש"י כתב: 'כמו שאומר על הנסים בחנוכה ופורים.' ולכאורה לא שייך זה לזה כלל, דהתם הודאה הוא וכאן רק תפלה, וצ"ע.

This question was already anticipated in the sefer "תולדות יעקב" מהרב יעקב קאסטרו, in his commentary to *Mesechtas Beitzah (17a)*. Commenting on the above-mentioned words of Rashi, "כמו שאומר על הנסים בחנוכה ופורים", the Toledos Yaakov contends that Rashi here was well aware of our problem of how one can legitimately insert a petition into the thanksgiving section of the Amidah prayer. He solved this problem by suggesting that indeed, according to R' Eliezer, if we are to insert יעלה ויבוא in the הודאה section, then we must change the whole structure of this prayer. It is no longer to be read as a petition but is rather to be considered like Al HaNissim, which is recited on both Chanukah and Purim.

רש"י ז"ל "כמו שאומר על הנסים בחנוכה ופורים": הרגיש איך יסובר ר' אליעזר שאומרה בהודאה, והלא הזכרת ראש חדש שאלה היא, יעלה ויבא כו', ואיך יזכירה בהודאה שהיא להודות על מה שכבר נתן, שנמצאו שני הפכים בברכה אחת לכן אמר שפי' "בהודאה" אינה שיאמר נוסחת יעלה ויבא, אלא שיאמר כמו שאומר על הנסים בחנוכה.

VII

Explaining R' Eliezer's View

We might suggest a way to understand R' Eliezer's view based on the following insights (See *The Commentators' Al HaNissim — Chanukah*).

In *Mesechtas Shabbos 21b*, the Gemara tells us that because of the miracle of Chanukah, our Sages instituted the eight-day festival of Chanukah, "to give thanks and to praise Hashem" — "להודות ולהלל". Rashi here comments:

לא שאסורין במלאכה שלא נקבעו אלא לקרות הלל **ולומר על הנסים בהודאה**.

> Chanukah is not a "holiday" in the sense that work is forbidden, rather it is celebrated by reciting Hallel and saying the prayer of Al HaNissim in the thanksgiving section of the Amidah prayers.

Thus we see that according to Rashi there was a special ruling by our Rabbis to insert the prayer of Al HaNissim in the thanksgiving section of the Amidah prayer. The Rambam, however, does not hold this opinion. In his Hilchos Chanukah, he does not mention the requirement of reciting Al HaNissim at all. He did, however, mention this requirement in *Hilchos Tefillah 1:13*. There we find the following statement:

בחנוכה ובפורים מוסיפין בהודאה על הנסים.

> On Chanukah and Purim we add to the prayers of thanksgiving — Al HaNissim.

The reason the Rambam did not mention this requirement in

Hilchos Chanukah was because he believes that it is not unique to the laws of Chanukah. Rather, because of the miracle of Chanukah we are obligated to give thanks and express our gratitude. This obligation is to be viewed as an extension of the overall obligation of gratitude which we articulate every day of the year in the prayers of "מודים אנחנו לך". It is interesting to note that in the Rambam's "סדר תפלות כל השנה" which is found at the end of the "ספר אהבה", where he delineates the prayers recited throughout the year, he writes regarding Al HaNissim as follows:

נוסח ברכות התפלה וסידורון.

בפורים מברך ברכת שמונה עשרה בנוסח זה: מודים אנחנו לך שאתה הוא ה' אלוקינו על חיינו המסורים בידך, על נשמותינו הפקודות לך, על נסיך שבכל יום ויום, ועל נפלאותיך שבכל עת כו', **על הנסים** ועל הגבורות ועל התשועות כו' ועל כולם ה' אלוקינו מודים לך הטוב כי לא כלו וכו'.

בחנוכה מברך ברכה זו בנוסח זה מודים אנחנו לך וכו' עד ועל נפלאותיך שבכל עת ערב וצהרים על הנסים וכו' עד ואחר כך באו בניך וכו'...

Thus we see that the Rambam includes על הנסים *within* the מודים, the thanksgiving prayer itself and not *after* it. Therefore, we are to view the על הנסים as an *extension* of the thanksgiving prayer. This reinforces our contention that whenever the word "ומוסיף" is used, it is to be understood, not as an "addition", but rather as an "extension" (see Part I of our discussion here).

Rashi, however, does not share this view. He does not consider the recitation of על הנסים to be an extension of the "מודים" thanksgiving prayer. It is rather to be viewed as an independent separate prayer, recited according to the ordinance of the Sages that it be said on Chanukah within the הודאה section of the Amidah.

Rashi writes, "ולומר על הנסים בהודאה". He explains that it is not that we are to express thanksgiving, but rather that the על הנסים which we recite should be inserted in the thanksgiving section of the Amidah. The על הנסים alludes to the events of the day, namely the Chanukah miracle. However, one can not just insert a prayer into the Amidah. Our Sages ordained that one can not add it within the section of praises, petitions or thanksgiving, but only at the end of the מודים thanksgiving section. The subsequent prayer of "וכל החיים יודוך סלה" is said to end the beracha of "מודים" with a concluding theme of thanksgiving, when we say: "ברוך..ולך נאה להודות".

The law stipulates that a concluding beracha must be similar to what is said just before it. In addition, our Sages wanted על הנסים to be recited within the context of a beracha.

From this we can see that according to R' Eliezer, we are being taught here a principle regarding the makeup of the Amidah. Namely, if any addition is to be made within a prayer, in particular a matter pertaining to the occasion of the day, מעין המאורע, it is to be said only at the conclusion of the מודים thanksgiving prayer. As for the addition on a fast day of "עננו", and the "נחם" recited on Tisha B'Av, and inserted into the prayers, we have already explained that these particular prayers are to be viewed as an *extension* of the existing prayer and thus an integral part of that prayer. The על הנסים, on the other hand, is an independent prayer, according to R' Eliezer.

The רש"ש, in his commentary on *Mesechtas Beitza 17a*, maintains that the position of R' Eliezer is that the prayer of יעלה ויבא is to be inserted in the thanksgiving, הודאה, section. He makes the following observation:

ר' אליעזר אומר בהודאה: וכן הוא אומר בהבדלה בפרק
ה' דברכות במשנה...

R' Eliezer follows here his manner of thinking as recorded in Mesechtas Berachos, where he contends that Havdalah should be recited in the thanksgiving prayer.

We might suggest, rather, that R' Eliezer maintains that Havdalah should be recited at the end of the thanksgiving prayer, not because of the consideration of thanksgiving, but rather as a way of referring to the occasion of the day. For as we have seen, according to R' Eliezer a מעין המאורע is to be said only at the end of the מודים thanksgiving prayer.

With this in mind, we can now understand the following words of Rashi: "כמו שאומר על הנסים בחנוכה ופורים". He maintains that יעלה ויבוא is to be recited, just as על הנסים on Chanukah is said, at the end of the הודאה prayer. This is based on the principle that anything to be added must be inserted at the end of the Amidah prayer. Consequently, although the יעלה ויבוא is viewed essentially as a petition, yet there is no infraction involved in inserting a petition into the thanksgiving section of the Amidah. For a petition is prohibited only when it is recited as an actual part of the thanksgiving prayer (since this section is reserved exclusively for expressing gratitude, and therefore it may not include petitions). Here however, we have permission to add the יעלה ויבוא prayer, and therefore a new prayer, which justifiably can be inserted, must be inserted at the end of the thanksgiving section, even if it happens to be a petition. Thus we need not alter its content or נוסח, and it can be recited as it is, according to the opinion of Rav Eliezer.

VIII

Justifying R' Eliezer's View

The Torah has "seventy faces" — ע' פנים לתורה, and therefore there are many different ways of viewing a matter. And even though this view of R' Eliezer that יעלה ויבא may be inserted in the הודאה section is valid, we may explore other possibilities as well.

As we have discussed, the requirement to recite יעלה ויבא is based on two considerations. The first one is that Rosh Chodesh is a day of remembrance, יום זכרון, as we know from the Torah, where it is written (in *Bamidbar 10:10*):

וביום שמחתכם..ובראשי חדשיכם..והיו לכם לזכרון לפני ה׳.

The second consideration is that we are obligated to articulate that today is Rosh Chodesh, because of קדושת היום, the holiness of the day, so designated as a result of the special sacrifice, the Korban Mussaf, which is offered on this day.

Based on this, we might attempt to explain the thinking of Rav Eliezer in another light. We learn in *Mesechtas Beitza, 17a:*

ת״ר: שבת שחל להיות בראש חודש...מתפלל שבע ואומר מעין המאורע בעבודה...ר׳ אליעזר אומר בהודאה...

The Gemara here discusses the following question: when Rosh Chodesh occurs on a Shabbos, where are we to insert the prayer of יעלה ויבא? Since we recite only seven berachos on Shabbos (the first three blessings of praise, the last three of thanksgiving and the middle section, which articulates the holiness of the day, קדושת היום), where do we insert יעלה ויבא? On the Shabbos day we do have a section designated for the holiness of the day, which we do not have in our weekday prayers. Should we insert the יעלה ויבא in that section? On the other hand, since the קדושת היום on Shabbos concerns itself exclusively with the uniqueness of Shabbos, it does not seem appropriate to insert the Rosh Chodesh יעלה ויבא there.

The תנא קמא contends that we insert יעלה ויבוא in the same place we insert it any other time, that is, in the Avodah section of "רצה". According to this opinion, we are not to insert it in the Shabbos קדושת היום, but rather leave it where it belongs, namely, in the Avodah section.

Rav Eliezer, however, maintains that when Rosh Chodesh occurs on a weekday, when there is no קדושת היום section in the prayers, we concentrate on the aspect of זכרון, a remembrance of the day. Consequently, since we are to remember and petition for the restoration of the Avodah in the Bais HaMikdash, that is the appropriate place for יעלה ויבוא, since this prayer also emphasizes the concept of the restoration of the sacrificial offerings to the Basis HaMikdash. However, on Shabbos, since we cannot offer petitions, we cannot insert the יעלה ויבוא in the Avodah, רצה section. Therefore, maintains Rav Eliezer, we must concentrate on the קדושת היום aspect of the day, the requirement to articulate that today is Rosh Chodesh, "ביום ראש חודש הזה". Thus we insert יעלה ויבוא in the הודאה thanksgiving section.

However, we are still left with the problem of how we are to mention the זכרונות, the day of remembrance requirement, which requires us to petition Hashem to remember us on this day. To satisfy this requirement, we have two possible options. We can delete the זכרונות consideration and concentrate only on the aspect of the sanctity of the day, קדושת היום. Or, if we wish to include the זכרונות aspect, we must change the נוסח of these petitions so that they are no longer couched in the language of petition but rather become a general statement of remembering this day. This, then, would no longer constitute an infraction of offering petitions on the Shabbos day.

According to this view, Rav Eliezer contends that only when Rosh Chodesh falls on a Shabbos do the following considerations apply: The position of the יעלה ויבוא is to be changed from the רצה, Avodah section to the הודאה, thanksgiving section of the Amidah. However, when Rosh Chodesh is on a weekday, Rav

Eliezer would agree that יעלה ויבא is to be inserted in the Avodah section. Or, only on Shabbos is the נוסח of יעלה ויבא changed; however, on the weekdays, the יעלה ויבא remains in the Avodah section, as we have explained.

IX

A Different Approach

There is another way of explaining R' Eliezer's contention that we insert יעלה ויבא in the הודאה. Indeed the שיטה מקובצת in *Mesechtas Beitza 17a* comments as follows on R' Eliezer's view:

ר' אליעזר אומר בהודאה: פי' דקסבר אף **בחול** אומרת שם כמו על הנסים בהודאה, ולא קי"ל כותיה.

R' Eliezer contends that יעלה ויבא is to be said in the הודאה section of the Amidah prayer not only when Shabbos falls on a Rosh Chodesh, but even in the ordinary weekday prayer.

Therefore, we might suggest that the יעלה ויבא included in the הודאה section was not amended, but was said, as we say it, in the Avodah. And as for the question how we are to justify the fact that יעלה ויבא is a petition in this section of הודאה, we might attempt an answer based on the following insight.

As explained previously, the essence of יעלה ויבא alludes to the יום הזכרון mentioned in *Bamidbar 10:10*, which says, "ביום שמחתכם...והיו לכם לזכרון". Yet the pasuk just before this verse reads:

וכי תבאו מלחמה בארצכם על הצר הצרר אתכם והרעתם בחצצרת ונזכרתם לפני ה' אל-היכם ונושעתם מאיביכם.

And when you go to war against the adversary that oppresses you, then you shall sound an alarm with the trumpets; and you will be remembered before Hashem; and you will be saved from all your enemies.

The Sifri comments on this pasuk by saying:

וכי תבאו מלחמה בארצכם...ר' עקיבא אומר: אין לי אלא מלחמה, שדפון וירקון ואשה מקשה לילד וספינה המטרפת בים מנין? תלמוד לומר: על הצר הצורר אתכם, על כל צרה שלא תבוא על הצבור. וזכרתם ונושעתם, הא כל זמן שנזכרים ישראל, אין נזכרים אלא לתשועות.

Rabbi Akiva told us that not only in times of war but whenever danger or calamity befalls Yisrael, they need only cry out to Hashem and they will be delivered from all manner of troubles. And by appealing to Hashem they will be remembered by Him and saved.

The verse here sets down a precondition. If Klal Yisrael want to be helped by Hashem, they must petition Him — "והרעתם בחצצרת" — and then He will remember them — "ונזכרת וכו'". The underlying principle here is that once Hashem is reminded, Yisrael's deliverance from all trouble is assured — "אין נזכרים אלא לתשועות".

We are being told here that when we petition Hashem, He will remember us and bring us salvation "ביום שמחתכם...ובראשי חדשיכם".

According to this view, we can see that the petition here is a prerequisite for assured Divine salvation. Thus, יעלה ויבוא is not considered a petition in itself, but rather, as we have explained, it is a *precondition* for attaining Divine salvation.

If this is so, we can understand how Rav Eliezer is of the opinion that since we are being assured that Hashem will remember us — "ונזכרתם לפני ה'" — then the prayer of יעלה ויבוא can be viewed as an expression of thanksgiving, הודאה. We are grateful for Hashem's concern for our plight and His assurance that He will grant us salvation. However, in order that we be helped, we must first spell out our petition in the words of יעלה ויבוא. Thus we can now understand exactly why Rav Eliezer maintained that יעלה ויבוא must be inserted in the הודאה section of the Amidah, for its heartfelt recitation here will lead us to Divine salvation.

X

Explaining R' Eliezer - Homiletically

We might suggest a homiletic justification for R' Eliezer's placing of יעלה ויבוא in the thanksgiving section of the Amidah. We commonly understand that this section expresses gratitude for Divine kindnesses performed for us. Yet the "הודאה" section could conceivably have another interpretation. The Sefer HaChinuch, in Parashas Ekev, explains the deeper meaning of a seemingly puzzling problem. How do we *"bless Hashem"*? Does He need our blessing? Are we even capable of "blessing" Him. The answer he gives here is enlightening.

> שעניין הברכה שאנו אומרים לפניו איננו רק (אלא) הזכרה לעורר נפשנו בדברי פינו כי הוא המבורך ומבורך יכלול כל הברכות וכו' להודות אליו שכל הטובות כלולות בו והוא המלך עליהם וכו' ובלשון יתברך שאנו מזכירים תמיד, שהוא מתפעל, נאמר שהכוונה בו שאנחנו מתחננים אליו שיהי רצון מלפניך שכל בני העולם יהיו מיחסים הברכה אליך **ומודים** כי ממך תתפשט בכל וכו'.

The significance of the blessing which we recite before Him is nothing but a reminder, to arouse our spirit with the words of our mouths to know that He is the Blessed One; and the Blessed One thus contains all blessing...to gratefully acknowledge to Him that all good favors are contained in Him and He rules over them to send them wherever he wishes.

Thus "הודאה" is to be understood not so much as an expression of gratitude and thanksgiving for kindnesses rendered to us by Hashem, but rather recognition that He is the Master of the Universe. For He is the Creator and sustains all that exists in the world. Thus the הודאה section alludes to the fact that we all recognize and acknowledge that everything emanates from Him, rather than asserting that everything comes from our own efforts.

Rav Yosef Dov Soloveitchik points out that this concept is alluded to in the Grace after Meals, as set down in the Torah in *Parashas Ekev (8:10)*. There we read:

ואכלת ושבעת וברכת את ה' אלוקיך על הארץ הטובה אשר נתן לך.

And you shall eat and be satisfied and bless Hashem, your G-d, for the good land which He has given you.

The next verses (11-17) read:

השמר לך פן תשכח את ה' אלוקיך וכו'. פן תאכל ושבעת ובתים טובים תבנה וישבת. ובקרך וצאנך ירביון וכסף וזהב ירבה לך וכו'. ורם לבבך ושכחת את ה' אלוקיך המוציאך מארץ מצרים מבית עבדים וכו' המאכילך מן במדבר וכו' ואמרת בלבבך כחי ועצם ידי עשה לי את החיל הזה.

Beware, lest you forget Hashem...lest when you

have eaten and are satisfied and have built goodly houses and have dwelt therein...And when your herds and flocks multiply and your silver and gold multiply... Then your heart will be lifted up and you forget Hashem, Who took you out of Egypt, out of the house of bondage ...Who fed you in the wilderness with manna...and you say in your heart, "My power and the might of my hand has brought me this wealth."

The proximity of these verses teaches us that the purpose of our expression of gratitude in the Grace after Meals is to remember that it is Hashem, rather than our own efforts, who brought us all these blessings. The thanksgiving section of the Amidah calls upon us to recognize that every blessing originates from Him. Thus, when we petition Him on Rosh Chodesh to remember us, we are essentially acknowledging that He is able and willing to provide us with the blessings which we ask for in the prayer of יעלה ויבוא.

XI

IF ONE FORGOT TO SAY יעלה ויבוא — TWO OPINIONS

There is a difference of opinion between these two schools of thought on the issue of how one is to rectify an inadvertent omission of יעלה ויבוא from his prayers. In *Mesechtas Berachos 26b,* Tosafos writes:

> כתב רבינו יהודה אם טעה ולא הזכיר ראש חדש במנחה [ר"ח] לא יתפלל עוד בלילה [במוצאי ר"ח], דלמא יתפלל עוד, הרי כבר התפלל כל תפלת המנחה מבעוד יום לבד ר"ח שלא הזכיר, אם כן אין מרויח כלום אם יחזור ויתפלל במוצאי ר"ח, הרי לא יזכיר עוד תפלת ר"ח [יעלה ויבוא] וי"ח [שמונה עשרה] כבר התפלל..

Rabbenu Yehudah wrote, if by mistake one omitted to mention יעלה ויבוא in the Mincha prayer, he is not required to repeat the prayer at night. For why should he be required to recite a makeup prayer? As for the Amidah prayer required in the afternoon, he already offered this prayer, and by making up the recitation of יעלה ויבוא [which he inadvertently omitted], he gains nothing, for he will not be able to add this prayer of יעלה ויבוא to the evening prayer. Therefore, what does one gain by praying an additional prayer at night, when nothing is accomplished?

The חכמי פרובינצא, cited in the commentary of the תלמידי רבינו יונה, disagree with this decision of Rabbenu Yehudah and contend that if one inadvertently omitted to insert יעלה ויבוא in the Mincha prayer, he is in fact required to pray two Amidah prayers at night (one is the required regular Maariv and the other is a makeup prayer, תשלומין). Their rationale here is that omitting יעלה ויבוא from the Mincha prayer is tantamount to not having prayed at all. Therefore, one is required to offer a makeup prayer at night, even though at that time יעלה ויבוא will not be recited.

Rav Chaim Brisker explains the difference between these two approaches in the sefer "כתבים המיוחסים בשם הגר"ח, זצ"ל". The Scholars of Provence are of the opinion that failure to include יעלה ויבוא in the Amidah prayer of Rosh Chodesh means that in effect one has not prayed at all. For the יעלה ויבוא on Rosh Chodesh is an integral part of the Amidah prayer. This omission then requires one to make up the Amidah prayer by reciting it again.

However, Rabbenu Yehudah is of the opinion that as far as the Amidah prayer is concerned, even without the inclusion of יעלה ויבוא, it is still considered a valid recitation of the Amidah, except for the fact that one has failed to fulfill one's obligation to recite יעלה ויבוא. This can be compared to the case when one fails to mention the Havdalah prayer in the Shemoneh Esreh on Motzei Shabbos, and he also does not have a cup of wine over which to recite Havdalah. In such a case, the halacha stipulates that one must repeat the Amidah, even though he has already prayed and is credited with a legitimate prayer. One must repeat the Amidah in order to fulfill one's obligation to recite Havdalah, just as one must repeat the Amidah on Rosh Chodesh if he omitted יעלה ויבוא, even though he is credited with a legitimate Amidah on that occasion as well. However, on the following night, when it is no longer Rosh Chodesh, there is no way one can make up for the omitted יעלה ויבוא, and thus there is no reason to repeat the Amidah.

QUESTIONING THE DECISION OF THE REMA

It is stated in the Shulchan Aruch, Orach Chaim, סימן קח, סעיף י"א, that if one forgot to recite יעלה ויבוא in the Mincha prayer on Rosh Chodesh he should offer a makeup prayer at night in the form of a נדבה, a "gift offering", as a voluntary prayer. The explanation for this is that according to the Scholars of Provence one who failed to say יעלה ויבוא is as if he failed to pray at all. We take this view into consideration, based on the fear that perhaps these commentators are correct and we therefore require a repetition of the Amidah.

If so, we are confronted with the following halachic question. The Rema in Orach Chaim (סימן תכב סעיף א') rules that if one is in doubt as to whether or not he recited יעלה ויבוא, it is not necessary to repeat the Amidah prayer. The halacha also reads that if one is in doubt as to whether or not he prayed at all, then he is required to repeat the Amidah. This ruling is based on the consideration of the position of Rav Yochanan that even if we were to pray all day, "דהלואי שיתפלל כל היום כולו", yet there would still be room for additional prayers. Consequently, one might ask, if it is as the Scholars of Provence maintain, and the omission of יעלה ויבוא is tantamount to not having prayed at all, how can one say that if he is in doubt as to whether or not he mentioned יעלה ויבוא in his Amidah prayer, he need not repeat the Amidah? For if the omission of יעלה ויבוא is tantamount to not having prayed, why is one not required to repeat the Amidah, which is certainly called for if one is in doubt as to whether or not he davened at all? Indeed, the Rosh does mention that according to the Scholars of Provence, if one is in doubt as to whether or not he said יעלה ויבוא, he is obligated to repeat the Amidah. Thus the Shulchan Aruch, in סימן קח, סעיף א', does take into consideration the opinion of the Scholars of Provence and maintains that perhaps the halacha is in accordance with their opinion. Why, then, does the Rema rule that one need not repeat the Amidah prayer if he is in doubt as to whether or not he recited יעלה ויבוא?

To answer this, we might suggest the following. It is true that we take into account the opinion of the Scholars of Provence, but only when one is *certain* that he did not recite יעלה ויבוא. Only in this case do we consider it tantamount to not having prayed at all. However, if one is in doubt as to whether or not he recited יעלה ויבוא, the issue to be considered is not whether he has davened, but only whether he has fulfilled his obligation to recite יעלה ויבוא. And the question to be decided is whether or not an omission of יעלה ויבוא requires a repetition of the Amidah. In other words, when it is a case of *doubt* whether or not one recited יעלה ויבוא, we do not take into consideration the opinion of the Scholars of Provence. We do so only when we are *certain* that one did not recite יעלה ויבוא.

XII

Another way to view this difference of opinion

Other commentators explain these two opinions (See the sefer "אשר לשלמה -מועד", סימן א'). According to Tosafos in Mesechtas

Berachos 26a, ד"ה איבעיא להו, the Mussaf prayer has no way of being compensated for, no תשלומין, for when the time for Mussaf has expired, we apply the principle of "עבר זמנו בטל קרבנו", that once the time period in which the sacrifice was to be brought has expired, then the sacrifice is null and void and can no longer be offered. This applies to the Mussaf sacrifice. However, in regard to the daily weekday Amidah, even though an Amidah is required every day, so too is a petition for Hashem's mercy, רחמים. One must pray for mercy from above. And if one failed to pray at the prescribed time, although he can never make up the prayer he missed, since the time has passed, he is nevertheless still obligated to recite an Amidah prayer to petition the Almighty for mercy.

This is the reason why the Baalei Tosafos contend that a prayer without the inclusion of יעלה ויבוא is still considered a valid prayer, as far as the requirement of petitioning for mercy is concerned. And therefore there is no need to offer a makeup prayer. However, the Scholars of Provence maintain that there are several possible options.

We might contend that a prayer not recited properly, that is, having prayed without the required יעלה ויבוא, does not constitute a proper prayer, even as far as petitioning for mercy is concerned. Therefore a second makeup evening prayer would be required. Or we might say that even a prayer without the inclusion of יעלה ויבוא fulfills the requirement of petitioning for mercy, בקשת רחמים. Yet having prayed without the required יעלה ויבוא means that one did not fulfill his requirement of offering the daily Mincha prayer, and therefore a makeup prayer is called for.

Another possible explanation

There is another way to explain this disagreement between Rabbenu Yehudah and the Scholars of Provence. This is discussed in the sefer "תורת גרשום" מהרב יהודה גרשוני. Chazal tell us in *Mesechtas Shabbos 24a*:

איבעיה להו מהו להזכיר של חנוכה במוספין כיון דלית ביה מוסף בדידיה לא מדכרינן או דילמא יום הוא שנתחייב בארבע תפלות. רב הונא ורב יהודה דאמרי תרווייהו: אינו מזכיר רב נחמן ורבי יוחנן דאמרי תרווייהו: מזכיר.

> They inquired in the yeshiva: what is the law regarding whether one is required to mention the Chanukah blessings in the Mussaf prayer (i.e., on Shabbos and Rosh Chodesh Teves)? Do we say that since there is no Mussaf prayer on Chanukah we do not mention it in the blessing? Or perhaps it is a day that requires four Amidah prayers (Ma'ariv, Shacharis, Mussaf and Mincha), and so we do recite the Al HaNissim in the Mussaf prayer. Rav Huna and Rav Yehudah both say that one *does not* mention the Chanukah blessing in Mussaf. However, Rav Nachman and Rav Yochanan both maintain that one *does* indeed mention it.

The rationale behind their opinion is that the phrase "it is a day that requires four Amidah prayers" is understood to mean that the addition of Al HaNissim was not simply an addition to the prayers, but rather the קדושת היום, the sanctity and uniqueness of the day, caused this prayer to be included in all the prayers said on this day. Thus, Al HaNissim has now become an integral part of the nusach, the structure of the Amidah prayer. Consequently, the קדושת היום, the uniqueness of the day, requires that all prayers said on this day, including Mussaf, should include the Al HaNissim.

Similarly, we may say that the recitation of יעלה ויבוא on Rosh Chodesh is not merely an additional prayer tagged onto the Amidah, but rather because of the קדושת היום, the holiness of the day, it has become an integral part of the day's prayers. Thus failure to recite יעלה ויבוא means that all the prayers of the day were not recited properly and must be rectified by reciting a makeup prayer.

On the other hand, the opinion that Al HaNissim is not called for in the Mussaf prayer considers the addition of Al HaNissim not as the result of קדושת היום but merely as a requirement that these words be said on an auspicious day. The יעלה ויבוא can also be viewed in this vein, and therefore omitting its recitation would mean that the daily prayer was said properly, and it was only the additional segment of יעלה ויבוא that was missing.

SUGGESTING A RESOLUTION

We might suggest that the position of Rabbenu Yehudah is based on the conclusion drawn here from the statements cited in the *Gemara Berachos 26b:*

> תנו רבנו: טעה ולא התפלל מנחה בערב שבת מתפלל בליל שבת שתים. טעה ולא התפלל מנחה בשבת מתפלל במוצאי שבת שתים של חול...

> If one mistakenly did not pray Mincha on Erev Shabbos, a makeup of two Amidah prayers are called for...and both prayers are of the Shabbos Shemoneh Esrei. If one mistakenly did not pray Mincha on Shabbos day, then one prays two Amidah prayers on Saturday night...And both prayers of a weekday prayer.

It is from this last statement that Rabbenu Yehudah concluded that these makeup prayers are only required when one failed and did not pray Mincha at all, and therefore a makeup prayer is called for. However, the fact is that by not praying Mincha on Shabbos day one also failed to make the required mention of Shabbos in the Amidah prayer of Shabbos. One might expect this omission in itself to require a makeup prayer. Yet we might conclude that since on Motzei Shabbos we can not add a mention of Shabbos in our prayers, therefore no makeup prayer is possible. Extending this principle to Rosh Chodesh, Rabbenu Yehudah maintains that if one failed to say יעלה ויבוא on Rosh Chodesh day at Mincha, then no makeup is possible, for, as we have explained, after Rosh Chodesh is over, it is not possible to mention it as the occasion of the day.

DEFENDING THE MAGEN AVRAHAM

We will encounter a problem if we adopt the position that if one fails to mention יעלה ויבוא, this is considered as if one never prayed at all, and not simply that one neglected to mention the occasion of the day, מעין המאורע.

The Shulchan Aruch in סימן קכד, סימן יו"ד states:

> מי ששכח ולא אמר יעלה ויבוא בראש חודש או בחולו של מועד או בכל דבר שצריך לחזור בשבילו, יכוין דעתו וישמע מש"ץ כל י"ח ברכות.

> If one forgets and did not say the prayer of יעלה ויבוא on Rosh Chodesh, Chol HaMoed, or forgot to say anything else which requires one to go back and pray again if he omitted it, he should concentrate and listen to the reader of the communal prayer when he recites the Eighteen Blessings from beginning to end.

The Magen Avraham comments on this. He says:

דאף על גב, דקי"ל דש"ץ אינו מוציא אלא דווקא מי שאינו בקי שאני הכא שהתפלל אלא ששכח ולא הזכיר ולכן אף על פי שהוא בקי הש"ץ מוציא.

For even though we rule that a communal prayer leader can solely make his blessings serve for someone to fulfill his obligation when that person is not capable of saying them himself, the circumstances here are different, since he already prayed, but merely forgot to include the prayer of יעלה ויבוא.

This leads us to ask the following question. If indeed the failure to mention יעלה ויבוא is tantamount to not reciting the prayer at all, how then can one simply listen to the prayer of the ש"ץ, the communal reader, if he is a בקי, that is, capable of praying for himself. For the law reads that the reader does not discharge this type of listener's obligation to pray (see מאסף תורני "ישורון-ב" עמ' שס"ה).

To answer this question, we might suggest that there is a difference between the case of a בקי, one proficient in reading on his own - in which case the reader can not discharge the listener's obligation- and our case, when one failed to recite יעלה ויבוא in the Amidah prayer on Rosh Chodesh. A communal prayer leader can not discharge the obligation of one who can read, but as yet did not pray. However, in our case, when one did pray but failed to recite יעלה ויבוא, perhaps the reader can help. The Scholars of Provence maintain that a failure to say all that was required means that a proper prayer was not offered. However, in essence, the reader *prayed* and even though he is required to repeat the prayer, he is still viewed as one who offered a valid prayer. Thus when does the halacha stipulate that the communal prayer leader can not discharge the obligation of one who can read on his own, a בקי? Only when the person did not pray at all but sought to rely on the prayer leader to fulfill his own obligation. However, it seems logical to assume that if he did pray, then all he needs is that his obligation to mention יעלה ויבוא be fulfilled, and this can only be done within the context of an Amidah prayer. Thus it suffices to fulfill his obligation if he simply listens to the complete repetition of the Shemoneh Esrei by the chazan.

XIII

If one mentioned Rosh Chodesh in the שמע קולנו

The sefer "שלמי חגיגה", written by HaRav Shlomo Algazi, in דיני יעלה ויבוא בראש חודש, סימן ב' או"ק ג' tells us:

כתב הרב ברכי יוסף הי"ו [זצ"ל]...דאם אמר בשמע קולנו בקשה, שהזכיר בה ראש חודש ושכח ולא אמר יעלה ויבוא, אין צריך לחזור ע"כ.

The Birkei Yosef writes that if in the prayer of שמע קולנו one made a petition in which he mentioned Rosh Chodesh (if, for example, one asked Hashem, "Help me on this day of Rosh Chodesh.") and then proceeded in his prayers and forgot to say יעלה ויבוא in its proper place, he need not repeat the Amidah prayer (because, in the Amidah prayer he has just recited, he *did* mention Rosh Chodesh, even though not in its proper place).

In the sefer (סימן כד, פרק ד) על מסכת ברכות "בכורי ארץ", by HaRav Avraham Yitzchak Tucker, the author points out that HaRav Shlomo Kluger differs from the decision of the Birkei Yosef. In his commentary on the Shulchan Aruch, "חכמת שלמה", in סימן תכ"ב, או"ק א', HaRav Kluger writes as follows:

שנשאל במי שאמר יעלה ויבוא בין שומע תפלה לרצה מה
דינו אם צריך לחזור ולהתפלל? והשיב שם דצריך לומר
על הסדר, תחלה רצה ואחר כך יעלה ויבוא, ולא להיפך,
ודינו כדין אם לא זכר יעלה ויבוא כלל, יעו"ש.

We were asked the question concerning one who recited the יעלה ויבוא sandwiched between the prayer of שמע קולנו and רצה. What is the law? Is one obligated to repeat his prayers? And the חכמת שלמה answered: "One is indeed obligated to repeat his prayers, for one is obliged to recite his prayers in order, first רצה and only afterwards יעלה ויבוא; and if one *changed the order*, it is to be viewed as if he omitted the יעלה ויבוא."

Thus we can conclude, maintains the "בכורי ארץ" that the "חכמת שלמה" is of the opinion that only if one recites יעלה ויבוא in its proper place is one's obligation to mention Rosh Chodesh thereby fulfilled. However, if it is inserted in any other place, even in the שמע קולנו, this is considered to be out of order, in contrast to the previously cited opinion of the Birkei Yosef.

We might contend that this assumption may not be true, and that the "חכמת שלמה" is concerned here with an entirely different issue, one that does not touch upon the opinion or the question discussed by the Birkei Yosef. The "חכמת שלמה" makes the point that the prayer of יעלה ויבוא cannot be recited or inserted in the Amidah prayer independently, but rather it must be said as part of an existing beracha. Chazal chose the beracha of the Avodah, רצה, as the proper place in which to insert it (See *Tosafos Shabbos 24a*, "ד"ה "בבונה ירושלים").

Therefore, the "חכמת שלמה" points out that if one inserted יעלה ויבוא between רצה and שמע קולנו, one thereby recited יעלה ויבוא *before* רצה, and this is considered to be out of order. And it is as if one did not include יעלה ויבוא in the beracha of רצה.

Rather, one recited יעלה ויבוא on its own, instead of within the context of a beracha. And this means that one has not fulfilled his obligation to mention Rosh Chodesh.

The simple reading of Ha Rav Shlomo Kluger's comments confirms this contention. The "חכמת שלמה" writes:

אך גם הזכרה לא הוי במקום הזה, דמקומו הוא בעבודה ולא קודם לו. ואינו דומה לאם סיים הברכה דיכול לומר יעלה ויבוא, דהתם ב**סוף** הברכה הוי ברכה אריכתא, אבל קודם **שהתחיל** בעבודה ודאי אינו הזכרה בעבודה ולא יצא.

Yet the mention of Rosh Chodesh here is not in the proper place, for its place is in the Avodah and not before it. This is not to be compared to the situation in which one only remembered to mention יעלה ויבוא at the very end of the beracha of the Avodah, where the halacha allows one to insert יעלה ויבוא. For there we view it as an extended beracha of the Avodah prayer. This means that יעלה ויבוא was actually recited in its proper place, that is, in the Avodah. However, if one mentioned it before he started the Avodah, it is certainly considered as if one did not mention it at all in the Avodah.

We can support this explanation, continues Rav Shlomo Kluger, by pointing to a decision made by the Magen Avraham regarding the beracha of "רפאינו". He rules that once the beracha here is made at the conclusion of the "רפאינו" prayer, one cannot continue praying for those who are ill. For this would mean that we would have to recite the blessing of "רפאינו" all over again. And adding a petition here would mean that our prayers were being said out of order. And so it is with the matter of the יעלה ויבוא prayer; if it is said *before* the Avodah, it is to be viewed as being recited out of order. This explanation seems proper and clear, asserts Rav Kluger regarding this opinion of the Magen Avraham.

ויש סמך לזה ממה שכתב המגן אברהם סימן קכד, לענין אם גמר ברכת רפאינו דאינו יכול לומר ענינו, דאם כן יצטרך לחזור ולומר רפאינו, דצריך לומר **על הסדר**. הכי נמי צריך לומר **על הסדר**, תחלה "רצה" ואחר כך, יעלה ויבוא, ולא להיפך. כנלפענ"ד נכון וברור...

We can see that the explanation here of being "out of order" is that a prayer that is not recited in its proper place is not to be included as part of the beracha just recited. For example, a petition for someone who is ill, which is recited *after* the completion of the beracha is not allowed, but is considered to be out of order. We may suggest that the same is true of יעלה ויבוא when it is said before "רצה". It is not to be viewed as part of the Avodah beracha, and therefore it is out of order. It is not considered to be out of order simply because it was said before the Avodah.

From this we can understand that the issue touched upon by the "חכמת שלמה" is not the same issue as the one addressed by the Birkei Yosef.

XIV

THE מאמר מרדכי DISAGREES

However, the מאמר מרדכי (as quoted in the "שלמי חגיגה") disagrees with this decision of the Birkei Yosef and maintains that even if one mentioned יעלה ויבוא in the blessing of שמע קולנו and even if it was mentioned elsewhere in the Amidah prayer, it still does not count, for it was not said in its proper place. This is positive proof that the מעין המאורע, the "occasion of the day", must also be inserted in its proper place. This is based on the following statement made in Mesechtas Berachos (מח, ב).

> The order of the blessings in Bircas HaMazon is as follows: The first blessing is the blessing of "הזן". The second is the blessing for the land, "נודה לך". The third is the blessing for the rebuilding of Yerushalayim, "ובנה ירושלים". The fourth is the blessing of "הטוב והמטיב".

On Shabbos, one begins the blessings with words of consolation, either "רחם" or "נחמנו" and concludes with words of consolation, "רצה".

Rav Eliezer says, if one wishes, he may say "רצה" in the blessing of consolation or he may say it in the blessings of the land. And if one wishes he can say it in the "הטוב והמטיב". Our Sages, however, contend that one may not say it anywhere except in the blessing of consolation, for that is its proper place.

The Magen Avraham, in סימן קפח, agrees that the law is in accordance with the opinion of the Sages. Thus if one deviates from the designated format, he has not fulfilled the mitzva.

אמנם בספר מאמר מרדכי חלק על זה וכתב וזה לשונו: נראה לי דאף על פי שהזכיר ענין ראש חודש בשומע תפלה או באחת מן האמצעיות, לא יצא. וראיה ברורה ממה שאמרו בברכות (דף מח, ע״ב) דמה שאמרו לענין הזכרת שבת בברכת המזון מתחיל בנחמה ואומר קדושת היום כו׳. רבי אליעזר אומר רצה לאומרה בנחמה אומרה, בברכת הארץ אומרה כו׳, וחכמים אומרים אינו אומרה אלא בנחמה בלבד, ואמרינן עלה, חכמים היינו תנא קמא, איכא בינייהו דיעבד, דלרבנן בתראי מהדרינן ליה. וכתב המגן אברהם (סימן קפ״ח). דהכי קיימא לן.

הנה מבואר דכל שלא הזכיר המאורע במקום המיוחד לו,

שינה ממטבע שטבעו חכמים כו', קל וחומר הדברים בנדון שלפנינו...

The שלמי חגיגה at this point agrees with the מאמר מרדכי that the mere mention of יעלה ויבוא in the שמע קולנו does not suffice, yet he contends that one need not bring proof from the Gemara Berachos. However, the very sugya in the Gemara that concerns itself with the laws of יעלה ויבוא, the Gemara in *Berachos* (כט,ב) itself can serve as proof of this theory that one cannot fulfill the requirement of reciting יעלה ויבוא anywhere but in the Avodah, in the exact place where it was specified. For the Gemara there states: If one erred and did not mention in the prayer of Rosh Chodesh, in the Temple blessing (עבודה - רצה) he returns to the Avodah. If he remembered his omission during the blessing of thanksgiving (מודים), then he returns to the Temple service (רצה). If he remembers his omission in the blessing of "שים שלום" he returns to the "רצה".

Thus we can conclude that if one did not return to the רצה, but rather inserted יעלה ויבוא — the theme of Rosh Chodesh as soon as he remembered his omission, then one would still not have corrected the omission of יעלה ויבוא properly, and thus he is still required to insert it in the Avodah section. Thus we see that one is not allowed to insert "יעלה ויבוא" anywhere but in the place originally designated for it by our Sages — that is, in the Avodah.

ואני אומר לו מה לו להביא ממרחק לחמו, כי לפי הדמיון הזה שדמה בדעתו אין צריך להביא עצות ממרחוק כי אם ממקומו הוא מוכרע בהזכרת ראש חודש דאמרו בש"ס (ברכות דף כ"ט, ע"ב) טעה ולא הזכיר של ראש חודש בעבודה חוזר, נזכר בהודאה חוזר לעבודה, בשים שלום חוזר לעבודה, ומשמע ודאי דאם לא חזר לעבודה אלא שהזכיר שם במקום שנזכר בהודאה או בשים שלום, לא עשה כלום, דאי לאו הכי אלא בדיעבד אהני אזכרתה במקום שנזכר, למה אמרו שיחזור לעבודה, הרי זה דיעבד גמור הוא ששכח וכבר בירך ברכתו, ואמאי חייבוהו לחזור ולברך

ולעשות ברכתו שבירך כבר ברכה לבטלה, טוב היה יותר לומר דבדיעבד אם לא אמרה במקומה יאמר במקום שנזכר, אלא ודאי דכל שלא אמרה כתקנת חז"ל הוי שינוי מטבע שטבעו חכמים.

Refuting both proofs

The שלמי חגיגה rejects both these proofs. Rather he suggests another solution to the problem. There is a vast difference between whether the prayer of Rosh Chodesh is recited after the Avodah, in "מודים", or in the "שמע קולנו". Chazal tell us, in *Mesechtas Avodah Zarah* that one can make a personal petition in the "שמע קולנו", even to the point that if one failed to add "ותן טל ומטר" in the beracha of "ברך עלינו", it can be "made up" in the section of "שמע קולנו". This compensation applies exclusively to "שמע קולנו" and not to any other beracha.

This is the reason why we cannot insert יעלה ויבוא in the prayers that follow the Avodah section of the Amidah, for these sections cannot serve as makeup sections for other berachas or petitions which were omitted. And so, if we were to insert יעלה ויבוא there, this would accomplish nothing. However, שמע קולנו, which serves as an all-inclusive prayer, is an acceptable place for making up omissions and for adding petitions which we forgot to mention earlier. And since יעלה ויבוא can be considered a petition, it too can be "made up" here in שמע קולנו, even before we reach the proper place for its recitation in the Avodah. And thus we can say that if we did mention Rosh Chodesh in this prayer, it would suffice to fulfill our obligation to mention Rosh Chodesh. However, in the Grace after Meals, we do not have one particular prayer that can serve as an all-inclusive prayer. Therefore the prayer of רצה said on Shabbos must be recited in its proper place, and mentioning it elsewhere serves no purpose.

Consequently, the שלמי חגיגה now contends that the decision of the Birkei Yosef is to be upheld. If one inserted a petition including the mention of Rosh Chodesh in the קולנו שמע, he need not repeat the Shemoneh Esreh. He explains this as follows:

דהתשובה הנזכרת לא איירי אלא כשהזכיר ראש חודש בשומע תפלה. ונראה ודאי שדוקא בכהאי גוונא אהנייא הזכרתו לשם, לפי שברכת שומע תפלה היא ברכה כללית להזכיר בה כל מילי כמו שאמרו [בגמרא עבודה זרה, דף ז, ע"ב], שואל אדם צרכיו בשומע תפלה, ופשיטא ודאי דאם שאל גשמים בברכה אחרת לא אהני כלום, דדוקא בשומע תפלה אמרו דהוי מזור למחלתו... ואם כן גבי יעלה ויבוא שכל הנוסח הוא לשון תפלה, אם הזכיר ראש חודש בשומע תפלה בבקשתו ושכח ולא הזכיר בעבודה, מהני הזכרתו למפרע בשומע תפלה, דמה לפנים ומה לאחור... ומעתה מה הדמות כלל יש לזה להזכרת שבת בברכת המזון, דבההיא לא תיקנו חז"ל ברכה אחת פרטית לכלול בה כל שאלותיו כמו שתיקנו בתפלה ברכת שומע תפלה, ולכן בברכת המזון כל ששינה מקום ההזכרה הוי שינה מטבע כמו בשאר ברכות התפלה חוץ מברכת שומע תפלה...

In conclusion, the שלמי חגיגה concurs with the position of the Birkei Yosef that the mere mention of Rosh Chodesh in the שומע תפלה suffices. Yet we would contend that the ruling of the מאמר מרדכי is the correct decision here. We base this on the following two considerations.

The Shemoneh Esrei is made up of various sections, each serving a unique purpose. The Amidah prayer begins with praises and only afterwards are we allowed to offer petitions. These petitions, צרכיו, are the "middle berachos" of the Amidah. After this section the Avodah follows, which includes the petition for the restoration of the Temple service. We then conclude the order of the prayers with the הודאה, expressing gratitude for the many kindnesses bestowed on us by Hashem. Given this composition of the prayers, one might ask, if indeed the Avodah is to be viewed as a petition, why was it set apart after that section of petitions, צרכיו, which conclude with the שמע קולנו? Why was it not inserted in the petition section which ends with the שמע קולנו?

From this arrangement of the prayers we can understand that since the Avodah section follows the שמע קולנו, the Avodah is not to be viewed as part of the section of petitions, even though it too is essentially a petition. If this is so, then it would follow that whereas the שמע קולנו serves as a makeup prayer for all the previous petitions, it cannot serve as a makeup prayer for the Avodah itself, which follows שמע קולנו.

Consequently, if one already mentioned in the שמע קולנו that today is Rosh Chodesh, this is considered to be out of order, since as we have discussed earlier, the שמע קולנו does not serve as a proper place for the יעלה ויבוא petition. This leads to the following question. As we have pointed out, יעלה ויבוא has two aspects: it fulfills the requirement of remembrance, for this day was established for that purpose, and it fulfills the requirement to articulate that today is Rosh Chodesh, based on the קדושת היום. Therefore, although שמע קולנו can not serve as the proper place for remembrances, since that petition belongs exclusively in the Avodah section, it is in fact the proper place to spell out that today is Rosh Chodesh.

As we have pointed out, no prayer can be placed in the Amidah prayer unless it is within an existing beracha, and it must be the appropriate beracha for it to be inserted. Thus, since remembrances belong in the Avodah section, that Avodah alone is to be seen as the appropriate beracha for the קדושת היום to be articulated, and thus, if it were to appear in שמע קולנו or in any other place, it would be considered out of order.

Chapter Three
The Half Hallel of Rosh Chodesh

I

Half-Hallel on Rosh Chodesh — a minhag

According to the formula set down in the Gemara, ער:ין יו"ד, ב, Hallel is recited only on a day which the Torah designates as a holiday, מועד, and on which work is forbidden, איסור מלאכה, or a day on which a miracle transpired. According to this halacha, it would seem that Rosh Chodesh would not require the recitation of Hallel. The Gemara states: "ראש חודש דאיקרי מועד לימא?" — "Rosh Chodesh is called a festival. Why do we not then recite the Hallel on this day?" To which the Gemara replies:

לא איקדיש בעשיית מלאכה, דכתיב (ישעיהו, ל, כט) השיר יהי' לכם כליל התקדש חג: לילה המקודש לחג טעון שירה, ושאין מקודש לחג אין טעון שירה.

> Rosh Chodesh is not sanctified regarding prohibition of work, and it is written, "You shall have a song as in the night when a festival is hallowed", i.e., only the night sanctified by the prohibition against work requires a song. However, Rosh Chodesh, which does not have a prohibition against work, does not require a song (Hallel).

The Gemara then asks: "חנוכה דלאו הכי ולאו הכי וקאמר?" — "Chanukah possesses none of these prerequisites (it is neither called a festival nor is work prohibited), and yet Hallel is recited. How is this possible?" The following answer is then given: "משום ניסא" — "We say Hallel because of the miracle."

Yet we do say half-Hallel on Rosh Chodesh, omitting certain designated sections, apparently to indicate that this day does not require the recitation of the regular full Hallel. The source for this practice is the Gemara cited in *Mesechtas Ta'anis 28b*, where we are told:

רב איקלע לבבל, חזינהו דקא קרו הלילא בריש ירחא. סבר לאפסוקינהו, כיון דחזא דקא מדלקי דלוקי, אמר שמע מינה, מנהג אבותיהם בידיהם.

Rav happened to be in Bavel and saw that the people there were reciting Hallel on Rosh Chodesh. He considered stopping them, because the recitation of Hallel is not called for on Rosh Chodesh. But when he saw that they were omitting certain sections, he said: "From this it is evident that the recitation of Hallel on Rosh Chodesh is based on a custom of their fathers which they are observing."

The obvious question here is what is the source for this minhag or custom, since according to the halacha Rosh Chodesh does not warrant the recitation of Hallel?

II

Various explanations of why Half-Hallel

There were a number of explanations offered by the classic commentators as to why we recite half-Hallel on Rosh Chodesh, even though according to the halacha no recitation of Hallel is required.

As a memorial to the Kiddush HaChodesh ceremony

Both the שיטה מקובצת and the ריטב"א in their commentaries to *Mesechtas Berachos* (י"ד, א, ד"ה דלא), contend that the recitation of half-Hallel on Rosh Chodesh serves as a memorial to the ceremony of Kiddush HaChodesh that took place at the time when the new month was determined by eye-witnesses.

> ובראש חודש אפילו בצבור, אין קורין אותו [ההלל] אלא משום מנהגא **זכר לקידוש החודש**...

The recitation of Hallel when Kiddush HaChodesh takes place is alluded to according to the (סימן קע"ה) "שבולי הלקט", in *Psalm 150*. Twelve exclamations of "הללו" — "praise to Hashem," are to be found in this psalm, and these refer to the twelve new moons of the year. The customary repetition of the concluding verse of "כל הנשמה וגו'" alludes to the additional New Moon added in a leap year. And the key word here of "בקדשו", mentioned at the outset of this psalm, refers to the "קדוש החדש" ceremony that took place in the Bais HaMikdash.

To publicize that today is Rosh Chodesh

The Meiri, in his commentary to *Mesechtas Ta'anis 28b*, explains that we recite the half-Hallel on Rosh Chodesh to publicize that today is Rosh Chodesh. It is important that this fact be made known, for one must be aware that there are special prayers which must be recited today. These special prayers include, primarily, "יעלה ויבוא" and the Mussaf of Rosh Chodesh day.

> אבל הלל של ראש חודש מנהג קבוע לכל בני בבל כדי שיתפרסם הדבר לכל שהוא ראש חודש...

Similarly, the ראב"ד writes in his השגות on the Rambam in chapter eleven of *Hilchos Berachos, Halacha 16:*

> אבל של ראש חודש בברכה תקנוהו כדי לפרסמו שהוא

ראש חודש...אבל קריאת ההלל בימים המוקדשים וקרבן מוסף בהם, אם תקנו בהם ההלל, **משום היכר לקדושתן.**

The custom of reciting Hallel on Rosh Chodesh calls for a beracha [although one usually does not recite a beracha for a practice that is based on a custom]. For the purpose of this Hallel was to publicize the fact that today is Rosh Chodesh, and so this justified the insertion of a beracha...even though on other days when we recite the Hallel, it is because of the particular sanctity of the day.

The Meiri points out that only in Bavel did they recite the Hallel in order to publicize that today was Rosh Chodesh; whereas in Eretz Yisrael the mere fact that they still sanctified the new month by means of eye-witnesses, "קדוש על פי הראייה" was in itself sufficient to publicize the new month.

QUESTIONING THE MEIRI'S RATIONALE

As we have explained, the Meiri, along with other commentators, maintains that the reason half-Hallel is recited on Rosh Chodesh is to publicize that this day is Rosh Chodesh. One might justifiably ask, however, how half-Hallel could be chosen to publicize the day of Rosh Chodesh, when, as we have previously pointed out, the Gemara in ערכין (יו"ד, ב), rejects outright the recitation of Hallel on Rosh Chodesh, because work is not forbidden on that day, and the forbidding of work is the usual criterion for determining when Hallel is to be recited. "ראש חודש דאיקרי **מועד** לימא? לא איקדיש בעשיית מלאכה."

How, then, can we say that Hallel is the vehicle for announcing that today is Rosh Chodesh?

וכל התבונן בזה יתמה, שהרי הגמ' בערכין מיעטו בפירוש
ראש חודש מהלל, משום שאינו אסור בעשיית מלאכה,
ואיך משום פירסום תקנו דוקא דבר שנתמעט בפירוש.

We might suggest a possible answer to this problem. As we have explained, Rosh Chodesh ought to qualify as a day on which Hallel should be recited, for it is referred to as a "מועד". Yet since work is not forbidden on this day, Hallel is not strictly required. We might then ask, how are we to understand the Gemara here? Does it mean to tell us that since on Rosh Chodesh day work is not forbidden, therefore this diminishes the status of the day being referred to as a מועד? In other words, although the Kisvei HaKodesh refers to this day as a מועד, yet it is not to be considered a מועד that requires Hallel to be said. Or perhaps, we might say that Rosh Chodesh does indeed qualify as a מועד, a full-fledged holiday. However, in order to be able to recite Hallel, another condition must be met—that on this day work is forbidden. Consequently, since Rosh Chodesh cannot fulfill this additional requirement, Hallel is not required on Rosh Chodesh.

If we view this from the second perspective, we can perhaps understand the phenomenon of half-Hallel being recited on Rosh Chodesh. Since in essence Rosh Chodesh qualifies as a מועד, the only reason we do not recite all of Hallel is because there is no prohibition against work on this day. However, in recognition that this day is a מועד, half-hallel was instituted, and the fact that we do not recite the entire Hallel indicates that this day is Rosh Chodesh. For Rosh Chodesh hovers "halfway" between a full-fledged yom tov, which calls for a full recitation of Hallel, and a "partial" yom tov, which calls for some kind of recognition — and therefore only half of Hallel.

Thus we can see that we publicize Rosh Chodesh with a recitation of half-Hallel, for the Gemara rejects only a complete recitation of Hallel on Rosh Chodesh, but not a recitation of half-Hallel.

III

A MEMORIAL TO THE BAIS HAMIKDASH

HaRav Moshe Soloveitchik maintains that during the period when the Bais HaMikdash was in existence, there was great rejoicing in Yerushalayim on Rosh Chodesh. This joy — שמחה — required a recitation of the entire Hallel. The Kohanim offered a Mussaf sacrifice in accordance with the dictates of the Torah, the Levi'im sang special hymns in honor of this day, and the rest of Klal Yisrael worshipped with great joy by reciting Hallel. However, after the fall of Yerushalayim and the destruction of the Bais HaMikdash, Rosh Chodesh ceased to be a joyous day. A real danger now existed that the uniqueness of this day would be forgotten. Therefore, the half-Hallel was introduced in the prayers, in order to serve as a זכר למקדש, a memorial to that joy which took place on the days of Rosh Chodesh in the Bais HaMikdash.

דיש מקום לומר דבמקדש היו אומרים הלל שלם בראש חודש, ומנהגנו לומר חצי הלל בראש חודש הוא בהמשך לדין זה, שמדינא נתחייבו לומר הלל שלם במקדש, דקדושת היום דראש חודש, שפיר יש לה משמעות במקדש לחייב בהקרבת המוספים, ולומר שירה על הקרבן. וממילא יש לומר דאיכא הלל שלם במקדש מכח הך **חיוב שמחה**, דבמקדש שפיר איקרי ר"ח מועד, וכן משמע באמת מלשונו של הרמב"ן הנ"ל [בספר המצוות, שורש א] שכתב, שרק מיעטו ראשי חדשים בגבולין, ומשמע דראש חודש במקדש לא נתמעטו, ושפיר אית בהו חיוב הלל שלם, מדאורייתא. — ראה ב"מסורה", חוברת ג, ניסן תש"נ.

HALLEL OF ROSH CHODESH — SONG OF THE FUTURE

Ha Rav Yosef Dov Soloveitchik addresses this question of how we are to justify the recitation of Hallel on Rosh Chodesh, when, as we have discussed, it is neither a day when work is prohibited, nor a day on which a miracle occurred in the past. In addition, he touches on the issue of why Hallel is said in such a way that we omit two chapters from the full Hallel. He concludes that Hallel is predicated on belief in the Ultimate Redemption and the coming of Moshiach, a belief which is cherished by Klal Yisrael. And just as the moon disappears and then makes its reappearance, so too will the Jew reappear in full glory in the near future, with the coming of Moshiach. This is based on the verse which says:

ואני בחסדך בטחתי, יגל לבי בישועתך, אשירה לה' כי גמל עלי.

In Your lovingkindness I trust, my heart will exalt in Your deliverance. I will sing to Hashem, for He has dealt kindly with me.

This firm belief of the Jew in the Ultimate Redemption calls for a response of "shirah", and this is the recitation of Hallel. But one might ask, why recite Hallel only on Rosh Chodesh, when this hope for the Ultimate Redemption is cherished each and every day of the year? The answer to this question is that Rosh Chodesh symbolizes the future. Besides the allusion to the new moon as a reflection of the reappearance of Yisrael's glory, this day is also associated with David HaMelech, who personifies the kingdom of the Moshiach. Indeed, in the Kiddush Levana ceremony, the sanctification of the moon, we include the phrase "דוד מלך ישראל חי וקים" — "David, the king of Yisrael, lives and endures forever." King David's kingdom is compared to the moon, as it states in *Psalm 89:37-38:* "his throne shall be like the sun before me; like the moon, it shall be established forever." David's dynasty is compared to the moon, and it too shall be renewed, just like the moon.

And so, on the day of Rosh Chodesh we express our hope and joy in anticipation of the Ultimate Redemption. The Hallel recited on Rosh Chodesh is not to be compared to the Hallel recited on the festivals, but rather it is a unique Hallel of shirah, recited out of the joy of anticipating the future redemption. We do not speak of those trials and tribulations of the period of upheaval that is prophesied to take place just before the coming of the Moshiach — ימות המשיח. Therefore we skip those chapters of "לא לנו" and "אהבתי", which allude to this period of upheaval. For we do not wish to dampen our feeling of joy and hope or temper it with a mood of despair.

And so the half-Hallel is a Hallel of Shirah, but only a partial Shirah. For we omit those chapters which would serve to diminish our joy.

IV

Two forms of Hallel

The Gemara in *Shabbos 18b* states:

אמר ר' יוסי: יהא חלקי מגומרי הלל בכל יום.

Rav Yose said: May my portion be among those who complete the Hallel every day.

The Gemara questions this practice:

איני, והאמר מר: הקורא הלל בכל יום הרי זה מחרף ומגדף.

Is this so; did not the master say, "One who recites the Hallel every day is thereby belittling and blaspheming Hashem?" How, then, could Rav Yose have considered reciting it daily to be a worthy practice?

To which the Gemara answers:

כי קאמרינן בפסוקי דזמרא.

In regard to what we say to the claim that one should recite the Hallel every day, we recite Psukei D'Zimra.

Thus we conclude from the Gemara that there are two forms of Hallel: the Hallel of the Psukei D'Zimra, and the Hallel consisting of *Psalms 113-118*, recited on festivals and Chanukah, at the time when a miracle transpired.

The Hallel of the Psukei D'Zimra may be said every day of the year; however, the Hallel referred to as "הלל המצרי" may not be said except on the festivals and on Chanukah. Indeed, if one recites Hallel on any days other than those prescribed in the baraisa mentioned in מסכת ערכין, that person is guilty of blasphemy against Hashem. But why are we permitted to recite the Hallel of Psukei D'Zimra every day, whereas the other Hallel, "הלל המצרי" is prohibited, except on those few specified days?

The answer to this question is that the Hallel of the Psukei D'Zimra praises Hashem and refers to His miracles *within* the laws of nature, נסים מתוך דרך הטבע. The Hallel of the holidays and Chanukah, הלל המצרי, alludes to the miracles performed by Hashem *beyond* the laws of nature, מחוץ לדרך הטבע. This is the reason we refer to this type of Hallel as "הלל המצרי", for in Egypt the miracles went beyond the laws of nature. We are allowed to praise Hashem for His participation in the laws of nature every day. However, we are forbidden to verbalize every day those miracles which go beyond natural laws and which were performed for our benefit on very rare occasions throughout our history. And one who attempts to mention them as if they were everyday occurrences is guilty of blasphemy. The rationale for this position is explained by Rabbenu Yona in his commentary to *Mesechtas*

Berachos, פרק אין עומדין. We will discuss this later.

V

HALLEL COMMEMORATES EXTRAORDINARY MIRACLES

In the sefer הרב צבי הירש חיות by "דרכי משה" (עמ' תס), there is an insightful explanation as to why Hallel is recited for miracles beyond the laws of nature. This insight is based on the verse in *Koheles 3:14*:

> ידעתי כי כל אשר יעשה האל-הים הוא יהי' לעולם, עליו אין להוסיף וממנו אין לגרוע. והאל-הים עשה שיראו מלפניו.

I realize that whatever Hashem does will endure forever. Nothing can be added to it and nothing can be subtracted from it and Heaven has acted so that man shall stand in awe of Him.

The Rambam, in *Moreh Nevuchim ("Guide for the Perplexed")* explains what this statement really means:

> ומה נחמד פי' רבינו ז"ל [הרמב"ם] במורה כח לשני, על הקרא "וכי כל אשר עשה האל-הים הוא יהי' לעולם, עליו אין להוסיף וממנו אין לגרוע", ונתן עלה שיהי' כן לעולם, כאילו אמר כי הדבר אשר ישתנה. אמנם ישתנה מפני חסרון שיש בו ויושלם על ידי השתנות או אם יש בו תוספות אשר אין צורך בו, ותחסר התוספות ההוא. אכן פעולת הש"י אחר שהם בתכלית השלימות, ואי אפשר בהם תוספות וחסרון, אם כן יעמדו כפי שהם עליו לא ישתנו סדר טבעם מפני שאין חסרון נראה בהם...

He imparts in this verse the information that the world is a work of Hashem and it is eternal. He also states the cause of its being eternal, for nothing can be added to it and nothing can be taken away from it...for anything which is changed is because of a deficiency in it, that it should be made good or some excess that is not needed should be gotten rid of. Now the works of Hashem are perfect and regarding them there is no possibility of an excess or a deficiency. Accordingly, they are necessarily permanently established as they are, for there is no possibility of something calling for change in them...

The Rambam asks, why do we find miracles that change the course of nature, "ניסים מחוץ מדרך הטבע"? And he offers the following insights into this question.

וסוף הפסוק באמרו "והאלקים עשה שיראו מלפניו" הוא נתינת טעם על הנסים שעשה השם לישראל אחרי שבריאת העולם והילוך הטבע הוא נאה ומהודר, ואין חסרון במעשי ידיו של הקב"ה אם כן למה עשה הנסים לישראל, ומסיים "שיראו מלפניו" כי היה מהצורך להראות להם למען יכירו וידעו כל באי עולם שיש בורא אחד, ממציא כל נמצא, וכל הנמצאות המה ברשותו: ועל ידי זה יכירו וידעו לירא ולכבד שמו כל הימים...כי ההלל נקבע אצלנו על זכר הנסים שנעשו לישראל בדברים יוצאין מגדר הטבע והשתנות סדרי בראשית וניכר לכל כי יד ה' עשתה זאת, כמו יציאת מצרים, קבלת התורה, והקפת ענני הכבוד והדומה...

The verse, "and Hashem had made it so that they fear Him" alludes to the fact that He produces miracles in times of distress in order to bring about the salvation of His people. When this happens, the recitation of Hallel is called for in order to commemorate these occasions. These miracles are performed for the sake of Yisrael, so that they and the entire world should be aware that there is but One Creator.

And so we might say that if Hallel can only be said for a miracle created beyond the laws of nature, we might then ask, how can we account for the fact that Rosh Chodesh calls for Hallel, for it is neither a festival, מועד, on which work is forbidden, nor does it commemorate a miracle beyond the laws of nature? Thus it would seem clear that the recitation of Hallel is not required. What then is the justification and what is the source for the innovation of reciting half Hallel on Rosh Chodesh? And how can this not be an infraction of the prohibition against reciting Hallel on days when it is not called for?

VI

Rashi: Hallel Recited Only For Something New

We know from the Gemara in Pesachim 117a that Hallel is recited by Klal Yisrael when a miracle is performed to bring about their salvation. It is also recited on specified holidays during the year, such as on the three Pilgrimage Festivals. The commonly accepted interpretation of the Gemara's statement "על כל פרק ופרק" — "the prophets instituted the recitation of Hallel *for each and every season*" — is that this refers to the festivals. And the subsequent statement, "ועל כל צרה וצרה" — "*if a calamity threatens to befall Bnai Yisrael and they are saved*", is taken as a reference to the times of Hashem's salvation. What is puzzling, however, is the following comment of Rashi on *Mesechtas Pesachim 95b*. He writes:

ולקמן (קיז) אמרינן נביאים שביניהם תקנו להם שיהיו אומרים על כל פרק וכל דבר חידוש.

Later on, we are told that the prophets among them inaugurated that Hallel be said *for each and every season* and *the times when something new occurs.*

Two questions arise here: Why does Rashi allude only to the issue of "על כל פרק ופרק" — "for each and every season", and omit the entire issue of "על כל צרה וצרה", being saved from calamity? Additionally, why did Rashi add the matter of "וכל דבר חידוש"?

Many commentators suggest that one question answers the other. For "וכל דבר חידוש" essentially alludes to miracles beyond the laws of nature which were performed to save the Jewish people from situations of imminent danger. Thus we can understand that the two phrases, "וכל דבר חידוש" and "על כל צרה וצרה", both allude to the same thing, a "new" miracle which was created beyond the laws of nature in order to bring about salvation for the Jewish people. But if this is so, why didn't Rashi simply say "על כל צרה וצרה" in *Mesechtas Pesachim*, as the Gemara later states. Why substitute another phrase, that of "וכל דבר חידוש"?

A POSSIBLE ANSWER

The sefer "עמק ברכה", by הרב ארי' פומרנציק ז"ל, discusses the classic question of "הלל על הנס", reciting Hallel to commemorate a miracle beyond the laws of nature. He contends that the reason we do not recite Hallel to commemorate a miracle of salvation which occurred *within* the laws of nature is not that we do not recognize this as a miracle; we certainly do. We know this from the fact that the beracha of "אשר יצר", which expresses our gratitude for a natural act performed within the laws of nature. This beracha contains the words, "ומפליא לעשות", that "wonders are now being performed" as everyday occurrences. From this we can see that everything that happens even within the laws of nature is a miracle, if we are only spiritually sensitive enough to recognize it as such. And the only reason we do not recite Hallel for such things is that only those miracles which can be identified as supernatural occurrences by human beings require Shirah.

On the other hand, the appreciation of a miracle is left up to each individual's discretion, and if one can not discern that an act of Hashem has just taken place, then Hallel is not called for. Therefore it is only those miracles which can be proclaimed by everyone as supernatural occurrences brought about by the direct intervention of Hashem in human affairs that call for a recitation of Hallel. (See *The Commentators' Shabbos*, pp.65-67.)

The Gemara in Megillah 14b presents various reasons why Hallel is not said on Purim. This might lead us to ask, why do we need to search for reasons to prove that no recitation of Hallel is required on Purim? For, as we know, the miracle which occurred on Purim was a miracle which was "hidden" within the laws of nature. And we have just established the principle that no Hallel is called for when miracles come about through natural means.

However, our Sages made an intriguing comment on the following verse in Psalms (תהילים צ"ח, ג): "ראו אותו כל אפסי ארץ". — "All the ends of the earth saw the salvation of our Lord." When did this occur, asked our Sages? To which they replied: "בימי מרדכי ואסתר" — "In the days of Mordechai and Esther."

The meaning behind this discussion is that even though the Purim miracle was performed within the laws of nature, yet everyone in the world attested to the truth that the Divine hand was at work in the Purim story, in that events were manipulated behind the scenes by Hashem Himself. And because everyone attested to the miraculous nature of Purim, one might think that Hallel should be recited. Therefore, *Mesechtas Megillah 14b* outlines a number of specific reasons why we do not recite Hallel on Purim. Were it nor for these reasons, we would have recited Hallel on Purim.

For those other miracles, there is a prerequisite is that everyone must be able to attest to the fact that a new phenomenon has come about. This *new* aspect inspires and motivates us to praise Hashem and therefore we are moved to recite Hallel. On the other hand, miracles which occur every day do not inspire us to the same extent, since we have become accustomed to them, and thus they do not call forth Hallel from the depths of our souls, as do supernatural miracles. Perhaps this is how we should understand Rashi's words here in *Pesachim 95b,* when he adds the phrase "וכל דבר חידוש". He means that in order for Hallel to be required, a miracle must be accompanied with something new, a feeling of exhilaration, which inspires us.

With this concept in mind, we might suggest that when we view the new moon we are overcome with a feeling of inspiration, that Hashem has once more brought a new moon into its proper course. In Eretz Yisrael they acknowledged this by declaring "מקודש מקודש". In Bavel, however, where Jews did not take part in this ceremony of Kiddush HaChodesh, the sanctification of the new moon, they showed their appreciation and recognition of Hashem's Hand in the world by reciting half-Hallel. Of course, all of Hallel could not be recited, since this phenomenon in essence is not to be viewed as a miracle that calls for a full recitation of the Hallel. Nevertheless, the Jews of Bavel were motivated to express their appreciation to Hashem for the renewal of the new moon by reciting Hallel.

The three components of Hallel

The structure of Hallel is similar to the structure of the Amidah prayer. In both, we begin with praise, שבחות; we follow this with petitions, צרכיו, and we conclude with expressions of thanksgiving, הודאה.

Chapters 113 and 114 from the *Book of Psalms,* the psalms of "הללו-יה" and "בצאת ישראל", fulfill the requirement of praise,

שבחות. Chapters 115 and 116, "לא לנו" and "אהבתי" fulfill the petition requirement, צרכיו. And finally, Chapters 117 and 118, the psalms of "הללו את ה'" and "הודו לה'" fulfill the thanksgiving requirement, הודאה.

This leads to the following question. If the Hallel prayer is an expression of gratitude, why does it have a petition section? We might suggest an answer by looking at the Mishna in *Berachos 54a,* which tells us: "נותן הודאה על שעבר וצועק על העתיד" — "One should give thanks for the protection afforded him in the past and he should cry out in supplication regarding the dangers of the future."

When one receives Hashem's blessing, apart from expressing gratitude for past kindnesses, one is obligated to petition for future blessings. The rationale behind this is explained by Ha Rav Yosef Dov Soloveitchik. Since man is mortal, there is no guarantee that our present blessings will be eternal. For example, even if we are blessed with health and livelihood now, this does not mean that these blessings will remain with us tomorrow. Therefore, when we are showered with Hashem's blessings, we must petition Him to extend these blessings indefinitely for our benefit.

If the structure of the Hallel prayer is predetermined, what can we say about the structure of the half-Hallel prayer of Rosh Chodesh? We can attempt to understand this by looking at the source for the half-Hallel, which is to be found in *Mesechtas Ta'anis 28b.* There we read:

> Rav visited Bavel and saw the people there were reciting Hallel on Rosh Chodesh. He considered stopping them, but when he saw that they *skipped certain sections* of the Hallel, he realized that their recital of Hallel on Rosh Chodesh was based on a custom of their fathers, which they were upholding.

However, in light of the above structural requirement, how could they have possibly skipped certain chapters, given that the makeup of Hallel requires the inclusion of all three components — all the chapters that constitute Hallel? The answer here might seem obvious—they skipped the sections of petitions, צרכיו, in order to show that they were not reciting Hallel on a day which, according to the halacha, did not require a recitation of Hallel. In addition, by doing this, they also avoided the prohibition against reading Hallel on a day not considered a proper occasion for a Hallel recitation. This means that they intentionally changed the structure of Hallel in order to circumvent these halachic problems.

VII

Two types of Hallel

We might suggest another reason why we omit the two sections of "לא לנו" and "אהבתי" from the Rosh Chodesh Hallel and a justification for this practice. According to the halacha, there are two distinct types of hallel: Hallel of song — הלל דשירה, and Hallel of recitation — הלל דקריאה.

Hallel of Shirah

This Hallel of song is said at the very moment of deliverance, when a miracle has transpired. It is characterized by a spontaneous outpouring of gratitude to Hashem in song for the miracle He has wrought for our benefit.

Hallel of Kriyah

This is the Hallel recitation which was instituted by our Rabbis to be recited on the anniversary of a miracle. It therefore commemorates the miracle which we previously experienced.

There are a number of differences between these two types of Hallel. The Hallel of Shirah does not require us to recite the entire Hallel, for even a partial recitation is considered sufficient to fulfill our obligation to praise Hashem. Proof of this is that on Pesach night we recite only the first two chapters of Hallel before the meal, and it is this section which we refer to as "Hallel". This partial recitation of Hallel fulfills the requirements of Shirah. On Pesach night we see ourselves as if we personally left Egypt, and this is why we sing this Hallel of Shirah, which consists of the first two chapters of the regular Hallel. The Hallel of Kriyah, on the other hand, requires that the entire text of Hallel be recited. Additionally, Hallel of Shirah may be said at night; whereas Hallel of Kriyah can only be said during the day. Hallel of Shirah can also be said while being seated, whereas Hallel of Kriyah must be said standing.

Thereby, based on our previous contention, that the Hallel of Rosh Chodesh is said in consideration of "Shirah", in anticipation of the Ultimate Redemption, therefore, as articulated here, הלל דשירה suffices with a partial Hallel (half-Hallel). We therefore delete the petition section of the Hallel and thereby do not recite all of Hallel. Indeed, even according to those who maintain that Hallel on Rosh Chodesh is recited in consideration of publicizing the fact that today be Rosh Chodesh, thus even a half-Hallel would suffice to accomplish this requirement of פרסום, publicizing.

However, one might still remain puzzled why it is these particular sections of "צרכיו", petitions, are the ones that were selected to be deleted. To this we would answer based on the insight previously mentioned, that the justification of including "petitions" in a prayer said in consideration of gratitude for miracles and kindnesses done in our behalf is due to the requirement to articulate petitions after expressions of gratitude. Thereby, we might say, this is so only if the present requirement to say the Hallel be due out of consideration of gratitude. However, if Hallel is said based on the consideration of either "Shirah" or in order to publicize that today is Rosh Chodesh, this consideration that petitions follow expressions of gratitude would not apply here. Thereby, we justifiably delete these petition sections of the regular Hallel.

Another reason for half Hallel

Perhaps we can suggest another reason why only half of the regular Hallel is said on Rosh Chodesh. In the sefer "דרשות אבן שועיב", the author explains why the Torah tells us exactly when each holiday will be, except for the holiday of Shavuos, about which the Torah makes no effort to give a specific date. The reason for this, contends the "אבן שועיב", is that Shavuos is perceived as the conclusion of the Pesach holiday. The Torah commands us to count fifty days, and upon completing this count, a Yom Tov is to be celebrated. This Yom Tov is Shavuos. Thus the entire period of fifty days is to be viewed as an extension of Pesach, and Shavuos is the day when the fifty-day count ends.

Based on this explanation of the structure of Pesach and Shavuos, we can perhaps better understand why the Torah only required a half-Hallel to be recited on the last day of Pesach. For only a holiday which is complete in itself warrants a recitation of the entire Hallel. And thus it is only the first day of Pesach, which represents the beginning, and Shavuos, which marks the conclusion of this fifty-day period, which warrant a recitation of the entire Hallel. Thus the last day of Pesach is not a self-contained holiday, but rather is seen as part of an ongoing process. Therefore it warrants the recitation of only half of Hallel.

We can apply this rationale to Rosh Chodesh as well. As we have pointed out, the celebration of Rosh Chodesh is based on the concept that it heralds the future time of Ultimate Redemption. Therefore it is not a full holiday but rather serves as an introduction to that anticipated future holiday of complete redemption at the time of the Moshiach. Therefore it only warrants the recitation of half of Hallel.

ולכן לא נתייחד לו זמן בתורה בפסח שהוא ביום י"ד בניסן או בסוכות בט"ו או בראש השנה או ביום הכפורים. לא אמר בו' בסיון אלא שעשאו התורה סניפין לחג פסח, דכתיב בחג הפסח, וספרתם לכם ממחרת השבת וגו' ממחרת השבת השביעית תספרו חמישים יום והקרבתם. והנה לפי זה מכלל הפסח והוא יום אחרון שהם מ"ט יום... כן לא נתקדש יום האחרון של פסח בקרבן חלוק משאר הימים, **ואין בו הלל גמור** עד יום החמישים הנזכרים...

JUSTIFYING THE ABRIDGED VERSION

Yet, we have another problem here in regard to reciting only half-Hallel. The abridged version of the Hallel omits the first eleven verses of both *Psalm 115* (לא לנו) and *Psalm 116* (אהבתי). It is only their second halves (מה אשיב and זכרנו ה') that are recited. Thereby, the question is asked: The Gemarah in ברכות יב, ב states: We have a tradition that any passage of the Torah that Moshe Rabbeinu divided, we may divide. But, any passage that Moshe Rabbeinu did not divide, we may not divide.

כל פרשה דלא פסקה משה אנן לא פסקינן.

This law applies not only to the passages of the Torah, but to all of Tanach, נביאים וכתובים as well. If this be so, how do we divide *Psalms 116-117* and recite only half of them?

This question is addressed by הג' ר' ישעיה פיק (quoted in the sefer, תפארת צבי by (הרב צבי הירש חיות) and he offers the insight, that the prohibition of dividing a passage only applies if the beginning of the chapter was just said. However, if one begins a passage from the middle, there would be no infraction. Thus, we read only the second halves of *Psalms 116-117*, in order to avoid transgressing the law of כל פרשה דלא פסקה משה אנן לא פסקינן.

VIII

THE SOURCES FOR THE SEQUENCE OF HALLEL

The Mishna in *Mesechtas Megillah 17a* tells us that one who reads the Megillah out of sequence (i.e., including words, sentences, and paragraphs out of sequence) has not fulfilled the mitzva of reading the Megillah. The Gemara then adds that this requirement of not disrupting the sequence also applies to the recitation of Hallel, "וכן בהלל". The Gemara proceeds to find a source for this requirement of maintaining the sequence in the recitation of Hallel: "?הלל מנלן" — "From where do we know that Hallel must be recited in sequence?" The Gemara then cites various sources:

"רבה אמר: דכתיב, ממזרח שמש עד מבואו.

> Rabba said: For it is written in Hallel: "From the rising of the sun to its setting." *(Psalms 113:3)*

The end of the verse reads: "מהלל שם ה'" — "Hashem's Name is praised." Therefore, just as the rising and the setting of the sun are never reversed, so too the praising of Hashem [i.e., the recitation of Hallel] should not be reversed.

רב יוסף אמר: זה היום עשה ה'.

Rav Yosef said: For it is written in Hallel: "This is the day Hashem has made." *(Psalms 118:24)*

Just as the hours of the day are never reversed, so too must Hallel not be recited in reverse.

רב אויא אמר: יהי שם ה' מברך.

For it is written in Hallel: "The Name of Hashem shall be blessed." *(Psalms 113:2)*

The word "יהי", shall be, implies that it shall always be as it is, i.e., the praise of Hashem and His blessing shall always be in the same order.

ורב נחמן בר יצחק ואיתימא ר' אחא בר יעקב אמר מהכא, מעתה ועד עולם.

And Rav Nachman bar Yitzchak and others say it was Rav Acha bar Ya'acov who said that it can be derived from here: "From this time and forever." *(ibid.)*

This phrase is the continuation of the verse mentioned above. It teaches us that Hallel must remain in the same form forever.

IX

WHY DO WE NEED THIS SOURCE?

There are a number of sources which teach us that there is a sequence, a set formula for the recitation of Hallel. Yet, based on our previous discussion, we might point out that the formulation of Hallel is based on the structure and sequence to be found in the Amidah prayer. This includes the set order of praise, שבחות, followed by petition, צרכיו, and concluding with thanksgiving, הודאה. Just as the Amidah must follow this sequence, so too must Hallel. Why then do we require any other source to prove the necessity for the appropriate sequence for Hallel?

To answer this, we might suggest the following. We find an interesting statement in *Mesechtas Megillah 17b*:

ת"ר: מנין שאומרים אבות, שנאמר "הבו ה' בני אלים."

> Our Rabbis taught in a baraisa: From where do we know that we are to say a blessing dedicated to the Patriarchs? For it is said, "Render unto Hashem, you sons of the powerful." *(Psalms 29:1)*

The first blessing of the Amidah prayer is called "אבות", "Patriarchs". The psalm here states that we are to mention before Hashem "the powerful of the earth" (i.e., the Patriarchs). The Gemara continues with the following question:

ומנין שאומרים גבורות: שנאמר "הבו לה' כבוד ועוז."

> From where do we know that we are to say a blessing dedicated to Hashem's might? For the verse continues and says, "Render to Hashem honor and might." *(ibid.)*

ומנין שאומרים קדושה: שנאמר "הבו לה' כבוד שמו השתחו לה' בהדרת-קדש."

> From where do we know that we are to dedicate a blessing to Hashem's holiness? For the verse continues, "in the splendor of holiness." *(ibid, v.2)*

The Gemara then continues to prove that there are verses which support the sequence of the entire Amidah prayer. Here too, one might ask, why the need for these verses, when we already know of the requirement for a particular sequence in the Amidah?

The answer to this is that without spelling out the exact order of אבות, then גבורות, and finally קדושה, we might inadvertently reverse the order and yet still have fulfilled the requirement of beginning with praise. This possibility arises from the fact that the section of praises contains the אבות, גבורות and קדושת השם. Therefore, if we were merely to rely on the general principle of first reciting praise, one might run this risk of reversing the order. Therefore, by pin-pointing the sources and proving that we must first recite אבות, then גבורות and only after that קדושות, we succeed in establishing the appropriate sequence *within* the section of praises itself.

We might further ask, why do we need the Gemara to tell us that the proper order of Hallel requires that we first recite praises, then petitions and finally thanksgiving, when we already have a set order based on those verses from *Psalm 103?* The answer here is that were it not for the Gemara's clarification, we would not realize that the sequence we are required to follow is the same sequence as that of the Amidah prayer. For the order spelled out in the Book of Psalms, as explained in *Mesechtas Megillah 17a,* is not specific enough in regard to Hallel and we might therefore mistakenly think that we are to follow this sequence for the Amidah, but not necessarily for Hallel. Therefore, we are told that *whenever* we address Hashem, we must first offer praise, then petition and conclude with thanksgiving. Thus we are made aware that we must follow this sequence in the Hallel prayer as well.

Reverting to our original question, which was why the Gemara needed to spell out the sequence from the Book of Psalms, when we already know of the requirement of praise followed by petition and concluding with thanksgiving, we can now answer that if we only had the general principle of the required sequence, then we might mistakenly think that within the section of praises one could reverse the sections of "הללו עבדי ה'" and "בצאת ישראל", since these are both chapters of praise. Thus, in order to avoid this confusion, we are told explicitly to follow the specified order set down in the Book of Psalms.

X

THE MANNER OF HOW TO SAY HALLEL

The Shulchan Aruch in סימן תפ"ז, סעיף ד' states:

גומרין את ההלל בצבור **בנעימה**...

Hallel is to be recited by the congregation *pleasantly*.

In סימן נא, סעיף ח' we find:

אין אומרים הזמירות במרוצה כי אם **בנחת**.

One should not recite the verses of song rapidly, but rather in a *leisurely manner*.

The באר היטב comments here: "'in a *leisurely manner*', as if one were counting money."

The requirement of "נחת" here seems to indicate something that is done slowly. However, HaRav Yosef Dov Soloveitchik offers a different interpretation of the word "בנחת". The "זמירות", that section of the "פסוקי דזמרה" — "verses of praise", must be said "בנעימה", pleasantly and with sweetness. Proof of this translation of the word "בנחת" comes from Chazal, who say:

דברי חכמים בנחת נשמעים.

The words of the Sages are said pleasantly, assuring that they will be listened to.

Here the word "בנחת" alludes to "a pleasant manner", rather than "slowly". And thus we say in our daily prayers:

להקדיש ליוצרם **בנחת רוח** בשפה ברורה ובנעימה.

...to sanctify the One who formed them with *tranquility*, with clear articulation and with sweetness.

Here "בנחת" is understood as "tranquility", "pleasantness". In סימן נא סעיף ט', the Shulchan Aruch states:

מזמור לתודה יש לאומרו בנגינה.

One should say the psalm for the Thanksgiving offering *melodiously*.

This refers to the "מזמור לתודה", and the melodious manner of its recitation is in contrast to the Psukei D'Zimra, which must be said *pleasantly and sweetly*, "בנעימה". This means that if Hallel is to be viewed as an exercise in praise, it would follow that it too must be recited pleasantly, "בנעימה". However, as we have pointed out, the Hallel prayer is made up of several components, including a section of praise and a section of thanksgiving. This implies that the "thanksgiving" section of Hallel (הודו-הודאה) must be recited "melodiously". And in fact it is our custom to sing the הודו verses of the Hallel.

והנה בהלל יש ב' עניינים. שבח והודאה. שבח" זהו כל
ההלל. והודו לד' כי טוב, זה "הודאה". כשאומרים הלל היינו
שבח, שמשבחים ומהללים ה' באופן כללי, ולפיכך אומרים
בנחת ובנעימה. אבל כשאומרים "הודו", שזה הודאה פרטית
ומודים על מה שעשה ליחיד לישראל, צריך לנגן ולשיר.
ובביהמ"ד של הגר"א שרו בהודו בהלל...

In light of the above, we could attempt to explain the following verses in *Psalm 107*. In verse 8, we read:

יודו לה' חסדו **ונפלאותיו לבני אדם**.

Let them give thanks to Hashem, for His kindness and His *wonders to the children of man.*

In explaining this verse, the Radak comments that the phrase "ונפלאותיו לבני אדם" requires us to *relate to man* the wonders that Hashem has wrought for us.

In verses 21-22 we read:

יודו לה' חסדו **ונפלאותיו לבני אדם**. ויזבחו זבחי תודה ויספרו מעשיו ברנה.

Let them give thanks to Hashem for His kindness, and *His wonders to the children of man.* And let them offer thanksgiving and *relate* His wonders with joyful songs.

The obvious question here is why repeat what we have already been told in verse 8, which is that we are required to relate the wonders of Hashem. However, in light of what we have just pointed out, we can answer this question by saying that there are two ways of "relating" the wonders of Hashem—one is "pleasantly", and the second, "melodiously" (in song). Thus, in verse 8 we are told of the requirement to *relate the wonders of Hashem to others*. But in verses 21 and 22 we are informed of the *manner* in which we are required to relate the wonders of Hashem — "ברנה" — melodiously, and in song, as we are called upon to do in the thanksgiving section, הודאה. And so when we give thanks here to Hashem, "יודו", we are obligated to do it in a melodious manner.

XI

RECITING HALLEL IN POETIC FASHION

HaRav Shlomo Fisher, *shlita*, in his sefer "דרשות בית ישי" (דרוש ו' הערה טו) suggests another reason why verse 8 and verse 22 are not redundant.

The classical commentators all ask the following questions: What is unique about the mitzva of Sippur Yetzias Mitzrayim, reading the Haggadah narrative on Pesach night? For don't we mention the Exodus from Egypt every day of the year in the Kriyas Shema which we recite each night. What is so different about the recitation of the Exodus in the Haggadah? Furthermore, why are women not required throughout the year to mention the Exodus from Egypt; yet on the night of Pesach, they too are obligated to read the Haggadah, with its central theme of the Exodus?

HaRav Fisher suggests that all year the Exodus is mentioned in the Kriyas Shema, which is primarily an exercise in the mitzva of *Talmud Torah*. And since women are exempted from this particular mitzva, they are also exempted from the obligation to mention the Exodus every day of the year. However, on Pesach night, the recitation of the Exodus as Sippur is viewed as an exercise in Shirah, as the verse states: "ויספרו מעשיו ברנה" — "to relate His deeds with song". Thus we can now answer the above questions.

The mitzva of Pesach night is different from all other nights, for on all other nights we *relate* the story of the Exodus; whereas on Pesach night we *sing out* the deeds of Hashem. Furthermore, although women are exempt from S*ippur*, they are obligated in S*hirah*.

Proof of this can be found if we examine the structure of the Haggadah. We begin with the statement of "עבדים היינו" — "we were slaves and are now free". We then go back and recount our history, beginning with the fact that we were once idol worshippers, "מתחילה עובדי ע"ז היו אבותינו". For this is the manner of a song, the poet begins with a sentence outlining the main theme and then he goes back and draws our attention to all the events which lead to that main theme. Thus we see that the Haggadah represents Shirah and is to be recited in the manner of song.

With this in mind, we can understand the reason for the apparent repetition in verse 22. Its purpose is to inform us that we must recite our words of appreciation in the manner of Shirah, and our praises must be organized as poetic utterance.

XII

The Exodus: A miracle outside the Land of Yisrael

As we have previously discussed, even though Rosh Chodesh is referred to as a holiday, "מועד", yet since work is not forbidden on this day, Hallel is not required. This prerequisite, that work must be forbidden, finds its source in the verse in *Isaiah 30:29:*

השיר יהי' לכם כליל התקדש חג.

The song shall be for you like the night of the festival's consecration.

This verse refers to the song of thanksgiving which the Jews will sing when they are redeemed from exile, and this is compared to the Hallel that is recited on the first night of Pesach to commemorate the Exodus from Egypt.

A night that is consecrated as a festival is defined as a night on which it is prohibited to perform any work — מלאכה.

The Gemara in *Megillah 14b* asks why we do not recite Hallel on Purim. And the following answer is given:

לפי שאין אומרים הלל על נס שבחוצה לארץ.

Because we do not recite Hallel for a miracle that occurred outside the land of Yisrael.

If so, asks the Gemara:

יציאת מצרים דנס שבחוצה לארץ, היכי אמרינן שירה?

The Exodus from Egypt was a miracle which took place outside the Land of Yisrael. How then may we sing a song of praise?

The טורי אבן makes the following comment: How are we to understand the question posed here in the Gemara? If that question is directed to the first day of Pesach, then it would mean, how are we to justify the recitation of Hallel on the first day of Pesach, when the miracle of the Exodus transpired outside the land of Yisrael?

If this is the question, then there would seem to be a simple answer. Indeed, we do not recite Hallel because of the miracle of the Exodus, but rather because the first day of Pesach is referred to by the Torah as a holiday, "מועד", and therefore, we recite Hallel as we do on all holidays. This requirement to recite Hallel on a מועד has nothing to do with whether or not a miracle transpired. Proof of this fact is that the Gemara in ערכין י"ד, ב lists several other occasions that are referred to by the Torah as מועדים, even though no particular miracle occurred. And it is only due to other considerations that Hallel is not said on some of these occasions. For example, Rosh Chodesh is referred to in Kisvei HaKodesh as a מועד, yet as pointed out only because of the consideration that it is different from other such holidays, since on Rosh Chodesh we are not forbidden to do work, therefore a recitation of Hallel is not called for. And this is reinforced by the fact that no miracle occurred on Rosh Chodesh. The same kind of rationale applies to the first day of Pesach. Hallel is recited because of the consideration that the Torah refers to this day as a מועד.

> וקשה לי, מאי פריך מיום טוב ראשון של פסח שאומרים הלל, דילמא לאו משום נס אומרים אותו, אלא מפני שהוא "מועד", מידי דהוה אעצרת וסוכות דלא נעשה בהם נס, ואפילו הכי אמרינן אותו [הלל]. ואפילו ראש חודש הוי לי' למימר אלא דלא דאיתקדש בעשיית מלאכה. והכי נמי הלל דראש השנה ויום הכפורים הוי לי' למימר אלא משום דמלך יושב על כסא דין... אם כן יום טוב ראשון של פסח מהראוי לומר בו הלל מצד עצמו דאיקרי מועד דאיקדש בעשיית מלאכה ולא משום לתא דניסא?

Therefore, contends the טורי אבן, we must specify that we are referring to *the night of Pesach* when we ask how can we justify reciting Hallel when the miracle transpired outside the Land of Yisrael. For on this unique night, we recite Hallel in commemoration of the miracle that took place that very night—the night of the Exodus. Thus the determining factor which justifies the recitation of Hallel is not that this day is a מועד, but rather the miracle which took place on that night. Proof of this is that on all other holidays when Hallel is said because it is a holiday, a מועד, we never include the *night*. And because we do so on Pesach night, our recitation of Hallel must be out of consideration for the miracle that transpired then.

ויש לומר, דהא דפריך "והרי יציאת מצרים". אהלל שאומרים **בליל** יום טוב ראשון של פסח קא קשיה לי', דהא לאו משום דתא דרגל אמרינן לי'. אלא משום דתא דניסא הוא. דהא בשאר רגלים אין אומרים הלל בלילה אלא ביום לחוד, והכא אמרינן הלל, כדתנן בפסחים פרק ט, (דף צה, ב). שמע מיניה משום דתא דניסא אמרינן לי' בלילה.

THE QUESTION OF THE טורי אבן

The טורי אבן is puzzled by the Gemara's statement in ערכין י"ד, ב that Rosh Chodesh does not require a recitation of Hallel because it is not a day on which work is forbidden. However, the pasuk informs us that in the future time of the Ultimate Redemption, Shirah will be said on this night and work will be prohibited. This would then qualify as an occasion on which Hallel could justifiably be recited. But at present, Rosh Chodesh is ruled out as a day on which Hallel should be said. Why is this so, asks the טורי אבן, for this pasuk of "a night consecrated" is an allusion to Pesach night?

Thus we are being taught here that the only night when Hallel is recited is this night of Pesach. Not, however, the night of Pesach Sheni, even though that night also commemorates the miracle of the Exodus from Egypt with a Pesach sacrifice. The reason we do not recite Hallel on that night is because work is not prohibited on Pesach Sheni. Thus this pasuk rules out any other night as an appropriate occasion for reciting Hallel, even if it commemorates the miracle of the Exodus, if there is no prohibition against work on that night. The טורי אבן contends that we can deduce from this that the consideration of prohibiting work relates to the night of Pesach Sheni, ruling it out as an occasion on which Hallel may be said. But how does this principle relate to Rosh Chodesh, where work is not prohibited, when the issue being addressed relates only to ruling out Pesach Sheni?

מכל מקום אכתי קשי' לי, דהא דפריך התם. "ראש חודש דאיקרי מועד לימא?" ומשני "לא איתקדיש בעשיית מלאכה", דכתיב "השיר הזה יהי' לכם כליל התקדש חג", ליל המקודש לחג טעון שירה, שאין מקודש לחג אין טעון שירה', והשתא אי הלל זה [דליל פסח] אינו מעין הלל דמועדות מאי ראיה מהא דאין אומרים **ביום** של ראש חודש דאיקרי **מועד** משום דלא אתקדיש בעשיית מלאכה, הא אינו **ממעט אלא לילה דכוותיה**, דהשיר אינו בא בגלל מועד, דהא שיר של כל המועדות אינם אלא ביום אבל לא בלילה, וקא ממעט פסח שני דאין טעון הלל בליל אכילתו כדאמרינן התם, הואיל ולא איקדש בעשיית מלאכה, אבל ראש חודש דאקרי **מועד**, הכי נמי דטעון הלל ביומו אף על גב דלא איקדש בעשיית מלאכה.

We can summarize the position of the טורי אבן as follows: The issue of whether or not work is prohibited is not taken into consideration for those holidays which are commemorated because of a miracle. This relates to those holidays when Hallel is recited only during the day. Thus, even if work is permitted on this day, Hallel is still to be recited. Examples of such holidays are Purim and Chanukah, when Hallel is said even though work is permitted.

For those holidays when Hallel is recited to commemorate a miracle, Hallel can be recited at night only if work is forbidden on this night. This would apply to Pesach night, but not to Pesach Sheni. For even though the night of Pesach Sheni commemorates the Exodus from Egypt which took place at night, yet since work is not prohibited, Hallel can not be said.

If Hallel is to be recited because the day is a festival, מועד, then the issue of whether or not work is prohibited is not taken into consideration in determining the recitation of Hallel. Therefore, we are left with the question of why Rosh Chodesh, a "מועד", was ruled out from saying Hallel because work is not forbidden on that day?

OTHER QUESTIONS

In light of these conclusions of the טורי אבן the following questions arise: If it is true that Hallel can be said even at night, when the Hallel is recited as the result of a miracle, then we can ask, as do many commentators, what about the Hallel of Chanukah? For if we say that we recite Hallel on Chanukah because of the miracle of the oil, which happened at night, why do we not recite Hallel at night on Chanukah?

It has been pointed out that the concept of "קרייתא זו הלילא" — that the reading of the Megillah is equivalent to the recitation of Hallel — applies only to the daytime reading of the Megillah. However, since we also read the Megillah at night, the nighttime reading of the Megillah is not considered equivalent to the recitation of Hallel. However, since we have established that for a miracle Hallel can be recited at night, why isn't the nighttime reading of the Megillah also considered a valid substitute for Hallel?

Furthermore, Hallel is always viewed as a time-bound mitzva, "מצות עשה שהזמן גרמא" for it is said by day and not at night, based on various verses in the Tanach (for example, "ממזרח שמש עד מבואו"). What, then is the rationale for allowing the Hallel of Pesach to be read at night? What is the difference whether Hallel is being said because of a מועד or because of a miracle? In any case, Hallel is recited only during the day.

Finally, if the justification of reciting Hallel at night is because that it was 'at the moment of the miracle' then why would we assume that Hallel should be said on Pesach Sheni, no miracle occurred then?

XIII

Answering these questions

As we have discussed, there are two types of Hallel. The first type is הלל דשירה — Hallel of Shirah, which is said at the very moment of the miracle, even at night. The second type is הלל דקריאה — Hallel of Kriyah, recited on the anniversary of a miracle that has already transpired. However, the הלל דקריאה is the result, not only of the miracle itself, but also of a Rabbinical enactment requiring us to memorialize that particular miracle by an annual recitation of Hallel.

An example of this is the Hallel of Chanukah. Chazal tell us that it was only in the year after the miracle of the oil had taken place — לשנה אחרת — that the Sages instituted the recitation of Hallel. The same rationale can be applied to Hallel recited on Pesach night. On the *night of the Exodus*, Hallel of Shirah was certainly said. In fact, we can imagine that it arose spontaneously out of the depths of gratitude from the hearts of Bnai Yisrael as they witnessed the miracle of their redemption by the Hand of Hashem. The following year, however, it was the Rabbis who instituted this reading of Hallel as a commemoration of the miracle of the Exodus which had happened a year before. We can perhaps understand this in the following manner.

If indeed the holiday of Pesach is to be celebrated as a מועד, then, according to the dictates of the Torah, it requires a recitation of Hallel. In addition, because on this day a miracle transpired — the Exodus from Egypt — this miracle needs to be commemorated by reciting Hallel. Our Sages chose to recite the Hallel of Pesach on a day which was decreed a מועד, a day when work is prohibited. To make up for the fact that Hallel is never said at night, the Sages applied the rationale of "בשעת הנס" (Hallel being said "at the moment of the miracle") to justify the fact that Hallel was to be recited at night. And so, in order to facilitate a true commemoration, Hallel had to be recited at the moment of the miracle, which was at night. Thus we can understand that when הלל דקריאה was instituted on the first night of Pesach, this resulted from the miracle of the Exodus.

However, it was not the miracle itself that *requires* us to say Hallel, but rather the ruling of our Sages to inaugurate a Hallel recitation. They therefore chose an appropriate day for Hallel to be recited — a day which was a מועד and when work was forbidden. Thus Pesach Sheni was ruled out as a day for reciting Hallel, since it was not a מועד on which work is forbidden, and therefore Hallel could not be recited on that day.

In other words, when the Gemara ruled out Pesach Sheni because work is not forbidden on that day, this does not mean that the Gemara was attempting to establish a general principle that Hallel which commemorates a miracle can only be said if the miracle is accompanied by a prohibition against work. Rather Pesach Sheni was ruled out because it is not a מועד and the issue of prohibition of work only brings home to us the significance of this fact that Pesach Sheni is not a מועד.

The Gemara asks a pertinent question. "יציאת מצרים נס דחוץ לארץ". How can we justify saying Hallel for the miracle of the Exodus from Egypt, since it took place *outside the land of Yisrael* and Hallel is recited for miracles which happen in Eretz Yisrael? But we can answer that if we focus on the aspect of מועד, and not that of the miracle, this justifies our reciting of Hallel. But this is not a complete answer. For a מועד is not a factor that obligates us to recite Hallel, but it is simply an appropriate occasion on which to recite Hallel over a miracle. Thus the Gemara's question remains.

Answering Our Other Questions

Even if a miracle happened at night, this alone is not a sufficient reason to allow us to recite Hallel at night. But this fact does neutralize the requirement that Hallel is never said at night. In other words, since the miracle did occur at night, we waive the requirement that Hallel be recited only by day. However, the decisive factor — the מחייב — which allows us to recite Hallel on Pesach night is the combination of the following two factors, as we have previously explained. These are that the occasion on which Hallel is recited must be a מועד, since this is the appropriate time for Hallel. Also there must be a miracle — נס — which inspires us to institute a Hallel recitation.

Thus on Chanukah, even though there was a miracle, which would normally require us to recite Hallel, and that miracle transpired at night, yet the Rabbinic Sages instituted the Hallel recitation for Chanukah as "הלל דקריאה", and according to the halacha regarding this kind of Hallel, the appropriate time for reciting it is only by day. Thus even though the nighttime was the "moment of the miracle" — "שעת הנס", this consideration is put aside and Hallel is not recited on Chanukah night but rather during the day. On Pesach night, on the other hand, we do indeed recite Hallel (though the Hallel on Seder night is considered to be a Hallel of Shirah, rather than a Hallel of Kriyah, as on Chanukah) since not only was the "moment of the miracle" at night, but because the recitation of Hallel occurs on a day which is a מועד, a festival day, which includes the night, on which work is prohibited.

This rationale also allows us to answer the question why Hallel is not read on Purim night. On Purim we apply the principle of "קרייתא זו הלילא", that the Reading of the Megillah is equivalent to the recitation of Hallel (and this refers to the Hallel of Kiryah). Purim is not a מועד, and therefore, as we have established, the miracle in itself is not sufficient to call for a nighttime reading of the Hallel, which, in any case, would have to be a recitation of Hallel of Shirah.

Hallel is to be read only during the day based on various verses from the Tanach. However, if Hallel is said in consideration of the "moment of the miracle", בשעת הנס, which was at night, then at the moment of the miracle Hallel would have been recited at night. Thus the Hallel of Kriyah, which commemorates the miracle, allows for Hallel to be said at night because of the aspect of שעת הנס, i.e., because the moment of the miracle was at night. In general, Hallel is meant to be recited during the day rather than at night. However, when we take into account the aspect of when the miracle took place — "הלל בשעת הנס" — then we can say that Hallel may be recited "בשעת הנס", even at night.

Although the miracle of the Exodus did not take place on Pesach Sheni, yet since on this night we eat the Korban Pesach, which serves as a memorial to the Exodus, then one might contend that we might join the Hallel of commemoration with the eating of the Korban Pesach. But since Pesach Sheni is not an actual מועד, for work is not prohibited, therefore Hallel may not be recited.

XIV

The Halachic Status of Half-Hallel

In seeking to clarify the halachic status of the half-Hallel which is recited on Rosh Chodesh, the following questions arise. As we have discussed, we are prohibited from reciting Hallel on any day of the year other than the ones designated by Chazal and enumerated in מסכת ערכין יו"ד, א. We might wonder whether this prohibition also applies to the recitation of half-Hallel. That is, if we were to recite half-Hallel on any random day of the year that was not Rosh Chodesh, would we be guilty of an infraction?

If we were unable to recite Hallel on one of the days designated by Chazal as a day on which we are obligated to recite Hallel, would we be permitted to recite half-Hallel instead? Or is it a situation of "all or nothing" regarding the recitation of Hallel?

When half-Hallel is said, is this viewed as a legitimate Hallel recitation or simply as an exercise in reciting a collection of psalms?

Answering these questions

If we accept the half-Hallel of Rosh Chodesh and Chol HaMoed Pesach as a legitimate recitation of the requirement of Hallel, then the following question arises. Is there a prohibition against reciting half-Hallel on days other than Rosh Chodesh or Chol HaMoed Pesach?

On the other hand, if we view half-Hallel as a mere recitation of psalms, then the question of whether or not we are allowed to recite it has no real meaning. We might suggest that even if we accept half-Hallel as a legitimate Hallel, there would still be no infraction of the prohibition against reciting half-Hallel (without a beracha, of course). Let us establish the rationale of this prohibition against reciting Hallel on any day other than one designated by Chazal as a day on which Half-Hallel can be recited.

The rationale of the Meiri and the Maharasha

According to the Meiri (שבת, קיח, ב) and the Maharasha (ibid.), the prohibition against reading Hallel on any day other than one designated by our Sages is based on the following consideration.

Hallel was intended to publicize the miracles of Hashem performed on the particular day when Hallel is said. Thus Hallel calls for recognition of the ability of Hashem to perform miracles by changing the laws of nature. If one were to read Hallel every day, then on the day when the reading of Hallel is required, there would no longer exist this recognition of the special power of Hashem to perform miracles. The reason for this is that His miracles would no longer be given any particular importance, since Hallel as the commemoration of His miracles would not be anything unusual or special, but would be just an everyday occurrence.

ז"ל המאירי:

הקורא הלל בכל יום הרי הוא כפורק עול מן התפלה שההלל לא נתן אלא להודאה על מה שעבר [באי זה נס או באי זה גאלה] וכל שקובעו בכל יום דומה במי שאין לו לצעוק ולהתפלל לזמן העומד או להבא. ועל דבר זה הוא קוראו מחרף...

וז"ל המהרש"א:

משום דהלל נתקן בימים מיוחדים על הנס לפרסם כי הקב"ה הוא בעל היכולת לשנות טבע הבריאה ששינה בימים אלו, ונמצא מי שאומרו בכל יום, לא יתפרסם אומרו על הנס גם בימים הראוים לפרסם נסי הש"י, והרי זה מחרף ומגדף שאין בידו חלילה לשנות טבע הבריאה.

The reading of Hallel on other days minimizes the impact that should be felt on the day when Hallel is required. Thus it would follow that if one were to recite half-Hallel throughout the year, however on those days when Chazal designated Hallel to be read to commemorate the miracles of Hashem, one would now read *all* of Hallel. And this means that the appropriate recognition would be given to Hashem as Master of the laws of nature. And there would be no fear of infraction, even if one were to recite half-Hallel every day of the year.

The Rationale of the Yerushalmi

Rav Yehudah HaChassid, in his commentary to Mesechtas Berachos, cites the Yerushalmi, which gives another rationale for not allowing Hallel to be said daily. In the Hallel we find:

עצביהם כסף וזהב.

Their idols are silver and gold.

If one were to recite this statement every day, it would be as if we are constantly taunting Hashem by intimating that "their idols" still stand today; why do Your miracles not destroy them?

ובירושלמי נותן טעם אחר משום דכתיב ביה עצביהם כסף וזהב, וכשאומר אותו בכל יום נראה כשמתכוין לחרף ולגדף כלפי מעלה ולומר שאינו יכול לבטלם מן העולם.

The Rationale of Rabbenu Yona

In his classic commentary to Mesechtas Berachos, Rabbenu Yona explains that Hallel acknowledges Hashem's miracles. If we were to recite Hallel every day, it would be as if we were commemorating the fact that Hashem once performed miracles, but He is no longer capable, God forbid, of performing them today. For what we read today is a commemoration of what transpired in the past.

נראה למורי הרב נר"ו שטעם הדבר הוא מפני שעיקר קריאת ההלל הוא על כל צרה וצרה שלא תבא על הצבור ואנו אומרים אותו שעה כמו שאמרו דוד על הצרות שעברו עליו, וכשאומר אותו בכל יום נראה כמי שאומר שאין

הקב"ה עושה נפלאות בכל יום ולפיכך קורא הנסים שעברו כבר, ונמצא שמחרף ומגדף כלפי מעלה.

We could understand this point of view if we are referring to all of Hallel. However, it does not apply if one recites only half-Hallel, omitting the middle sections. And therefore, according to the rationale of Rabbenu Yona, there would be no prohibition against reading half-Hallel.

XV

Is Half-Hallel a legitimate Hallel

The Maharil offers an explanation as to why Hallel is not recited on Rosh Hashanah or on Yom Kippur. He bases this on the verse in Hallel which states: "כי חלצת נפשי ממות" — "For You have delivered my soul from death."

The Maharil points out that it is not appropriate for us to recite this verse, for on these awesome days of Judgement our souls hangs in the balance and we have not yet been delivered from death. Thus we do not recite Hallel either on Rosh Hashanah or on Yom Kippur. And if we were to suggest that we might conceivably omit this verse and simply recite half-Hallel, as we do on Rosh Chodesh, the Maharil answers with the reply of the Gemara to the question the angels asked the Holy One, Blessed be He, as to why Klal Yisrael does not sing Hallel on Rosh Hashanah and Yom Kippur. "How is it possible, when the King sits on the Throne of Judgement with the books of life and death open before Him, that Yisrael should sing a song before Him?"

וז"ל המהרי"ל:
וזה לחד טעמא, שאין אומרים הלל בראש השנה, לפי

שנאמר בו "כי חלצת נפשי ממות", ואין יכול לומר כן בראש השנה. אך עדיין יאמרו אותו בדילוק כמו בראש חודש, ואז יהי' אותו פסוק מדולק. אלא טעמא אחרת איתא בגמ', שמשיב הקב"ה למלאכי השרת, אפשר אשר המלך יושב על כסא דין וספרי חיים ומתים פתוחים, וישראל יאמרו שירה?

From here we see that the Maharil is of the opinion that if it was possible to omit a chapter of Hallel and recite half-Hallel as we do on Rosh Chodesh, this would be considered a legitimate Hallel recitation.

However, we can dismiss this proof. For when Chazal in Mesechtas Megillah address the issue why Hallel is not recited on Purim, one of the answers given is that one of the verses we recite in Hallel celebrates the fact that we are servants of Hashem and not of any other ruler. We proclaim: "הללוי' - הללו עבדי ה'" — "Give praise, you servants of Hashem."

The significance of this is that at the time of the Purim miracle, we could not justifiably make this declaration. For even though the Jewish people were redeemed from death, they continued to remain servants of Ahashuerus, a human king: "אכתי עבדי אחשורוש אנן".

Therefore we can not recite Hallel on Purim, for it can only be recited by those who are free to pledge their sole allegiance to Hashem.

Yet we might still ask, according to the Maharil, why could we not simply omit this chapter and recite the rest of Hallel? For didn't we attempt to do the same thing with the verse "כי חלצת נפשי ממות"? The answer to this question is that there is a vast difference between these two chapters of Hallel. For if we omit the chapter containing the phrase "כי חלצת נפשי ממות", we are left with half-Hallel, which has a precedent in the half-Hallel of Rosh Chodesh, where we also omit the chapter [אהבתי] containing this verse. However, if we were to omit the *opening* chapter of Hallel, the one which contains the phrase "הללו עבדי ה'" there is no precedent for this, and it would be highly irregular to offer Hallel without its opening chapter.

We might suggest that perhaps what the Maharil meant here by asking why we can not omit the chapter containing the phrase "כי חלצת נפשי ממות" was that since we cannot recite the complete Hallel on Rosh Hashanah, perhaps we can leave out a chapter and this might be acceptable, for we have the precedent of Rosh Chodesh, when half-Hallel is recited. Thus perhaps we do not have here a proof of the general principle that reciting half-Hallel in place of the complete Hallel is acceptable, but rather the issue here pertains only to Rosh Hashanah, and we are being told that we are allowed to omit a chapter here and that a recitation of half-Hallel is acceptable on this day.

Another commentator, the Rokeach, in "הלכות ראש השנה" also addresses the issue of why Hallel is not said on Rosh Hashanah. He cites the Gemara in Mesechtas Rosh Hashanah in which Hashem Himself explains that since Klal Yisrael is in the process of being judged, it is not appropriate for them to recite Hallel at this time, with its inclusion of the verse "כי חלצת נפשי ממות".

There are several important differences between the position of the Maharil and that of the Rokeach. The Rokeach does not raise the question of why we do not simply omit this verse of "כי חלצת נפשי ממות".

The Maharil separates the two issues of "כי חלצת נפשי ממות" and the answer of the Gemara in Rosh Hashanah that since Klal Yisrael are in the process of being judged, they can not say Hallel. The Rokeach, on the other hand, combines these two concepts and presents them as one. In this way we can understand the underlying difference between these two commentators.

According to the Maharil, there is a vast difference between the verse "כי חלצת נפשי ממות" and that of "הללו עבדי ה'". The difference is that it is possible to omit the verse of "כי חלצת נפשי ממות" on Rosh

Hashanah, since it is inappropriate to recite it on the Day of Judgement. However, he makes no effort to omit the verse of "הללו עבדי ה'", for without this verse it becomes impossible to say Hallel at all, either the complete Hallel or even half-Hallel, since we remain servants of a human king and are not free to give our full allegiance to Hashem.

The Rokeach, however, is of the opinion that the verse of "כי חלצת נפשי ממות" means that any possible recitation of Hallel is ruled out on Rosh Hashanah, because it is a day of Judgement, when the life of every living creature hangs in the balance. On such a day no recitation of Hallel can be justified, and therefore there is no question of omitting a single chapter, for it is not the verse alone which is problematic, but the general mood of the day.

The legitimacy of half-Hallel

According to the חות יאיר (סימן רכ"ה), one can only fulfill his obligation of offering Shirah if he recites the entire Hallel. A partial recitation, such as half-Hallel, is not considered sufficient.

> דבשלמא הלל בשלימתו וכשגומרין אותו הוי "שמחת אלקים", כדרז"ל פרק כיצד מברכין, על מה שכתוב גבי "יין ישמח אלקים ואנשים", אם אנשים משמח [ביין] אלקים במה משמח? ולמדו מזה שאין אומרים שירה אלא על היין והוא גמירות הלל בניסוך היין...**והלל שלם דוקא שירה מיקרי**, כדילפי רז"ל מקרא דהשיר יהי' לכם כליל התקדש חג...מה שאין כן מה שאמר דוד "הללו-יה" בעלמא, וכן מה דקרינן הלל בדילוק, אין לפניו ית' שמחה הואיל ואינו בשלימות...

However, it would appear that this approach of the חות יאיר seems to clash with that of the הגרי"ז הלוי. For the latter commentator delineates the differences between the Hallel of Kriyah, recited in commemoration of a miracle, and the Hallel of Shirah, recited at the time the miracle transpires. One of the differences is that Hallel of Kriyah requires a complete recitation of all the chapters of Psalms that make up the Hallel prayer. Whereas when reciting the Hallel of Shirah, all the chapters of Hallel need not be said. Even a partial reading is sufficient.

Proof of this can be found in the law regarding the offering of the Korban Pesach. This sacrifice must be accompanied with the singing of Hallel — הלל דשירה. The Mishna describes this ceremony by telling us that when the third group who crowded into the Bais HaMikdash to offer the sacrifice did not recite the whole of Hallel, for by the time they reached the section of "אהבתי", the service had already ended. (See *Mesechtas Pesachim*, Chapter 5, Mishna 7). Thus we see that even a partial reading of the Hallel does indeed fulfill the requirement of Shirah. This appears to contradict the opinion of the חות יאיר, who maintains that half-Hallel, a partial recitation, does not constitute a valid Hallel of Shirah.

In order to attempt to reconcile these views, we might suggest that these are not two contradictory views, but rather each view addresses a different issue regarding Hallel. As we have discussed, there are two kinds of Hallel — Hallel of Kriyah and Hallel of Shirah. The חות יאיר addresses the issue of Hallel of Kriyah. In order to fulfill this aspect of Hallel, one must read a "שיר", and the חות יאיר tells us that what constitutes a "שיר" is that one must read all the chapters of Hallel in their entirety. This alone is considered to be a sufficient recitation of Shirah, and not a partial reading of these chapters. The גרי"ז הלוי, on the other hand, addresses a different issue — that if one is obligated to offer Hallel of Shirah, how much of the Shirah of Hallel does one have to recite? And he answers that even a partial reading of the chapters is sufficient if they are recited in the appropriate manner of song. Thus we can see that the חות יאיר concerns himself with the issue of *what constitutes the Hallel of Shirah*. Whereas the גרי"ז הלוי addresses the issue of *what is the proper manner of reciting Shirah*.

The גרי"ז הלוי presents another valuable insight in his commentary on the Haggadah. He tells us there that before we begin to recite the Hallel in the sippur of the Haggadah, we make the following declaration:

בכל דור ודור חייב אדם לראות את עצמו כאילו **הוא עצמו** יצא ממצרים. לפיכך אנחנו חייבים להודות ולהלל...

In every generation one is obligated to see himself as if he personally has gone forth out of Egypt...Therefore we are to give thanks, and to praise His mighty acts.

The גרי"ז explains why we must make this declaration before we begin to recite Hallel. And he explains that the obligation to recite Hallel in the Haggadah is, as Rav Hai Gaon contends, that we are to offer Shirah, a song of praise unto Hashem — הלל דשירה. To be able to offer a justifiable הלל דשירה, a song of Hallel, one must be personally involved. Thus if *he himself* experienced the miracle of the Exodus from Egypt, then that person is obligated to express his gratitude with emotion and in song. However, if one is not personally involved, even though a miracle did take place for the benefit of his fellow Jews, then he is not obligated in the Hallel of Shirah. The reason for this is that this type of Hallel calls for deep emotional involvement, and this can only be realized when one experiences a miracle in his own life.

Thus we preface the recitation of Hallel here with the stipulation that every one must personally experience the Exodus, and only then will we be capable of offering a deeply-felt Hallel of Shirah. This means that the essential element in the Hallel of Shirah is not necessarily a complete recitation of all the chapters included in the Hallel text, but rather a genuine emotion of gratitude and praise which arises from our personally experiencing the miracle of redemption. Thus we can fulfill our obligation of the Hallel of Shirah with even a partial recitation of Hallel, providing that we are able to sing these psalms in the appropriate manner.

HaRav Shlomo Fisher, *shlita* in his sefer "בית ישי-דרשות" explains the Gemara in *Sanhedrin 94a,* which tells us that Hashem desired to make King Hezikiah the Messiah and to make the war against Sancherib the war against Gog and Magog, which will precede the coming of the Messiah. However, since Hezikiah failed to offer a Hallel recitation after the defeat of Sancherib, he was rejected as the Messiah. The obvious question here is why didn't Hezikiah offer an expression of Hallel at the moment when, according to the halacha, he was obligated to do so? HaRav Fisher suggests that Hezikiah was unable to offer a whole-hearted recitation of the Hallel of Shirah because he had tried to avert a full-fledged confrontation with Sancherib. However, he would have been able to offer a complete recitation of the Hallel of Kriyah, if that had been required of him. However, what was called for here was the Hallel of Shirah, as the prophet stated: "השיר יהי' לכם כליל התקדש חג".

According to Chazal this alludes to the downfall of Sancherib. (See the commentaries of Rashi and Radak here.) King Hezikiah was unable to offer this kind of Hallel because it must be sung with a full heart and in total recognition and appreciation of the miracle. However, as the Gemara in Sanhedrin points out, Hezikiah tried to avoid this war with Sancherib. Thus even though he gained victory, it was not a joyful victory, and this is why he was unable to offer a wholehearted Hallel of Shirah and thus disqualified himself from being the Messiah.

This reinforces the concept that Shirah does not depend on the *quantity* of verses to be recited, but rather what is decisive is the *quality* of emotional response which accompanies the Hallel recitation. (See sefer "רשימות שיעורים" of HaRav Yosef Dov Solevetchick, ע"מ סוכה, עמוד רל"א, ד"ה ונראה.)

Chapter Four
The Prohibition Against Working on Rosh Chodesh

I

Contrary Indications in the Gemara

The Shulchan Aruch, in Orach Chaim, סימן תי"ז, סעיף א' states:

ראש חודש מותר בעשיית מלאכה...

It is permitted to do work on Rosh Chodesh.

The source for this halacha is found in several Gemaras. For example, in *Mesechtas Chagigah 18a* we find the following statement:

ראש חודש שיש בו קרבן מוסף **ומותר** בעשיית מלאכה...

Rosh Chodesh contains a Mussaf offering in its Temple service and yet the performance of labor is **permitted**.

In the Gemara ערכין יו"ד, ב' we learn:

ראש חודש... לא איקדיש בעשיית מלאכה.

Rosh Chodesh is not sanctified regarding the prohibition against work.

In *Mesechtas Shabbos 24a*, the Gemara ponders the question whether the prayer of יעלה ויבוא is required in the blessings of the *Grace after Meals:* "Perhaps since one is *not forbidden* to engage in the performance of labor on Rosh Chodesh, we need not mention יעלה ויבוא."

The Prohibition Against Working on Rosh Chodesh

Thus we can see clearly that the Gemara takes it for granted that work is permissible on Rosh Chodesh. However, what becomes problematic is the statement made in *Mesechtas Megillah 22b*:

זה הכלל כל שיש בו ביטול מלאכה לעם כגון תענית צבור ותשעה באב קורין ג' ושאין בו ביטול מלאכה לעם כגון **ראשי חדשים** וחולו של מועד קורין ד'.

This is the general rule: Any day on which there is a loss of work to the people by keeping them late in the synagogue, such as on a public fast day or on Tisha B'Av, three people are called up to read the Torah. And days on which there is no loss of work caused to the people by keeping them late in the synagogue, such as Rosh Chodesh, and Chol HaMoed, four people are called up to read the Torah.

Tosafos (ibid.) poses an obvious question. It would seem from this statement that work is *prohibited* on Rosh Chodesh, and therefore an additional person is called up to the Torah, for there is no loss of work caused to the people. And yet in *Mesechtas Chagigah 18a* (cited above) the Gemara states that Rosh Chodesh is a day on which work is permitted.

To this Tosafos makes the following reply. Even though it is a day when work is permitted for men; yet women are forbidden to work. They are given this consideration because it was the Jewish women who refused to participate in the making of the Golden Calf. Therefore Hashem granted them the day of Rosh Chodesh as a "yom tov", a day on which they are forbidden to work.

ויש לומר דודאי מותר לעשיית מלאכה **לאנשים** אבל **נשים** אסורות במלאכה, לפי שלא פרקו נזמיהן במעשה העגל.

II

Questions Arising from the Gemara

This Gemara and the comments made here by the *Ba'alei Tosafos* lead us to ask the following questions:

The Mishnah in the beginning of the third chapter of Megillah, presents the formulation of how many are to be called up to the Torah on various occasions.

זה הכלל, כל שיש בו מוסף ואינו יום טוב, קורין ארבעה.

> This is the general rule: Any day when there is an addition [i.e., when the Mussaf sacrifices were offered during the time of the Bais HaMikdash and nowadays, when the corresponding Mussaf prayers are recited] but it is not a Yom Tov, four people are called up to read the Torah.

From this statement it would appear that the additional reader on Rosh Chodesh was the result of the Mussaf sacrifice and not of the fact that today work is prohibited and therefore there would be no loss of work if we add to the number of Torah readers.

We understand why on Chol HaMoed it would be forbidden to do work, due to the dictate of the verse מקראי קדש, "a holy convocation", which calls for a cessation of work during this period. However, in regard to Rosh Chodesh, there is no such supporting pasuk. Where, then, would we find a reason why work might be forbidden on Rosh Chodesh? And if there were a prohibition against doing work on Rosh Chodesh, why would there be a difference between men and women?

The most obvious question here in regard to this position of Tosafos, that only women are prohibited to work, is touched upon by the טורי אבן here. To be called up to the Torah is an exclusive right reserved for men. Women are not obligated in this mitzva of Kriyas HaTorah. Thus, if it is as Tosafos contends, that men are permitted to work on Rosh Chodesh and it is only women who do not work on this day, then why is the consideration "that there be no loss of work" given to explain why we add a fourth reader? For women are not obligated to read the Torah or to attend the synagogue service, since the mitzva of Kriyas HaTorah does not apply to them. However, as far as the menfolk are concerned, prolonging the Torah reading by calling up an additional reader would indeed constitute a "loss of work" for men who are not prohibited from work.

> ועוד אי האי אין בו ביטול מלאכה, היינו טעמא, מפני שאין הנשים עושות ביטול מלאכה, הא מכל מקום, הא איכא ביטול מלאכה לאנשים שהן מותרין בעשיית מלאכה בראש חודש, והרי נשים פטורים מקריאת התורה ואין חיוב אלא לאנשים ולהם יש ביטול מלאכה...

HaRav Yitzchak Isaac HaLevi, in his classic sefer "דורות הראשונים" (ח"א עמ' 330), raises the following question. The Baraisa here in *Mesechtas Megillah 22b*, lists Tisha B'Av as a day on which work is permitted. However, as we well know, all of Klal Yisrael has adopted the custom of not working on Tisha B'Av. Yet the Gemara here refers to Tisha B'Av as a day on which work is permitted, and for this reason no additional reader is called up to the Torah. If this is so, how can we account for the fact that on Rosh Chodesh, when there is a custom for women alone to abstain from work, the Gemara refers to this day as "a day on which there is no loss of work", and for this reason an extra reader is called up to the Torah, as if work is prohibited on this day?

If the consideration of there being "no loss of work" determines the calling up of an additional reader to the Torah, then it should follow that on Chanukah too, there should be four people called up to the Torah, at least according to those commentators, such as the Tur (טור) and the Bach (ב"ח), who contend that on Chanukah too women are forbidden to do work. Yet we never find such an opinion expressed or even suggested. (See שו"ת שיח יצחק מהרב יצחק וייס, סימן קצ"ד").

In our Mishnah, we find that on a holiday five people are called up to the Torah. The Gemara in *Megilla 23b* presents the following rationale to explain the addition of a fifth reader on Yom Tov:

> נקוט האי כללא בידך, כל דטפי ליה מילתא מחבריה, טפי ליה גברא יתירה, הלכך בר"ח ובחולו של מועד דאיכא קרבן מוסף קורין ארבעה, וביום טוב דאסור בעשיית מלאכה, חמשה.

> Take this general rule in your hand: any day that has something more than another day, has an extra person reading on that day."

This might lead us to ask: if we are told that labor is forbidden on Rosh Chodesh as well, why do we add a fifth reader on Yom Tov but not on Rosh Chodesh? In an attempt to address this question, the "נחל אשכול" (הלכות ראש חודש, או"ק י"ד) points out that there is an addition to the text of the "ספר האשכול", which reads:

> וכל שאין בו ביטול מלאכה לעם כגון ר"ח... קורין ד'. יום טוב דאסור בעשיית מלאכה קורין חמשה.

> On Yom Tov, when work is forbidden, five readers are called to the Torah.

This additional statement indicates that only on Yom Tov do we have a prohibition against work, and not on Rosh Chodesh. If this is so, then one could ask, how are we to understand the statement here in the Gemara that "Rosh Chodesh has no loss of work"? For this statement indicates that there is in fact a prohibition against working on Rosh Chodesh. And how are we to understand the difference between Rosh Chodesh and Yom Tov in this respect?

III

RASHI: AN APPARENT CONTRADICTION

In *Mesechtas Megillah 22b,* Rashi cites the same source as does Tosafos to explain why Rosh Chodesh is a day on which work is forbidden for women only.

ראשי חדשים: אין בו ביטול מלאכה כל כך שאין הנשים עושות מלאכה בהן... ושמעתי מפי מורי הזקן ז"ל שנתנו להם מצוה זו בשביל שלא פירקו נזמיהן בעגל. ומקרא מסייעו דכתיב אשר נסתרת שם ביום המעשה (שמואל א, כ) ותרגום יונתן ביומא דחולא, והתם נמי גבי ראש חודש קאי, דקאמר ליה מחר חודש, וקרי ליה לערב ראש חודש "יום המעשה" אלמא **ראש חודש לאו יום המעשה** הוא...

Apart from giving the source for the custom that women do not work on Rosh Chodesh, Rashi concludes that the following verse in *Shmuel I (20:19)* gives further proof to this contention. There we read how Jonathan and David plan that David will hide until the intentions of King Shaul towards him are clarified. This dialogue took place the day before Rosh Chodesh. "ובאת אל המקום אשר נסתרת שם **ביום המעשה**." — "And you should come to the place where you hid on a day of work…"

Rashi explains here that David was already in hiding and the day referred to is the same day, that is, the day before Rosh

Chodesh. And since that day is referred to as a "day of work", "יום המעשה", the implication is that the following day, which is the day of Rosh Chodesh, is not a day of work, either for men or for women.

However, Rashi's comment here leads us to ask the following questions: The verse here seems to indicate that both men and women refrained from work on Rosh Chodesh. But this would appear to contradict Rashi's contention that it was only women who did not work on Rosh Chodesh. Additionally, the verse cited in *Shmuel I* seems to indicate that Rosh Chodesh is not a day of work, either for men or for women. Why then didn't Rashi use this verse to support this idea rather than to support the contention that it was women alone who did not work on Rosh Chodesh?

To answer these questions, we might suggest that the implication of "לאו יום המעשה", alluded to in *Shmuel I* does not really indicate that work is completely forbidden on this day, but rather that *this day is not an ordinary workday, יום חול*. There are three different kinds of days. We have Shabbos, when work is forbidden; the usual weekdays, ימי חול, when work is permitted; and finally, we have a "לאו יום המעשה", a day which is like an ordinary work day, but not quite. On such a day, even though work is allowed, there are some who choose not to work, for it is preferable not to work on such a day. Thus, since some are prohibited from working, this day is not considered to be a regular working day. Thus Rashi points out that this verse in *Shmuel I* is to be understood to mean that not everyone desisted from work on this day, but only the women. And so, after we point out that women customarily do not work on Rosh Chodesh, in consideration of the reward they received for not taking part in the Sin of the Golden Calf, we can now understand who were the people who did not work and thus made this day into something other than an ordinary working day.

In light of this explanation, we can now answer the questions we raised earlier. It would appear from the verse cited in *Shmuel*

I that everyone, both men and women, did not work on Rosh Chodesh. However, in view of our explanation, we can now see that this was not necessarily the case. But rather the verse indicates that only some did not work, namely, the women.

Why didn't Rashi use this verse from *Shmuel I* to prove that work was forbidden on Rosh Chodesh, but rather he used it only to support his contention that women were rewarded with a day of rest for their refusal to participate in the Sin of the Golden Calf? This verse is ambiguous, and it is only after we know of Rashi's source and explanation that we can fully understand the pasuk.

IV

The Approach of the טורי אבן

The טורי אבן answers many of the above questions when he maintains that the main reason why work was forbidden on Rosh Chodesh was because of the Mussaf offering on this day. This approach is based on the rationale of Tosafos, which is cited at the beginning of the fourth chapter of *Mesechtas Pesachim*. The law maintains that on Erev Pesach work is forbidden from midday onwards. The source for this law is the Yerushalmi Pesachim, and it is based on the consideration that since all Jews offered a Korban Pesach on this day, everyone was therefore forbidden to work. The rationale behind this is that it would not be proper for a person to engage in everyday work while his Pesach offering was being sacrificed. In addition, the Rambam, in "הלכות כלי המקדש (פרק ו', הלכה ט) tells us that when an individual offers a sacrifice, that day is to be considered a yom tov for that person and he is forbidden to do work on that day.

ומה הוא קרבן עצים? זמן קבוע היה למשפחות משפחות
לצאת ליערים להביא עצים למערכה ויום שיגיע לבני
משפחה זו להביא עצים היו מקריבין עולות נדבה. וזהו קרבן

העצים. והיה להם כמו **יום טוב** ואסורין בו בהספד ובתענית ובעשיית מלאכה.

What is a "wood sacrifice"? When Bnai Yisrael returned from the Babylonian exile and prepared to offer sacrifices, there was no firewood in the Bais HaMikdash. In order to carry out the sacrificial service, families came forward and volunteered to contribute wood to light the sacrificial fire. In recognition of this gesture, the prophets decreed that in future years these families would continue to contribute wood, even if the wood chamber of the Bais HaMikdash was already full. On the day when the families brought the wood, they would offer a voluntary sacrifice and celebrate the day as a festival. Eulogies, fasting and *labor* were all forbidden on these days.

These prohibitions for one who offered a sacrifice did not apply only to an individual, but to a צבור, the congregation of Klal Yisrael. When they offered a communal sacrifice they too were prohibited from doing any work. As stated, the source for this law is to be found in the Yerushalmi, quoted by Tosafos at the beginning of the fourth chapter of *Mesechtas Pesachim*. The Yerushalmi asks, if one is forbidden to do work when one brings a sacrifice, shouldn't it follow that when the Korban Tamid, the daily sacrifice, is offered, work should be forbidden every day? The following answer is given by the Yerushalmi:

שאני תמיד, שהתורה הוציאה מן הכלל, דכתיב, ואספת דגנך, ואם כל ישראל יושבים ובטלים, מי יאסף להן דגן.

The daily sacrifice (Korban Tamid) is to be viewed in a different manner, in that the prohibition against work does not apply. This is in consideration of the fact that the Torah dictated that we must gather our produce, and if work were to be forbidden, how would it be possible for us to gather our produce? Therefore these prohibitions do not apply to the daily sacrifice.

From this we can see that were it not for this consideration, even a communal sacrifice would call for the cessation of work. Therefore, since the Korban Mussaf, the additional Rosh Chodesh offering, is to be viewed as a communal sacrifice, קרבן צבור, this would require all of Klal Yisrael, both the men and the women, not to work on Rosh Chodesh.

The טורי אבן concludes that during the time of the Bais HaMikdash, work was indeed forbidden on Rosh Chodesh, in keeping with the fact that there was an additional aliyah during the Torah reading, that is, another person was called up to the Torah. Today, although we no longer offer a Mussaf sacrifice, yet the practice of calling up a fourth reader on Rosh Chodesh has remained intact.

This seems to contradict the statement in the Gemara in *Chagigah 18a* that even though a Korban Mussaf was offered on Rosh Chodesh, yet work was nevertheless permitted. But what the Gemara means here is that even though work is not expressly forbidden on Rosh Chodesh because of the holiness of the day, קדושת היום, yet it is forbidden because of the consideration, which we have just discussed, that since a communal sacrifice was offered on this day, this obligated the community to abstain from working.

THE VIEW OF HaRav Yosef Dov Soloveitchik

HaRav Soloveitchik defends the position of the Baalei Tosafos in making a distinction between men and women regarding the prohibition against working on Rosh Chodesh. He also traces the source of this prohibition, איסור מלאכה, back to the offering of the Korban Mussaf on Rosh Chodesh. However, he explains the effect of this prohibition differently than does the טורי אבן. When an individual offers a sacrifice, the day is to be considered a holiday for him and ordinary work is prohibited. The reason for this is not just because work is usually forbidden on a holy day, as in the case of Shabbos, but rather, when one offers a sacrifice, one should spend the day in contemplation and spiritual pursuits, because if we were to engage in ordinary work, the spirit of the day would be lost. This is also true of Chol HaMoed, when work is not forbidden for its own sake, but rather because working takes away from the spirit of holiness of the day. This is why the Tanna in *Pirkei Avos (3:15)* tells us that one who "cheapens the festivals has no share in the World to Come." — "המבזה את המועדות... אין לו חלק לעולם הבא". Chazal tell us that this refers to Chol HaMoed, the intermediate days of a festival. For by working, one "cheapens" the sanctity of Chol HaMoed, which is considered a time of "holy convocation", מקראי קדש. This is also the reason why an individual is encouraged to refrain from engaging in ordinary work on the day when he offers a sacrifice. However, when a communal sacrifice, קרבן צבור, is offered, the responsibility rests with the congregation as a whole rather than with the individuals who make up the community, to keep the day holy and to refrain from mundane work on it. In this situation of communal responsibility, it was the women who were called upon to accept upon themselves this responsibility of not engaging in work on Rosh Chodesh day. This served to release the menfolk from this communal prohibition and thus freed them to be able to engage in work on this day.

Therefore the Gemara stated that Rosh Chodesh is a day on which there is no "loss of work", ביטול מלאכה. This is to be understood to mean that this is indeed a special day on which it is desirable to refrain from work. This explains why an additional reader is called up to the Torah on this day, for even though it is the women who refrain from work on Rosh Chodesh, the offering of the Korban Mussaf accounts for the additional reader being called up to the Torah, as the Mishna explains.

Other Explanations of Prohibiting Work on Rosh Chodesh

The Rishonim have various ways of explaining whether or not there is a prohibition against work on Rosh Chodesh.

The Ritba explains the Gemara's statement that there is no "loss of work", ביטול מלאכה, on Rosh Chodesh to refer to the custom prevalent at the time when the Talmud was written, when men as well as women did not work on Rosh Chodesh. This then was sufficient reason to justify the addition of an extra Torah reader on the day of Rosh Chodesh. In our time, however, only women continue the custom of not working on Rosh Chodesh. Thus the statement in the *Gemara Megillah 22b* alludes to the period when men also did not work on Rosh Chodesh.

הא דאמרינן כל שאין בו ביטול מלאכה לעם כגון ראש חודש לפי מנהגם אמר כן, שהיו נוהגין שלא לעשות מלאכה בר"ח, ומנהג ראשונים, כמו שכתב [שמואל א, כ, יח-יט] בדוד ויהונתן, אשר נסתרת שם ביום המעשה, שהי' יום לפני ראש חודש, כדכתיב "מחר חדש" לממירא דחדש עצמו אינו יום המעשה להם. אבל אנו אין אנו נוהגים בכך אלא הנשים בלבד. ובפרק מ"ה מפרקי דר"א כתיב כן, לפי שלא קבלו הנשים עליהם ליתן נזמיהם לעגל, נתן להם הקב"ה שכרן בעוה"ז [בעולם הזה] שהם משמרות ראש חודש יותר מן האנשים.

The Meiri shares the same opinion as Rashi regarding the prohibition against working on Rosh Chodesh. He maintains that it applies only to women and therefore it is relevant even today. The ספר האשכול suggests a unique interpretation of the following statement in the Gemara:

כל שיש ביטול מלאכה כגון תענית צבור וט' באב. וכל שאין בו ביטול מלאכה כגון ר"ח וחול המועד.

The focus of this statement is not so much on the issue of prohibition of work but rather on the addition of extra prayers on the days of Tisha B'Av and Rosh Chodesh. Thus we are told that on fast days and on Tisha B'Av, when many additions are added to the daily prayers, there is no room for calling up additional readers to the Torah. However, on Rosh Chodesh and on Chol HaMoed, there are not so many additional prayers, and thus there is enough time to allow for adding an extra reader without detaining the congregation for too long.

> והאי דאמרי בטול מלאכה לעם, על **תוספת תפלה ותחנונים** שאין בראש חדש וחולו של מועד כמו תענית, ולא בטול מלאכה ממש, דהא ראש חדש, לא דמי לחולו של מועד, שראש חדש מותר במלאכה, וחולו של מועד אסור...

In the sefer of "עטורי מגילה על מסכת מגילה", written by הרב אליקים געציל פשקס נ"י, the author offers the following explanation of the Gemara to account for the apparent contradiction between the statement made here and that which is stated in the Mishna. In the Gemara the justification given for adding another reader is that there would thereby be no loss of work. The Mishna, on the other hand, gives a different reason, which is that of the Korban Mussaf offered on this day. We might resolve the issue by asserting that these two sources focus on two different issues.

The Mishna suggests that we add to the number of readers called to the Torah on Rosh Chodesh because of the Korban Mussaf, which makes the day special. The Gemara, however, addresses a different issue. Even though it is justified to call up another reader on this day, yet this will lead to a genuine problem, that is, it will considerably delay the congregants in the synagogue and prevent them from going to work on time. The Gemara deals with this problem by maintaining that since women do not work on Rosh Chodesh as a matter of custom, we are to view this day not as an ordinary working day, and this is what justifies the addition of an extra reader on this day. Thus the issue of ביטול מלאכה, "the loss of work", is not a *cause* for adding an extra reader, but rather it is a reason to *preserve* the practice of adding an extra reader, even though it will result in the loss of work.

V

Publicizing Rosh Chodesh with Various Mitzvos

The following strategy may serve to answer all our above questions. If we were to examine all the various mitzvos of this particular Rosh Chodesh day, we would find a common denominator for all of these mitzvos. This common denominator is the element of פרסום, publicizing that today is Rosh Chodesh. In particular, we find the opinion of the ראב"ד, cited in *Hilchos Berachos,* that the reason for reciting half-Hallel on Rosh Chodesh is to publicize the fact that today is Rosh Chodesh. The requirement to have a special festive meal on this day finds its source in the historical process of Kiddush HaChodesh, when the new month was determined by the testimony of eye-witnesses. At that time, a special meal was eaten to signify that this day was Rosh Chodesh. Even the Bircas HaChodesh prayer, recited on the Shabbos before Rosh Chodesh which announces the exact date and time when the new month will commence, is also based on the concept of publicizing the day of Rosh Chodesh. (See *The Commentators' Shabbos,* pp. 254-259.)

The issue of the prohibition of work on this day, איסור מלאכה, is also related to this consideration of publicizing the day of Rosh Chodesh. As we have discussed, working on Rosh Chodesh is not forbidden per say, for Rosh Chodesh is not considered to be a day which the Torah depicts as a sanctified day, מקראי קודש, which requires the absolute cessation of all work, איסור מלאכה. But rather the prohibition against work on this day is for the purpose of calling our attention to the fact that this day is Rosh Chodesh and we should be careful to observe all the required mitzvos.

We can add to this list the call for a Torah reading on Rosh Chodesh. HaRav Moshe Feinstein, זצ"ל, in his "אגרות משה", ח"א, סימן קא, ענף ב explains why there is a special Torah reading on Rosh Chodesh. The inclusion of a Torah reading in the prayer service on Shabbos mornings and on Yom Tov, as well as on Mondays and Thursdays and on Shabbos Mincha, was instituted by Moshe Rabbenu and expanded upon by Ezra HaSofer. The purpose of this innovation was to insure that everyone participated in the study of Torah, תלמוד תורה ברבים. It is also mentioned in the Gemara that the Torah reading was instituted in order that Klal Israel not go three days without hearing words of Torah. (See *The Commentators' Siddur*, pp. 353-360.)

However, there is another category of public Torah reading whose purpose is not Talmud Torah, but rather to inform the public of specific obligations. For example, on the Shabbos of Parashas Shekalim, this particular Torah portion is read in order to make the congregation aware that they are required to contribute a half shekel, מחצית השקל, at this time. And there are three other occasions on Shabbos when specific mitzvos are publicized. These are the Parashios of Zachor, Parah, and HaChodesh. And so, too, on a public fast day, the Torah reading does not merely serve the purpose of Talmud Torah, as it does on Shabbos, but rather it is a call to the people to repent. Thus we may say that this also applies to the Torah reading on Rosh Chodesh. We read the chapters in the Torah which speak of Rosh Chodesh and the special sacrifice which was offered on this day in order to bring to the attention of the congregation that today is Rosh Chodesh and to inform them that the particular mitzvos which belong to this day must be properly performed.

This aspect of the Torah reading was not the one based on the pasuk in *Vayikra (23:1)* which states: "וידבר משה מועדי ה'". For this particular pasuk alludes to the "three Pilgrimage Festivals" of Pesach, Shavuos and Succos and does not include the Rosh Chodesh Torah reading.

With this in mind, we can answer the following question. When a holiday occurs on Shabbos, why is it that the Torah reading consists of the parasha related to that particular holiday and it supersedes the regular Shabbos Torah reading? In light of our previous discussion, the answer now seems obvious. For on the three festivals we have a dictate directly from Moshe Rabbenu that the Torah reading must concern the matter of the day. Thus it supersedes the regular Shabbos Torah reading, which is primarily an exercise in Talmud Torah. On Rosh Chodesh, however, even if it occurs on a Shabbos, the Shabbos Torah reading takes precedence and the Rosh Chodesh reading is only added at the end. The reason for this is now quite clear. For the only purpose of the Rosh Chodesh reading is to publicize that today is Rosh Chodesh. Thus it is sufficient to add this parasha at the end of the regular Shabbos Torah reading.

HaRav Moshe Feinstein cites proof for this theory from Chapter 13 of *Hilchos Tefillah*. There the Rambam outlines the requirements for the particular Torah readings of the day. In Halacha 4, he elucidates the order of the Rosh Chodesh reading, even when it coincides with Shabbos. On the other hand, the laws of the Torah reading for the three festivals are outlined later, in Halacha 8. There he mentions that when one of these festivals falls on Shabbos, the regular Shabbos Torah reading is suspended in favor of the Torah reading for that particular festival. He also mentions that the festival Torah reading was an innovation introduced by Moshe Rabbenu; whereas the reading for Rosh Chodesh is not included in this category. Thus we can conclude that the introduction of the Torah reading for Rosh Chodesh was not similar to that of the Monday and Thursday Torah readings, which were instituted by Moshe Rabbenu.

וצריך לומר דיש שני עניני קריאה: **חדא** דחייבו **ללמוד התורה ברבים** בשבת ובשני ובחמישי ובמנחה בשבת, כמפורש בבבא קמא דף פ"ה מצד **מצות למוד התורה**. וכן ביום טוב מצד **מצות למוד התורה**, כדאיתא בסוף מגילה מוידבר משה מצותן שיהיו קורין כל אחד ואחד בזמנו, והוא רק למצות למוד בעלמא... ויש **עוד קריאה** שתקנו **לפרסם ולהודיע** כמו שקלים פרה וחדש, כדאיתא ברש"י במגילה דף כט. וכן קריאת "זכור" הוא כדי לזכור בפה... ואם כן אינם מצד מצות לימוד. וכן קריאת דתענית, שהוא **לעורר בתשובה**. וכן בחנוכה ובפורים, **שהוא לפרסומי ניסא**. וכן **קריאת דראש חדש**, משמע שאינה בכלל תקנת משה מקרא מוידבר משה, ואף שראש חדש איקרי מועד... שעכ"פ צריך לקרא של ראש חודש... **לפרסם** ולהודיע...

If we accept this contention, then the prohibition against doing work on Rosh Chodesh is due to the need to publicize that today is Rosh Chodesh. Thus if only women abstain from work on this day, this would be sufficient to publicize that today is Rosh Chodesh. This was also suggested by HaRav Yosef Dov Soloveitchik. Based on this premise, we can now understand the Gemara in *Megillah 22b* in the following way:

The reading of the Torah portion on a fast day serves the purpose of bringing to the attention of the listener that he must repent on this solemn day. This is accomplished by having three readings from the section of the Torah whose theme is teshuvah, repentance. Three readers thus reinforce the desired effect. On Rosh Chodesh, however, the Torah reading serves the purpose of publicizing that today is Rosh Chodesh. This is accomplished by women abstaining from work on this day. Publicizing that today is Rosh Chodesh is a matter of great concern to the congregation. And therefore, apart from having three readers read from the Torah portion which deals with Rosh Chodesh, we add to the number of readers in order that this manner of publicizing the day be realized, and this is the reason why four readers are justified.

Answering Our Previous Questions

The Mishna appears to justify the addition of another reader on Rosh Chodesh as a result of the Korban Mussaf, whereas the reason given by the Gemara seems to be that there is "no loss of work", ביטול מלאכה. To resolve this apparent contradiction, we might suggest that there is one underlying principle in both the Mishna and the Gemara. The Korban Mussaf, apart from serving a special function on Rosh Chodesh, also calls to our attention that this is a unique day. So, too, does the "loss of work", ביטול מלאכה call to our attention that today is Rosh Chodesh, a special day. As we have previously discussed, many of the mitzvos of this day were intended to publicize that today is Rosh Chodesh. Thus adding an extra reader here is justified, since this serves, along with the Korban Mussaf and the ביטול מלאכה, to publicize that today is Rosh Chodesh.

We can also answer the question of where is the source that forbids work on Rosh Chodesh, even though there is no pasuk of מקראי קודש written in relation to Rosh Chodesh. The answer can now be understood that forbidding work on Rosh Chodesh was based on the consideration of publicizing that today is Rosh Chodesh.

We can also now understand why only women are prohibited from doing work on Rosh Chodesh. This is because it is the women who are given the task of publicizing the day by refraining from work. They are the ones chosen for this honor because they did not participate in the Sin of the Golden Calf.

Although Klal Yisrael accepted upon themselves not to work on Tisha B'Av, this was due to the fact that this day calls for great solemnity, since on this day the Bais HaMikdash was destroyed. However, refraining from work on Tisha B'Av would not necessarily justify an additional Torah reader. For it is only when we wish to publicize the day that we add another reader. And on

Tisha B'Av we have no desire to "advertise" this day, since it is well known and deeply felt by all of Klal Yisrael without the need for it to be publicized.

And similarly, even though women do not work on Chanukah, the reason for this is not to publicize the day, but rather because women were involved in the miracle of Chanukah. And so, if the day does not need to be publicized, there is no justification for adding another Torah reader on Chanukah.

VI

ROSH CHODESH: A SPECIAL GIFT TO THE WOMEN

As we have explained, Rosh Chodesh was a special gift to the women in consideration of their refusal to participate in the creation and worship of the Golden Calf. This is pointed out in פרקי דר' אליעזר, פרק מ"ה.

This raises the following two questions. It would seem that a pasuk in *Devarim 33:9* contradicts the view that women did not participate in the worship of the Golden Calf. The verse here deals with the recognition given to the tribe of Levi by Moshe Rabbenu at the time when he blessed all the tribes just before he died. The pasuk tells us: "...האמור לאביו ולאמו לא ראיתיו ואת אחיו לא הכיר" — "The one who said to his father and mother, 'I have not seen him,' his brothers he did not recognize."

The meaning here refers to the incident when Klal Yisrael sinned by creating and worshipping the Golden Calf. Moshe thereby declared "מי לה' אלי" — "Whosoever is for Hashem, to me" *(Shemos 2:26)*. The tribe of Levi responded to Moshe Rabbenu's call. Thus it would seem that the entire tribe of Levi rejected the worship of the Golden Calf. Yet because the pasuk comments that Levi "did not recognize his own parents", this is a clear indication that Levi's parents, who were themselves Levites, did in fact participate in the worship of the Golden Calf. This leave us with the following question. How can we say that the women totally rejected the worship of the Golden Calf when we know that the mothers of the tribe of Levi took part in the worship of the Golden Calf?

An answer is suggested by Chazal in *Mesechtas Yoma 66b*. The Gemara here makes the statement that the entire tribe of Levi did not worship the Golden Calf. The Gemara then asks, how can such a statement be made when the pasuk in the Torah clearly states, "But he [Levi] did not recognize his own father and mother"? Surely, his father and mother must have been Levites, otherwise he himself would not be a Levi. Thus it would appear that some of the tribe of Levi did indeed participate in the Sin of the Golden Calf. The Gemara answers by saying that "אביו" is not to be taken literally, to mean one's own father. But rather it is to be understood as referring to one's *grandfather*. A grandfather is referred to as "one's father". Thus the pasuk here alludes to the father of the Levi's mother, who was an Israelite and not a Levi. And similarly, "his brother" alludes to the son of his mother, whose first husband was not a Levite.

This interpretation can lead us to an unusual way of understanding the pasuk of "האמור לאביו ולאמו לא ראיתיו...". This verse is not to be understood to mean that the Levi did not have any compassion on his own mother for her having worshipped idols. But rather the meaning here, based on the above insight of the Gemara in Yoma, is that since the Levi did not show any compassion to his grandfather and slayed him for his participation in idol worship, this indicates that the Levi "did not recognize his own mother." In other words, he did not refrain from slaying his own mother's father, even though he realized how much this act would hurt his mother. Seen from this perspective, we can not prove from the pasuk that the women participated in the worship of the Golden Calf, and thus our original contention still holds, that the women did not take part in this sin.

We can ask a second question here. How are we to understand the principle of measure for measure, מדה כנגד מדה? What does the women's refusal to participate in the Sin of the Golden Calf have to do with their reward of not having to work on Rosh Chodesh?

We can suggest a possible answer to this question based on an insight offered by the בעל העקידה, who defines for us the meaning of the mitzva of Kiddush HaChodesh. The Torah helps us to combat our natural tendencies towards idol worship. Thus the very first mitzva in which Klal Yisrael was commanded was the mitzva of Kiddush HaChodesh, sanctifying the new month. The purpose of this mitzva was to demonstrate that the heavenly bodies—including the moon, which was a primary source of idol worship—were powerless on their own. Only the Ribbono shel Olam, the Master of the Universe, is in total control of the heavenly bodies.

With this in mind, we can understand that the observance of Rosh Chodesh is to teach us how to reject idol worship. For it was the women who resisted this temptation to worship idols, by not taking part in the Sin of the Golden Calf, a classic case of idol worship. Therefore, they were rewarded with the gift of Rosh Chodesh, and this is an appropriate gift for resisting idol worship. This then explains the significance of the aspect of מדה כנגד מדה, regarding women and Rosh Chodesh.

Chapter Five
The Mitzva of Kiddush Levanah

I

The Message of Kiddush Levanah

The Czar of Russia, Nicholas II, was an ardent antisemite. He spent his summers in his villa just outside Moscow. One evening, during a summer vacation, the Czar stepped out onto his balcony and noticed a group of people congregated nearby with torches in their hands. Fearing that they might be plotting his overthrow, he immediately dispatched his guards to investigate the matter. The soldiers rounded up the group and brought them to the Czar. They consisted of a minyan of elderly Jews who held torches in one hand and prayer books in the other.

"What are you doing?" demanded the Czar.

"It has been cloudy all this past week and only tonight is the moon visible. Therefore we have taken this opportunity to sanctify the moon," answered the leader of the group, trembling as he spoke.

"What is this ceremony of sanctifying the moon? Do you worship the moon?" asked the irate Czar.

"Certainly not, your Royal Highness. Jews serve only the one true God. What we pray for is this. According to our Sages, at the time of Creation, both the sun and the moon were the same size. However, the moon complained that two kings cannot rule at the same time; and so God made the moon smaller. We pray for the moon to be restored to its original size," explained the group's leader.

The Czar was amazed at his explanation, and before dismissing the obviously harmless group, he shouted at them, "What fools I have for subjects. There are so many problems in the world, and you idiots pray for the moon to be restored to its former size!"

But the Czar had missed the point. For within the ritual of Kiddush Levana lies a deep concern with the solution of all the problems of the world. For the trembling Jew who had been hauled before the arrogant Czar did not disclose to him the real reason we pray for the restoration of the moon to its former size. It was made smaller because it was consumed with jealousy. Hidden within this allegory is a lesson for human beings. We pray that all tensions among people be resolved and we all learn to live in peace and harmony with each other. And we pray for the restoration of the moon to its former glory for yet another reason – and this the leader of the small minyan very wisely did not mention to the Czar – because the moon symbolizes Klal Yisrael. Just as the moon declines and completely disappears, and then it is reborn and regains its former power; so too do we look forward to the time in the future when the glory of Yisrael will be restored and we will regain our sovereignty among the nations.

II

THE SOURCE FOR THIS MITZVAH

The laws, customs and blessings associated with this mitzva are explained in *Mesechtas Sanhedrin 41b-42a*, where we read:

ואמר רב אחא בר חנינא, אמר רב אסי, אמר רבי יוחנן:
עד כמה מברכין?

And R' Acha bar Chanina said in the name of Rav Assi, who in turn said in the name of R' Yochanan: Until when may we recite the blessing for the new moon?

Rashi comments here as follows:

עד כמה מברכין: אם לא בירך היום יברך למחר.

> "Until when may we recite the blessing of the new moon?" If one failed to do so today, then he can make the blessing on the morrow.

This initial statement of Rav Yochanan's raises several questions. The first of these questions is the following. The Gemara here presupposes that there is such a mitzva as blessing the new moon. Yet one might ask, exactly where is this mitzva presented? No mention of it is found either in the Torah or in the Mishna, nor is there an allusion to its source anywhere else. Indeed, the last chapter of Mesechtas Berachos is concerned with the issue of when one is to offer a blessing *upon seeing,* הרואה. An example of this law of הרואה is given in the Gemara, which discusses the situation where one sees a place where a miracle was wrought for Klal Yisrael or one sees such wonders as a comet, lightning, thunder or a tempest. In all these instances, a beracha is to be recited. Yet no mention is made in the Mishna or in the Gemara of the situation where one sees a new moon and whether a beracha is required. It must be noted however that in the Yerushalmi Berachos, in the chapter of הרואה, we do find it mentioned that one who sees the new moon must recite the beracha of "מחדש חדשים". The Yerushalmi tells us: "הרואה את הלבנה בחידושה אומר: מחדש חדשים".

Yet we may still wonder why neither the Mishna nor the Gemara in the Bavli Berachos mentions the origin of this mitzva at all.

A second question arises from Rav Yochanan's position. It might have been more appropriate for the Gemara here in Sanhedrin to initially mention when we may *first begin* to recite the beracha for the new moon. For in this regard we find a difference of opinion between the Rishonim and the Achronim as to when exactly we may begin to recite this blessing upon sighting the new moon.

The Rambam is of the opinion that one should recite this beracha *on the very first night* the new moon makes its appearance. He articulates this position in *Hilchos Berachos 10:16-17*, where he writes:

הרואה לבנה בחדושה מברך...אם לא בירך עליה **בליל הראשון** מברך עליה עד ששה עשר בחדש...

> One who sees the renewal of the moon recites the beracha...If one failed to make the blessing on the *first night* (of the new month) he may do so until the sixteenth of the month.

The תלמידי רבינו יונה, cited in פרק תפלת השחר of *Mesechtas Berachos*, maintains that we may recite this blessing only after three days have elapsed from when the new moon has first made its appearance.

The gaon, Rav Menachem Azarya contends that only on the seventh day after the new moon appears may we make the blessing.

The Kabbalist, מוהר"י ג'קטילא, quoted by the Bais Yosef in סוף סימן תכ"ו is of the opinion that only *after* seven days have elapsed may we recite the blessing. The diversity of opinion here serves to underline the question why the Gemara delved into the issue of how long one has to recite the blessing before it dealt with the question of when we may *first begin* to recite this beracha.

III

Answering these questions

We might suggest an answer to our first question, as to why this mitzva of sanctifying the new moon is not mentioned in the

Mishna in *Berachos,* based on insight related to the similar question raised regarding Chanukah. Why is the mitzva of kindling the Chanukah lights not mentioned in the Mishna? (This question was discussed in *The Commentators' Al Hanissim – Chanukah,* pp. 48-49.) A classic answer to this question is based on the commentary of the Rambam in the fourth chapter of מסכת מנחות, where we read:

ודיני הציצית והתפילין והמזוזה ועניין מלאכתן והברכות שחייבין לברך עליהן וכל העניינים התלויים בכל זה מן הדינין ומה שנאמר עליהן והמשנה לא דברה על אלה המצוות דבר מיוחד לכלול דיניהם עד שיהא חייב לפרש אותו.

וסבת זה בעיני לפי שהיו הדברים האלו **מפורסמים** בזמן חבור המשנה והיו עניינים ידועים ונוהגים ביד כל העם פרט וכלל ואין עניין מהם נפלא משום אדם. ועל כרחך לא ראה לדבר בהן כמו שלא הסדיר התפלה ר"ל נוסחיה ואיך יתנהג שליח צבור, לפי שהיה מפורסם...

The details of the laws of tzizits, tefillin and mezuzah and their manufacture are not discussed in the Mishna. This is probably due to the fact that they were so much a part of universal and daily practice at the time of the writing of the Mishna, that it was unnecessary to incorporate within the Mishna these detailed laws, since they were common knowledge. Similarly, the Mishna never set forth the specifics of the text of the daily prayers, for as a result of their daily practice their laws were well known.

We may say something similar in regard to this mitzva of Kiddush Levana. Since this ceremony of blessing the new moon was commonly practiced by the masses, there was no need for the Mishna to explain the requirement or the details of this beracha.

Regarding our second question – why the Gemara deals with "עד כמה" — "until when may we recite this beracha" instead of concentrating on when we may *begin* to recite it – we might suggest an answer based on the makeup of the Gemara. For the Gemara here concerns itself with statements made by the amora Rav Acha bar Chanina. The preceding Gemara deals with the question based on a statement made in the Mishna on page 40a, that "if a person is not aware of the exact day of the calendar month, due to the fact that a witness was not clear as to exactly on which day Rosh Chodesh occurred, and therefore in his testimony he was off by a day, the law reads that this witness is not thereby disqualified." The Gemara on page *41b* asks: "עד כמה"?

The reason the witness gave the wrong date was because he did not know that the bais din had added an extra day to Rosh Chodesh, and therefore he is one day ahead. This is why the Gemara raises the question of how far into the month we can say that a person was not aware when Rosh Chodesh occurred. To this question the Gemara replies:

אמר רב אחא בר חנינא, אמר רב אסי, אמר רבי יוחנן: עד רובו של חודש.

Rav Acha bar Chanina said in the name of Rav Assi, who in turn said in the name of R' Yochanan: "Only until most of the month has passed; after that we say that the witnesses already know the exact date of the month…"

Thus since the Gemara here cited a law of Rav Acha bar Chanina, in the name of Rav Assi, who in turn cited a law in the name of R' Yochanan, the Gemara, as it does in many places, cites another statement by R'Acha bar Chanina, which also begins with the question of "עד כמה" — "how long do we have to recite the blessings of the new moon."

The Gemara is not oblivious to the question of when do we *start* to make the beracha, but rather it focuses here on the question of "how long", for that was the question prior to this law being discussed and thus the Gemara continues this theme of "עד כמה".

Although this answers the question of why the Gemara here does not simply address the issue of when we may begin to recite the beracha, we may still ask why that question is not addressed elsewhere. Why did the Gemara completely bypass this question, especially since there is a difference of opinion regarding exactly when we are allowed to begin reciting this beracha?

To answer this question, we might suggest a return to our initial search for the source of this mitzva. If we go back to the makeup of this beracha of Kiddush Levana, we can perhaps find the answers to both our questions. In the blessing of Kiddush Levana we give thanks to Hashem for the renewal of the natural cycle of the moon. Thus we say in the concluding blessing, "ברוך אתה ה' מחדש חדשים" — "Blessed are You, O Lord, Who renews the months." This blessing acknowledges Hashem's mastery over nature and it indicates both the source and the timing of this mitzvah — at the moment of renewal. From this we can see that the source of this mitzva is that the renewal of the moon requires this blessing to be recited. Yet if we recognize that the moment of renewal is still a matter of contention among the Rishonim, why did the Gemara not clarify this matter for us once and for all?

To this we might point out that we have a similar precedent in regard to the mitzva of Kiddush HaChodesh. For although the Torah calls for this mitzva, yet there is a difference of opinion as to when exactly we may sanctify the moon. Some say that it is six hours after the molad, yet others maintain that it is twenty-four hours later. All the Gemara tells us is that there exists a mitzva of Kiddush HaChodesh, which requires that we determine and declare a new month according to the first sighting of the new moon by witnesses. However, the exact moment when we may do so is left to the determination of the Rishonim. And similarly, here, too, in relation to the mitzva of Kiddush Levana, we are told that we must recite a beracha at the moment of renewal. However, what constitutes the exact moment of renewal is left to the Rishonim to clarify for us.

IV

Until when may we bless the new moon?

Rav Yochanan suggests an answer to the Gemara's question of "עד כמה". His answer is: "עד שתתמלא פגימתה" — "Until its cavity is full." To which the Gemara asks: "וכמה?" – "How much is that?"

The Gemara then cites two opinions.

אמר רב אחא בר אידי, אמר רב יהודה: עד שבעה.

R' Ya'acov bar Idi said in the name of R' Yehudah: Until the seventh day of the month.

נהרדעי אמרי: עד ששה עשר.

The Nehardeans say: Until the sixteenth day of the month.

ותרווייהו כר' יוחנן סבירא להו, הא למיהוי כי יתרה, הא למיהוי כי נפיא.

And both R' Yehudah and the Nehardeans concur with R' Yochanan, that the blessing is not said after the cavity became full, but they disagree as to when that occurs.

According to R' Yehudah, this is when the moon becomes half full, like a bow filled up to its bowstring. However, according to the Nehardeans, it is only when the moon becomes completely full, like a round sieve.

The Gemara then asks, "וליברך הטוב והמטיב" — "But let one recite the blessing of 'who is good and does good.' Here we have a difference of opinion as to how we are to understand this question.

RASHI'S OPINION

Rashi contends that this question applies to the opinion of R' Yehudah. Even though R' Yehudah does not allow the beracha of "מחדש חדשים" to be recited after seven days of the new month have elapsed, he should nevertheless require the blessing of 'who is good and does good' to be said after the seven days, since the increasing reflection of light from the moon to the earth is beneficial to all.

אדרב יהודה פריך, נהי נמי דמשבעה ואילך ליכא למימר "מחדש חדשים" ליברך מיהא "הטוב והמטיב", שכל שעה הוא מטיב לנו במילואתה תמיד שמוספת להאיר לעולם.

THE VIEW OF THE MAHARSHAL (מהרש״ל)

The Maharshal, in his commentary חכמת שלמה, prefers to say that the question why not say the beracha of "הטוב והמטיב" is directed to both R' Yehudah and the Nehardeans, and not, as Rashi contends, exclusively to R' Yehudah. And if we were to ask, as the Nehardeans do, why two berachos should be recited, those of both "מחדש חדשים" and "הטוב והמטיב", the answer, according to the Maharshal, would be that we find a precedent for two berachos in the law regarding the drinking of wine. When we are about to begin to drink wine, we recite the blessing of "בורא פרי הגפן", and if we then drink another kind of wine, an additional blessing of "הטוב והמטיב" must be said.

And so here too, we recite two berachos with the appearance of the new moon. One beracha, that of "מחדש חדשים", is related to the creation of the new moon, and the second beracha, that of "הטוב והמטיב", expresses the benefit man receives from the moon's light.

And the Maharshal contends that there is another case where two berachos are recited, and this is when one's father dies. On this sad occasion, the beracha of "ברוך דיין אמת" is said to justify the harsh decree of death. And then an additional beracha, that of "הטוב והמטיב", is recited to express gratitude for the inheritance received by the heirs. This situation, where two berachos are recited, can be compared to the situation of the blessings recited on the new moon. For, as we have explained, first we say "מחדש חדשים" for the renewal of the moon and then "הטוב והמטיב" for the benefit of the light we receive.

The Maharshal explains this as follows:

בד"ה וליברך הטוב וכו' אדרב יהודה פריך כו': נ"ב כבודו [של רש"י] במקומו מונח, כי אין אנו צריכין לזה. דלכולי עלמא מקשה. יברך "הטוב והמטיב" ומה שיש לו ברכה אחרת דהיינו "מחדש חדשים" מה בכך, הלא אותה ברכה קאי על בריאת השם ומעשהו, וברכה "הטוב והמטיב" קאי על הנאת האדם, כמו על היין דמברכין "בורא פרי הגפן" וגם "הטוב והמטיב" וכל שכן דברכת "מחדש חדשים" מברך על אתחילת חדושה, וברכת "הטוב והמטיב" יברך על מילואה, לכל הפחות אחר שבעה, שאז הוא ואחרים נהנין

בשלימותה. ועוד דלא גרע ממת אביו דמברך "דיין האמת" על המיתה, ועל בשורות הירושה "הטוב והמטיב..."

The objection of the Maharsha (מהרש"א)

The Maharasha rejects this interpretation of the Maharshal, although on the surface it appears to be logical. He presents two objections to the Maharshal's approach. If, as the Maharshal contends, the question here is whether we should make two berachos, then the reading here should be "וליברך נמי הטוב והמטיב" — "that we should *also* make the blessing of הטוב והמטיב". Secondly, there is a vast difference between blessing the new moon and drinking different kinds of wine. For in relation to the blessing of "הטוב והמטיב" recited over wine, this is the result of drinking *different kinds* of wine, which calls for an additional beracha; whereas in the case of the blessings on the new moon, it is the *same* moon upon which we are required to recite two separate blessings, and we normally do not recite two berachos over a single entity.

And as for the comparison between the blessing of the new moon and the laws of inheritance, there is also a vast difference. For the two berachos here address two separate issues. דיין האמת relates to the death of one's father, whereas the beracha of "הטוב והמטיב" is concerned with the actual inheritance, which involves concrete monetary gain. However, in regard to the blessings on the new moon, both berachos refer to the benefit of the light derived from the moon. How can we justify reciting two berachos over the same concept?

We can explain this difference of opinion between the Maharshal and the Maharsha as to how we are to understand the blessings of the new moon, in the following manner. The Maharshal contends that the beracha of "מחדש חדשים" is concerned with the recognition of God's creations, whereas the blessing of "הטוב והמטיב" relates to the benefit one derives from the light of the moon.

The Maharsha, on the other hand, maintains that both berachos relate to the benefit, הנאה, man derives from the light of the moon.

V

What kind of blessing is Kiddush Levana?

There are three general categories of berachos. The first is ברכות שבח והודאה — Blessings of praise to Hashem. For example, in our daily prayers the concluding beracha of the ברוך שאמר is "מלך מהולל בתשבחות", "the King Who is lauded with praise" falls into this category. The second is ברכות נהנין – Blessings recited upon deriving enjoyment or benefit. For example, a blessing before partaking of food or drink would be this type of blessing. The final category is ברכות המצוות – Blessings recited before performing a mitzva, such as when eating matza at the Pesach seder, when we say: "אקב״ו על אכילת מצה", or when taking the lulav and esrog, when we say: "אקב״ו על נטילת לולב".

We might ask to which category of berachos Kiddush Levana belongs. And the answer would be that this depends on the reason given for the fulfillment of this mitzva. Some maintain that the purpose of Kiddush Levana is to articulate our gratitude to Hashem for His wondrous creations. This is the opinion of Rabbenu Yona, who writes as follows at the end of the chapter on Tefillas HaShachar in Mesechtas Berachos:

כאילו מקבל פני השכינה: מפני שהקב״ה אע״פ שאינו נראה לעין, נראה הוא על ידי גבורותיו ונפלאותיו כעניין שנאמר "אכן אתה קל מסתתר אלוקי ישראל מושיע," כלומר אף

על פי שאתה מסתתר אתה הוא אלוקי ישראל, שעשית
להם כמה נפלאות, ואתה מושיע בכל עת ובכל שעה, ועל
ידי תשועתך רואים אותך בני אדם, **ואתה מתגלה להם
ומכירין אותך** גם כן בכאן על ידי **מה שמחדש החדשים** הוא
מתגלה לבני אדם והוא כאילו מקבלין פניו...

Thus this beracha could be seen as an exercise in praising Hashem for His wondrous creations, that is, it would fall into the category of berachos characterized by praise and thanksgiving, ברכות השבח והודאה.

Yet others contend that we are not to recite this beracha on the moon until *after* we derive benefit from its light, which means only after three days from the initial appearance of the new moon — referred to as the מולד. In this case, it would seem that this beracha falls into the category of ברכות נהנין.

And yet others view this ceremony of Kiddush Levana as a challenge to receive the Divine Presence, מקבל פני השכינה, at least once a month, as we acknowledge in the beracha itself when we say:

תנא דבי ר' ישמעאל: אלמלא לא זכו ישראל אלא להקביל
פני אביהן שבשמים כל חדש וחדש דיים.

R' Yishmael taught: Had Yisrael been privileged to greet the countenance of their Father in Heaven only once in each and every month, it would have sufficed them.

Rashi explains that even if Bnai Yisrael were privileged to perform only this one mitzva, it would have been sufficient. Thus we see that the ceremony of Kiddush Levana is to be viewed as a mitzvah, and therefore the beracha here may be considered to belong to the category of Bircas HaMitzvos.

Each of these opinions has its halachic consequences and also raises questions regarding those consequences. For example, if we are to view the beracha of the Kiddush Levana ceremony as a ברכת נהנין, then the following objections arise.

The halacha states that a ברכת נהנין may be recited while sitting, and yet we know that the beracha here must be said while standing, מעומד. However, this objection may be readily dismissed, for the requirement to stand while reciting this beracha is based on another consideration altogether. It is not the particular category to which this beracha belongs which is the determining factor, but rather it is because we stand before the Divine Presence, מקבל פני השכינה, and in the presence of the Shechinah we must certainly stand. And so, even if this beracha were to be viewed as a ברכת נהנין, we would still be required to stand when reciting it.

Additionally, if the blessing of the moon, ברכת הלבנה, is due to the benefit we receive from the light of the moon, then one could ask why we recite this beracha only once a month? Why do we not recite it every night, or at least until the sixteenth of the month, during which period of time the light increases?

But this, too, is not a strong objection. For the halacha stipulates that this beracha is to be recited when the moon is בחידושה. This period of בחידושה commences at the beginning of the month and extends until the sixteenth day of the month. At any time during this period we may recite this beracha of appreciation for the light of the moon, and once we have done this, we need not recite it on every night that we derive this benefit. So writes the "יד המלך" מהרב אלעזר לנדא, פרק יא מהלכות ברכות, הלכה ד':

> והא דלא נתקנה ברכת הירח זאת הרבה פעמים בכל חודש בכל פעם על קבלת אור חדש אשר נתוסף והולך בכל רגע אשר רואה אותה עד מלואותה טז יום היינו משום דכל חודש בפני עצמו שם חידוש אחד הוא והלכך אם ברך פעם אחת בחודש שוב אינו מברך באותו חודש, וכמו שמצינו בברקים ורעמים, דכל זמן שלא נתפזרו העבים, אם בירך

פעם אחד, שוב אינו מברך עוד על ברקים ורעמים ששמע אחר ברכתו. ומכל מקום אם לא בירך עדיין על שמיעת הרעמים וראיית הברק בפעם ראשון, מברך על השני או על השלישי...

Another objection to this theory that this beracha of Kiddush Levana is a ברכת נהנין is cited in the sefer ד' ס"ק תכ"ו סימן "ברכי יוסף", where the author goes to great lengths to disprove the contention that we must recite the blessing for the benefit we receive from the light of the moon. According to the opinion of the Rambam, we must offer this beracha on the very first day of the new moon. For on this night, the light of the moon is minimal and so, even though a beracha is required, it is not a beracha for the benefit we receive from the light of the moon.

עוד נראה להביא ראיה דלא בענין שיהנה מאור הלבנה ממה שכתב הרמב"ם פרק י' דברכות, אם לא בירך עליו בליל הראשון מברך עליה עד י"ו בחודש...הרי למדנו מהרמב"ם...דאף על ירח בן יומו מברכין, ומאי הנאה איכא בריש ירחא, בר יומיה הוה, אלא מוכרח דאין צריך ליהנות ממנה...

THE GEMARA'S SOLUTION

According to the Rebbe of Belz (among others), this issue of what type of beracha we consider the Beracha of Kiddush Levana is alluded to in the statements made in the *Gemara Sanhedrin 41a*, where we find the following:

תנא דבי ר' ישמעאל: אילמלא לא זכו ישראל אלא להקביל פני אביהן שבשמים כל חדש וחדש דיים. אמר אביי: **הילכך** נימרינהו מעומד.

The school of R' Yishmael taught: Had Yisrael

been privileged to greet the countenance of their Father in Heaven only once each and every month, it would have sufficed them. Abaye said: Therefore, we should recite the blessing while standing.

As we have previously explained, we find several differences concerning whether a beracha is a ברכת נהנין or a ברכת המצוות. The ברכת נהנין need not be recited while standing; whereas a ברכת המצוות requires one to stand when reciting the beracha. In addition, it would seem that if the beracha is in recognition of benefit we receive, then we should recite that beracha every time we receive that same benefit from the moonlight. Yet since R' Yishmael stated here that all that is required is to recite this beracha once a month, we can thus see that this beracha must not be viewed as a ברכת נהנין, but rather a ברכת המצוות. Thus Abaye concluded: "If this is a beracha recited on a mitzva then we must recite it while standing, מעומד."

שמעתי לפרש ענין "הילכך" זה, לפי שישנן ברכות הנהנין וברכות המצוות. ברכת הנהנין מברכין בכל פעם שנהנין. אבל ברכות המצוות רק בזמנם הקבוע. בברכות הנהנין מברכין בין מיושב בין מעומד, וברכות המצוות רק מעומד. והנה אור הלבנה מהניא בני אדם ואם נאמר שברכתה מסוג ברכות הנהנין היו צריך לברך כל לילה. אבל אחר שאמרו שפעם אחת בחודש די, נמצא שאין זו ברכות הנהנין רק כברכת המצוות. ובכן אמר אביי, **הילכך** נימרינהו **מעומד**, כדין ברכות המצוות.

We might suggest that indeed the Bircas HaLevana is to be considered a blessing of praise, ברכת השבח. We praise Hashem and acknowledge our recognition of all His works. However, even though this is a ברכת השבח we also benefit from the light of the moon. The reason for this is at the time of Creation, Hashem fashioned two luminaries, one to rule by day and the other by night. "To rule" means to function. The moon functions by providing the benefit of light in the nighttime. Thus the beracha we recite on the light of the moon acknowledges the fact that benefit comes to man from the moon. For, as we have discussed, only when we receive that benefit can we praise Hashem for all His works.

VI

THE CONCLUDING BERACHA — "מחדש" OR "מקדש"

The name of this ritual is headlined in our siddurim as קידוש לבנה, the "Sanctification of the Moon". But why do we refer to this ritual in this way, when nowadays we do not strictly speaking *sanctify* either the month by means of witnesses or the new moon itself. For in modern times we have a fixed calendar, and thus there is no need to "sanctify the moon" at all. In fact, sanctifying the new moon has no place in the halacha. Therefore, the obvious question we here is why refer to this ritual as קידוש לבנה at all?

The answer given by the commentators is that this was the name that was given to this ceremony in the time when the month was determined by eye-witnesses — קידוש על פי הראייה — and subsequently it was proclaimed as Rosh Chodesh by the Bais Din. For in those days the Bais Din literally *sanctified* the new month in accordance with the sighting of the moon — the לבנה — by witnesses. The "greeting of the moon" by the people of that period was referred to as חידוש לבנה, literally the "renewal" of the moon. Therefore, as a memorial to the קידוש לבנה ritual of ancient times, we today use the same name for our modern "greeting" of the moon, we also refer to it as קידוש לבנה.

Other commentators contend that the name קידוש לבנה crept into our ritual of חידוש לבנה, even though קידוש, literally "sanctification", has no place in our present-day ritual. This is the opinion of the Ha Rav Shimon Greenfield, who writes as follows in his sefer (שו"ת מהרש"ג (סימן ה'): "

לכן נ"ל קצת לומר דקריאת שם זה נשתרבב ממה שבזמן
שהי' בזמן המקדש קיים, וגם קצת אחר כך, היו הבית דין
מקדשין החדש כשהעידו העדים שראו הלבנה החדשה, ושם
שפיר שייך לשון קידוש...

THE OPINION OF THE תניא רבתי

According to our custom, the concluding beracha is מחדש חדשים. However, there are a number of different versions of the concluding beracha cited that read מקדש חדשים. For example, the תניא רבתי, in סימן לא' writes that one may conclude the beracha with the words, מקדש חדשים. And the שבולי הלקט also cites this same nusach. Indeed, we find this same conclusion to the beracha in *Chapter 20, Halacha I* of *Mesechtas Sofrim*, where we read:

ואין מברכין על הירח אלא במוצאי שבת כשהיא מבושם
ובכלים נאים... ברוך אתה ה' **מקדש** ראשי חדשים.

The sefer "עמק ברכה" מהרב לייבעלע פומרנציק (ערך ברכת הלבנה) would have us believe that this nusach of מקדש חדשים was only said during the period when we determined Rosh Chodesh by the testimony of eye-witnesses. Today, however, when Rosh Chodesh is determined by a fixed calendar and follows a set procedure, only מחדש חדשים is the appropriate conclusion of the beracha here. He then cites a source for this opinion. In the *Midrash Rabbah Shemos, Bo, Parashas 15,* we find:

הרואה את הלבנה איך צריך לברך? בזמן שהיו ישראל
מקדשין החודש. יש מרבנן אמרין ברוך **מחדש** חדשים. ויש
מהם אומרים: מקדש חדשים. ויש מהם אומרים: מקדש
ישראל, שאם אין ישראל מקדשין אותו אין אותו קידוש
כלום.

For one who sees the moon, how is he to make the blessing? At the time when Yisrael sanctified the moon by means of eye-witnesses, they said, "Who renews the month". Yet others contend that they said, "Yisrael, who sanctified". For if it were not for Yisrael sanctifying the moon, then we have no sanctification.

The עמק ברכה concludes that the beracha of מקדש ישראל was only accepted as the appropriate conclusion at the time when the new month was determined by the Bais Din. Today, however, when this is no longer the case, all would agree that the appropriate blessing should be מחדש חדשים.

THE TEXT OF THE MIDRASH RABBAH

The text which we find in the Midrash Rabbah, which we have quoted here, raises several questions regarding the correct reading of the text. The classic commentators all point out that there is a discrepancy here. At the beginning of the Midrash we find "הרואה את הלבנה", which seems to indicate that we are speaking of an individual Jew when he first sees the new moon. Yet the following statement, "בזמן שהיו ישראל מקדשין החודש", seems to indicate that we are referring here to the Bais Din, who were responsible for sanctifying the new month. And therefore the question arises, what kind of beracha are they required to recite? The disagreement seems to be over how we are to conclude the blessing of the new moon. Is it with the words מקדש, מקדש ישראל, or מחדש? It would appear that the blessing of מקדש ישראל was the appropriate conclusion of the blessing at the time when the Bais Din determined the new month. However, everyone would agree that the appropriate concluding beracha in our day should be מחדש חדשים. Thus one who tries to recite מקדש in its place has not fulfilled his obligation (see the classic commentators on the Midrash Rabbah here פרי תואר, פירוש מהרז"ו, חדושי הרד"ל.)

Although these commentators present different rationales, when we come to evaluate their opinions we find that there are really only two opinions (מקדש ישראל or מקדש) and not three (מחדש or מקדש ישראל, מקדש). The question is related to the period when the Bais Din determined the new moon. To correct the reading of the text, the version should read that we have only two opinions, either מקדש ישראל or מקדש. The third version, מחדש, should be deleted from the text. This version relates only to our time, when the Bais Din no longer practice the ceremony of קידוש, actually *sanctifying* the month. The commentary of תורה שלמה in Parashas Shemos, יב, בא, או"ק לה, points to the text which was available to him, that is, the Oxford manuscript of this Midrash. Here the following *two* opinions were explicitly cited:

הרואה את הלבנה האיך צריך לברך. בזמן שישראל מקדש את החדש. יש מרבותינו אומרים: מקדש חדשים. ויש אומרים: ברוך מקדש ישראל וראשי חדשים, שאם אין ישראל מקדשין אותו, אין אותו קידוש כלום.

We can see from here that we have only two versions here, and not three. They are מקדש ישראל and מקדש חדשים. The text thus proves that the Midrash refers only to the time when Rosh Chodesh was determined by means of eye-witnesses. Therefore, no one held the opinion that מחדש חדשים was recited in those days. However, today we recite this as the concluding beracha.

Answering the Commentators

To understand and resolve the apparent discrepancy among the commentators here we might suggest the following. We begin with the statement of "הרואה", literally "*one* who sees", and conclude with the statement of "בזמן שהיו ישראל מקדשין החודש" — "when the *Bais Din* sanctified the month". We must move the question mark, from the way it was understood by the commentators, and place it at the end of the statement. According to the commentators, the reading is "הרואה את הלבנה איך צריך לברך?" — "How should the one who sees the moon make the blessing?" But let us rearrange the sentence to give us a slightly different reading:

הרואה את הלבנה איך צריך לברך בזמן שהיו ישראל מקדשין החודש?

How was the one who sees the moon supposed to make the blessing at the time when Yisrael [the Bais Din] sanctified the new month?

During the time when the Bais HaMikdash stood and the Sanhedrin sanctified the new month, the mitzva of Kiddush Levana by the ordinary Jew was practiced in addition to the mitzva of Kiddush HaChodesh by the Bais Din. Thus the question was raised: At the time when the Bais Din acted to officially establish the month by means of the sighting of the moon by eye-witnesses, what was expected of the ordinary Jew to mark the occasion?

When we say Kiddush Levana, should we end with the beracha מקדש חדשים? For even though this ceremony did not sanctify the month, yet when we see the light of the moon, this reminds us that we were obligated to acknowledge the role of the moon at the time when the month was determined by its sighting. This then would justify the recitation of מקדש חדשים.

Or should we say only מחדש חדשים, for this would imply that we now have a new month because of the new moon. Thus we are faced with three possible opinions. The first is מחדש חדשים — to acknowledge a new month has already been established by means of the new moon.

The second opinion is מקדש חדשים. Although in our day and age, we are not acting to sanctify the moon, yet since it was *this* moon that was used by the Bais Din to sanctify the month, we too, recite these words of מקדש חדשים in recognition of the role the moon played at the time when designating a new month depended on its first appearance. What is required, now that this is no longer the case, is that we simply acknowledge the renewal of the new moon in this new month, מקבל פני השכינה.

The third opinion is מקדש ישראל וכו'— based on what we have just discussed, that we now wish only to acknowledge the role of the moon in determining the new month, therefore we must also acknowledge the role of Yisrael, manifested by the Bais Din, for they too played a crucial role in determining the new month.

If this is so, then all we need to recite today is מחדש, for this is the only role the moon fulfills today. Thus we need not "correct" the text of the Midrash Rabbah or seek out corrected texts. But we must simply understand what is intended here. We are speaking of the time when the Bais Din alone acted to determine the new month, and the only question we need to ask now is how are we to respond to what they accomplished, what should be our contribution.

VII

Is Kiddush Levana a time-bound mitzvah?

There is a basic question raised here in regard to the mitzva of Kiddush Levana. Is it to be considered a time-bound mitzva, "מצות עשה שהזמן גרמא" (מעשהז"ג), from which women are exempt? We find various opinions regarding this matter. The Magen Avraham, for example, in סימן תכ"ו ס"ק א' contends that Kiddush Levana is certainly to be viewed as a time-bound mitzva.

Furthermore, he states that even according to those who are of the opinion that although women are not obligated in time-bound mitzvos, they still retain the option to fulfill these mitzvos if they so wish. However, regarding the mitzva of Kiddush Levana, we say that they are totally ruled out from performing this mitzva. The rationale for this is that since it was a woman (Chava) who was responsible for diminishing the moon's light (see here Part II), it would not be appropriate for women to participate in sanctifying the moon.

נשים פטוריות: דמ"ע שהז"ג הוא, ואע"ג דהם קיימות כל מצוה עשה כגון סוכה, מכל מקום מצוה זו אין מקיימים, מפני שהם גרמו פגם הלבנה (של"ה).

This position of the Magen Avraham caused Rav Shlomo Kluger, in his commentary here, חכמת שלמה, to speculate on how the Magen Avraham could have possibly considered the mitzva of Kiddush Levana to be time-bound, for this class of mitzva must satisfy the condition of being possible to fulfill the mitzva all year long, even if it was limited to a particular time period. For example, matzah can be eaten all year round. Yet the Torah called for it to be eaten *as a mitzva* only on Pesach. This is why we view this mitzva of אכילת מצה as one of the time-bound mitzvos. However, in relation to Kiddush Levana, the mitzva here is not to sanctify the moon in general, but rather to sanctify the moon בחידושה, that is, while it is still new at the beginning of the month. After the middle of the month we no longer have a new moon, and therefore the mitzva of Kiddush Levana is no longer required. In light of this approach, we can understand that Kiddush Levana is not to be viewed as a time-bound mitzva, for as we have seen, it can only be performed when the moon is new, בחידושה, and thus time is not the determining factor here, but rather the condition of there being a new moon.

A different opinion is held by the gaon, Ha Rav Yehoshua Leib Diskin, in his sefer קו"א סימן ה, אות כו, "שו"ת מהרי"ל דיסקין".

This opinion does indeed view Kiddush Levana as a time-bound mitzva. He contends that the moon could have been sanctified all month long, and yet it is only at the beginning of the month, when the moon is new, בחידושה that we are to fulfill this mitzva. Thus it can legitimately be considered a מצות עשה שהזמן גרמא.

Perhaps we may attempt to reconcile these two opinions. The basic question being addressed is whether this mitzva requires a new moon, לבנה בחידושה, in order to be sanctified. If so, then after a certain time has passed there is no longer a moon to sanctify. Or are we called upon to sanctify a moon, and the time to do this is when that moon is seen to be new. According to this first way of understanding the matter, Kiddush Levana would not be seen as a time-bound mitzva; whereas according to the second view, it would indeed be considered a מצות עשה שהזמן גרמא.

It is interesting to note that these two possible approaches are touched upon in the following seforim. It is the contention of Ha Rav Yosef Dov Soloveitchik, as cited in the sefer "נפש הרב" (עמ' קעו), that Kiddush Levana is not to be counted among the time-bound mitzvos. The reason for this is that the mitzva is only required when the moon is new, בחידושה. The rest of the month, the moon does not qualify for fulfilling this mitzva.

הרואה לבנה בחידושה חייב לברך, **ובשיעור** של בחידושה יש זמן מסויים, אך אין זאת אומרת **שהזמן גורם** לחייב לברך ברכה זו, ואשר על כן בודאי נראה, שאין כאן ענין של זמן גרמא עיקר.

However, in the sefer "משמרת חיים", להרב ח.פ. שיינברג שליט"א (ערך ברכות, אות ז), the author adopts the second view we have just cited that the entire month is an appropriate period in which to offer a beracha, even though only the beginning of the month was designated as the proper time for this mitzva. Consequently, Kiddush Levana is to be viewed as a time-bound mitzva.

אבל הכא גבי ברכת הלבנה בעצם שייך לברך על לבנה אף
בחסרונה, דעצם הברכה **על הלבנה**, והרי יש כאן לבנה.
ורק לסוף החדש ממש דאינו נראה כלל אין על מה לברך,
אלא דחז"ל **תקנו** דרק יברך **בחידושה**, הרי **דהגבילוהו בזמן**
וזה ממילא חשיב מצות עשה שהזמן גרמא.

This is essentially the basis of the disagreement between the position of Ha Rav Shlomo Kluger and that of Ha Rav Yehoshua Leib Diskin, and it reflects the way we are to view this divergence of views regarding the question of whether or not Kiddush Levana is to be considered a time-bound mitzva.

VIII

Man's role in restoring the moon to its original size

As we have discussed, the Magen Avraham rules out women from this mitzva of Kiddush Levana, based on the consideration that it was a woman who caused the moon to be diminished in the first place. Thus it would not be proper that they participate in this mitzva. This leads us to ask the following question. The Gemara in *Chullin 60a* (quoted by Rashi in his commentary on *Bereishis 1:16*) tells us that at the time of Creation both the sun and the moon were the same size. However, Hashem reduced the size of the moon because it complained that it was "not possible for two kings to share the same crown". If the moon was diminished from the very dawn of Creation because of its own arrogance, how can we attribute its diminution to the first woman?

The suggested answer to this question is that at the time of Creation it was the light of the two heavenly bodies which were equal, and after the moon complained, its *light* was diminished. Later on, after the woman sinned, the moon was also diminished in *size*.

In the sefer by HaRav Shlomo Zalman Auerbach, "הליכות שלמה" (הערה 32, עמ' קפ"ז) the author quotes Ha Rav Yitzchak Yerucham Diskin, who explained why after reciting the prayers of Kiddush Levana, there is a custom to touch the tzitzis – למשמש בציצית. And he explained that in the future, when the *light* of the moon will be restored to its original state, and its light will again be equal to the light of the sun, then the mitzva of tzitzis will be practiced at night as well as during the day. For at present it is not practiced at night due to the fact that we cannot see the tzitzis at night, and the Torah insists in regard to this mitzva that we must be able to see the tzitsis, וראיתם אותו. In the future, though, when the light of the moon will shine at night with the same intensity as the sun shines during the day, "שיהי' אור הלבנה כאור החמה", then this mitzva will also be practiced at night. And so, after the Kiddush Levana ceremony, when we pray for the moon's restoration we touch the tzitzis to allude to the consequences of the moon's restoration.

However, the question still remains as to why the moon was punished for the sin of the first woman, Chava. Why should the moon be held responsible for her wrongdoing? The answer, which also answers our previous question, is that the moon was not punished directly because of its own sin, but rather the sin of the woman caused the size (light) of the moon not to be restored to its original condition until the time of the Ultimate Redemption. For the sin of Chava in eating from the forbidden fruit, עץ הדעת, caused the evil inclination, the יצר הרע, to be implanted in man, thus preventing him from being restored to his former spiritual level of perfection. This diminution of spiritual status also prevented the moon from being restored to its former condition.

We might conclude this discussion with another insight of HaRav Shlomo Zalman Auerbach which is cited in the same sefer. The אדר"ת, HaRav Eliyahu David Tumim Rabinovitz, sought to emend the concluding petition in the Kiddush Levana prayer, which reads: "ויהי רצון מלפניך ה' אלוקי ואלוקי אבותי" — "May it be your will, Hashem, my God and the God of my forefathers."

The אדר"ת asks, why do we stress here the singular, אלוקי — "*my* God", אבותי — "my forefathers", instead of changing it to the plural, אלקינו — "our G-d" and אבותינו — "our forefathers"? HaRav Shlomo Zalman contends that homiletically we can retain the singular form, based on an insight offered in the *Gemara Kiddushin 41b,* where the Gemara tells us:

> ר' אלעזר בר' שמעון אומר: לפי שהעולם נידון אחר רובו, והיחיד נדון אחר רובו, עשה מצוה אחת אשריו שהכריע את עצמו ואת כל העולם לכף זכות. עבר עבירה אחת, אוי לו שהכריע את עצמו ואת כל העולם לכף חובה...

> R' Elazar, the son of R' Shimon said: Because the world is judged on the basis of the deeds of the majority of its inhabitants and the individual is judged on the basis of his deeds, one should always regard the world as populated by righteous and evil individuals equally. And furthermore, he should regard himself as half guilty and half meritorious. Hence if he performs a single mitzva, he is fortunate, for he has tipped the scales for himself and for the entire world towards the side of merit. But if he commits a single transgression, woe to him, for he has tipped the balance for himself and for the entire world towards the side of guilt.

HaRav Shlomo Zalman concludes that it is important for an individual to view the restoration of the moon as dependent on his own actions. Therefore the individual, as articulated in the singular is stressed here, "ויהי רצון מלפניך ה' אלוקי ואלוקי אבותי".

CHAPTER SIX

THE PRAYERS AND CUSTOMS OF ROSH CHODESH

I

THE PSALM OF THE DAY RECITED ON WEEKDAYS

At the time of the Bais HaMikdash, the daily sacrifices — both the תמיד של בין הערבים and the תמיד של שחרית — were accompanied with a daily psalm. The psalm, called a shir — "שיר", was sung with the offering of the wine libation, "נסכים". This is articulated in (יא, א) מסכת ערכין, where we find the following statement:

> אמר ר' שמואל בר נחמני אמר ר' יונתן: מנין שאין אומרים שירה אלא על היין שנאמר "ותאמר להם הגפן החדלתי את תירושי המשמח אל-הים ואנשים". אם אנשים משמח אל-הים במה משמח, מכאן שאין אומרים שירה אלא על היין...

> R' Shmuel bar Nachmani said in the name of R' Yonason: From where do we know that the shira is not sung except over wine? Because it is said, "and the vine said unto them, since it cheers man, can it also cheer God? *(Judges 9:13)*" From this it is evident that shira is not sung except over wine.

The purpose of this mitzva, writes the author of the sefer "שו"ת בנין שלמה" להרב שלמה הכהן מווילנה, was to articulate our gratitude and praise to Hashem for the gift of His Divine Presence (Shechinah) which rests on the Bais HaMikdash, and this afforded Him a sense of satisfaction.

> השיר של קרבן עיקר מצוותו אינו אלא כדי לתת שבח והודיה לפני מלך מלכי המלכים הקב"ה, שהשרה שכינתו בבית הגדול והקדוש, וזה היה נחת רוח לפניו יתברך שמו...

Therefore the question arises, since today we no longer have a Bais HaMikdash nor the daily sacrifices, why do we still offer this

שיר, psalm of the day, every day of the week, including Shabbos day? A number of possible answers are suggested to this question. Based on the Mishna in *Mesechtas Sofrim 18:1*, it would appear that indeed a שיר may be recited even without the accompanying wine libation offering or the daily sacrifices. (See the commentary of the "נחלת יעקב" here, who cites additional sources justifying the recitation of the daily Psalms.) We are challenged to such an extent to recite the daily psalm that the above Mishna concludes:

שכל המזכיר פסוק בעונתו מעלה עליו כאילו בונה מזבח חדש ומקריב עליו קרבן.

> Whenever one makes mention of a Biblical verse at its proper time, it is regarded by Hashem as though he had built a new altar and offered sacrifices upon it.

Others contend that this ritual is based on a זכר למקדש, a remembrance of what once transpired in the Bais HaMikdash when it was intact. This can be proved by the fact that prior to reciting the psalm of the day we preface this prayer with the following words:

היום יום...בשבת, שבו היו הלוים אומרים בבית המקדש.

> Today is the...of the Shabbos on which the Levites used to recite in the Bais HaMikdash.

We shall later attempt to show that there is an entirely different reason for this practice of reciting the daily psalm, the song of the day. But first we must address the obvious question, why do we offer this psalm only during the morning service, why not also at Mincha? This question was already touched upon by Ha Rav Moshe Alshich, cited in the Magen Avraham (או"ח, סימן קלד, או"ק ד). There we find that the Magen Avraham contends that the psalm of the day is decisive—מעכב—only in relation to the morning service, קרבן שחרית. Thus the daily psalm is recited only at Shacharis.

The Chasam Sofer, in his commentary on *Mesechtas Beitzah 4b,* explains the reason why we do not recite the psalm of the day again in the afternoon at the Mincha service. Tosafos in Mesechtas Rosh Hashanah contends that we repeat the same psalm twice on the same day only in emergency situations or else, when we are in doubt as to which psalm is to be said, then we are to say no psalm at all. And therefore today, since we are not clear which psalm they used to recite at Mincha, therefore we say no psalm at all. Perhaps the daily psalm was divided in half, with part of it said in the morning and the rest in the afternoon. Therefore today, since we do not know how the psalm was divided, we recite it only in the morning.

II

THE PSALM OF THE MUSSAF SACRIFICE

The singing of the daily psalm was also included in the Mussaf service. However, when a קרבן מוסף, an "additional sacrifice", was offered, a different psalm was sung than the one which was sung when the תמיד של שחר was offered. Consequently, on Shabbos day, Rosh Chodesh and Yom Tov (including Rosh Hashanah) a special psalm was sung.

ON SHABBOS DAY

We are told in the Mishna in *Mesechtas Sofrim 17:1* and at the end of Mesechtas Tamid that the psalm of Shabbos was "מזמור שיר ליום שבת". And the Gemara in *Rosh Hashanah 31a* addresses the question of what psalm was recited at Mussaf:

במוספי דשבתא מה היו אומרים? אמר רב ענן בר רבא אמר רב: הזי"ו לך.

With the Mussaf offerings of the Shabbos what hymn would the Levi'im recite? Rav Anan bar Rava said in the name of Rav: they recited the six Torah passages represented by the mneumonic *Haziv Loch*.

The reference here is to the song of Haazinu *(Devarim 32:1-43)* which is divided into six segments. The mneumonic הזי"ו לך contains the first letters of the opening words of each segment. These are: הַאזינו (verses 1-6), זַכור ימות עולם (verse 7-12), יַרכבהו (verses 13-18), וַירא ה' וינאץ (verses 19-26), לוּלי כעס אויב (verses 27-35), כִּי-ידין ה' עמו (verses 36-43).

The Maharasha points out that a song from the Torah rather than from the Book of Psalms was selected to accompany the Shabbos Mussaf service, because this day is holier than the others.

On Rosh Chodesh

Some contend that the daily song was the same one said every day, and the song of Mussaf was the ברכי נפשי. Others, however, like the Gr'a, for example, maintain that the only song of the day was ברכי נפשי. We will shortly expand on the role of ברכי נפשי as the song of the day for Rosh Chodesh.

On Yom Tov

Most commentators are of the opinion that we do not know exactly which psalm was said on Yom Tov, either in the Shacharis or the Mussaf service. The (סימן כה) שו"ת הרמ"ע מפאנו", and the Chasam Sofer in his commentary on *Mesechtas Beitzah (ibid.)* both contend that although the song of the day for ordinary weekdays is recited today in the Morning service, yet since we do not know whether or not this was the prayer recited by the Levi'im in the Bais HaMikdash, we should not include the usual opening phrase of: "השיר שהיו הלוים אומרים וכו'". In fact, the Gr'a lists a new set of psalms to be said on Yom Tov.

According to Rashi, in מסכת ערכין י, א, the song of Yom Tov was Hallel. The Mishna (ibid.) states that on all the holidays, instruments were played while the Levi'im sang the Hallel, which replaced the usual psalm of the day.

ובשעת הקרבה היה שיר זה. והיו הלויים משוררים בפה את ההלל באותן יב ימים...

Therefore, since we do not know exactly what the psalm was— whether it was Hallel or another psalm — if today we recite the psalm of the regular weekday service, then the accompanying phrase of "שהיו אומרים בבית המקדש" should not be said.

III

Various problems

If the song of the day, as we recite it today, was the one sung at the service in the Bais Haikdash of the daily morning sacrifice, תמיד של שחר, and the psalm of ברכי נפשי was the psalm of the Korban Mussaf on the day of Rosh Chodesh, then we are faced with several difficulties.

It is the custom of the Sefardim to recite the psalm of the day and the ברכי נפשי at Shacharis. The Ashkenazim, on the other hand, have the custom of reciting both of these hymns after the Mussaf Amidah prayer. Thus, based on the Sefardic tradition, we have the following difficulties to resolve.

It is understandable that the psalm of the day was said during the Morning prayers, for this psalm was said at the time of the תמיד של שחרית service. However, why do they also include ברכי נפשי in the Shacharis prayers, when it was sung at the time of the Mussaf offering?

According to the Gemara (סוכה, נד,א) we are not to sing two hymns at one service. How, then do the Sefardim justify joining both the song of the day with the ברכי נפשי in the Shacharis service?

On the other hand, the custom of the Ashkenazim to recite both the song of the day and ברכי נפשי in the Mussaf service leads to the following questions.

How are we to justify the reciting of the song of the day after Mussaf, when we know very well that it was recited at the time of the offering of the daily morning sacrifice, תמיד של שחרית? The same question arises here as it does for the Sephardim, that is how can we offer two hymns at one prayer service, when we know that this is forbidden? And finally, how can the Ashkenazim justify their custom of reciting the psalms of Shabbat and Yom Tov after the Mussaf prayers, when they both really belong to the prayers of Shacharis?

These questions are raised by the Aruch HaShulchan in סימן קלג, ס"ק ג', where we find the following:

ודע דביום שיש מוסף היו הלוים אומרים שיר דשחרית אחר תמיד של שחר, ולמוסף היה שירים אחרים, כמבואר במסכת סופרים שם, לראש חודש וליום טוב. ומן הדין לומר בשבת ויום טוב וראש חודש, השיר של יום דשחרית אחר תפלת שחרית, וכן מנהג הספרדים ונכון הוא, ואנחנו לא נהגו כן שאומרים אחר מוסף. וגם שירי מוסף לא נהגנו לומר כלל,

> והוא פלא. והספרדים אומרים בר"ח ברכי נפשי שהוא שיר
> של מוסף ר"ח, וביום טוב גם הם אין אומרים, ולא ידעתי
> למה...

As a result of these questions, the sefer "מועדים וזמנים", מהרב משה שטרנבוך, חלק ז, סימן קכו, suggests a new formula which will help us avoid the above problems. On Shabbos, the שיר של יום should be recited in the Shacharis prayers as the Sephardim recite it. On Yom Tov, in Shacharis the weekday psalm of the day should be said with the omission of the phrase, "שהלויים היו אומרים", for, as we have previously pointed out, we do not know for sure whether the psalm of the day was the song that the Levi'im recited on Yom Tov. On Rosh Chodesh, the שיר של יום דחול should be said at Shacharis, and the ברכי נפשי at Mussaf.

This might be a good solution to our difficulties, yet it does not answer the question of how the respective customs of the Sephardim and the Ashkenazin originated.

A POSSIBLE SOLUTION

It is not certain whether or not the psalm of ברכי נפשי was the psalm recited at the time of the Korban Mussaf of Rosh Chodesh. The Tur, in סימן תכג, maintains that we recite ברכי נפשי on Rosh Chodesh because of the pasuk "עשה ירח למועדים" — "He made the moon for festivals" (i.e., we are being informed that the moon and its cycle were created to facilitate the lunar calendar, upon which the Torah bases the determination of the holidays.) Thus it might seem that the psalm of ברכי נפשי was not recited because it represented the psalm which accompanied the Korban Mussaf, but simply because it alludes to Rosh Chodesh. And similarly, the "תפארת ישראל", in פ"ו אות י"א "חומר בקודש", writes that the exact psalm of Rosh Chodesh was not mentioned anywhere in the Gemara and indeed we have completely forgotten what psalm was sung.

Consequently, if the ברכי נפשי is not said because it represents the psalm which accompanied the Rosh Chodesh Korban Mussaf, then we can resolve the questions that were raised by the Aruch HaShulchan cited here. This view is expressed by Ha Rav Moshe Halberstam, נ"י, in his responsa to this issue which is presented at the end of the sefer (עמ' רמח) "עלת החדש" by HaRav Meir Lieberman, נ"י. We do not recite the Mussaf psalm in any of our prayers on Shabbos, Rosh Chodesh or Yom Tov. Therefore, if ברכי נפשי were to be said, it would not have any particular reference to the Korban Mussaf, and therefore it need not be said after Mussaf.

Consequently, the recitation of ברכי נפשי can be justified based on the suggestion made by the Tur that since the verse of "עשה ירח למועדים" is mentioned there, it is appropriate that we recite ברכי נפשי on Rosh Chodesh. If this is so, then the regular song of the day should be said in the Shacharis prayer every day and even on Rosh Chodesh, accompanied by ברכי נפשי, due to the rationale offered by the Tur.

However, this still leaves us with the following question. What was the rationale behind the Ashkenazic custom of reciting both the song of the day and the psalm of ברכי נפשי at the end of the Mussaf prayer?

IV

ANSWERING ALL OUR PREVIOUS QUESTIONS

HaRav Shlomo HaKohen of Vilna, in his sefer "שו"ת בנין שלמה" (ח"ב, סימן א, אות קנ"ח) presents an insight which might help us solve all the outstanding questions and give a rationale for both the Sephardic and the Ashkenazic positions here.

The psalm which we recite each day is not to be viewed as a substitute for the psalm which was sung when the Bais HaMikdash stood. As we know, when we recite the Korbanos today, it is considered the equivalent of actually offering the sacrifices, whether the daily sacrifice, the sin offering, or any other which we articulate with all its details, "ונשלמה פרים שפתינו". However, when we recite the psalm which was thought to accompany the daily sacrifice, the שיר של יום, which the Levi'im sang, this is not considered today to be a fulfillment of the mitzva of שירה. For the purpose of this שירה when the sacrifices were offered was to express our deep sense of gratitude to Hashem and to praise him for the gift of His Shechinah which rested on the Bais HaMikdash. Our hope then was that this expression of gratitude through the psalm would bring satisfaction to the Almighty.

השיר של קרבן עיקר מצותו אינו אלא כדי לתת שבח והודאה לפני מלך מלכי המלכים הקב"ה, שהשרה שכינתו בבית הגדול והקדוש, וזה היה נחת רוח לפניו יתברך שמו, וכמו שאמרו אשרי המלך שמקלסין אותו בביתו כך...

However, after the destruction of the Bais HaMikdash, the mere recitation of the שיר של יום would not serve to give a sense of satisfaction, "נחת רוח", to the Almighty, for we are not praising him *in His Home*. Therefore, the psalm of the day in recent times was instituted for another reason altogether—to allude to the particular event which took place on the corresponding day of Creation. For example, on the first day of Creation, the heavens and the earth were created, and this is alluded to in the שיר של יום ראשון בשבת, where we find: "לה' הארץ ומלואה" — "The earth is the Lord's and its fullness..." (Psalm XXIV). And so each day's psalm alludes to the particular work of creation that was fashioned on that day. (See *The Commentators' Siddur*, pp. 380-383, and *The World of Prayer*, pp. 191-192.)

Even the psalms recited on Yom Tov, Rosh Hashanah, Yom Kippur and Rosh Chodesh each contain a theme of the particular event of the day. This, then, will help answer our question why we do not recite the psalm of Mussaf on Shabbos day, even though we know for certain which psalm was said (הזיו ל"ד). Since the psalm of the day is said today only out of consideration for the fact that we wish to emphasize the unique nature of the day, it suffices that we recite it just once a day, in the Shacharis prayer, and we need not repeat the psalm in the Musssaf service. This is also the reason we need not recite the psalm at Mincha. So writes the "בנין שלמה":

> אבל עכשיו בעו"ה שחרב בית המקדש ואין לנו לא מזבח ולא קרבן ולא מנחה ולא ריח ניחוח, א"כ איפשר דבאמירת השיר אין מגיע מזה נחת רוח לפניו ית'...ולכן במעמדות וסדר קרבנות שתקנו לנו רבותינו לא מצינו שתיקנו לנו השירים והמזמורים שאמרו הלוים במוספין של שבת יו"ט ור"ח, רק השיר של תמיד של שחר שבכל יום תיקנו. משום ד**הוזכר בכל אחד מעין היצירה** שבכל יום, ולכן תקנו לאומרם. ע"ד דאמרינן במס' סנהדרין דף קא, דכל הקורא פסוק בזמנו מביא טובה לעולם... ורק שרבינו ז"ל תיקן לומר גם המזמורים שאמרו הלוים על המוספין של ר"ח ור"ה ויו"כ ומועדים, לפי המבואר בגמ' ובמס' סופרים, משום **שבהם גם כן הוזכר מעיינא דקרא, אבל לא משום לעשות זכר למקדש**...

> והלכך ביום שיש שני מזמורים לא תיקן לומר רק אחד כיון שכבר הזכירו במזמור אחד מעניינא של יום די בכך ותדע דהא הלוים אמרו שני פעמים את השיר של יום דהיינו בתמיד של שחר ובתמיד של בין הערבים, ואם כן למה אין אנו אומרים השיר של יום גבי מנחה. אבל הוא הדבר אשר דברתי דמה שאנו אומרים שיר של יום **אינו משום זכר למקדש**, רק להזכיר מעין יצירת היום ולכן די בפעם אחד...

Thus, as we have explained, the psalm of ברכי נפשי is said on Rosh Chodesh because of the pasuk that articulates the theme of the day: "עשה ירח למועדים". Others contend that the theme of this psalm — "יתמו חטאים מן הארץ" — is that sin is removed from the earth and the sinner is no longer guilty of sin. Thus Rosh Chodesh can be considered a day of atonement. With this in mind, we can now attempt to explain the rationale of both the Sephardic and the Ashkenazic customs of reciting this psalm on Rosh Chodesh.

The Ashkenazim say both שיר של יום and ברכי נפשי after the Mussaf prayer, and, as we have pointed out, this prompts us to ask why it is not recited after Shacharis, since at the time of the Bais HaMikdash, the psalm accompanied the morning sacrifice, the תמיד של שחרית. However, based on what we have just explained—that neither the שיר של יום nor the ברכי נפשי are said today because of the sacrifices, but rather we still recite them because each articulates a particular theme of the day—thus there is no halachic requirement to recite the שיר של יום only during the Shacharis prayer. Rather, it can be said at any other time, including during Mussaf, as is the case here. Thus, since the theme of ברכי נפשי is Rosh Chodesh, the most appropriate place for this psalm is after the Mussaf prayer. This means that once it was determined that the appropriate place for the theme of the day was after Mussaf, then we are justified in placing the theme of the day of the week here as well, and this is the reason why the שיר של יום, in addition to the psalm of ברכי נפשי, is said after Mussaf. Thus we can say that it is the psalm of ברכי נפשי that determines where the שיר של יום should be placed.

The Sephardim, on the other hand, are of the opinion that the psalm of the day was said during the Shacharis prayer, and that is why they recite it on Rosh Chodesh and at other times during Shacharis. And because we emphasize the unique nature of each day of the week by reciting the psalm of the day at Shacharis, we also mention the uniqueness of Rosh Chodesh here as well, by reciting ברכי נפשי during Shacharis, for, as we have explained, this psalm alludes to the uniqueness of the new month.

V

Raising other questions

According to the customs of both the Ashkenazim and the Sephardim, both psalms are said at the same time, whether at

Shacharis (according to the Sephardic custom) or after Mussaf (according to the Ashkenazic custom) and the psalm of the day is recited first and ברכי נפשי only afterwards. This particular order raises several questions.

The Gemara in *Mesechtas Succah 54b* cites two opinions regarding the situation when Rosh Chodesh falls on a Shabbos. One opinion is that in such a case the psalm of Rosh Chodesh *supercedes* the psalm of Shabbos. But the meaning of "supercedes" here involves a difference of opinion between ר' אחא בר חנינא and the Sages.

Rav Acha is of the opinion that "supercedes" is not to be understood literally. Rather the issue which dominates our choice is that of *publicizing the uniqueness of the day* of Rosh Chodesh, פרסומי ראש חודש, and this is the reason why the psalm of Rosh Chodesh takes precedence over the psalm of Shabbos. For even though the psalm of Shabbos is recited more frequently, תדיר, and that which is more frequent (Shabbos, which comes every week) usually precedes that which is less frequent (Rosh Chodesh, which comes only every month), yet here the psalm of Rosh Chodesh takes precedence in order to publicize the fact that Rosh Chodesh was established in its proper time.

The Sages, however, maintain that "supercedes" has a different meaning altogether, and that is that we recite the psalm of Rosh Chodesh *instead of* that of Shabbos. Thus in both cases, the psalm of Rosh Chodesh precedes the psalm of the day. In the sefer "כל בו" in the section on Hilchos Rosh Chodesh, we find the following statement:

שיאמר שיר של ראש חודש ואחר כך של יום.

> The psalm of Rosh Chodesh should be recited first and only afterwards the psalm of the day.

But why should we recite the psalm of the day before the psalm of ברכי נפשי, whose theme is Rosh Chodesh? (See the sefer "חקרי לב," סימן לב.)

Perhaps we can answer this question based on what we have discussed up to this point. For Rav Acha, the consideration of publicizing that today is Rosh Chodesh takes precedence over the general rule that what is *more frequent* precedes that which is *less frequent*. This is the case when we are obligated to do both mitzvos *at the same juncture* and for the same reason. In other words, the additional offering of the Shabbos day, the קרבן מוסף, requires an accompanying psalm, שירה, and so does the additional offering, the קרבן מוסף, of Rosh Chodesh. Thus, according to Rav Acha, by reciting שיר של חודש, the psalm of Rosh Chodesh first, we indicate the overriding importance of Rosh Chodesh day. However, regarding the שיר של יום, the song of the day, and ברכי נפשי, no one maintains that they must be recited at the same time. Rather, as we have suggested, according to the Sephardim, ברכי נפשי is said only at Shacharis. The reason for this is that we have already recited the psalm of the day, and therefore *this juncture* then becomes the appropriate place for articulating the uniqueness of the day, and that is why we add ברכי נפשי here, for this is the psalm which alludes to Rosh Chodesh and its uniqueness.

And according to the Ashkenazim, since the juncture of Mussaf best serves to emphasize the uniqueness of the day, this is where we add the psalm of ברכי נפשי, for this is the *best place*, though certainly not the only place, for us to articulate both the שיר של יום and the ברכי נפשי. And since our intention is now to find the *best* rather than the *only* place for these hymns, we now bring into play the consideration of תדיר— the most frequent preceding the less frequent mitzva—and we need not consider the aspect of publicizing the occasion of the day (the recitation of ברכי נפשי) to take precedence over the more frequently recited psalm of the day (שיר של יום).

VI

Reciting the Prayer of "ובראשי חדשיכם"

We find different practices regarding the custom of reciting "ובראשי חדשיכם", the chapter which deals with the offering of the Mussaf sacrifice, prior to the recitation of Psukei D'Zimra (פסוקי דזמרא).

The Tur, in Orach Chaim, סימן תר"א, cites the custom of the German community to recite the "ובראשי חדשיכם" after the chapter of the daily Tamid service. In Spain, though, they were not accustomed to reciting this section, since it would eventually be read in the Torah portion of the day [which is "ובראשי חדשיכם"].

The Shulchan Aruch, in סימן מח, also expresses the view that since the Korbanos of Rosh Chodesh will be recited in the Mussaf prayer, therefore it is not necessary to recite this prayer before beginning the daily prayers.

בטור שלחן ערוך סימן תר"א:
נוהגין באשכנז שאומרים ובראשי חדשיכם שחרית אחר פרשת התמיד. ובספרד אין נוהגין לאומרה לפי שעתידין לקרות אותה בספר תורה.

בשלחן ערוך סימן מח:
דבראשי חדשים אין אומרים ובראשי חדשיכם בשחרית מפני שקורין בתורה בפסוקי מוסף.

וברמ"א שם:
דנוהגין להזכיר גם בראש חודש כדי לפרסם שהוא ראש חודש.

Thus we have two schools of thought here. We need not read this chapter in the morning section of the Korbanos, since it will be read subsequently in the Torah reading of the day. We should read it, since by doing so we publicize the theme of Rosh Chodesh.

In addition, there are two issues which must be clarified. Why was the objection to the recitation of this chapter based on the fact that we read it later in the Torah reading, Kriyas HaTorah? Why not simply say that we recite the theme of the Rosh Chodesh offerings in our Mussaf prayers? What is the rationale behind the opinion of the Tur and the Shulchan Aruch? Why do they reject the position of the Rema?

HaRav Moshe Feinstein, ז"ל suggests an insight which might help us understand the opinions presented here. This insight was previously discussed in the chapter on the prohibition of work on Rosh Chodesh.

The innovation of Moshe Rabbenu in instituting a public reading of the Torah has two aspects: It fulfills the requirement of Talmud Torah by the masses, and it publicizes various special events in the life of the Jewish people.

Thus the Kriyas HaTorah on Monday and Thursday and on Shabbos morning and afternoon, as well as the reading of the Torah on the holidays, all result from the mitzva of Talmud Torah. However, the readings of the "Four Parshios" (זכר, שקלים, פרה, והחודש) as well as the Torah reading on Rosh Chodesh are the result of the requirement to publicize the unique nature of the day. (See HaRav Moshe Feinstein's sefer "אגרות משה", חלק א, סימן קא, ענף ב".)

Thus, we might perhaps say that the Rosh Chodesh reading of the Mussaf Korbanos both in the morning section of the prayers and in the Torah serve the same purpose — that is, both publicize the uniqueness of the day. Therefore the Sefardic custom was not to say this prayer at the beginning of Shacharis, for as we have discussed, it would be "publicized" later, in the Kriyas HaTorah. However, they did not reject its recitation in the morning prayers because it would be said later in the Mussaf prayer, since these two readings serve two completely different purposes. As we have pointed out, the reason we read the parasha of the Mussaf offering of Rosh Chodesh in the Shacharis prayer is to publicize that today is Rosh Chodesh. Whereas the reason for mentioning the Korbanos in the Mussaf prayer is that it is an integral part of the additional prayer of the Mussaf service.

The Rema, on the other hand, is of the opinion that publicizing Rosh Chodesh has two separate dimensions: We publicize that today is Rosh Chodesh so that everyone will be aware that this is the day on which special mitzvos are required of us. These include the recitation of Half-Hallel and the addition of "יעלה ויבוא". We simply wish to advertise the holiness of the day, קדושת היום. Thus the recitation of "ובראשי חדשיכם" in the morning serves to publicize that today is Rosh Chodesh and one should be sure to recite the special prayers required on this day. However, the purpose of reciting the Mussaf sacrifice of Rosh Chodesh in the Torah reading of the day is simply to advertise the sanctity of the day.

The חכמי ספרד, the Sephardic Sages, are of the opinion that both instances of publicizing that today is Rosh Chodesh serve the same purpose, and that is to make us aware of the uniqueness of the day so that we will be sure to fulfill all the special mitzvos required of us on this day.

Answering the Objections of the "המנהיג"

Based on these insights we might attempt to answer the objection which is raised in the sefer "המנהיג" to the custom of reciting "ובראשי חדשיכם". As we have seen, the Tur cited the custom of the Jews of Spain to recite this parasha on the day of Rosh Chodesh. The reason that "המנהיג" objected to this custom was this: How, he asked, are we allowed to mention the Korbanos of Rosh Chodesh before we have even recited the Morning prayers? For the sacrifices of Rosh Chodesh belong to the Mussaf service, and we must first pray Shacharis before we can even mention Mussaf. In addition, he continues, we do not mention the holiday Mussaf sacrifice in this section of the morning sacrifices. Why, then, should the Mussaf of Rosh Chodesh be mentioned?

In light of our previous discussion, however, we might say that the mention of the Rosh Chodesh Mussaf offering is the result of the need to *publicize* that today is Rosh Chodesh. With this in mind, these two objections can thus be dismissed.

As for the question of how we are allowed to mention the Korban Mussaf before we have prayed the Shacharis prayer, we might say that we are not here praying or offering the Mussaf sacrifice, but rather before we begin the Shacharis prayers we bring to attention the fact that today is Rosh Chodesh. We do this so that when we come to pray Shacharis, we will remember to include "יעלה ויבוא".

To explain the reason why the sacrifices of the שלש רגלים, the Three Pilgrimage Festivals, are not mentioned here, we might reply that these holidays do not require any particular act of being publicized, whereas Rosh Chodesh most certainly does. That is why only the Mussaf Korbonos of Rosh Chodesh and not that of any other holiday is said prior to the beginning of Shacharis. Yet we might still ask, why don't we mention the other holidays before Shacharis in order to remind us to recite "יעלה ויבוא" in the Amidah of Shacharis? To this we might reply that Yom Tov needs no reminder in order that the "יעלה ויבוא" be recited, for this publicizing of the nature of the day is accomplished when we begin the Amidah Yom Tov prayers with a different opening than we do on ordinary weekdays ("אתה בחרתנו וכו"").

On Rosh Chodesh, on the other hand, we begin the Amidah prayer with the same words as we do on any other weekday. Thus a reminder is very much in order and this is provided by the recitation of "ובראשי חדשיכם".

VII

The Laws of the Mussaf Prayers

The Gemara in *Berachos 30b* states:

והתניא טעה ולא הזכיר של ראש חודש בערבית אין מחזירין אותו מפני שיכול לאומרה בשחרית. בשחרית אין מחזירין אותו מפני שיכול לאומרה במוסיפין. במוסיפין אין מחזירין אותו מפני שיכול לאומרה במנחה. ...אמר ר' יוחנן בצבור שנו.

It has been taught in a baraisa: if one erred and he did not mention the paragraph of Rosh Chodesh in Ma'ariv, we do not make him return and repeat that prayer, because he is able to mention Rosh Chodesh in the Shacharis prayer. If he did not mention Rosh Chodesh in Shacharis, we do not make him return and repeat that prayer, because he is able to mention it in the Mussaf prayer. If he did not mention Rosh Chodesh in Mussaf, we do not make him return and repeat that prayer, because he is able to say it in Mincha. R' Yochanan said: they taught this only in regard to a congregation.

There are two explanations as to what is meant by this statement "in regard to a congregation" means. When the person is praying with a congregation he has the opportunity to hear the "יעלה ויבוא" recited by the shaliach tzibbur when he repeats the prayer. However, one who prays alone is required to repeat the Amidah prayer. Rashi cites the BeHag, who explains this statement to refer to the chazzan. If he failed to say "יעלה ויבוא", he does not repeat the Amidah prayer, because this would be too burdensome for the congregation. And so we rely on the fact that he will mention Rosh Chodesh in the next [Mincha] prayer.

וכה כתב רש"י:
בצבור שנו: דאין מחזירין משום דשמע ליה מש"ץ ואיכא מקצת הזכרה. אבל ביחיד צריך לחזור. ובה"ג מפרש לה בש"ץ משום טירחא דצבורא אבל יחיד הדר.

The רי"ף does not include the statement here which refers to Mussaf, namely, if one forgot to mention the theme of Rosh Chodesh in the Mussaf prayer, he need not repeat the Amidah, for he will mention Rosh Chodesh subsequently in the Mincha prayer.

The רא"ש explains the rationale for not including Mussaf here, even though one will mention Rosh Chodesh in the Mincha prayer, and he suggests a formula for this law. One can only depend on the forthcoming prayer and not what was already said to act as a compensation for what one forgot. For example, if one failed to mention Rosh Chodesh in the Mussaf prayer he can not rely on the fact that he already mentioned Rosh Chodesh in Shacharis. Only if both prayers are usually said together can the failure to mention Rosh Chodesh in the first prayer (Shacharis) be compensated for in the second prayer (Mussaf). However, if one failed to mention Rosh Chodesh in the Mussaf prayer, he can not rely on the Mincha prayer, for Mussaf and Mincha are not usually said one after the other.

THE QUESTION OF THE צל"ח

This rationale of the רא"ש is questioned by the צל"ח in his commentary to *Mesechtas Berachos (ibid.)*. Why did the רא"ש say that Mussaf is ruled out from the process of compensating for missed prayers because this law only applies to two prayers which are usually recited in close proximity to each other (such as Mussaf and Shacharis, but not Mussaf and Mincha, for these two prayers are usually recited at different times). Why did the רא"ש not simply say that since the main theme in Mussaf is the special sacrifices of Rosh Chodesh, and the Mincha prayer does not include any mention of these special sacrifices for Rosh Chodesh and thus can not possibly make up for those not mentioned in Mussaf. For this reason, one cannot justifiably make up for the Mussaf prayer in the prayer of Mincha.

"הלא בלאו הכי אין שום סברא לומר במוסף שיסמוך על מה שיזכיר במנחה, דבשלמא הני ג' תפלות [מעריב, שחרית ומנחה], דהיינו שמונה עשרה, הזכרת היום שוה בהו דמזכירין קדושת היום בעבודה [יעלה ויבוא], אבל מוסף שעקרה נתקן להזכיר קרבן מוסף, ואם טעה ולא הזכיר הקרבנות מה יועיל לזה הזכרת המנחה, שאין שום זכרון להקרבן!"

The צל"ח concludes that indeed according to the רא"ש it is only necessary to mention the special sanctity of the day in the Mussaf prayer. However, the failure to articulate the nature of the Rosh Chodesh sacrifices here is not decisive. And therefore if one just mentioned the sanctity of the day, קדושת היום in the Mussaf prayer without mentioning the sacrifices, he would not need to repeat the Amidah prayer. Thus one could compensate in the Mincha prayer for the failure to mention the קדושת היום in Mussaf, were it not for the fact that we are not allowed to make up a prayer by another prayer which is not usually said in close proximity to the first one.

The צל"ח therefore questions the decision made by the Magen Avraham in סימן רס"ז that if one inadvertently recited the Mincha Shemoneh Esreh on Shabbos morning instead of the Shemoneh Esreh of Shacharis, then he has fulfilled his obligation and need not repeat the prayer. For the most important prayer of all the Shabbos prayers is "רצה במנוחתינו" which is said in all the Shabbos prayers. Thus, even if one inadvertently said the wrong prayer (i.e., if he recited Mincha instead of Mussaf, for example) then he has still managed to fulfill his obligation, since he has succeeded in saying "רצה במנוחתינו". However, if instead of saying the Mussaf prayer he said one of the other prayers, even though he did say, "רצה במנוחתינו" yet because he did not include a mention of the Mussaf sacrifices of the Shabbos day, קרבנות מוסף, he has still not fulfilled his obligation. This is the opinion of the Magen Avraham.

The צל"ח questions this by saying, we see from the above mentioned רא"ש that indeed all that is needed in the Mussaf prayer is the mention of the קדושת היום, the special sanctity of the day, and the mention of the sacrifices, קרבנות, is not decisive (מעכב). Therefore, if one did say the "רצה במנוחתינו" in Mussaf, which articulates the קדושת היום, of Shabbos day, why would one have to repeat the Mussaf prayers in order to now mention the matter of the קרבנות, when we have just said that all that is required is the mention of the sanctity of the day, קדושת היום, and not the קרבנות?

VIII

Answering the צל"ח

The sefer (משנת יעב"ץ (מהרב בצלאל זולטי, חאו"ח סימן ג) attempts to answer the question of the צל"ח in the following manner. There is a vast difference between the obligation to mention the sacrifices in the Shabbos Mussaf prayer and the mention of the sacrifices in the Rosh Chodesh prayer. On Shabbos the קדושת היום, the unique sanctity of the day, derives from the fact that on this day work is forbidden, איסור מלאכה. The additional sacrifices offered on Shabbos day are not exclusively responsible for the sanctity of the Shabbos day, קדושת היום. Thus in the Shabbos Mussaf prayers both elements are decisive, i.e., we must mention the special sanctity of the day — מקדש השבת — and also the unique Mussaf sacrifices. Even the very name of this prayer,

תפלת מוסף, the "additional prayer", alludes to the special Mussaf sacrifices offered on this day.

Therefore, it does not suffice simply to mention the קדושת היום of the Shabbos day, when we say "מקדש השבת", rather, there must also be a mention of the additional special sacrifices offered on this day, קרבנות מוסף, and failure to mention this requires that we repeat the prayer. Thus we can understand the rationale behind the decision of the Magen Avraham. For if one inadvertently said the wrong prayer on Shabbos, for example, if one said Mincha instead of Mussaf, then he has not fulfilled the requirement to mention the additional [Mussaf] sacrifices of this day.

On Rosh Chodesh, however, the situation is different. . The Gemara in ערכין י,ב informs us that even Rosh Chodesh is referred to as a מועד, a holiday, not by virtue of the prohibition against work, since work is not prohibited on Rosh Chodesh, but rather because of the unique Mussaf sacrifices of Rosh Chodesh. Consequently, in the Mussaf prayer if one made mention of the קדושת היום (by saying ברוך...וראשי חדשים) it fulfills the requirement that the mentioning of the Mussaf korbonos were designated.

Therefore the previously mentioned רא"ש whose comments are only directed to the laws of Rosh Chodesh contends the failure of the mentioning of the korbonos of Rosh Chodesh doesn't call for a repetition (as long as the קדושת היום of Rosh Chodesh was spelled out somewhere in the Mussaf prayers).

The משנת יעב"ץ endeavors to prove his contention by citing the following Gemara in *Rosh Hashanah 35a*:

> אמר רב חננאל אמר רב: כיון שאמר "ובתורתך כתוב לאמר" שוב אינו צריך.

> Rav Chananel said in the name of Rav: Once one has said, "And in Your Torah it is so written", he is no longer required to recite the actual verses [i.e., those that describe the sacrifices of Rosh Hashanah].

And Rashi comments on this as follows:

כלומר כיון שאמר ונקריב לפניך כמצות רצונך כמו שכתבת
עלינו בתורתך.

What we mean here is if one reads the statement that says, "we will perform and bring near to You, according to the Commandments of Your Will, as You have written in Your Torah."

There is a difference of opinion over what exactly was said here. Rabbenu Tam contends that this statement refers to the requirement of reciting the verses of מלכיות זכרונות ושופרות in the Mussaf prayer. And this does include a mention of the sanctity of the day, the קדושת היום, when we say "מקדש...יום הזכרון".

Thus if one fails to mention these verses (מלכיות, זכרונות, ושופרות), but simply says "as you have written in your Torah", then it is still considered as if he actually recited the verses of מלכיות, etc.

The רא"ש, however, holds a different opinion. He believes that what is meant here is that even if one does not specifically mention the various sacrifices of Rosh Hashanah enunciated in the Torah, but he only recites the statement of "נעשה ונקריב...כמו שכתבת עלינו בתורתיך", then he has still managed to fulfill his obligation of mentioning the sacrifices of Rosh Hashanah, and it is still considered as if he spelled them out in all their details.

Thus, contends the משנת יעב"ץ, if the statement "נעשה ונקריב וכו" suffices to fulfill one's obligation to mention the sacrifices in the Mussaf prayer of Rosh Hashanah, how much more so is the mention of the sanctity of the day, קדושת היום, on Rosh Chodesh to be considered equivalent to a mention of the Rosh Chodesh sacrifices. For, as we have explained, the essence of the קדושת היום of this Rosh Chodesh is the קרבנות היום, the sacrifices of this day, and thus mentioning the particular sanctity of this day (when we recite

"מקדש...וראשי חדשים") is to be viewed as if one actually mentioned the day's sacrifices.

Taking issue with this view

Based on what we have said elsewhere, we might take issue with the conclusion of the משנת יעב"ץ. In the *Commentators' Machzor Companion, pages 286-289*, we cited the opinion of the "שערי תשובה" (סימן תקפ"ב סעיף קטן ד') regarding the question if one omitted the words in the bracha "מלך על כל הארץ" in the Rosh Hashanah prayer, however, he did mention in the section of קדושת היום the words "מקדש ישראל ויום הזכרון", thus in the prayer in which מלכות is an integral requirement one certainly must repeat the prayer. However, the question has merit in the Shacharis prayer where he only is required to make mention of the קדושת היום and not מלכות. In this situation, the שערי תשובה maintains that there he has no need to repeat the Amidah prayer.

However, Rav Chaim Brisker argues with this decision of the שערי תשובה and he contends that one would in fact have to repeat the Amidah, even in Shacharis, if one had failed in the concluding beracha to recite the phrase "מלך על כל הארץ". The rationale here, according to Rav Chaim, is that the essence of the קדושת היום of Rosh Hashanah is the concept of מלכיות זכרונות ושופרות, for we are told "כי זה עצם תיאור קדושת היום גופא".

Therefore, when one mentions the word "מלך" in the concluding beracha, he is actually describing the essence of the day's holiness, which is kingship, מלכיות. Thus if one fails to mention "מלך על כל הארץ" even in Shacharis one has also failed to mention the specific holiness of the day, קדושת היום, even though he did conclude with the words "מקדש ישראל ויום הזכרון".

Thus we see from Rav Chaim's position that it is not sufficient to merely allude to the essence of the day by reciting the phrase of קדושת היום ("מקדש ישראל ויום הזכרון"), but rather we must spell out clearly the concept which articulates the essence of the day.

Consequently, merely alluding to the sacrifices of the day by mentioning the קדושת היום of Rosh Chodesh does not suffice to fulfill one's obligation. Rather, we are required to spell out that additional sacrifices must be offered on this day, even though we are not required to articulate the exact details of these sacrifices. This is in contrast to our requirement regarding the Mussaf sacrifices of Rosh Hashanah, when merely reciting "...נעשה ונקריב" is considered to be enough to fulfill our obligation.

IX

The Nusach of the Mussaf Rosh Chodesh Prayer

It is important to clarify the nature of the fourth beracha in the Mussaf prayer of Shabbos Rosh Chodesh. This prayer is:

או"א רצה במנוחתנו וחדש עלינו ביום השבת הזה את החודש הזה לטובה ולברכה, לששון ולשמחה, לישועה ולנחמה, לפרנסה ולכלכלה, לחיים ולשלום, למחילת חטא ולסליחת עון ("בשנת העיבור" ולכפרת פשע)...כי בעמך ישראל בחרת מכל האמות ושבתות להם הודעת, וחקי ראשי חדשים להם קבעת. ברוך אתה ה' מקדש השבת וישראל וראשי חדשים.

In this fourth beracha of קדושת היום recited on Yom Tov, Rosh Hashanah and Yom Kippur we include in this section the theme of Shabbos by adding the phrase of:

קדשנו במצותיך ותן חלקנו בתורתך, והנחילנו וכו', וינוחו בו ישראל מקדשי שמך.

The Aruch HaShulchan in אור"ח, סימן תכ"ה, סעיף ב' is puzzled as to why on Shabbos Rosh Chodesh when we substitute "אתה יצרת" for the prayer we ordinarily recite every Shabbos, "תכנת שבת", we omit the key phrases of "קדשנו במצותיך", etc. Consequently, he tells us that he, personally, adds these phrases, since he sees no reason why they should not be included in the Shabbos Rosh Chodesh Mussaf prayers.

ודע שמעולם תמהתי על נוסח שלנו שבסוף "אתה יצרת" שאחר "למחילת עון" אומרים, כי בעמך ישראל בחרת וכו' ושבת קדשך וכו' למה אין אומרין "קדשנו במצותיך ותן חלקנו וכו' והנחילנו וכו', וינוחו בו ישראל מקדשי שמך, כי בעמך ישראל וכו'", והרי כל יום טוב שחל בשבת, ור"ה ויוה"כ שחלו בשבת אומרים בסוף הברכה האמצעית נוסח זה שזהו תורף קדושת שבת, ולמה לא יאמרו זה בראש חדש שחל בשבת, ובנוסח ספרד ישנו באמת זה הנוסח. ולענ"ד בנוסח אשכנז חסר זה מהדפוס ואני נוהג לאומרה ואין שום טעם שלא לומר זה ולא מצאתי מי שהעיר בזה.

[The נוסח ספרד cited by the Aruch HaShulchan is in reality נוסח חב"ד and not the regular נוסח ספרד.]

The Shabbos Rosh Chodesh prayer of "אתה יצרת"

Why, on Shabbos Rosh Chodesh, do we depart from the regular Mussaf prayer of "אתה תכנת" and substitute instead "אתה יצרת"? Why do we not simply add to the prayer of "תכנת שבת" those phrases which emphasize the theme of Rosh Chodesh? We might attempt to answer this question by pointing out that the Mussaf Rosh Chodesh prayer recited on a weekday contains a unique structure which elaborates on the theme of Rosh Chodesh. Thus even though on Shabbos we have available to us a Mussaf prayer which has an allusion to Rosh Chodesh, and we do not have this on a weekday, yet we do not rely on this allusion alone, but rather substitute another Mussaf prayer which elaborates on the theme of Rosh Chodesh.

The Rishonim address a similar question and offer a different answer. The שלטי גבורים למרדכי extends this question to Shabbos Yom Tov and asks, why do we not simply add to the regular Shabbos prayers a mention of the theme of Yom Tov instead of introducing a completely new נוסח of the Yom Tov prayer —"אתה בחרתנו". And the answer given is that the prayer of "אתה בחרתנו" substitutes for the Shabbos prayers of Maariv, Shacharis and Mincha in which the theme of "אתה קדשת" blends well with the theme of "אתה בחרתנו" much better than Rosh Chodesh and Yom Tov would fit into the regular Shabbos prayers.

> פסקי מהר"ם: יש שואלין למה מניחין בשבת ברכה אמצעית של שבת ואומרים של יום טוב שהיא אתה בחרתנו וכוללין בה של שבת. וכן במוסף שבת ובראש חודש מניחין "תכנת" ואומרים "אתה יצרת"? והטעם משום דברכות של שבת שהם "אתה קדשת", "ישמח משה", "אתה אחד" לא יפול בהם ערוב יפה של שבת ויום טוב וראש חודש כמו שנוכל לומר ב"אתה בחרתנו" ו"אתה יצרת". ולכן מניחין וכוללן של שבת וב"אתה בחרתנו" וב"אתה יצרת" ומתחילין בכולן בשל שבת כלומר מזכיר בהן של שבת תחלה.

And then he adds the following reason:

> ויש אומרים טעם אחר למה מניחין של שבת ואומרים של יום טוב, **כדי לפרסם שהוא יום טוב.**

We make the change in order to publicize the holiday.

This includes the reason for the change on Rosh Chodesh. And consequently a justification for the omission by the Ashkenazim of the phrases of "קדשנו במצוותך וכו'" in order to concentrate on the theme of Rosh Chodesh. This is in line with the rationale here—that we go out of our way to publicize the fact that today is Rosh Chodesh.

In the year תשכ״ב, Rosh Chodesh Iyar came out on a Shabbos. Ha Rav Ephraim Shmuel Lerner Fefferman, a gabbai of the HaGra shul in the Shaarei Chesed neighborhood of Jerusalem, announced in the newspaper "HaModea" that according to the Aruch HaShulchan one should add the above-mentioned phrases in the prayer of "אתה יצרת". Subsequently, there was great controversy in the Torah journals "מבקשי תורה" (קובץ יג) and "מעין התורה" over this announcement and various opinions, both pro and con, were printed. In the following issue, קובץ יד, the opinion of the great posek, Ha Rav Shlomo Zalman Auerbach, was cited:

נכון שהרב פפרמאן בשערי חסד היה אומר נוסח זה אבל
יש גם טעם למה שלא לומר נוסח זה.

One of the arguments for not adding these phrases to the Mussaf Rosh Chodesh prayer was that the Gra and other gedolim never endeavored to make changes in the נוסח of the Shabbos Mussaf Rosh Chodesh prayer, for apparently they found nothing wrong with it as it was.

X
"תמידים כסדרם ומוספים כהלכתם"

In the Mussaf prayer on Rosh Chodesh and on the festivals we say:

ושם נעשה לפניך את קרבנות חובותינו תמידים **כסדרם**
ומוספים **כהלכתם**.

There we will perform before You our obligatory

offerings, the continual offerings according to their *order* and the additional offerings according to their *law*.

The question arises, why is the expression "כסדרם" — "according to their order", used in relation to the continual offerings; whereas "כהלכתם" — "according to their law" is used for the additional offerings?

This issue was addressed by the eminent gaon, HaRav Bezalel HaCohen of Vilna (cited in his brother's sefer, "שו"ת בנין שלמה", סימן א, and in the siddur "אשי ישראל", in the commentary there "שיח יצחק" in the Mussaf prayer of Rosh Chodesh). The following answer emerges. The daily sacrifices, the תמידים, were offered exactly as their order is indicated in the Torah. This accounts for the phrase "כסדרם" — "according to their order". However, when it came to the additional (Mussaf) offering of Rosh Chodesh and the festivals, including Rosh Hashanah and Yom Kippur, we know from the Torah that another sacrifice was offered first, i.e., the עולה, burnt offering, followed by the חטאת, sin offering. The Oral Law, on the other hand, required the sin offering to precede the burnt offering, עולה, and therefore we read in the prayer here "מוספים כהלכתם", to indicate that the Mussaf was offered according to its *law* (as dictated by the Oral Torah) and not as prescribed in the written Torah.

What we may say here is based on that which we suggested in *The Commentators' Pesach* (pp.254-261). The Ba'al Haggadah states "חסל סדור פסח כהלכתו" — "the order of the Pesach is complete according to its laws". And then we say, "כאשר זכינו לסדר אותן, כן נזכה לעשותו" — "Just as we merited to perform it (לסדר אותו) so may we merit to offer (לעשות) the sacrifice in deed."

In the Mussaf prayer of Rosh Chodesh we say "תמידים כסדרם" and "ומוספים כהלכתם". To explain the difference between the phrase "כסדרם" and "כהלכתם", we might point out that there is a basic halachic distinction between the Shacharis and the Mussaf prayers.

Essentially, Shacharis and Mincha are petitions to Hashem for mercy, "משום רחמים". Chazal tell us that women are obligated to pray Shacharis and Mincha, even though they are time-bound mitzvos, מצות עשה שהזמן גרמא, and women are usually exempt from such mitzvos. But since women are also in need of Hashem's mercy, they too are required to pray. The Rabbis instituted this prayer for mercy to correspond to the Korban Tamid, the continual offering, which was sacrificed in the Bais HaMikdash. However, the Korban Mussaf is not a petition for mercy, but rather the Mussaf prayer is tantamount to offering the *sacrifice itself.* This is why the order of the korbanos are mentioned only in the Mussaf prayers. This insight is presented by Ha Rav Yosef Dov Soloveitchik in his sefer "קונטרס בעניין עבודת יום הכפורים". There he writes (in pages ל-לא):

וכלשון רב האי (ברי"ץ גיאות עמ' סג-סד)... כדרך שאין אומרים סדר קרבנות היום לא בשבתות ולא בימים טובים ולא במועד ולא בראשי חדשים אלא במוסף. והיינו מפני שקיום מוסף ביסודו הוא, ונשלמה פרים שפתינו כלומר, שהתפלה **כמוה כקרבן** והיא באה במקומו מה שאין כן בשאר התפלות שקיומן היסודי אמירת רחמי ורק תיקנו כנגד קרבנות, כלומר **במקום הקרבן**, אך לא שתפלת שחרית ומנחה **כקרבנות תמיד**.

In light of this, we might attempt to explain the prayer of "תמידים כסדרם". We beseech the Almighty to rebuild the Bais HaMikdash so that we may once again offer actual sacrifices rather than the substitute prayers which we offer today in their place. For in these days it is not considered as if we actually offer them but only that we fulfill our obligation by reciting the prayers *in their order* — כסדרם —and we pray that He will accept them as such. At Mussaf, however, we say "כהלכתם". This indicates that our prayer is considered as if we truly offered the sacrifice itself "according to its law" — "כהלכתם".

On Pesach night there are mitzvos which must be performed whether or not the Bais HaMikdash is standing. And there are other mitzvos which serve as a memorial to what was done in the Bais HaMikdash. Examples of such mitzvos are Korech and Afikoman, which is a memorial to the Korban Pesach. Therefore we say here: "חסל סדור פסח כהלכתו".

This signifies that we have performed these mitzvos and we pray that they be accepted as the actual fulfillment of Torah law, and we have also performed those mitzvos which are only memorial enactments of what we once did at when the Bais HaMikdash existed. Therefore we pray: "כאשר זכינו לסדר אותו", that in the near future we may merit to perform those mitzvos which we performed only as a memorial, "כן נזכה לעשותו" as actual sacrifices, just as they are required to be offered on the Altar of the rebuilt Bais HaMikdash.

XI

THE STRUCTURE OF THE CONCLUDING BERACHA

The concluding beracha of the fourth blessing of the Mussaf Rosh Chodesh Shemoneh Esreh is: "מקדש ישראל וראשי חדשים". But what if one made a mistake and concluded this beracha with the words, "מקדש ישראל והזמנים", which is the appropriate ending for a festival. This question was raised by the Acharonim. The ("שו"ת מנחת אלעזר" חלק ג, סימן י"ט) deals with this issue at length. Initially, it would appear that since Rosh Chodesh is also referred to as a festival, מועד, it should qualify for the same ending beracha as that recited on the other holidays — "מקדש ישראל והזמנים". Yet he concludes that since the Sages composed a specific ending for this beracha on Rosh Chodesh, namely "מקדש ישראל וראשי חדשים", one who does not conclude the fourth beracha with these words has not managed to fulfill his obligation and must repeat the entire Amidah prayer.

In the sefer "הליכות שלמה", which contains halachic decisions made by Ha Rav Shlomo Zalman Auerbach regarding the laws of prayer, we find concurrence with this view that one who does not recite the proper concluding beracha for Rosh Chodesh in the Mussaf Rosh Chodesh prayer has not fulfilled his obligation. This is based on the following rationale. If on Rosh Hashanah one recited the wrong concluding beracha, by saying "מקדש ישראל והזמנים" instead of "מקדש ישראל ויום הזכרון", then he would be obliged to repeat the prayer. Therefore this would most certainly be the case as well on Rosh Chodesh, when we must conclude with the words composed by our Sages for this occasion. (See pages הערה ט, קפה-קפו).

שהרי אף הטועה במוסף דראש השנה ואמר מקדש ישראל והזמנים במקום יום הזכרון, כתב המטה אפרים דלא יצא, ואם כן **כל שכן** בנדון דידן. — כתבי תלמידים.

We might suggest that even though the comparison to the Rosh Hashanah prayer may have some justification, yet we would not use the phrase "כל שכן" — "most certainly" in regard to Rosh Chodesh. For essentially the Amidah prayer on both occasions requires a repetition, if "מקדש ישראל והזמנים" was inadvertently said, for the very same reason, as we shall explain.

We have touched upon this issue of the ending beracha, "מקדש ישראל והזמנים", recited on the Three Pilgrimage Festivals. Rav Baruch Epstein, in his sefer, "ברוך שאמר" על תפלת השנה suggests that the concluding blessing of "מקדש ישראל והזמנים" which is common to all three pilgrimage festivals, is the result of a misreading, and each festival should really have its own unique ending to the blessing. Thus on Pesach the concluding beracha should be "מקדש ישראל וחג המצות". On Shavuos it should be "מקדש ישראל וחג השבועות". And on Succos it should be "מקדש ישראל וחג הסוכות". This misreading came about because of the fact that in old machzorim the final word, "והזמנים", was written either in smaller print or in parentheses in order to save space, and one was supposed to insert the appropriate ending here for the particular holiday. The later printers of machzorim made the mistake of disregarding the parentheses and joining the word "הזמנים" in larger letters to the words "מקדש ישראל". In the course of time, it became generally assumed, quite incorrectly, that this was literally the ending for the blessing of קדושת היום for all three festivals. We find proof for this contention in the fact that on Rosh Hashanah, the blessing that concludes the Kiddush and the קדושת היום (the fourth beracha of the Amidah) is indeed distinctive: "מקדש ישראל ויום הזכרון". (See the discussion of this issue in the sefer "נפש הרב" by HaRav Yosef Dov Soloveitchik, page 182.)

We might draw a distinction between Rosh Hashanah and Yom Kippur, both of which have distinctive endings to the fourth beracha (On Rosh Hashanah we say "ויום הזכרון", and on Yom Kippur "מקדש ישראל ויום הכפורים") and the three pilgrimage festivals, which all end in "מקדש ישראל והזמנים". On the holidays of Rosh Hashanah and Yom Kippur, it is the *day itself* which is unique. The uniqueness of Yom Kippur is based on the principle of "עיצומו של יום מכפר", that it is the day itself which offers atonement, even if one failed to pray or to fast. Thus the appropriate blessing requires a specific mention of "יום הכפורים". This is also the case on Rosh Hashanah, when the day itself is a time of Judgment, יום הדין, regardless of whether or not one observed the appropriate mitzvos specific to this day. Thus we say on Rosh Hashanah, "מקדש ישראל ויום הזכרון".

On the three pilgrimage festivals, on the other hand, the days themselves have no special significance apart from what we impart to them. Pesach, for example, is not a day of matzos, but rather a day on which we have the opportunity to fulfill the mitzva of eating matza. Similarly, the holiday of Succos on the fifteenth of Tishrei is a day when we have the opportunity to fulfill the special mitzvos of succah and lulav. Time is given a unique significance and this is why we refer to these days as הזמנים.

In this regard, Rosh Chodesh can be compared to Rosh Hashanah. For here it is the day itself which is unique. It is the beginning of a new month and that holiness is separate from the mitzvos which must be performed on this day. Therefore Rosh Chodesh has its own unique concluding beracha, and "הזמנים" would not be the appropriate blessing on this day. Thus if one inadvertently concluded the beracha with this ending, he would not have fulfilled his obligation.

XII

THE HAFTARAH OF ROSH CHODESH

Chazal tell us in *Mesechtas Megillah 31a*:

ראש חודש שחל להיות בשבת מפטירין "והיה מידי חדש בחדשו..."

When Rosh Chodesh falls on the Shabbos, the Haftarah is read from the book of *Isaiah 66:1-24:* "And it shall come to pass that at every new moon"...

Since there is a reference here to Rosh Chodesh, it was chosen as the Haftarah of Shabbos Rosh Chodesh. The Gemara tells us:

חל להיות באחד בשבת, מפטירין: ויאמר לו יהונתן **מחר** חדש.

If Rosh Chodesh falls on a Sunday, then on the preceding day, which is Shabbos, we conclude with the Haftarah of : "And Yonason said to him [David], tomorrow is the new moon." *(I Shmuel 20:18-42)*.

Here the important concept is "מחר חדש". Yonason warns David not to attend the festive Rosh Chodesh meal to be observed by King Shaul on *the following day*. Therefore we read this Haftarah when "the following day", Sunday, will be Rosh Chodesh. The Rambam, the Tur and the Shulchan Aruch all cite this halacha from the Gemara here. However, the "ספר כל בו" amends this statement based on the requirement set down by the Gemara that a Haftarah must have the same theme as the Torah reading one has just completed. Or else it must echo the theme of the day, such as Rosh Chodesh. Thus since on the Shabbos before Rosh Chodesh (on Sunday), the Torah reading has nothing to do with Rosh Chodesh, we do not read this Haftarah of "מחר חדש". Rather this Haftarah is read only when we have *two* days of Rosh Chodesh, that is, Shabbos day and Sunday. The reason for this is that since Shabbos day is Rosh Chodesh, the appropriate theme of the day is Rosh Chodesh and this justifies reciting the Haftarah of "מחר חדש".

ויש חולקין בזה המנהג לפי שלעולם אין מפטירין אלא מענינא דיומא ומה דסליק מיניה, וזאת אינה אחת מהנה, לכן לא נהגו להפטיר מחר חודש אם לא בהיות ראש חודש באותו היום, וכן נהגו גדולי צרפת.

This argument is also cited in the (שער א אות ח) "ספר הבתים":

יש מי שכתב שלא נאמר זה, אלא כשחל ראש חודש בשבת ובאחד בשבת הואיל ונדחית אבל אין ר"ח אלא בא' בשבת בלבד אין דוחין הפטרת היום מפני מחר חודש. ויש מי שכתב שאפילו אין ראש חודש בשבת מפטירין מחר חדש מפני שהוא **כהכרזה**, וכן נהגו העולם.

Here in the ספר הבתים we find a clarification of the rationale behind each of the positions we have cited here. It clarifies the position of those who contend that only if Rosh Chodesh occurs on two days, both Shabbos and Sunday, does the theme of the day "push aside" the regular Shabbos Haftarah and instead we read "מחר חדש". On the other hand, there are some who maintain that even if Rosh Chodesh is one day, namely Sunday, we can still read "מחר שבת" on the preceding Shabbos. The justification here is that "מחר חדש" serves as a means of announcing that tomorrow will be Rosh Chodesh — "מחר חדש". Thus, even though we do not have on this Shabbos day any of the reasons mentioned above which would justify the reading of the Haftarah of "מחר חדש", yet we can take into consideration the need to publicize the fact that the next day is Rosh Chodesh, and this constitutes a valid justification for reading this particular Haftarah on the Shabbos which falls a day before Rosh Chodesh.

XIII

Justifying the Haftarah of "מחר חדש"

We can suggest a defense of the position that "מחר חדש" can be said even if there is only one day of Rosh Chodesh (Sunday). HaRav Shimon Schwab, in his sefer, ("מעין בית השואבה" הפטרת מחר חדש) presents a rationale for reading this Haftarah of "מחר חדש" on the Shabbos preceding Rosh Chodesh and a justification for it to supercede the regular Haftarah reading. Ha Rav Schwab explains that at first sight it might appear that the theme of this Haftarah has nothing to do with Rosh Chodesh, and simply because the words "מחר חדש" are mentioned is not sufficient reason to "push aside" the regular Shabbos Haftarah reading in favor of this one.

But in fact the theme of Rosh Chodesh is indeed alluded to in this parasha of "מחר חדש". For when Yonason advises David not to flee until *after* Rosh Chodesh, what he means is this. Rosh Chodesh is a day of atonement and it carries with it a chance for new beginnings. We can renew our commitment to the Torah and its Commandments on this special day, for the theme of the day is one of spiritual renewal for the new month. Thus Yonason was expressing his hope that his father, King Shaul, would be influenced by the spirit of Rosh Chodesh to undergo a change of heart and abandon his relentless pursuit of David. And so we see that this chapter emphasizes the theme of Rosh Chodesh, which is to give us a new perspective for the coming month, and therefore it is appropriate to read this Haftarah on the Shabbos preceding Rosh Chodesh, even if Rosh Chodesh is only one day. For, as we have pointed out, Erev Rosh Chodesh is a day of atonement and this challenges us to renew our commitment to Torah principles.

XIV

When do we read "מחר חדש"?

We previously presented the opinions of both the "כל בו" and the "ספר הבתים", that the Haftarah of מחר חדש is only read when Rosh Chodesh is on both Shabbos day and Sunday. Only then do we read "מחר חדש" on the first day of Rosh Chodesh, that is, on Shabbos. And yet, if we were to examine their statements carefully, we might discover some fundamental differences in reasoning between these two commentators.

The "כל בו" writes:

ולכן לא נהגו להפטיר מחר חודש אם לא בהיות ראש חודש באותו היום.

Only if Rosh Chodesh is also on Shabbos do we read the Haftarah of מחר חדש.

However, the ספר הבתים writes:

שלא נאמר זה [שקורין מחר חדש] אלא כשחל ראש חודש בשבת ובאחד בשבת הואיל ונדחית.

Only if Rosh Chodesh falls out on Shabbos and Sunday, since we superceded the regular Haftarah…

Thus it would seem that the only justification for inserting מחר חדש on Shabbos Rosh Chodesh is that the regular Haftarah has already been pushed aside, since it is Rosh Chodesh, and if we did not read "מחר חדש" we would be reading the regular Haftarah for Shabbos Rosh Chodesh, that of "השמים כסאי".

Thus we could say, according to the sefer "כל בו", if Rosh Chodesh falls on a Shabbos, and it is also the eve of the next day of Rosh Chodesh, then the Haftarah for this week will be "מחר חדש" and not the regular Haftarah of the week.

On the other hand, the "ספר הבתים" contends that the justification for inserting "מחר חדש" is only that the regular Shabbos Haftarah has already been suspended due to the theme of Rosh Chodesh, and therefore we can now read the Haftarah of "מחר חדש" in its place. This does not mean, though, that initially "מחר חדש" is to be considered the Haftarah of the day.

We find an interesting Chazal in *Mesechtas Megillah 31b*:

ראש חדש אב שחל להיות בשבת מפטירין, חדשיכם ומועדיכם שנאה נפשי היו עלי לטרח.

When Rosh Chodesh falls on the Shabbos, we conclude with the Haftarah, "Your New Moons [Rosh Chodesh] and your festivals, My soul hates them. They have become a bother to Me." *(Isaiah 1:14)*

Tosafos here mentions that we follow a different custom, which adopts the order laid down by the פסיקתא for the Haftaros for the Three Weeks. This is "שמעו דבר ה'", "דברי ירמיה", and

"חזון ישעיהו". This means that the vision of Yeshayahu, חזון ישעיהו (Isaiah I:1-27), which includes the verse "חדשיכם וגו'" (1:14) is read on the Shabbos immediately before the Fast of Tisha B'Av. Thus, on Shabbos Rosh Chodesh we do not read "חזון", but rather "שמעו דבר ה'".

Yet the מרדכי and others contend that on Rosh Chodesh Av we read the Haftarah which has the theme of Rosh Chodesh, namely "השמים כסאי", and this supercedes "שמעו דבר ה'". However, an objection to this line of reasoning of the מרדכי is raised by other commentators. For they maintain that it would seem from the Gemara that on Rosh Chodesh Av we are confronted with two themes, that of Rosh Chodesh, and that of the period of the Destruction of the Bais HaMikdash.

Thus, since the Gemara here is of the opinion that the Haftarah is taken from Isaiah I (חזון), we find that Rosh Chodesh is completely rejected as the dominant theme of the day. The theme of the punishments which befell the Jewish people in that dark period which preceded the Destruction of the Holy Temple takes precedence, while the theme of Rosh Chodesh is "pushed aside". Therefore, even though we do not follow the custom of reading "חזון" on Rosh Chodesh (but rather we substitute "שמעו"), yet we can not add the theme of Rosh Chodesh here, for it is superceded by the theme of destruction.

In the sefer (ח"ג, סימן כד) "מנחת אליהו מהרב יצחק קולץ נ"י", we find the following explanation for this. When the Gemara states that the Haftarah of Rosh Chodesh Av is "חדשיכם ומועדיכם", and this also happens to be the chapter of "חזון ישעיהו", this is not due to the consideration that this is the very Haftarah which alludes to the Destruction of the Bais HaMikdash, but rather the presence of the crucial verse of "חדשיכם" accounts for the reason why Chazal chose this particular Haftarah to represent Rosh Chodesh. Thus this means that they did not reject the theme of Rosh Chodesh in favor of the theme of the Destruction, but rather they chose the Rosh Chodesh theme alluded to here to be the most appropriate Haftarah for this particular Rosh Chodesh.

Therefore, it is not that the theme of the Destruction pushed aside the theme of Rosh Chodesh, but rather some commentators insist that the Haftarah of "השמים כסאי" best serves as the most appropriate Haftarah for this particular Rosh Chodesh.

Thus we can summarize the situation as follows. According to the "כל בו" it is the Haftarah of "מחר חדש" that Chazal chose as the most appropriate Haftarah for Rosh Chodesh when Rosh Chodesh occurs on two days, Shabbos and Sunday. On the other hand, the "ספר הבתים" maintains that it is only because the regular Shabbos Haftarah has been set aside that we can now insert the Haftarah of "מחר חדש" into the Shabbos service.

Chapter Seven
The Mitzva of Kiddush HaChodesh

I

Sefer Bereishis and Kiddush HaChodesh

We are told that the first mitzva commanded of Bnai Yisrael by Moshe Rabbenu was Kiddush HaChodesh. This led Rashi to ask, in the name of R' Yitzchak, if Rosh Chodesh is the first mitzva, then why didn't the Torah begin with this mitzva?

אמר רבי יצחק, לא היה צריך להתחיל את התורה אלא מ"החודש הזה לכם", שהיא מצוה ראשונה שנצטוו בה ישראל.

The Ba'alei Tosafos, as well as other commentators, question Rashi's statement here that Kiddush HaChodesh was in fact the first mitzva, for they point out that this mitzva was preceded by the mitzvos of bris mila (circumcision) and gid haneseh (the prohibition against eating the sciatic nerve in the hindquarter of cattle). But they explain that there is a fundamental difference. For these mitzvos were commanded to individuals (bris mila to Avraham Aveinu) and gid hanaseh to Yaakov Aveinu), whereas the mitzva of Kiddush HaChodesh was commanded to the entire nation.

שקורא אותה מצוה ראשונה, לפי שנאמרה לכלל ישראל בתחלה, לאפוקי מילה, שלא נאמרה אלא לאברהם, וגיד הנשה לא נאמרה תחלה אלא ליעקב.

Perhaps we could explain here the deeper implications of the distinction between mitzvos given to individuals (Avraham, Yaakov) and mitzvos given to Klal Yisrael as a congregation, based on an insight by the Maharal, addressing the question why the Torah was not given at the beginning of Creation or to the Patriarchs, Avraham, Yitzchak and Yaakov. The answer he gives is that Torah was intended to be given to the nation of Yisrael and not to any individual, no matter how great. Thus, when the Baalei Tosafos refer to the Patriarchs as individuals, the point they wish to emphasize is that when bris mila was commanded of Avraham and gid hanaseh of Yaakov, these were not to be viewed as mitzvos, for only what is commanded of Yisrael as a nation is to counted as a mitzva. The sefer (להראנ"ח) "אמרי שפר" in Parashas Bo explores this concept that only those commandments given to Moshe at Sinai are to be taken as mitzvos, even though bris mila and gid hanaseh were given to the Avos and through them to their descendants.

In light of this, we may appreciate the following. The Gemara in מסכת הוריות ח,ב tells us:

איזו היא מצוה שהיא נאמרה בתחלה, הוי אומר זו עבודת כוכבים.

What was the first mitzva given to Klal Yisrael? It was the prohibition against idol worship.

The Gemara then asks:

והא אמר מר, עשר מצות נצטוו ישראל במרה...

This is not so, for we were taught that already at Marah ten mitzvos were commanded of Klal Yisrael. [The seven mitzvos of Bnai Noach, plus the mitzvos of Shabbos, the Red Heifer and the commandment to establish courts of law.] Thus how can you say that the prohibition against idol worship was the first?

To this statement Tosfaos (ibid.) gives the following justification as to why the Gemara did not cite circumcision as the first mitzva. This commandment was given to Avraham, who was still considered to be a בן נח, a son of Noach, and not yet a member of the nation of Yisrael.

הא דלא מייתי מהני דכתיב בהדיא כגון מילה לאברהם, שפיכת דמים דכתיב שופך דם האדם, וגילוי עריות? משום דהכא **נצטוו ישראל** והתם **בני נח**.

Thus we see from the words of Tosafos that the directives given to the Avos are not to be viewed as mitzvos, for they were given to בני נח, the sons of Noach, and it is only the entire nation of Yisrael who may be viewed as the "official" recipients of mitzvos.

Answering the Question of the Griz HaLevi

Addressing the Gemara in הוריות ח,ב, the Griz HaLevi (See the stencil פרשת בא, "גרי"ז הלוי על התורה") remarks that the Gemara did not ask why the commandment of Kiddush HaChodesh preceded the prohibition against idol worship. He leaves this question unanswered. In attempting an answer, we might suggest that Klal Yisrael was given two types of mitzvos: those related to individuals alone, and those which are the responsibility of the congregation as a whole, the צבור.

See the "ג"רס, "ספר המצות לרס"ג", HaRav Perlow edition, which lists the Taryag (613) mitzvos which belong to individuals and those which are incumbent on the congregation, "המוטלים על הצבור".

Thus, for example, eating matza on Pesach and putting on Tefillin are mitzvos which apply to every individual Jew. However, appointing judges and offering the daily sacrifices are the responsibility of the entire congregation of Yisrael.

Consequently, when the Gemara in הוריות ח,ב cited idol worship as being the first mitzva commanded of Bnai Yisrael, this meant that each individual Jew was warned not to worship idols. This leads the Gemara to raise the following question. How is this possible? For at Marah we were commanded to observe the Shabbos, which means that each individual Jew must observe the Shabbos. This mitzva preceded the prohibition against idol worship. How then can we say that the prohibition against idol worship was the first mitzva? And, viewing this from our perspective, the Gemara could no longer ask why Rosh Chodesh was the first mitzva, for determining the proper date of Rosh Chodesh is the responsibility, not of the individual, but of the congregation of Yisrael as a whole.

II

Explaining Rashi

Rashi himself answers his question why the Torah begins with the mitzva of Kiddush HaChodesh. He writes:

> משום "כח מעשיו הגיד לעמו לתת להם נחלת גוים" (תהלים קיא, ו) שאם יאמרו אומות העולם לישראל לסטים אתם, שכבשתם ארצות שבעת גוים, הם אומרים להם כל הארץ של הקב"ה היא, הוא בראה ונתנה לאשר ישר בעיניו, ברצונו נתנה להם וברצונו נטלה מהם ונתנה לנו.

> Because of the idea expressed in the verse, "He has declared to His people the power of His works, that He may give them the heritage of the nations" *(Psalms 111:6).* Thus, should the nations of the world say to Yisrael, "You are thieves because you took the lands of the seven nations of Canaan by force," Yisrael can then say to them, "The entire

earth belongs to the Holy One, Blessed be He; He created it and gave it to whomever he saw fit. He gave it to the seven nations when He so desired, and when He so desired He took it from them and gave it to us."

Rashi's answer seems difficult to understand. The question here was, since the Torah is a book of laws, why not start with the first law, namely that of Kiddush HaChodesh? Therefore, to prove to the world that Eretz Yisrael belongs to the Jewish people does not answer this particular question.

However, we might suggest a way of looking at his question so that it alludes to the centrality of the Torah as a book of laws. According to the Rambam (See the *Sefer HaMitzvos,* positive commandment 153) the law reads that the day of Rosh Chodesh can be determined and decreed only in Eretz Yisrael. Therefore, the mitzva of Kiddush HaChodesh, which establishes when the month begins and the time of each festival, depends on there being a Jewish settlement in the land of Yisrael. If at any time there is no settlement in Eretz Yisrael, then the date of Rosh Chodesh could no longer be calculated.

Thus it is now clear why we must hear the story of Bereishis before we can hear the law of Kiddush HaChodesh. For if the first mitzva in the Torah can be observed when we are present in Eretz Yisrael, then the Torah must first make that presence invulnerable to doubt and dispute. The best way to do this is to preface the first mitzva with the story of Creation, thus declaring the power of His works to His people. For in this way the Torah discredits the nations' allegation against us of having stolen the land and justifies our presence in Eretz Yisrael. (See the sefer "שערי אורה" מהרב מאיר צבי ברגמן, פרשת בראשית.)

HaRav Moshe Leib Sachor, in his sefer "אבני שהם" also suggests that the Torah did indeed begin with the mitzva of Kiddush HaChodesh. He cites the above-mentioned Rambam that

Kiddush HaChodesh can only take place in Eretz Yisrael. Therefore the Torah had to first explain the uniqueness and sanctity of Eretz Yisrael.

דהואיל וקידוש החדשים והמועדות נקבע מקומו בארץ ישראל...לכן הקדימה התורה את השתלשלית קדושתה של הארץ, להסביר את מעלתה וסגולתה, להיותה מקדושת לקבוע בתוכה קדושת המועדות, ולאחר מכן כתבה התורה את מצות קידוש החדש.

Here we are presented with two reasons why it was necessary to begin with the story of the Creation in the Torah: to explain the uniqueness and sanctity of the land of Yisrael, and to ensure that everyone recognizes that Eretz Yisrael is the land of the Jewish people. In turn, this mitzva of Kiddush HaChodesh prompts us to remember that we are Jews and that we have a unique relationship with the Land of Yisrael.

III

Not the First but the Foremost Mitzva

We might suggest another possible answer to the question how we can refer to the mitzva of Kiddush HaChodesh as the very *first* mitzva that was given to Bnai Yisrael, when we know that there are other mitzvos that preceded that commandment. Perhaps we are not to understand Rashi's phrase, "מצוה ראשונה" to mean "the *first* mitzva", but rather "the *foremost* mitzva". For we can suggest several reasons why Kiddush HaChodesh can be considered to be the foremost of the mitzvos.

This mitzva of establishing a calendar year is composed of two processes, that of קידוש החדש — declaring a new month, and עיבור השנה — intercalating the year by adding an extra month The first process, that of Kiddush HaChodesh, involves declaring a calendar month as a result of the sighting of the moon by eyewitnesses. By this means we establish a lunar calendar. Yet we are also aware that there is a solar calendar year, and in order to reconcile these two systems we add an extra day to the month or a month to the year and thereby intercalate the year, עיבור השנה.

The solar year is based on the rotation of the earth around the sun and is viewed as a natural phenomenon. The word "שנה", "year" means "to repeat". This can be seen from the fact that there is nothing new in the way time passes. The sun we saw yesterday is the very same sun we see today and will see tomorrow. Therefore, we refer to this phenomenon as being "דרך הטבע", following the regular laws of nature.

The moon, on the other hand, is viewed as being constantly *renewed*. After its initial appearance at the beginning of the month, it grows bigger and shines brightly by the middle of the month, only to wane and grow smaller until it "disappears" by the end of the month and eventually "reappears" at the beginning of the new month. Thus we refer to the moon as "new", "חדש", and we say that it "renews" itself each month. In addition, the cycle during the month may vary in its speed of rotation and does not necessarily follow a set pattern. Therefore we may view the movement of the moon as being beyond the usual laws of nature, "שלא כדרך הטבע".

This then is the lesson we are to learn from this mitzva, that the regular laws of nature are bound together with those laws which go beyond nature. Thus we are to understand that the purpose of Torah in its entirety and its mitzvos is to teach us this important lesson, that natural and supernatural laws are all part of Hashem's Creation of the natural world, and it is Hashem alone who regulates both the regular workings of nature and what goes beyond the laws of nature. The existence of the world is dependent on the will of its Creator from minute to minute. This lesson is explained in the very first mitzva which we are given in the Torah, and thus we can see why it should be considered as the foremost of the mitzvos, for it teaches us how to understand the rest of the mitzvos and the teachings of the Torah. (See pages 113 and 114 in the sefer דברים, "ספר ממעמקים", which is based on the lectures of HaRav Moshe Shapira.)

IV

THE PURPOSE OF THIS MITZVA

Classic commentators like the Ramban, the Akeidas Yitzchak, Abarbanel, and the Derushas HaRan offer different explanations for this mitzva of Kiddush HaChodesh. They emphasize different reasons for the primacy of this mitzva. These reasons include combating the natural human tendency towards idol worship, especially worship of heavenly objects, such as the sun, moon and stars. Secondly, to emphasize the importance of the Oral Law, since many of the halachos pertaining to this mitzva of Kiddush HaChodesh are based on the Oral Torah. Thirdly, to emphasize the supreme importance of the Sages, since the determination of the new month depends exclusively on the authoritative declaration of the Bais Din. Finally, Kiddush HaChodesh serves as a constant reminder of the Exodus from Egypt, which was a central determining event in the life of the Jewish people.

MAN'S NATURAL TENDENCY TO BE FASCINATED BY THE HEAVENLY BODIES

From the dawn of human history, man was fascinated by idol worship and in particular he was drawn to the adulation of the heavenly bodies. This lured many away from a belief in monotheism, and therefore the Torah did not cease to admonish its followers: "do not raise your eyes heavenwards and be led astray" *(Devarim 4:19)*. The Rambam in *Hilchos Avodah Zarah 1:1* describes the beginnings of the worship of the stars and the heavenly bodies:

בימי אנוש טעו בני אדם טעות גדול, ונבערה עצת חכמי הדור, ואנוש עצמו מן הטועים היה וזו היתה טעותם:

אמרו: הואיל והא-להים ברא כוכבים אלו וגלגלים להנהיג את העולם, ונתנם במרום, וחלק להם כבוד, והם שמשים המשמשים לפניו וזהו כבודו של מלך. כיון שעלה דבר זה על לבם התחילו לבנות לכוכבים היכלות, ולהקריב להם קרבנות ולשבחם ולפארם בדברים ולהשתחות למולם, כדי להשיג רצון הבורא בדעתם הרעה...

ואחר שארכו הימים, עמדו בבני אדם נביאי שקר ואמרו, שהא-ל צוה ואמר להם עבדו כוכב פלוני או כל הכוכבים, והקריבו לו ונסכו לו כך וכך...

וכיון שארכו הימים, נשתכח השם הנכבד והנורא מפי כל היקום ומדעתם ולא הכירוהו. ונמצא כל עם הארץ, הנשים והקטנים אינם יודעים אלא הצורה של עץ ושל אבן וההיכל של אבנים שנתחנכו מקטנותם להשתחות לה ולעבדה ולהשבע בשמה...

During the time of Enosh (the grandson of Adam) man made a great mistake, and the wise men of that generation gave thoughtless counsel. Enosh himself was one of those who erred.

Their mistake was the following: They said that God had created stars and spheres with which to control the world. He placed them on high and treated them with honor, making them servants to minister before Him. Accordingly, it is most fitting to praise and glorify them and to treat them with honor. They perceived this to be the will of Hashem, Blessed be He, that they should magnify and honor those whom He magnified and honored. After conceiving of this notion, they began to construct temples to the stars and offer sacrifices to them. They would praise and glorify them with words and prostrate themselves before them, because by doing so, according to their false conception, they would be fulfilling the will of God…

After many years passed, there arose false prophets, who told the people that God had commanded them to say, "Serve this star…all the stars, sacrifice to it, offer libations to it…"

As the years passed, God's glorious and awesome Name was forgotten by the entire generation. It was no longer part of their speech or thought, and they no longer knew Him.

Thus all the common people, the women and children, knew only the images of wood or stone and the temples of stone to which they were trained from their childhood to bow down and serve and in whose name they swore…

It was therefore the Patriarchs who took the initiative to combat and dispel these false gods and notions. In particular, Avraham Aveinu proved to them that all of the heavenly bodies were merely tools that God uses to guide the progress of the universe. And so the above-mentioned Rambam continues.

ועל דרך זה היה העולם הולך ומתגלגל, עד שנולד עמודו של עולם והוא אברהם אבינו... כיון שהכיר וידע, התחיל להשיב תשובות על בני אור-כשדים ולערוך דין עמהם ולומר...שאין ראוי לעבוד אלא לאלו-ה העולם...

The world continued in this fashion until the pillar of the world — Avraham Aveinu— was born...When he recognized and knew Him, he began to formulate replies to the inhabitants of Ur Kasdim and to debate with them...to teach the people that it is fitting to serve only the one true God of the world...

As pointed out, Avraham's main argument was to show that the stars and the heavenly bodies were only created to serve both God and man. This concept is alluded to, according to the משך חכמה in the pasuk of (בראשית טו,יז) "ויהי השמש לבוא" — "And it came to pass that when the sun was going down..."

The משך חכמה explains the verse here to mean that until the time of Avraham, the sun was referred to as the "great luminary", "המאור הגדול". However, after Avraham appeared on the scene, he sought to prove to the people of Ur Kasdim that the sun was meant to be only a servant of God and not a god itself. He attempted to prove this by the fact that the sun always rises in the east and sets in the west in order to give light. Thus it is now referred to as "שמש", a mere servant.

דע, כי עד אברהם לא נקרא "שמש" רק "המאור הגדול" (בראשית א, טז). רק משבא אברהם בארץ ארם בחרן, ולימד כי השמש מוכרח מהיוצר, שתמיד עולה במזרח ושוקע במערב, והוא רק ,שמש — "לשמש פני קונו" קראהו בלשון ארמי "שמש"...

In the sefer "אבני שהם" מהרב משה ליב שחור, a similar insight is cited to explain the meaning of the dream of Yosef (Bereishis 37:9):

והנה השמש והירח ואחד עשר כוכבים משתחוים לי.

And behold the sun and the moon and eleven stars all bowed down to me.

Yosef was telling them that his dream implied that everything in creation, including the sun and the moon, were created to serve him. The sun and the moon are thus to be viewed as mere servants.

כלומר שנבראו בשבילי לשמשני, כי השמש והירח שמשים הם ולא יותר.

V

THE APPROACH OF THE "AKEIDAS YITZCHAK"

The "Akeidas Yitzchak" contends that the purpose of the mitzva of Kiddush HaChodesh is to dispel the false allusion of the masses in worshipping the sun, moon and stars. He begins to explain this by posing the following questions.

Considering all the efforts made in the Torah to combat man's tendencies towards idol worship, it seems puzzling that the very first mitzva given to the Jewish people should be to sanctify the moon. Indeed, the various ceremonies associated with this sanctification seem to raise the specter of idol worship.

The special Rosh Chodesh sacrifice in the Bais HaMikdash, the special blessing recited when declaring the new month, and the Hallel recited on this day all seem strange and lead one to wonder whether we are still addicted to idol worship.

Why was this mitzva given to the elders and scholars of Yisrael to authorize the sanctification of the forthcoming month?

To answer these questions, the Akeidas Yitzchak explains the rationale man has adopted for worshipping idols. And this goes to show that not all manifestations of idol worship are the same. In fact, idolatry can be divided in three categories:

Belief that the object worshipped is itself a deity; and worshipping this deity is to be seen as the most blatant form of idol worship.

One considers the object of worship to be close enough to the real deity to exercise some influence on that deity's decision-making powers. One hopes that the object worshipped will intercede with the inaccessible deity on behalf of the worshipper.

One worships the object in question only for the specific visible function it performs, since the continued performance of that function is considered vital to the welfare of the worshipper.

Therefore, we might say that the purpose which the mitzva of Kiddush HaChodesh serves is to disprove these three reasons for worshipping the moon and also to refute the possibility of worshipping any other heavenly body.

The moon itself, after reflecting progressively more light until it is full, then reflects progressively less light until at the end of its cycle it does not give any light at all. Thus it demonstrates that it is not a primary source of light. Astronomy has proved that unless the face of the moon is turned towards the sun it cannot reflect light. This teaches the Jewish people that it cannot possibly be a deity, since it has nothing of its own to contribute. Deities are by definition not passive recipients but those who bestow bounty on others. This should be ample proof that the moon should not be worshipped as a deity.

At the time of the new moon, both the sun and the moon appear close to one another in the west at sunset. It seems clear to the beholder that both follow a path imposed on them and that they are not free to move in the direction of their choice. For what free individual moves only in one direction forever?

Thus the moon has no independent influence at all, and this thereby disproves the second reason given here for worshipping the moon.

In the third aspect of Kiddush HaChodesh, we are no longer concerned with the moon or its orbit, but rather with the use we can make of it for the purposes of our yearly calendar. Since our holidays are determined in large measure by the calendar, the Almighty uses the moon to demonstrate His sovereignty over it. Jewish law provides us with the possibility of using the moon in such a way that it accommodates itself to the needs of the Jewish people, instead of serving as an object of worship.

Thus, we might answer our original questions in the following manner. The unchanging nature of the orbits of all the planets testifies to their impotence as potential deities. The purpose of the Rosh Chodesh offering, a male goat, is to atone for any lingering subconscious doubts we may still entertain regarding the true nature of the heavenly bodies. Furthermore, the reason we add songs and praises to Hashem to our prayers on Rosh Chodesh day is to emphasize that He alone is Master of the Universe and all that exists within it. The elders who are charged with establishing all the intricacies of the new moon observance cannot fail to realize that this commandment is the very antithesis of idol worship. And their task is to persuade the masses of this profound truth.

VI

The view of Abarbanel

According to Abarbanel, based on the fact that the designation of the new month was placed under the jurisdiction of the Bais Din HaGadol, The Great Sanhedrin, two salient features emerge. This serves to prove the existence of the Oral Law — תורה שבעל פה, and it also establishes the exalted position occupied by the Sages in applying the Oral Law.

The various laws regarding Kiddush HaChodesh are not explicitly detailed in the Written Torah. Rather it is the Oral Law that guides us in applying the laws and designates the ways in which we are to determine the month, the year and the calendar.

The early Sages were proficient in astronomy and astrological lore. So much so, that Ptolemy declared in awe that their solution of how to fashion a nineteen-year cycle in order to align the lunar and solar calendars was a clear indication that true prophecy belonged to the Jewish people. This is explained by Abarbanel in his commentary on *Kiddush HaChodesh (Shemos 12:2):*

נמסר קביעת החדשים ועיבור השנים לסנהדרין גדולה
מפני שהם היו חכמים מופלא' בחכמת התכונה ויחשבו
מהלך האמצעי והאמיתי...עד שמפני עוצם החכמה שהיתה
בחכמי ישראל בדבר הזה הפליג בתלמיוס היוני לשבח ולפאר
מי שהמציא זה המחזור של י"ט שנה במלאכת העיבור
אשר לבני ישראל וכתב שזה יוכיח שהיתה ביניהם נבואה...

There is a fascinating insight offered by אבן עזרא in his commentary here. He remarks that it is rather puzzling that this important matter of determining the calendar is allotted only one verse in the entire Torah, even though it is a subject that affects all of Bnai Yisrael for generations to come and involves matters as important as when to eat matza and when the prohibition against being in possession of chametz takes effect. On the other hand, the matter of leprosy, which applies only to an individual and was in effect for only a short period of time, was allotted an entire parasha in the Torah. The answer to this enigma must be that the determination of the calendar and all its details was delegated to the Oral Law and it is there that it is dealt with at length.

ויש לתמוה מזה תימא גדולה איך פירש דיני כל נגעי
המצורע שהוא באדם אחד ולא יעמוד בכל זמן, והניח דבר
המועדים שכל ישראל חייבים לשמרם בכל זמן ויש כרת
על אכילת חמץ בפסח ועל אכילת יום הכפורים, אם סמך

על המולד היה לו לפרש אם הוא כפי המהלך האמצעי או
כפי מולד האמיתי...וזה לאות כי סמך על קריאת בית דין
בכל דור ודור...

VII

THE VIEW OF THE דרשות הר"ן

According to the דרשות הר"ן, by Rabbenu Nissim Ben Reuven of Gerondi, a very important principle is alluded to here in the mitzva of Kiddush HaChodesh, which is that decision-making and the final determination of how the halacha is to be interpreted lies in the hands of the Sages of Yisrael. The right to designate, declare and sanctify the day of Rosh Chodesh was delegated to the Bais Din by the Torah itself, which states: "**החודש הזה לכם**". This alludes to Moshe Rabbenu, who represented the Bais Din HaGadol, as Chazal tell us: "משה במקום ע"א".

This means that all of the holidays are dependent on when the Bais Din determines Rosh Chodesh. Consequently, anyone who challenges their authority is essentially challenging the Torah itself. The Mishna in *Rosh Hashanah 25a* relates an incident which shows how literally this principle was applied. It once happened that R' Yehoshua challenged the decision of the Nasi, Rabban Gamliel, concerning the dates of Rosh Hashanah and Yom Kippur. Thereupon, Rabban Gamliel sent him the following message: "I decree upon you that you must come before me with your staff in your hand and your money in your purse on the day that according to your reckoning will be Yom Kippur." R' Yehoshua was compelled to do this, and thus he appeared before Rabban Gamliel on the very day he had declared to be Yom Kippur.

This proved that the final decision was to be determined by the Nasi, as the representative of the Bais Din. Furthermore, we conclude that a decision handed down by the Bais Din, even if it happens to be the opposite of the truth, is to be accepted and adhered to meticulously.

The דרשות הר"ן expands on this concept (and in fact it is repeated several times in דרוש שלישי and דרוש שביעי, and in some editions, also in דרוש חמישי). He contends that this is what is meant by the Gemara in *Chagigah 3b* which comments on the verse in *Koheles 12:11*:

דברי חכמים כדרבנות וכמסמרות נטועים בעלי אסופות נתנו מרועה אחד.

The words of the wise are like goads, and like nails, well driven are the sayings of the masters of assemblies, coming from one Shepherd.

"בעלי אסופות" אלו תלמידי חכמים שיושבים אסופות אסופות ועוסקין בתורה, הללו מטמאין והללו מטהרין, הללו אסורין והללו מתירין, הללו פוסלין והללו מכשירין.

"The masters of the assemblies" alludes to the wise scholars who sit in groups and occupy themselves with the study of Torah. There are those scholars who declare a thing ritually impure and there are those who pronounce it clean; there are those scholars who prohibit and those who permit; those who disqualify and those who declare fit (i.e., they debate whether or not one is fit to testify in court and whether one is fit or disqualified for the priesthood. — See Rashi on this verse.).

The Gemara continues:

שמא יאמר אדם האיך אנכי למד תורה מעתה, תלמוד לומר כולם נתנו מרועה אחד א-ל אחד נתן, פרנס אחד אמרן,

> מפי אדון כל המעשים ברוך הוא דכתיב, וידבר אל-הים
> את כל הדברים האלה...

Perhaps a man will say: How can I ever learn Torah and understand precisely, when every issue is subject to debate and disagreement?

To allay this concern, Scripture states that all of the various Rabbinic opinions are given by One Shepherd, and that One God gave them. [Both sides of any Talmudic dispute adduce proof for their respective positions from the Torah of our God and not from the "Torah" of any other god. See Rashi here.] One leader [Moshe Rabbenu] proclaimed them from the mouth of the Master of all masters, blessed be He. As it is written, "And Hashem spoke *all* these words." ["All" alludes to all the opinions expressed, and they are called Hashem's words.]

Thus *all* opinions are seen as "the words of Hashem", even the words of those opinions that were finally rejected. This raises a further question. How can we say that *both* arguments are valid, when we find that one opinion was ultimately pronounced as wrong and was thereby rejected? How can we say (ערובין יג,א) "אלו ואלו דברי אל-הים חיים" — "These and those are the words of the living God"? Bais Shammai says "this way", and Bais Hillel says "that way" and yet, asks the Gemara, how can we assert that both opinions are correct?

The דרשות הר"ן explains this based on a statement in *Mesechtas Megillah 19a*:

> ואמר רבי חייא בר אבא א"ר יוחנן מאי דכתיב, ועליהם ככל
> הדברים אשר דבר ה' עמכם בהר' מלמד שהראהו הקב"ה
> למשה דקדוקי תורה ודקדוקי סופרים ומה שהסופרין
> עתידין לחדש...

And R' Chiya bar Abba also said in the name of Rav Yochanan: what is the meaning of that which is written: "and the writing upon them [i.e., the Tablets] was in accordance with all the words that Hashem spoke to you on the mountain." *(Devarim 9:10)?* This teaches us that the Holy One, Blessed be He, showed Moshe the fine interpretations of the Torah, and the fine Rabbinic interpretations, and what the Sages would innovate in the future.

And the דרשות הר"ן explains:

"דקדוקי סופרים" הם המחלוקת וחלוקי סברות שבין חכמי ישראל, וכלן למדן משה רבינו עליו השלו' מפי הגבורה, ושתהי' ההכרעה כפי הסכמת חכמי הדור..."

"The fine Rabbinic interpretations" alludes to all the differences of opinion that transpired among the Sages; Moshe Rabbenu learned them from the mouth of Hashem, and the law that the final decision would be that which was decided by the Sages of every generation.

Thus the principles established here are the following: Hashem Himself reviewed the arguments of the Sages, and we thus refer to them by saying, "אלו ואלו דברי אל-הים חיים". Furthermore, final decisions are left up to the Sages. This important principle was also implied in the very first mitzva given in the Torah, that of Kiddush HaChodesh. As we have discussed, it was the Sages who were instructed by Hashem to designate and sanctify the day of Rosh Chodesh, and therefore they set the holidays in their proper times, and anyone who dared question their authority in this matter would be severely punished.

VIII

OTHER EXPLANATIONS OF THIS MATTER: RASHI

In addition to the explanation offered by the דרשות הר"ן as to why opposing opinions are to be viewed as equally acceptable, based on the consideration that "both these and those are the words of the living God", we find several other possible ways to explain this statement.

As we have pointed out, Rashi in *Mesechtas Chagigah 3b* writes that since each view justifies itself by citing a verse from the Torah to support its opinion, it is thereby considered to be a justification of the statement of "אלו ואלו דברי אל-הים חיים". See also the לקוטי רש"י cited here, where we find (קהלת יב,יא):

נתנו מרועה אחד: כל דבריהם דברי אל-הים חיים ורועה
אחד נתנן, משה מפי הגבורה.

However, Rashi in מסכת כתובות נז, א offers another explanation as to why opposing views are both to be seen as the word of the living God.

כי פליגי תרי אמוראי בדין או באיסור והיתר, כל חד אמר
הכי מיסתבר טעמא אין כאן שקר כל חד וחד סברא דידיה
קאמר, מר יהיב טעמא להיתרא וחד יהיב טעמא לאיסורא,
מר מדמי מילתא למילתא הכי ומר מדמי ליה בעניינא
אחרינא, ואיכא למימר **אלו ואלו דברי אל-הים חיים** הם,
זימנין דשייך האי טעמא וזימנין דשייך האי טעמא, שהטעם
מתהפך לפי שינוי הדברים בשינוי מועט.

When two Amoraim dispute a matter of reason, each one presents a logical valid point. One argues, for example, why something should be permitted, while the other argues why it should be prohibited;

one compares the situation in question to a certain precedent; while the other considers it more similar to a different precedent. Regarding such a dispute of reason, we apply the following maxim *(Eruvin 13b):* "These and those are the words of the living God", that is, both views are Torah-true opinions. For at times, one logical argument is more appropriate, as minor changes in a given situation call for different lines of reasoning.

THE INSIGHT OF THE RITBA

The ריטב"א comments in מסכת עירובין יג,ב on the statement of "אלו ואלו דברי אל-הים חיים". He writes as follows:

שאלו רבני צרפת ז"ל, האיך אפשר שיהיו שניהם דברי אל-הים חיים, וזה אוסר וזה מתיר, ותרצו, כי כשעלה משה למרום לקבל תורה, הראו לו על כל דבר ודבר מ"ט פנים לאיסור ומ"ט פנים להיתר, ושאל הקב"ה על זה, ואמר שיהא זה מסור לחכמי ישראל שבכל דור ודור ויהי' הכרעה כמותם, ונכון הוא לפי הדרש, ובדרך האמת יש טעם סוד בדבר.

The Ritba addresses the question of how we can assert that opposing positions both constitute the word of Hashem. And he answers that when Moshe ascended to Heaven to receive the Torah, he was shown forty-nine different ways of perceiving a matter, and it was left up to the Sages to make the decision how to rule on any particular matter.

In addition, we are told in the Gemara that the law is decided according to Bais Hillel, who offers a more lenient view, since he was more patient, kindly and modest — "מפני שנוחין ועלובין היו".

We are also told that in the future, the halacha will follow the opinion of Bais Shammai. How are we to understand this?

The קדושת לוי answers all these questions by interpolating yet another question. We are told that in the future all unsolved questions will be answered by Eliyahu HaNavi, the Prophet Elijah. This is alluded to in the words: "תיקו = תשבי יתרץ קושיות ואבעיות". The meaning of this is: "Eliyahu, from the city of Tishbi, will answer all undecided questions and resolve all unresolved issues."

And we might further ask: since in the future Moshe Rabbenu will reappear at the time of the Resurrection of the Dead, why must we rely on Eliyahu to reveal all the answers that need clarification? Why not simply ask Moshe Rabbenu, who heard the entire Torah and all its laws directly from the Source? This question was already anticipated in the sefer "בית אלהים" by the מבי"ט.

To resolve this seemingly confusing situation, we must consider that when one views the law from the perspective of mercy, one would rule in one way, usually according to the more lenient opinion of Bais Hillel. Whereas if one were to rule from the perspective of strict justice, considering only the letter of the law, then one would rule in another way, according to the stricter opinion of Bais Shammai. Thus the Sages of each generation must determine which mode of justice to apply, whether strict justice or mercy.

Chazal tell us that in our time the halacha follows the opinion of Bais Hillel, who were more patient, kindly and forgiving. This means that the Sages determined that the present generation needed a lenient ruling based on mercy, since we are not capable of withstanding a more stringent process of judgement. However, in the future, when the Ultimate Redemption will come about, the situation will change and halachic issues will be determined according to the ruling of Bais Shammai. This will be possible, we are told, because the world will be full of the knowledge of Hashem — "ומלאה הארץ דעה" — all mankind will develop the moral and spiritual strength to be able to live by the stringent halachic rulings of Bais Shammai, which are based on the principle of strict justice.

Consequently, concludes Rav Levi Yitzchak, only one who is sensitive to the needs and capabilities of his own generation can determine how to apply the law. Applying this to the original question of why we await Eliyahu HaNavi rather than Moshe Rabbenu to solve all unresolved halachic questions at the End of Days, we are well aware that Moshe Rabbenu was mortal but Eliyahu HaNavi never died. This means that he is aware of the particular needs of each generation and is thus the appropriate judge, able to determine how best to apply the law in every situation.

IX

It is a Mitzva to Count the Months

The Ramban, in his commentary on the Torah, contends that we are to begin counting the months of the year with the month of Nissan. By doing this, we remember the Exodus from Egypt, which took place in Nissan. Thus, when we mention the third month, for example, we imply that this is the third month *after the Exodus* from Egypt. According to the Ramban, in addition to the mitzva of Kiddush HaChodesh, sanctifying the new month, there is another mitzva here of *remembering the Exodus* from Egypt. This is the reason why the months do not have individual names in the Torah. Instead, Scripture refers to them by saying, "In the third month" *(Shemos 19:1)*, "And it came to pass in the second year in the second month..." *(Bamidbar 10:11)*. "And in the seventh month, on the first day of the month" *(Bamidbar 29:1)*. They are referred to in relation to the month of Nissan, when Bnai Yisrael were redeemed from slavery in Egypt. This is similar to the way in which we refer to the days of the week, always in relation to the Shabbos day.

Similarly, just as the months of the year are not referred to in the Torah by individual names, but are rather counted by their proximity to Nissan and the Exodus from Egypt, so too are the days of the week designated according to their proximity to Shabbos. For example, Sunday is "יום ראשון של שבת" — "the first day after Shabbos", Monday, "יום שני של שבת," — "the second day after Shabbat", and so forth.

The actual names of the Hebrew months, Nissan, Iyar, Sivan, etc. were introduced after the Jews returned from the Babylonian exile, when these names of the months served as a reminder of that exodus, as the prophet Jeremiah stated, "And it should no more be said: 'As the Eternal liveth, Who brought up the children of Yisrael out of the land of Egypt,' but as the Eternal liveth that brought up the children of Yisrael from the land of the north." From then on we began to call the months by the names they were called in the land of Babylon. These names — Nissan, Iyar, etc. are Persian in origin and are to be found only in the Books of the Prophets of the Babylonian era and in the Scroll of Esther."

וטעם "החדש הזה לכם ראש חדשים." שימנו אותו ישראל חדש הראשון, וממנו ימנו כל החדשים שני ושלישי עד תשלום השנה בשנים עשר חדש, כדי שיהי' זה זכרון בנס הגדול, כי בכל עת שנזכיר החדשים יהי' הנס נזכר, ועל כן אין לחדשים שם בתורה, אלא יאמר בחדש השלישי...וכמו שתהי' הזכירה ביום השבת במנותינו ממנו, אחד בשבת ושני בשבת...כך הגדירה ביציאת מצרים במנותינו החדש הראשון...לגואלתינו שאין המנין הזה לשנה שהרי תחלת שנותינו מתשרי...וזה טעם ראשון הוא לכם, שאיננו ראשון בשנה, אבל הוא ראשון **לכם** שנקרא לו לזכרון גאולתינו. וכבר הזכירו רבותינו זה הענין ואמרו: [ירושלמי ראש השנה, פרק א, הלכה ב] שמות החדשים עלו עמנו מבבל, כי מתחלה לא היו שמות אצלינו, והסבה בזה כי בתחלה היה מנינים זכר ליציאת מצרים, אבל כאשר עלינו מבבל ונתקיים

מה שאמר הכתוב "ולא יאמר עוד חי ה' אשר העלה את בני
ישראל מארץ מצרים כי אם חי ה' אשר העלה ואשר הביא
את בני ישראל מארץ צפון", חזרנו לקרא החדשים בשם
שנקראים בארץ בבל, להזכיר כי שם עמדנו ומשם העלנו
הש"י...והנה נזכיר בחדשים הגאולה השנית כאשר עשינו עד
הנה בראשונה...

X

VARIOUS INTERPRETATIONS OF THE RAMBAN

In the "ספר העקרים" (מאמר ג, ט"ז), by HaRav Yosef Albo, the author explains that the Rambam's intent here was to point out that after the return from Bavel, the first memorial to the Exodus from Egypt was eventually to be superceded by a second memorial, that of the Exodus from Bavel.

Thus, contends the ספר העיקרים, we can conclude from this that a mitzva of the Torah can be nullified. He also points out that we find that the script in which Moshe Rabbenu wrote the Torah, כתב עברי, was replaced by a new script, one which was introduced by Ezra HaSofer, כתב אשורי, (see *The Commentators' Gift of Torah, pp. 39-48),* again proving that one mitzva can be replaced by another.

וכן עשו דבר אחר (מלבד שינוי הכתב) זכר לגאולה השנית
והיא שהניחו מלמנות מנין החדשים מניסן כמו שהיו רגילין
למנות זכר ליציאת מצרים וחזרו למנות מנין אחר לחדשים,
וזהו שאמרו רבותינו ז"ל שמות החדשים העלו עמהם מאשור,
כלומר שהיו מונים החדשים בשמותם תשרי, מרחשון...
כמו שהיו מונים אותם באשור זכר לגאולה השנית, ולא שני
שלישי כאשר בתחילה, וכן כתב **הרמב"ן** ז"ל ונראה מזה
כי הם הבינו שצווי מנין החדשים היה זמני, רוצה לומר, כל
עוד שתתמיד הגאולה ההיא אבל אחר שגלו שנית ונגאלו

משם ונצטוו על ידי ירמיה "ולא יאמר עוד חי ה' וגו'" ראוי
להניח המנין הראשון שהיה לזכר מצרים וחזרו למנות מנין
אחר מתשרי לשנות עולם...

It goes without saying that this approach of the ספר העקרים was vehemently rejected by the scholars of his own day and by those of subsequent generations. His contention was dismissed by various means. Some simply dismissed his "proofs". Others challenged his interpretation and the Ramban's intent, by contending that what the Ramban here intended was that the Exodus from Bavel was not meant to displace the memorial of the Exodus from Egypt, but rather to be "added" to the overall memorial of our redemption from foreign dominion.

THE POSITION OF THE מהר"ץ חיות

HaRav Tzvi Hirsch Chayes, in his classic sefer "תורת הנביאים" Chapter 12, "חוקת עולם", dismisses the "proofs" of the ספר העקרים. Based on the concept of "אין הנביא רשאי לחדש דבר מעתה" — a prophet has no authority to introduce "new" laws and say that they are biblically ordained; and certainly they cannot nullify any existing law of the Torah. Thus if the prophet Yermiyahu did abrogate here a mitzva, we must say that this was already alluded to at Sinai. It would have already been decreed that there would come a time when the memorial to the Exodus from Egypt would be replaced by a memorial to the Exodus from Bavel. Yermiyahu must certainly have been well aware of this halacha and this means that there was no infraction of "אין הנביא רשאי לחדש". Or, we might say that he was of the opinion of Ben Zoma, mentioned in the last mishnah of the first chapter of Mesechtas Berachos. There Ben Zoma makes the statement "וכי מזכירין יציאת מצרים לימות המשיח". Based on the pasuk of "למען תזכור...כל ימי חייך" — "You are to make mention of the Exodus all the days of your life." The word "כל" here is to be understood to mean only at the present time, for in the future we will speak of greater redemptions.

Thus we indeed have a biblical source for eventually abrogating the mitzva of memorializing the Exodus from Egypt. And the same can be said regarding the changing of the script utilized by Moshe Rabbeinu to that of Ezra. The Torah already alluded to this change and referred to it as כתב העשויה להשתנות — a manner of writing which eventually will be changed. And so we find that we have no "proof" that a mitzva can be nullified.

אולם היטב אשר דברו הרמב"ן והר"י אברבנאל שם שמלשון הירושלמי שמות החדשים עלו מבבל, היינו שעשו זכר ליציאת בבל ו**סמכו על קרא** אשר נאמר בירמיה "הנה ימים באים נאום ה' ולא יאמר עוד חי ה' אשר העלה וגו', כי אם חי ה' אשר הביא מארץ צפון ומכל הארץ אשר הדיחם שם."

ובודאי היתה זאת הלכה מקובלת אצלם דביציאת מארץ בבל יתבטל מצוה דמנויות ראשון ושני ויתחיל מנין חדש זכר ליציאת בבל...דכיוון שידענו דאין נביא רשאי לחדש דבר מעתה, ומכל שכן לעקור דבר מן התורה, ואם כן היה להם הלכה בידם מסיני ואסמכי' ירמי' על קרא...

ועוד אפשר לומר דסמכי' על קרא דכתיב "כל ימי חייך" להוציא ימות המשיח. וכן הוא דרשות בן זומא בספ"ק דברכות, וכן משמע לשון בן זומא לחכמים "וכי מזכירין יציאת מצרים לימות המשיח..."

The Opinions of the מהר"ל and the ר"י בן חביב

The ר"י בן חביב understands the words of the רמב"ן to mean that we are not really obligated to count the months; however, if we do make a count, we must begin counting from Nissan.

The names of the months are insignificant. And so he writes (see בעין יעקב פ"ק דמגילה בפירוש הכתוב):

> ...שהמצוה היא רק אם בא ליתן מנין לחדשים לא יהא מונים אותם אלא מניסן, שיהא ניסן ראשון וממנו ימנו כל החדשים, וכשיתן להם מנין אחר כגון שימנה תשרי ראשון עובר בעשה זו, ומכל מקום הרשות בידו שלא ליתן להם שום מנין כלל...

The Maharal from Prague makes the same observation. Only if we desire to count the months are we obligated to count from Nissan. However, to simply mention that a certain event took place in a certain month, for example, that this loan took place in Tammuz, does not constitute an infraction.

> ...וכל דבריו של בעל העקרים אין בהם ממש...ודבר זה ודאי הבאי כי אין הפירוש שלא למנות רק מניסן שלא יאמר כי בחודש תמוז נעשה דבר זה או ההלואה הזאת נעשה בחדש אלול שנת כך וכך, כי דבר זה אינו כלל.
>
> אבל הפירוש הוא כאשר יבואו למנות החדשים בשם ראשון ושני אל ימנה תשרי ראשון. אבל אם לא בא למנות את החדשים בשם ראשון ושני כלל רק יאמר כי ההלואה נעשתה בחדש כסלו שנת כך וכך אין זה דבר...וכן היא דעת הרמב"ן ז"ל לא כמו שהבין בעל העקרים שרצה לומר כי מצות למנות החדשים מניסן ולא בענין אחר...

Yet others contend that based on the Ramban's own words (in his "דרשה לראש השנה"), he explicitly states that the counting of the months in recognition of the redemption from the Babylonian exile does not mean that we set aside the matter of the Exodus from Egypt. On the contrary, this "new" count compliments and *adds* to the recognition of the initial Exodus from Egypt.

> והסבה בזה לפי שמתחילה נצטוינו למנותם בזכרון גאולת
> מצרים, וכיצאנו מבבל ונצטוינו...חזרנו לקרות חדשינו
> לגאולת צפון, ולא שנשנה השמות הראשונים ונשכח גאולת
> מצרים, אבל **שנצטרף** שמות בבל להודיע ולזכור ששם
> עמדנו ומשם הוציאנו ה'...

A similar suggestion is offered by the Abarbanel:

> ונראה לי שלא עברו בזה על מצות החדש לפי שגם הם לא
> נמנעו מלקרוא את החדשים ראשון ושני במספרם כמו
> שצותה התורה, אבל מלבד זה כנו החדש באותו כנוי שהיו
> מכנים אותו בבבל...

XI

CLARIFYING THE POSITION OF THE RAMBAN

HaRav Yerucham Fischel Perlow, in his classic commentary to the "ספר המצוות לרס"ג" (The Book of Mitzvos according to Rav Saadiah Gaon), asks the following question in Mitzva 56. If indeed there is a mitzva to count the months (one, two, three, etc.), why did the Ramban not include it in his enumeration of the 613 mitzvos? We might suggest an answer based on the various opinions previously presented.

ACCORDING TO THE "מהר"ץ חיות"

As we have discussed, according to the מהר"ץ חיות the justification for replacing the memorial of the Exodus from Egypt with the memorial of the Exodus from Babylon is based on the statement of

Ben Zoma, who contends that the pasuk of "כל ימי חייך", which stipulates that we must mention the event of the Exodus from Egypt all the days of our lives, nevertheless allows for the eventuality of our no longer having to fulfill this mitzva when the Ultimate Redemption comes about. Thus we can see that this mitzva of mentioning the Exodus from Egypt was intended to be ultimately nullified. Therefore, we can now simply answer Rav Perlow's question of why the Ramban did not count this as one of the 613 mitzvos. To support this view, we need only point to the position of the Rambam, who informs us, in the principles which underlie his Sefer HaMitzvos, that a mitzva that is not eternal is not to be counted among the 613 mitzvos given at Sinai. And so he writes in 'Principle Three' (שורש ג'):

> שאין ראוי למנות מצוות שאין נוהגות לדורות, דע כי אמרם (מכות כג, ב) "תרי"ג מצוות נאמרו לו למשה בסיני", מורה על היות זה המספר הוא מספר המצוות הנוהגות לדורות. כי מצות שאינן נוהגות לדורות אין קשר להם בסיני. ואילו היה מכלל המנין מצות שאינן נוהגות לדורות הנה יחסר זה הכלל בזמן שיכלה בו חיוב המצוה ההיא ולא היה המאמר הזה שלם כי אם בזמן מוגבל...

> Know that their saying, "Taryag mitzvos were conveyed to Moshe at Sinai," indicates that this is the number of mitzvos that obtains throughout the generations. For the mitzvos that do not obtain throughout the generations have no connection to "Sinai"...But if those mitzvos which do not obtain throughout the generations were included, then this number would be lacking when the obligation of such a mitzva lapsed, which would make their dictum correct only for a particular period.

In light of this, we can understand why the Ramban did not include in his enumeration the mitzva of "counting the months", for as we have pointed out, this mitzva would eventually be nullified. Therefore, it does not qualify to be counted among the 613 mitzvos given for all eternity at Sinai.

According to the מהר"ל

If we accept the explanation that this mitzva will not be replaced but rather will be *added* to by giving names to the months in memory of the Exodus from Bavel, we may suggest the following answer. The Rambam, in his Sefer HaMitzvos, Principle 11 (שורש י"א) writes that the "parts" of a mitzva are not to be enumerated separately if they comprise a single mitzva. Sometimes one law constituting one mitzva consists of several parts, such as the mitzva of lulav, which is made up of the four species. We do not say that "the fruit of a tree that is hadar" *(Vayikra 23:40)* is a mitzva in itself; "a branch of a plaited tree", a mitzva in itself; "willows of a brook", a mitzva in itself; and "branches of date-palms", a mitzva in itself. For all of these are parts of one mitzva.

Thus if we accept the view that this mitzva was created to serve as a memorial to the Exodus, it is an essential part of the overall mitzva to remember the Exodus, זכר ליציאת מצרים, and this is a mitzva which includes many parts. Thus, as we have established, one "part" of a mitzva is not to be enumerated as a mitzva unto itself. Therefore, the mitzva here of counting the months as a "זכר", a memorial to the Exodus, is not to be included in the enumeration of the mitzvos.

XII

Applying the insight of the חתם סופר

This view, that counting the months is not to be considered a separate mitzva, is based on a concept introduced by the חתם סופר ("שו"ת חתם סופר", אור"ח סימן קפה). The Chasam Sofer was asked the following question regarding the opinion that the concept of

"אף הן היו באותו הנס" — "For they [the women] were also involved in the miracle", applies to mitzvos from the Torah.

The Gemara in *Kiddushin 29a* states that women are not obligated in those positive mitzvos (מצות עשה) which are time-bound (שהזמן גרמא). This halacha is based on the fact just as women are not obligated to put on tefillin, because it is time-bound, so too are they freed from all time-bound positive mitzvos. Regarding the mitzva of tefillin, we find in the Torah (שמות י"ג, ט"ז):

והי' לאות על ידיך ולטוטפות בין עיניך כי בחוזק יד **הוציאנו ה' ממצרים**.

And it should be for you a sign upon your hand, an ornament between your eyes, that by the strength of His Hand did Hashem bring us out of Egypt.

If the commandment to wear tefillin is justified as a commemoration of the Exodus from Egypt, then we should apply the concept of "אף הן" to include women, for they too took an equal part in the Exodus. Thus it should logically follow that women should be obligated to wear tefillin, and subsequently, they should be obligated in all the other positive mitzvos, whether or not they are time-bound.

The חתם סופר answers that there are two classifications of mitzvos related to the commemoration of the Exodus — זכר ליציאת מצרים. And of these, one is characterized by those mitzvos which result *directly* from the Exodus. These include such mitzvos as eating matza, maror and the Korban Pesach, which relate directly to the history of the Exodus.

The second class of commemorative mitzvos is not directly related to the actual event of the Exodus, but rather the Torah requires us to remember the Exodus when we perform them. This class of mitzvos includes putting on tefillin. Even though tefillin has no obvious connection to the Exodus, the Torah requires us to mention the Exodus from Egypt whenever we put on tefillin.

The practical difference between these two categories of memorializing the event of the Exodus is that in the first instance, because the mitzva came into being because of the actual Exodus, we can apply this principle of "אף הן היו באותו הנס", that women were equally involved in the Exodus process and therefore they too are obligated in the mitzvos. In addition, fulfilling the mitzva is considered a separate mitzva. Thus, if one eats matza, he fulfills not only the mitzva of eating matza, but in addition memorializing the Exodus from Egypt is counted as a separate mitzva. In contrast, in the second category of memorial, זכרון, the particular mitzva now being performed has no connection to the Exodus, and thus we do not apply here the principle of "אף הן".

This answers the question about tefillin, which, as we have explained, is not directly due to the Exodus, but rather the matter of the Exodus was only added as an extra element. In other words, we are asked "also to remember the Exodus" when we perform this mitzva. However, we do not apply the concept of "אף הן" in this case.

This is also true regarding the mitzva of Kiddush HaChodesh and keeping a count of the months in order to preserve the memory of the Exodus. The mitzva here is essentially that of Kiddush HaChodesh, even though we "attached" the matter of counting the months as a memorial to the Exodus. And so when it comes to enumerating the mitzvos, we only count Kiddush HaChodesh, but not the mitzva to count the months.

And in light of this, we can dismiss the "proof" of the ספר העקרים that a mitzva can be nullified, for we find this to be the case in relation to the mitzva of counting the months as a memorial to the Exodus from Egypt, which will be subsequently replaced by the mitzva of counting as a memorial to the Exodus from Babylon. However, as explained, this mitzva of counting was only attached to the mitzva in this particular instance. Thus we have no proof here that a mitzva which is an intrinsic mitzva (that is, a mitzva in and of itself), and is not merely "attached" to an existing mitzva, can be nullified.

XIII

BAIS DIN DETERMINES THE MONTH, YEAR AND SEASONS

The Jewish calendar is divided into three time periods: months, years and the four seasons. All these periods are determined by the Bais Din. The question arises: are all these determinations to be viewed as one mitzva and counted as such in the enumeration of the 613 mitzvos, or are they to be counted as separate mitzvos? There are two opinions here, one which views them as a single mitzva and another which counts them as separate mitzvos. The Rambam and the Sefer HaChinuch consider the mitzvos of Kiddush HaChodesh and adding a leap year (עבור השנה) as one mitzva. This is in contrast to the (בעל הלכות גדולות) בה"ג and the Ramban, who view them as separate mitzvos. The Sefer HaChinuch explains this:

מצוות קידוש החדש לקדש חדשים ולעבר שנים בבית דין גדול בחכמה סמוך בארץ. ולקבוע מועד השנה על פי אותו קידוש, שנאמר "החודש הזה לכם ראש חדשים", כלומר, כשתראו חדושה של לבנה תקבעו לכם ראש חדש, או אפילו לא תראוה מכיון שהיא ראויה להראות על פי החשבון המקובל.

The precept of establishing the month: To sanctify and intercalate years by the decree of the Bais Din that is greatest in wisdom and ordained with authority in the land of Yisrael, and to set the dates of the year's festivals according to that sanctification. For it is stated: "This month shall be for you the beginning of months" *(Shemos 12:2)*. In other words, when you see the renewal of the moon, you will establish for yourselves the beginning of the month; and thus do so, even if you do not see it once, it is due to be seen according to accepted reckoning.

The *Sefer HaChinuch* then states:

וכן תכלל מצוה זו מצוה עבור השנה, לפי שיסוד מצות קידוש החדש כדי שיעשו ישראל מועדי השם במועדם, וכמו כן מצות עבור השנה מזה היסוד היא, ואולם מלבד זה המקרא באו העדות בכתובי התורה יורו על מצות העבור, והוא מה שכתוב: ושמרת את החקה הזאת למועדה, וכן, שמור את חדש האביב.

The precept also includes the obligation to intercalate the year [by adding a lunar month when necessary]. The fundamental reason for the precept of sanctifying each month is that Bnai Yisrael might observe the holy days of Hashem at their proper times; and the intercalation of the year is for the same fundamental reason. Indeed, apart from this verse, there is evidence in other verses of the Torah which points to the precept of intercalation. Thus, it is written, "You shall keep this ordinance [of observing Pesach] at its season [of spring]" *(Shemos 13:10)*. And so too, "Observe the month of Aviv, the spring" *(Devarim 16:1)*.

From this we see that the Sefer HaChinuch is of the opinion that both determining the month and proclaiming a leap year are to be counted as one mitzva. Furthermore, both serve the same purpose, which is to fix the calendar in order that the holy days be observed at their proper times — Pesach in the spring, and Succos in the fall.

He concludes by saying, "זה שאמרנו הוא על דעת הרמב"ם" — "What we have stated here follows the view of the Rambam." In other words, the Rambam is of the opinion that in the enumeration of the mitzvos, both קידוש החדש and עבור השנה, establishing new months and setting a leap year, are to be counted as a single mitzva. For as we have said, the purpose of these two calculations is one and the same – that we may observe the holidays at their proper times.

THE OPINION OF THE RAMBAM

In the Sefer Hamitzvos, (מצוה קנז), the Rambam tells us:

היא שצונו לקדש חדשים [ס"א ולחשוב] ושנים, וזו היא מצות קדוש החדש, והוא אמרו יתעלה: החודש הזה לכם ראש חדשים.

To abide by the Exalted One's command relating to the reckoning of months and years, the mitzva of Kiddush HaChodesh, the sanctification of the New Moon. As the Exalted One said: "This month is to you the beginning of months."

Thus we see that he combines the reckoning of the months and the years and counts them as one mitzva. And so he writes at the beginning of his sefer, Mishneh Torah, [in his enumeration of the mitzvos]:

לקדש חדשים ולחשב שנים וחדשים בבית דין בלבד שנאמר: החדש הזה לכם ראש חדשים.

We are to sanctify the months and calculate the years and months as it is written, "This shall be for you the beginning of months."

The source for these mitzvos is the verse which states: "החדש הזה לכם וגו'". However, in *Hilchos Kiddush HaChodesh 1:7,* the Rambam writes:

מצות עשה מן התורה על בית דין, שיחשבו וידעו אם יראה הירח או לא יראה. ושידרשו את העדים עד שיקדשו את החדש. וישלחו ויודיעו שאר העם באי זה יום הוא ראש חדש, כדי שידעו באי זה יום הן המועדות, שנאמר: **אשר תקראו אתם מקראי קדש**, ונאמר: ושמרת את החקה הזאת למועדה.

It is a positive command of the Torah for the Bais Din to calculate and determine whether or not the moon will be sighted; to examine the witnesses until the moon can be sanctified; and to send forth messengers to inform the remainder of the people on which day Rosh Chodesh was observed, so that they will know the day on which to celebrate the festivals as implied in *Vayikra 23:2:* "that you will pronounce as days of holy convocation," and as implied in *Shemos 13:10,* "and you shall observe this statute in its appointed season."

The "לחם משנה" here points out that the Rambam's citing of the verse of "אשר תקראו אתם מקראי קדש" refers only to the statement made here "that messengers are to be sent to inform the people when Rosh Chodesh day will be". However, the mitzva to determine and designate Rosh Chodesh finds its source only in the verse of "החדש הזה לכם".

This approach of the "לחם משנה" is questioned by HaRav Aharon Kohen, in his sefer (סימן ג) "על המועדות - בית אהרן". He asks, why would the Rambam cite here a source for sending out messengers, when he should have cited a source for the overall mitzva of Kiddush HaChodesh? He writes:

> אבל דבריו דחוקים, דלמה הביא הר"ם פסוק רק על פרט זה "וישלחו ויודיעו" ולא הביא הפסוק "דהחודש הזה לכם" על עיקר המצוה. ופשטות דברי הר"ם מורים דמה שהביא הפסוקים ד"אשר תקראו אותם וכו'" הוא עיקר המצות עשה. ולפי זה לכאורה דבריו סותרים למה שכתב במנין המצות שמצוה זו נאמרה בפסוק, החודש הזה לכם.

The בית אהרן concludes that both verses allude to the mitzva of establishing the new month, even though both must be cited. For if we only cited the verse of "אשר תקראו אותם מקראי קדש", this calls only for the Bais Din to determine the month in order that the holy days be observed at their proper times. In this case, this pasuk would not be counted as a separate mitzva, but rather it must be included in the overall call for observing the holy days. However, the verse of "החדש הזה לכם" spells out clearly that the jurisdiction and the right to determine Rosh Chodesh was in the hands of the Bais Din. And thus it is this right which must be enumerated in the counting of the 613 mitzvos.

> אכן נראה דשני ענינים אמת, דמש"כ כאן דמ"ע על הב"ד לחשב ולידע וכו' מקרא ד"מקראי קדש" הוא משום דמהאי קרא נלמד באמת שיש חיוב על בית דין לקבוע את המועדות...אכן לטעם זה **לא היה נחשב למצוה מיוחדת בפני עצמה במנין המצות**, אלא חיוב זה הוא פרט וחלק ממצות המועדות...ומה שנחשב למצוה מיוחדת במנין המצות אינו מעשה המצוה של קביעות המועדות רק עיקר דין התורה שמסרה את קביעות החדשים והשנים רק לבית דין, **זה נחשב** למצוה **מיוחדת**.

XIV

THE RAMBAM'S POSITION ACCORDING TO THE גרי"ז הלוי

Based on our previous discussion, we may conclude that both Kiddush HaChodesh and establishing the leap year are to be seen as one mitzva, since both serve the same purpose of ensuring that the holidays are observed at their proper times. By establishing the day of Rosh Chodesh, we know exactly on which days Pesach and Succos will occur. (Shavuos, on the other hand, has different considerations.) A leap year ensures that Pesach will be observed in the spring, "חודש האביב", and Succos in the autumn, "חודש האסיף". Thus, as we have pointed out, both mitzvos serve the same purpose — to ensure the timely observance of the holidays.

Yet the גרי"ז הלוי suggests a different perspective. He maintains that the purpose of the leap years is to ensure the preservation of a lunar-solar calendar, which reckons the months according to the moon and the years according to the sun. This is mandated by the fact that the Torah requires Pesach to fall in the spring — חודש האביב — "the month of ripening" *(Shemos 13:4)*, since in Eretz Yisrael the grain ripens in the spring at Pesach time. Succos must fall in the autumn. If we were to employ a simple lunar calendar, the following would occur. A lunar year consisting of twelve months adds up to 354 days. A solar year is approximately 365 ¼ days. The difference is 11 ¼ days. A lunar calendar, left on its own, would "wander' from season to season, with the result that Pesach would not occur in the spring. Since the Torah requires that Pesach occur in the spring, in order to make sure that this happens, an extra month is added from time to time so that it will parallel the seasons of the solar year. The purpose then of a leap year, עבור השנה, is to adjust the lunar-solar calendar rather than to adjust the holidays. To prove his point, the גרי"ז הלוי offers the following insights. The Gemara in *Mesechtas Sanhedrin 11b* states:

תנו רבנן: על שלשה **דברים** מעברין את השנה: על האביב, ועל פירות האילן, ועל התקופה.

The Rabbis taught in a baraisa: because of three things we intercalate a month into a year — on account of the grain ripening after Nissan, on account of the tree's fruits' ripening after Shavuos, and on account of the seasons.

'On account of the grain ripening after Nissan.' As previously explained, Pesach, on the fifteenth of Nissan, is viewed as the 'month of ripening'. If the grain were not to ripen before Pesach, this would postpone Pesach for a month, in order that it would coincide with the ripening of the grain.

'On account of the tree's fruits' ripening after Shavuos.' There is an obligation to bring the first fruits of the seven species of produce to the Bais HaMikdash. Thus, if the fruits were not ripe by Shavuos, an extra month could be added by the Bais Din.

'On account of the seasons' that are scheduled to begin in the wrong calendar month. As previously explained, if the Bais Din reckons that the spring season is to begin after Pesach, this is enough reason to proclaim a leap year.

Thus it would seem that the above considerations would be sufficient to convince us that the reason for declaring a leap year was to ensure that the holidays occur in their proper seasons. Yet, points out the גרי"ז הלוי, when the Rambam cites this baraisa he makes a slight change, which thereby indicates that the purpose of declaring a leap year is due rather to the consideration of adjusting the lunar-solar calendar. Thus the Rambam states, in *Hilchos Kiddush HaChodesh 4:2*:

על שלשה **סימנים** מעברין את השנה: על תקופה, ועל האביב, ועל פירות האילן, כיצד? בית דין מחשבין ויודעין

אם תהי' תקופת ניסן בששה עשר בניסן או אחר זמן זה מעברין אותה השנה, ויעשו אותו אדר שני, כדי שיהי' הפסח בזמן האביב. ועל סימן זה סומכין ומעברין, ואין חוששין לסימן אחר.

An extra month is added to the year as the result of three indications: the vernal (spring) equinox, the ripening of the barley crop, and the blooming of the fruit trees.

What does this imply? When the court calculates and determines that the vernal equinox will fall on the sixteenth of Nissan or later, the year is made full. The month that would have been Nissan is made into the second Adar, and thus Pesach will fall in the spring. This factor alone is sufficient for the court to proclaim a leap year, and the other factors need not be considered.

The Rambam here substitutes the word "סימנים" — "indications", for "דברים" — "things, matters which we are to consider". Thus we can see that the reasons outlined here are not for the purpose of ensuring that Pesach occurs in the spring, but rather these "indications" signify that the year is "out of order" and that therefore the solar year needs to be rearranged. Thus the Rambam concludes, in *Halacha 4:*

ואלו הדברים שהן העיקר שמעברין בשבילן, כדי שיהיו השנים שני החמה.

These are the primary grounds for making the year full, so that the years will follow a solar calendar.

Similarly, in the Sefer HaMitzvos the Rambam writes, in מצוה קנג:

ואמרו "שמור את האביב" הורה כי שנותינו ראוי שנשמור
בה פרקי השנה ולכן תהי' שמשית.

And they said *(Devarim 16:1)* "Observe the month of spring" implies that in the reckoning of our years we must take account of the seasons of the year, so that they are solar years.

Consequently, we must concern ourselves with the seasons in order to adjust our solar-lunar calendar. And again, the Rambam points this out at the beginning of *Hilchos Kiddush HaChodesh 1:1*, where he writes:

השנים שאנו מחשבים הם שני החמה שנאמר שמור חודש
האביב.

The years we follow are solar years, as implied in *Devarim 16:1*: "Keep the month of spring."

And so we conclude that we are obligated to arrange the calendar so that the vernal equinox always falls in the month of Nissan.

XV

THE OPINION OF THE RAMBAN

The Sefer HaChinuch concludes by saying:

זה שאמרנו הוא על דעת הרמב"ם זכרונו לברכה. והרמב"ן
זכרונו לברכה יחשב קדוש החדש מצוה אחת ועבור השנים
מצוה אחת, וראיותיו בספר המצוות שלו, וכן בעל הלכות
גם כן. והפסוק המורה על מצות העבור, כלומר שנחשב

התקופות כדי שנעשה המועדים בזמן קבוע להם הוא:
ושמרת את החקה הזאת למועדה, וכן: שמור את חדש
האביב, כמו שכתבנו.

What we have stated here follows the view of the Rambam, of blessed memory. The Ramban, of blessed memory, reckons the sanctification of the month as one precept and the intercalation of the years as another. His proof for this is given in his Sefer HaMitzvos. So too is the opinion of the sefer, Halachos Gedolos. The verse of Scripture which indicates the precept of intercalation, i.e., that we should calculate the seasons in order to observe the holy days at the times set for them, is: "You shall therefore keep this ordinance [of observing Pesach] in its proper season." *(Shemos 13:10),* and so too: "Observe the month of Aviv [spring]". *(Devarim 16:11)* – as we have written.

These words of the Ramban are quoted in his commentary to the Rambam's Sefer HaMitzvos, in Root Principle One. He cites two proofs for this theory.

אבל בעל הלכות יעשה אותם שתים...ומצאתי לי ראיה
מדבריהם ז"ל אמרו בספרי "האזינו השמים". דבר אחר
שלא עשו מצות שנתנו להם מן השמים. ואלו הם **מצות**
שנתנו להם מן השמים עיבור שנים וקביעת חדשים, שנאמר:
והיו לאותות ולמועדים ולימים ושנים. "ותשמע הארץ",
שלא עשו **מצות** שניתנו בארץ לקט שכחה ופאה תרומות
ומעשרות שמיטים ויובלות. הרי שקראון קדוש החדש
ועיבור השנים בלשון רבים... "**מצות** שנתנו להם מן
השמים", מוכה מזה שהן נחשבות לשתי מצות.

Even though the Halachos Gedolos counts them as two mitzvos...I have found proof from the words of the Sages, of blessed memory, from that which is stated in the Sifri. Commenting on the verse, "Give ear, O heavens" *(Devarim 32:1)* and testify that they did not adhere to the mitzvos which pertain to the heavens, i.e., the mitzvos of sanctifying the months and intercalating the leap year...The word "מצות" is used here in the plural, proving that there are here two separate mitzvos, Kiddush HaChodesh and calculating leap years....

The Ramban presents a second proof as follows:

אבל חישוב תקופות שמנה בעל הלכות היא מצות עיבור שנים על התקופות דכתיב "שמור את חדש האביב" על פי מה שאמרו בגמרא ראש השנה (דף כא) "כד חזית דמשכא תקופות טבת עד שיתסר בניסן עבדא להיא שתא ולא תיחוש דכתיב שמור את החדש האביב, שמור את החדש שהוא סמוך לאביב, מלמד שמעברין את השנה שיהא אביב בזמנו. יכול אם היתה חסירה י"ד או ט"ו, תלמוד לומר חדש, לא פחות ולא יותר. יכול אם היתה חסירה ארבעים או חמישים, תלמוד לומר, חדש, לא פחות ולא יותר", וזו מצות עשה היא כמו שאמרו חכמים (מנחות לו,ב) השמר דעשה עשה...

When the בעל הלכות גדולות in his enumeration of the mitzvos, includes 'the seasons', what he means is that there is a mitzva to calculate whether a leap year is necessary in order that the solar seasons remain in place. This is based on the verse, "Guard the month of the first ripened produce (i.e., Nissan)" *(Devarim 16:1)*. This approach is based on the following statement in *Mesechtas Rosh Hashanah 21a*.

Rav Huna bar Aviv sent the following message to Rava: When you see the solar season of Teves is stretching until the 16th of Nissan [when the spring season is to begin], intercalate a month into that year and do not be concerned about it. For it is written: "*Guard* the month of Aviv", which means "Guard the spring season to ensure it will begin during the moon's renewal in the month of Nissan" [the "renewal" period alludes to the first fourteen days of the month, after which it is no longer seen as a "new" moon]. Thus we see the new season of spring begins on the fifteenth of Nissan. And thus if it does not begin until the sixteenth, [for the ripening of the grain has not yet taken place], then intercalation is required.

Thus the Ramban concludes that "Guard the month of Aviv" alludes to the mitzva of intercalation. And therefore this is a mitzva, for the word "guard" indicates a positive commandment, for we are told to be "on guard" to keep the mitzvos.

XVI

HaRav Perlow's objection to the Ramban's proofs

HaRav Yerucham Perlow, in his classic commentary to the "ספר המצות לרס״ג", the Book of Mitzvos as enumerated by Rav Saadia Gaon, dismisses these proofs of the Ramban in מצות עשה נו.

Regarding the first proof, that when the Sifri refers to Kiddush HaChodesh and the intercalation of leap years in the plural as "mitzvos" — "מצות", and thus we can assume that these are two separate mitzvos, this is not necessarily decisive. For there are other instances when we refer to "mitzvos" in the plural and yet all the components which go to make up that mitzva are ultimately enumerated as one single mitzva. For example, the esrog and the four species, including the lulav, myrtle and willow, are referred to as "מצוות". Yet in the enumeration of the mitzvos they are counted as a single mitzva. Indeed, in the Gemara in *Mesechtas Succah 37b*, the opinion of Rabbah is cited that the lulav should be held in the right hand and the esrog in the left hand. This leads to the question why the lulav is given preference (since the right hand is considered the preferred hand). The answer given is that the lulav constitutes three mitzvos – lulav, myrtle and willow branch – whereas the esrog is only one mitzva. Thus we see that even though we refer to this combination of lulav, myrtle and willow as "מצוות", yet in the actual enumeration of the 613 mitzvos, all three are counted as one. The same can be said regarding the mitzva of tzitzis. Even though we refer to the fringes placed on all four corners of a garment as "four mitzvos", yet we ultimately count the mitzva of tzitzis as a single mitzva.

And as for the Ramban's second proof from the Gemara of *Rosh Hashanah 21a* that if we find that the spring season will not arrive by the sixteenth of Nissan, then we intercalate a month into that year (based on the verse of "שמור את חדש האביב", which mandates that Pesach must fall out in the spring), Rav Perlow maintains that not only does this not prove the Ramban's position, but rather it even contradicts it. For the Gemara here tells us that it is only when the solar season of Teves (the winter season) stretches as far as the sixteenth of Nissan that we are compelled to add an extra month, עיבור השנה.

However, if it stretches only up to the fifteenth of Nissan, we need not add a full month, but rather need only add an extra day to the current month. This ensures that the spring season will fall out by the fifteenth of Nissan. From this we can see that the verse, "שמור את חדש האביב" — "Guard the spring season", includes both the mitzva of Kiddush HaChodesh and that of intercalating a leap year, for both methods are used to attain the same goal of ensuring that Pesach come out in the spring.

Thus, concludes Rav Perlow, it should follow that they be counted as a single mitzva, as the Rambam contends, and not as two mitzvos, in keeping with the opinion of the Ramban.

Defending the Ramban

Regarding the Ramban's first proof that "מצות" is used in the plural form even though in the final enumeration of the mitzvos this will ultimately constitute just one mitzva (as in the case of lulav and esrog or of tzitzis), the truth is that this question was anticipated in the classic commentary to the Sefer HaMitzvos, "מרגינתא דרב".

However, in the sefer "בית אהרן-על המועדות" by HaRav Aharon Kohen, we find a fascinating answer to this question. We can draw a distinction between these two categories of mitzvos of lulav and Kiddush HaChodesh and intercalating a leap year. On the one hand, the mitzva of lulav requires only a single action – that of taking the lulav – as the verse states: "ולקחתם". This one act includes not only the lulav but also the myrtle and the willow branch. Therefore, since there is only one act at one time, we therefore count this mitzva of lulav as a single mitzva. The same is true of the mitzva of tzitsis. We are required to wear a four-cornered garment with fringes on each of the four corners. The mitzva, though, relates to one act of wearing this garment and therefore it is counted as one mitzva, and not four.

On the other hand, in relation to the mitzva of establishing a new month and adding an extra month to the year, each of these mitzvos is mentioned in different places in the Torah. For example, Kiddush HaChodesh is mentioned in *Parashas Bo, 12:1*, and intercalating the leap year in *Parashas Devarim 16:1*. However, each requires a separate act to be implemented on a different occasion (Kiddush HaChodesh at the beginning of the month, and עיבור השנה at the end of the year in the month of Adar). And although both of these mitzvos relate to adjustments made to the calendar, they are still justifiably counted as two separate mitzvos.

אבל נראה בזה שיש לחלק משם בפשיטות, דגבי ד' מינים שבלולב שבלשון התורה הם כלולה בפועלת לקיחה אחת, הם נחשבים למצוה אחת, אף שכל דבר בפני עצמו הוא חלק מסוים מהמצוה דמשום זה חשוב אותם לארבע שמחות, וכן בציציות, אף שכל כנף הוא חלק מסוים, מכל מקום התורה כללה אותה בעשה אחת. אבל בקידוש חדשים ועיבור שנים שכתבה אותם התורה בשתי מקומות וגם הם פעולות מחולקות בזמנים שונים צריך לחשוב אותם לשני מצות כיון שכל דבר הוא חלק מסוים בפני עצמו שמטעם זה הם נקראים בלשון רבים, מצות מן השמים...

THE INSIGHT OF THE SEFER "אגן הסהר"

My rebbe, HaGaon HaRav Chayim Zimmerman, ז"ל, presents a new insight to defend the Ramban from the second question raised here, that since the mitzva of Kiddush HaChodesh and that of עיבור השנה are both included in the pasuk of "שמור את חדש האביב", they should be counted as only one mitzva. HaRav Zimmerman explains what the Ramban really meant here.

The בעל הלכות גדולות cited by the Ramban does not intend to imply that we have here the following two mitzvos, the mitzva of קדוש החדש, which establishes the calendar month, and עיבור השנה, enacting a leap year. Rather what we have are two different mitzvos: the mitzva of קדוש החדש, as we have explained, and the mitzva of ensuring that the festivals of Pesach and Succos fall in their proper seasons. This second mitzva can be accomplished in two ways. Either, if the winter stretches only until the fifteenth of Nissan, then we simply add a day to the calendar month. However, if it stretches to the sixteenth of Nissan, then we are compelled to add an extra month to the year – עיבור השנה.

Consequently, we are being told here that we have the legal right to apply either of these methods in order to be sure that the spring season, the "חודש האביב", coincides with the holiday of Pesach. With this in mind, we can now appreciate the statement made here in the Gemara, that if the length of time is more than a day or a month (i.e., 40 or 50 days) before the appearance of the spring season, then it can not be rectified by adding only one month of 30 days, and we do not do anything. For only a "חדש", a month, is referred to in the pasuk, nothing more and nothing less.

One might think that in order to ensure that the spring season coincides with Pesach, we might be allowed to add any amount of time we wish; therefore the Torah tells us that we might add a month, "חדש", and nothing else.

And so, according to the Ramban and the בעל הלכות גדולות, we have the following two mitzvos: קדוש החדש, a mitzva to establish Rosh Chodesh day even without having a direct or an indirect impact on establishing the spring season in its proper time. We also have קדוש החדש and עיבור השנה, when either of these methods can affect the adjustment of the spring season in its proper time for the holiday of Pesach, based on the pasuk which states: "שמור את חדש האביב".

This, then, is what the Gemara in Rosh Hashanah alludes to when it says, "if you see the solar season of Teves stretch out – add a month (or a day)". The mitzva here is that of calculating the seasons, and both קדוש החדש and עיבור השנה are ways of accomplishing this.

> ונראה לומר דבאמת לא נזכר כלל בדברי הבה"ג מצות
> עשה דקידוש חדשים ומצות עשה דעיבור שנים אלא מצות
> עשה דקידוש החדשים ומצות עשה ד**חישוב תקופות**, והיינו
> דבקרא ד"שמור את חדש האביב" נאמר שיהא זמן אביב

בתקופה חדשה אשר על ידי זה משתווים שנות החמה עם חדשי הלבנה...ולפי זה צריכים בית דין לחשוב התקופות ולראות שיהיו חלים בזמנם. ואם רואים שהתקופה החדשה מתאחרת צריכים לעבר את החדש שיהי' התקופה בזמנם ואם לא די בעיבור החדש צריכים לעיבור השנה. ונמצא דעיבור השנה אינה חלות קיום המצוה בפני עצמה אלא היא טצדקי במצוה של חישוב התקופה שנתנה התורה רשות אף לעבר השנה...אבל אם די בעיבור החדש אז צריכים רק לעבר החדש כדי שיהי' התקופה בזמנה. ונמצא דאין כאן דין מצות על הבית דין לעבר השנה אלא **לחשוב התקופות** ולצדד שיהיו בזמנם...

Chapter Eight
How the Month is Determined

I

Various Methods of Determining the "New Moon"

There are a number of ways to determine the new month: by means of astronomical calculation, by the sighting of the new moon by eyewitnesses, and by the Bais Din designating the month through the testimony of eyewitnesses on the 30th day, or for whatever reason, they can decide to sanctify the 31st day.

There are two methods of calculating the new moon. The first method is by calculating the "מולד האמיתי", the precise moment of conjunction. The moon moves eastward around the earth, completing its cycle once a month. At the beginning of the month, the moon will be aligned exactly between the earth and the sun. This stage is referred to as "מולד האמיתי" — true conjunction. The second method is by calculating the "mean conjunction". This is the moment of "conjunction" based on the mean or average motion of the sun and the moon. Its duration, which does not vary, is 29 days, 12 hours, 44 minutes, and 2.98 seconds — "כ"ט יום, י"ב שעות, ותשצ"ג חלקים". By applying this method, one month is thereby "full" — "מלא", consisting of 30 days, whereas another month will be "lacking" — "חסר", consisting of only 29 days.

Witnesses who sighted the new crescent moon have the obligation to appear and testify before the Bais Din. In a subsequent chapter, we will expand on the laws pertaining to these eyewitnesses. It would seem that since what is required here is merely to gain a glimpse of the new moon, thus sighting even a sliver of the new crescent moon would suffice. Yet there is a difference of opinion among the classic commentators, if it is sufficient to catch just a glimpse of the moon or whether there is a particular size (שיעור) of the crescent that must be sighted in order to qualify as a valid sighting of the new moon by eyewitnesses.

Rashi's comments here

Commenting on the pasuk in *Shemos 12:2*:

"החודש **הזה** לכם ראש חדשים וגו'."

This month shall be for you the beginning of the months, etc.

Rashi states:

"הזה": נתקשה משה על מולד הלבנה באיזו שיעור תראה ותהיה ראויה לקדש. והראה לו באצבע את הלבנה ברקיע ואמר לו כזה ראה וקדש..."

This [month]: Moshe was perplexed about the precise determination of the reappearance of the moon and did not know what "size" moon must appear for it to be fit to be sanctified. Therefore Hashem showed him with a finger, so to speak, the moon in the sky and said to him, "See it like this and sanctify it."

This comment of Rashi's leads us to ask several questions. Why was Moshe Rabbenu so perplexed? What was so difficult, since all that was required was a simple glimpse of the moon, which would suffice in determining the new moon? What 'size' is Rashi referring to here? It would seem that seeing even the smallest sliver of the new moon crescent would suffice. Why do we need to see a particular size, שיעור, of the moon? For what purpose is this required?

The Brisker Rav, R' Velvele, concludes that indeed a specific size, שיעור, is required, so that witnesses can claim that they saw the "new" moon. Any amount less than this particular size is not considered sufficient to warrant that a new moon be declared. This then is the meaning behind the pasuk, "כזה ראה וקדש" — "this is the amount that must be seen before the moon can be considered renewed".

Proof can be brought from the Rambam's remarks in his commentary to Mesechtas Rosh Hashanah. There he writes that even when the month was determined merely by calculation, these calculations had to take into consideration the fact that one could not sanctify the moon until six hours had elapsed after the "molad", the conjunction. This contention is based on the pasuk here: "כזה ראה וקדש", which includes the determining of the month either by eyewitnesses or by calculation. In both instances, the moon must appear to be of a definite size, a שיעור, in order for sanctification to take place. We can perhaps establish the validity of this assumption only if we conclude that the requirement that the crescent moon be of a specific size must apply in both cases — that is, both for eyewitnesses and for sanctifying the moon by means of calculation.

It is required that a period of six hours must elapse after the conjunction, for before this time it is impossible for the human eye to see the moon. Thus it should follow that if we are to determine the moon by means of calculation, then we should calculate the moon from its "true" conjunction, which was six hours earlier.

> והנראה מבואר מדברי רש"י, דבהך "כזה ראה וקדש" דינא נאמר בזה, דבזה השיעור היא ראויה לקדש, ובבציר מהכי אף אם היה אפשר לראות אותה גם כן לאו בת קידוש היא, וזו היא ההלכה של כזה ראה וקדש, על זה השיעור שהראה הקב"ה למשה באצבע.

> והנה יעיין שם בפירוש הרמב"ם לראש השנה דגם שמקדשין את החדש על ידי חשבון גם כן אין מקדשין אותו עד אחר שש שעות מהמולד, משום דקי"ל "כזה ראה וקדש" והחשבון והראיה בהדדי נינהו...וכל זה הוא אם עד שש שעות הלבנה מדינא לאו בת ראיה וקידוש היא, ועל כרחך

שייך זאת גם לעניין חשבון, אבל אם אין זה מהלכה, רק משום שאין אנו רואין אותה ולא משכחת ראיה קודם זמן זה, אם כן לעניין חשבון לא שייך זאת, ושפיר היה אפשר לחשוב משעת המולד. ולכאורה מבואר, גם מדברי הרמב"ם אלו יסוד זה דבהך "כזה ראה וקדש" נאמרה הלכה דבשיעור זה יכולין לקדש ולא בפחות מזה...

II

Not all agree

However, all the commentators do not necessarily accept this contention. Many, in fact, dismiss it completely. For example, the רא"ם, HaRav Eliyahu Mizrachi, in his classic commentary, writes that the appearance of the moon has no *minimum* requirement and therefore as soon as the moon is sighted, regardless of its size at that moment, it is qualified for sanctification right then and there. There is, however, a maximum requirement, and that is if it is not sighted a day or two after the *molad*, then it no longer qualifies to be sanctified when it is sighted after this time, for by now it has already been sanctified *in heaven*.

The רא"ם concludes that there may be a need for a minimum requirement in order to be able to distinguish between what appears to be the sighting of the moon and what is actually nothing other than a cloud. In fact, the Mishna tells us that the eyewitnesses were interrogated regarding what exactly they saw.

שאף על פי שאין ללבנה שיעור למטה שהרי בתחילת ראייתה **מיד** ראוייה לקדש מכל מקום יש לה שיעור למעלה, שאם לא נראית עד לאחר יום או יומיים ששיעורה גדול מאד אינה ראוייה לקדש שכבר קדשוהו מן השמים.

...ושמא יש לומר שמרוב קטנותה אינה נכרת אם היא עב קטנה או ירח, כדאמרינן בראש השנה, "כזה ראיתם

> או כזה ראיתם", דמשמע שיש ללבנה שיעור ידוע בתחלה
> הראותה.

Although the רא"ם expresses some doubt as to whether a שיעור is required, the Maharal of Prague is adamant in rejecting this notion. All that is needed, maintains the Maharal, is to catch a mere glimpse of the moon to ascertain that a new moon has appeared. He writes:

> דברי תימא הן דמה שיעור לדבר דאם נראה כל שהוא
> ממנה ראויה לקדש...אמנם בירושלמי מצאתי שיש שיעור
> לקדוש הירח דקאמר התם שאין מקדשין את הירח עד
> שנראה בה כשעורה. ואם תאמר הוי לי למימר: על מה
> שיעור הירח, כשעורה, שאז ראוייה לקדש. אין קשיא, כיון
> דשיעור "שעורה" אינה אלא למראית העין ולא כפי האמת
> אין לומר דשיעורה כשעורה, ופשוט.

THE SAGES DIFFER ON THIS ISSUE

According to the sefer "מרכבת המשנה", a classic commentary on the Mechilta, this issue of whether a prescribed size, a שיעור, is required here is characterized by a difference of opinion among the Sages of the Talmud. This parallels the discussion between Moshe Rabbenu and the Ribbono Shel Olam, which we have discussed previously.

In *Mesechtas Rosh Hashanah 24b-25a,* we are told:

> It once happened that two witnesses came and said: We saw the new moon in the morning in the east and in the evening in the west [i.e., they claimed to have seen the "old" moon in the morning and the "new" moon that same evening].

R' Yochanan ben Nuri declared: They are false witnesses [because there is a 24-hour period between the disappearance of the old moon and the appearance of the new moon. During that period *no moon* is visible. Thus witnesses who claim to have sighted both the old moon and the new *within* twelve hours are liars.]

But when the witnesses came to Yavneh [the seat of the Sanhedrin, presided over by Rabban Gamliel] and told the same story, Rabban Gamliel accepted them as valid witnesses.

The Gemara asks *(25a)*, why did Rabban Gamliel validate their testimony?

Rabban Gamliei said to the Sages who questioned how he could have accepted these witnesses: "Thus I have received a tradition from the house of my father's father [Rabban Gamliel, the Elder], that sometimes the moon travels a long route and sometimes it travels a short route."

He attempted to explain this by pointing out that the speed of the moon's motion is not constant. In most cases it takes 24 hours from the disappearance of the "old" moon until the "new" moon moves out of conjunction sufficiently to be seen. However, occasionally the moon moves with exceptional speed and thus the new moon will be visible within twelve hours of the disappearance of the old moon.

As a result of this reasoning, Rabban Gamliel did not consider the two sightings claimed by the witnesses as conclusive proof of falsehood.

Consequently, maintains the "מרכבת המשנה", if we say that the moon has a *set* motion, then one could contend that since six hours after the conjunction, when the moon becomes visible [according to Rashi] we can estimate the size of the moon and say that indeed there is a specified "size" that must be sighted in order to qualify for sanctification. Therefore, R' Yochanan ben Nuri requires a "שיעור", a specified size, in order for the sighting of the moon to be valid. And so Rabban Gamliel, who contends that the motion of the moon is not constant, maintains that we cannot determine a fixed שיעור for the sighting of the moon.

This then, according to the "מרכבת המשנה", reflected the give and take between Moshe Rabbenu and Hashem. Moshe was of the opinion that there is a *fixed size* required for sighting the moon, and therefore he questioned Hashem in order to ascertain what was this *exact size*. But Hashem answered that there is *no* set size and all that is required is to sight the new moon, even if that means catching just a "glimpse" of what *appears to be* the moon.

שמשה למד כשיטת ר"י בן נורי שלעולם הילוכה שוה, והוקשה לו, מדוע לא ניתן שיעור מאתנו יתברך בלמדו סוד העיבור? והשיב לו השי"ת, כזה ראה וקדש...שאין שיעור למדתם של הלבנה לקדשה, אפס כזה עשה, ראה וקדש כשיטת רבן גמליאל, שפעמים בא בארוכה וכו', ובראיה תליא מילתא, כשיעידו עדים שראו אותה, כשיטת ר"ג הנזכר.

III

EXACTLY WHEN CAN THE MOON BE SIGHTED?

There is a difference of opinion among the Rishonim as to when exactly the moon can be sighted after the molad (conjunction). Both Rashi, in his commentary to *Mesechtas Rosh*

Hashanah 20a (ד"ה אחר חצות), and the Rava'ad contend that the new moon can be seen *six hours* after the molad.

In the sefer "יסוד עולם" by Ha Rav Yitzchak Yisraeli, a student of the Rosh, the author contends in מאמר ד' פרק ח' that the moon can be seen *twenty-two hours* after the molad.

Both the Rambam and the הרז"ה (רבינו זרחיהו הלוי), in his commentary on the Gemara in *Rosh Hashanah 20b,* where he discusses the issue of whether the molad occurs before or after midday (נולד קודם חצות או אחר חצות), maintain that the new moon can be seen *twenty-four* hours after the molad. Still other commentators believe that the required period of time is *eighteen* hours.

This wide range of opinion leads us to raise the following questions. How can there be such a great time difference among the various opinions here? One would imagine that a number of minutes or at most an hour or two might constitute the difference among them; not a range of from six hours after the molad to twenty-four hours. And in addition to the first problem, these opinions are contradicted by modern astronomical calculations. The impression is thereby given that the early commentators lacked knowledge of the ways of the solar system or that their calculations were based on erroneous assumptions.

However, we earlier established the necessity for a שיעור, a required size of the moon, which must be sighted by witnesses before it can qualify for determining Rosh Chodesh. Thus the question to be asked here is not *when is the moon visible* after conjunction, מולד, but rather *what is the size of the moon that is required* as a שיעור. Each opinion presented here offers a different שיעור, and the reason for the differences will soon become apparent.

My rebbe, HaRav Chaim Zimmerman, ל"ז, in his classic sefer "אגן הסהר", addresses this issue (עמ' מג):

שיש שיעור לראיה הירח ויוצא לנו מזה ענין נכבד מאד,

שלא פליגי כלל רש"י והראב"ד וסייעתם, והרז"ה
והרמב"ם ובעלי התוכנים וסייעתם במציאות, אם יש
אפשרות של ראיית לבנה אחר שש שנה. **אלא שפליגי בדינה**
דראיית הלבנה. אם יש שיעור לראיית זריחת הלבנה, או בכל
שהוא סגי, שרש"י והראב"ד וסייעתם סובר שאין שיעור
לראיית הירח. והרז"ה והרמב"ם סוברים, שיש שיעור מסוים
לראיית הירח. וסובר הרז"ה ששיעור קשת הירח הוא כפי
התמונה שנראית קשת הירח לבני אדם לאחר כד שעות
מעת הקיבוץ...

The Maharal reconciles Torah and science

This approach was anticipated by the Maharal of Prague, in his sefer "באר הגולה" (ראה שם מדף פה והלאה-באר חמישי), where we find the insight expressed that it is from this issue of when exactly the Rishonim approximated the moment that the new moon could be sighted that we can appreciate the words of Chazal in relation to the findings of modern science. We sometimes find that not only are the words of Chazal contradicted by modern science, but they are also proven "wrong".

The Maharal points out that we are not to be overwhelmed by this, but rather we should be aware that Chazal based their words on halachic principles and focused on how they would affect halachic decisions. For example, here the issue is not *when* the moon can be sighted, but when halacha recognizes the size of the moon to qualify as designating Rosh Chodesh after it has been sighted. Thus even though modern astronomers contend that the moon can not generally be seen as early as six hours after the molad, yet even though it is very small, it can be seen by witnesses if they are positioned in such a way as to catch a brief glimpse of it. Thus when science tells us that the moon cannot be seen until after six hours, what this means is that it cannot be seen easily *by everyone*, even though the possibility exists for it to be seen in exceptional circumstances by *a few* individuals who happen to be strategically situated.

הנה הגבורי המלחמה היודעים בחכמת התכונה הקולעים אל השערה ולא יחטיאו, וזורקים אל המאמר הזה [שיש לראות הלבנה אחר שש שעות] אומרים דבר זה יכחיש חכמת התכונה, כי מה שנאמר שאפשר שתראה הלבנה אחר שש שעות לחדושה ליושבי מערב וזה אינו. כי התבאר בחכמת בתכונה שאין הירח נראה אחר מולדו עד אחר יום שלם או פחות מעט או יותר מעט וכן נמצא שהירח מתכסה ב' ימים יום לפני חדושה ויום לאחר חדושה מעט. וכן כתב הרמב"ם פרק א מהלכות קדוש החדש, יום שלם צריך קודם שתראה הלבנה בתחילת החודש ע"כ. וממילא יום שלם אין הישנה נראית, כי משפט אחד לחדשה עם הישנה. ומפני זה רבים אשר התחכמו בחכמה זאת, האריכו דברים על המאמרים אלו להשותם ולאחדם עם חכמי התכונה. ועם מה שמעיד עליו החוש שאין הלבנה נראית ו' שעות אחר חדושיה, וטרחו טרח מאוד מאוד, ואין להשיב על דברים שלהן אם האמת אתם או לא... כי חכמתם בנוי כאשר הירח נראה **מוחש לעין כל**, ואין זה חכמת התורה, והוא יסוד העבור בנוי על שיעור הירח כשנראה ממנו בשיעור שעורה, וזה נקרא שלא נראה הירח בעליל, רק נראה לפי שיכול להכיר...ולפיכך השיעור אשר נתנו חכמים כי אחר ו' שעות לחדושה אפשר שתראה הירח, היינו שאפשר בשום צד בעולם, והמדינה גם כן גבוה ואינה יושבת בעמק, והיא קרובה בתכלית אל המערב...

IV

Do Eyewitnesses Determine or only Indicate?

In the sefer (פרק ו' עמ' מה) "אגן הסהר", the following question is raised. If we conclude that the month is to be designated by eyewitnesses, what exactly does this mean? Does it mean that the sighting of the new moon by witnesses automatically designates a new month; in other words, that the witnesses *cause* Rosh Chodesh to occur — חלות? Or is it merely an *indication* that the molad has made its appearance? This would mean that it is essentially the *molad* which brings about Rosh Chodesh, and eyewitnesses only ascertain that the new moon has made its appearance. This question reveals a difference of opinion between the ראב"ח, Rav Avraham bar Chiya Ha Nasi, and the sefer "כפתור ופרח".

THE OPINION OF THE ראב"ח

HaRav Avraham bar Chiya, in his sefer "ספר העיבור", explains why in the Hebrew language we call a month "חדש" — "new", and why it is that from the appearance of this "new" moon we begin the counting of the new month. He also explains why we refer to a month as "חודש". Even though the new moon should be determined by means of mathematical calculations, this is not a simple matter, since very few people are knowledgeable in this science, and there are differences of opinion regarding how to apply these mathematical formulas. Therefore Hashem, in His infinite mercy, allowed us to determine the "new" moon simply by its being sighted by eyewitnesses.

> **חידוש** וקראו לו ''חדש'' מפני שאנו מתחילין למנותו אחר הלבנה, לא מעת חידושה ממש, וראש חידושה הראוי לקרוא אותה על שמה הוא מולד הלבנה...לולי שאיו שעת המולד גלוי' לבני האדם ואין אדם מגיע אלי' אלא מדרך חשבון וסברא, ושניהם קשין על רוב העולם והספקות באות בהן ואין מחשבות לבות בני אדם באים בהם אל דעת אחד.
>
> ומפני זה לא החמיר הקב"ה עלינו ולא צוה לשמור ראשי החדשים משעת התחלתן ברקיע אשר היא שעת המולד, אבל הרחיב לנו בדבר הזה ונתן לנו רשות לקבוע החדש על עצת חכמינו מפני שאין לנו אות שתהי' מעידה לנו על התחלתו ברקיע, והתחלתו היא למראית עינינו והיא הגלוי' לנו, והתחלה הזאת אינה שוה לעיני כל אדם ומפני

זה צריכה לסיוע ולסיג, והקב"ה נתן הרשות בזה והכח ביד
חכמינו וזקנינו כדי לסייגו לדעתם ועל חכמתם וכו'...

Thus it becomes apparent that the process of eyewitnesses determining Rosh Chodesh was a "קולא", a concession on the part of Hashem to make it easier for us to determine the actual time of the molad. For eyewitnesses verify for us that there was in reality a molad. In halachic terms we call this system "דין בירור", i.e., eyewitnesses do not designate a new month, but they merely *indicate* for us that there was an *appearance* of a new moon.

THE OPINION OF THE "כפתור ופרח"

The sefer (פרק י"ד) "כפתור ופרח" contends that it is indeed the testimony of eyewitnesses that determines the day of Rosh Chodesh. For when Hashem told Moshe Rabbenu, "כזה ראה וקדש" — "so you shall see and sanctify", He meant that the month would be determined as a new month by eyewitnesses actually seeing the moon with their own eyes.

אי לא מסתפינא מדברי ר' אברהם אבן עזרא הייתי אומר, שמה שאנו עושין שלא נקבע ראש חודש תמיד ביום המולד, ואף על פי שאנו בקיאין בקביעא דירחא הוא, לפי שראש חודש אינו תלוי ברגע המולד שהוא דיבוק שני המאורות במקום אחד מגלגל המזלות אלא שהוא תלוי אל עת התחלת ראיית הירח החדש באופק עיר אלקים ירושלים וארצו. וזה נמנע הוא שיהי' אלא אחר המולד, ויהי' אם כן הקביעות רודף ראיית הירח.

כתוב "החודש הזה לכם", ואמרו מלמד שהראה לו הקב"ה למשה דמות לבנה ואמר לו כזה ראה וקדש, כלומר, ראי' חושיית, שהרי חשבון נקודת המולד הוא ראי' שכלית וכבר ידעת מה בין המולד האמצעי שהוא ביד כל אדם היום ובין מולד האמיתי.

Explaining the Views of the Rishonim

Based on what we have discussed, we might raise the question of whether the sighting of the new moon calls for a שיעור, a fixed amount of the moon to be sighted, or whether *any amount*, "כל שהוא", is acceptable. If we say that eyewitnesses determine Rosh Chodesh (make a "חלות"), then it would be logical to assume that a שיעור, a fixed amount of the size of the moon, would be required. However, if we say that the sighting of the moon by eyewitnesses serves only as an indication that the molad took place, then we could say that all that is required is a mere sighting of the moon, no matter what size it might be.

We can outline the various opinions of the Rishonim as follows. Rashi, who accepts the sighting of the moon six hours after the molad, is of the opinion that we need no שיעור, as previously explained. Furthermore, the actual molad is what determines Rosh Chodesh, thus any indication that a molad has occurred suffices to determine the new month.

The other Rishonim do require a שיעור, for they believe that it is the eyewitnesses who determine Rosh Chodesh, and therefore only when everyone can see the moon can we accept the report of the eyewitnesses. This means that the eyewitnesses create the חלות, and it is they who conclusively determine that today is Rosh Chodesh.

Expanding on the View of the "כפתור ופרח"

The previously mentioned, "כפתור ופרח" requires the sighting of the new moon to take into account only that moon which appears on the horizon in the holy city of Yerushalayim. This has a number of halachic implications.

As we shall discuss further in a subsequent chapter, the halacha stipulates that if the greatest Sage in Yisrael finds himself for the moment in the Diaspora, even though Kiddush HaChodesh is to be designated in Eretz Yisrael, he may determine the day of Rosh Chodesh by his own astronomical calculations. However, these calculations must be based on when the new moon will make its appearance in Yerushalayim and not in the place where he presently finds himself. This is explained in the sefer "אגן הסהר" (עמ' ק"ט) where we read:

> ופשטות הדברים נראה, שאף בלא הניח כמותו בארץ ישראל או בנתנו בית דינו רשות לעבר שנים ולקדש חדשים בחוץ לארץ, ראיית הלבנה צריכה להיות לעולם באופק ארץ ישראל...ודוחק לומר שהכל תלוי ביומם בכל מקום שהם, שאם כן למה זה אמר הכפתור ופרח רק על אופק ירושלים וארצו...

This theory is also held by the Chasam Sofer, who explains the words of Rashi and the Mechilta, cited here previously, that Hashem showed Moshe the moon at twilight, for He spoke to Moshe only during the day. The Chasam Sofer explains this to mean that Hashem showed him the moon as it appeared in Eretz Yisrael. Thus, when it is twilight in Egypt, the sun has already set in Eretz Yisrael and the moon has made its appearance on the horizon of Eretz Yisrael.

The "אגן הסהר" writes as follows:

> ומצאתי מפורש בדברי החתם סופר שתפס כן לדבר פשוט (חלק ו, לקוטי שו"ת ח"ס, סימן לה) וז"ל אך מ"ש שאם אינן מחשיבין עידן וזמן על פי ירושלים עה"ק, יעשה כל אחד מועדו לפי נוף מדינתו, יפה כתב בזה...וכבר הארכתי במקום אחר, שלפענ"ד פי' החודש הזה שהראה הקב"ה למשה רבינו ע"ה הלבנה בחידושה, היינו שהראה לו במצרים על פי ארץ ישראל דאי לאו הכי, כיון שלא נדבר עמו ביום והלבנה בחידושה לא תראה אלא סמוך לאחר שקיעת

החמה, איך הראה לו הלבנה, ומה הועילו חז"ל באמרם, בין השמשות נדבר עמו.

...אלא על כרחך זה היה ברגע אחרון של היום במצרים וכבר שקעה החמה בארץ ישראל שהיא מזרחית למצרים... וקדשו ארץ ישראל על פי נוף ארץ ישראל...

The Rambam in *Hilchos Kiddush HaChodesh 3:1* states:

עדים שראו את החדש, אם היה ביניהם ובין מקום שיש בו בית דין מהלך לילה ויום או פחות, הולכין ומעידין. ואם היה ביניהם יתר על כן – לא ילכו, שאין עדותן אחר יום שלשים מועלת שכבר נתעבר החדש.

"When witnesses see the new moon and there is a journey of a night and a day or less between them and where the court holds session, they should undertake the journey and testify. If the distance between them is greater, they should not undertake the journey. For the testimony they deliver after the 30th day will be of no consequence, since the month was already made full."

The classic commentators all point out here that the Rambam appears to contradict his statement in *Halacha 15,* where he writes as follows:

בית דין שישבו כל יום שלשים ולא באו עדים והשכימו בנשף ועברו את החדש... ואחר ארבעה או חמשה ימים באו עדים רחוקים והעידו שראה את החדש בזמנו, שהוא ליל שלשים. [הלכה טז]...מקדשין אותו, וחוזרין ומונין לאותו החדש מיום שלשים, הואיל ונראה הירח בלילו.

If the court held session throughout the entire 30th day, but witnesses did not arrive, the judges arose early in the morning and made the month full…and after four or five days witnesses came from a distant place and testified that they had sighted the moon at the appropriate time, the 30th night… the moon is sanctified retroactively. We recalculate the dates of the month beginning from the 30th day, after the previous Rosh Chodesh, since the moon was sighted on the appropriate night.

The obvious question here is: why does the Rambam say that the witnesses should not undertake the journey unless they can arrive in time to sanctify the 30th day; for even if they come later, their testimony helps to overturn the decision of declaring a full month?

The sefer (סימן טז) "בני ציון" מהרב דוד שפירא offers a novel interpretation here to answer this question. The author, HaRav David Shapira, bases his assumption on the fact that the moon has to be sighted on the horizon in Yerushalayim. Given this condition, what the Rambam means here in Halacha I is not that there is a distance in traveling of more than a day, but rather if the moon was sighted a day or two further than from horizon of Yerushalayim, the witnesses should not go (not they should not come), for even if they were to arrive in time, their testimony would not be valid, since they sighted the moon *beyond the horizon of Yerushalayim*.

דהנה הרמב"ם לא כתב דאם **באו** עידי ראיה לאחר יום שלשים דאינה מועלת, רק כתב, "דאם" היה בינהן יתר ממהלך לילה ויום לא **ילכו** היינו משום דהראי' **לא מהני** רחוק מירושלים יותר ממהלך לילה ויום, משום דהמצות עשה המוטל על הסנהדרין לחשוב ולידע אם יראה הירח או לא הי' רק על אופק ירושלים ומהלך לילה ויום לכל צד...

V

DID MOSHE RABBENU RECEIVE PROPHECY AT NIGHT?

As we have previously discussed, Moshe Rabbenu was perplexed about the precise determination of the size of the new moon in order to qualify as appropriate to be sanctified. Therefore Hashem showed him the moon in the sky and said to him: "See it like this and sanctify it."

Rashi, citing the Mechilta, asks: But how could He have shown him the moon at night, when we are told that He did not communicate with Moshe at night, but rather only during the day?

והלא לא היה נדבר עמו אלא ביום. שנאמר: "ויהי **ביום** דבר ה'" (שמות ו:כח). "**ביום** צוותו" (ויקרא ז:לח). "מן **היום** אשר צוה ה' והלאה" (במדבר טו:כג), אלא סמוך לשקיעת החמה נאמרה לו פרשה זו והראהו עם חשכה.

For, indeed He did not communicate with Moshe except by day; as it says: "And it was on the *day* that Hashem spoke" *(Vayikra 7:38)*, "On the *day* of His commanding" *(Bamidbar 15:23)*, "from the *day* Hashem commanded and onward." *(Bamidbar 15:23)*."

All these pasukim show that Hashem only spoke to Moshe by day. How, then, did He speak to him at night, showing Moshe the moon and declaring, "See it like this"?

אלא סמוך לשקיעת החמה נאמרה לו פרשה זו, והראהו עם חשכה.

Rather, close to sunset this passage was told to him. And He showed the re-appearing moon to Moshe with the approach of darkness.

There seems to be a difference of opinion among the classical commentators regarding whether Moshe Rabbenu received his prophetic revelations only during the day or also at night.

THE OPINION OF THE IBN EZRA

The Ibn Ezra explains why the Torah portion dealing with the Menorah at the beginning of Parashas Behaloscha is placed next to the verse which states: "And Moshe went into the Tent of Meeting, that He might speak with him." This was in order to inform us that the Divine Communication came to Moshe also at night, for there the lamp would be burning and would not be extinguished."

ונסמכה זאת הפרשה [לסוף פרשת נשא] להורות כי הדבור יהיה **גם בלילה**, כי שם יהיה הנר דלוק ולא יכבה.

THE VIEW OF THE RAMBAN

The Ramban disagrees with this opinion of the אבן עזרא for it challenges what our Sages tell us, that the prophecy of Moshe Rabbenu took place only during the day (Mechilta).

ור"א...וזה איננו ככה על דעת רבותינו, שאמרו (מכילתא בא, א), והלא לא נדבר עמו אלא ביום, ואלו ידע ר"א מה בין נבואת משה לנבואת שאר הנביאים, לא חשב כן, והוא מה שאמר הכתוב (בהעלותך יב, ו, ז)...במראה אליו אתודע בחלום אדבר בו לא כן עבדי משה, שאין נבואתו בחלום, כי החלום בלילה ממש.

But this is not so according to our Sages, who say, "Did He not speak to Moshe only in the daytime?" And if Rabbi Abraham [Ibn Ezra] would have understood the difference between the prophecy experienced by Moshe and that of the other prophets, he would not have thought that the Divine communication came to Moshe Rabbenu also at night, as the Scripture states: "If there be a prophet among you, I, the Eternal, do not make Myself known to him in a vision, but I do speak to him in a dream. But concerning My servant Moshe, this is not so, for his prophecy was not through a dream, since dreams take place when it is night."

THE ABARBANEL DEFENDS THE IBN EZRA

The Abarbanel, however, defends the position of the Ibn Ezra by interpreting the words of Chazal, that Moshe's prophecy occurred by day, to mean that prophecy came to him while he was awake, in contrast to the revelations of the other prophets, whose prophecy came to them only when they were asleep. Abarbanel thus asserts that Moshe did in fact *receive prophecy at night*, but while he was awake.

ואומר אני שאין בזה קושיא כלל כי לא היה דעתם ז"ל בשלילות נבואתו בלילה, אלא להגיד שלא היתה נבואתו בחלום הלילה אלא בהקיץ והשתמשות חושיי וכמ"ש בחלום אדבר בו, לא כן עבדי משה, אבל נבואת בהקיץ מזולת חלום לא שללו חז"ל שתהיה למשה ביום ובלילה כי אם היה מנבא בכל עת שירצה יתחייב כי גם בלילה ברצותו לנבא תבואתו הנבואה...

QUESTIONING THE RAMBAN

Thus, according to the Ramban it would seem that Moshe's prophecy took place only during the day, and therefore the statement of the Mechilta that Moshe's prophecy took place only during the day was to be taken literally. This leads us to ask the following questions. The Rambam, as well as other commentators, point out that one of the differences between Moshe Rabbenu and the other prophets was that Moshe was able to prophesy at all times, "מתנבא בכל עת שירצה". This seems to include the night as well as the day. Also, the "שירת הים", the song of praise to Hashem which was sung by Moshe Rabbenu and Bnai Yisrael in the spirit of prophecy after the crossing of the Red Sea, was recited at night.

Chazal discuss the problem of how Moshe Rabbenu was able to distinguish between day and night when he was on Mount Sinai. This presupposes that he received prophecy at night as well as during the day throughout those forty days and forty nights.

The Gemara in *Shabbos 87a* tells us that Moshe Rabbenu initiated three actions on his own and Hashem subsequently concurred with him regarding those three acts. One of these was that he separated himself from his wife and abstained from marital relations. Moshe arrived at this idea through a קל וחומר, that is, he inferred a conclusion concerning a stringent case from a law applying to a lenient case. His reasoning was as follows. If Klal Yisrael, who received Divine revelation only once, at the time of the giving of the Torah, were instructed at that time to abstain from marital relations, how much more so must I remain in a state of purity by abstaining from marital relations, since Hashem can summon me at any moment. From this we can clearly see that Moshe was open to prophecy at any time, day or night; otherwise it would not have been necessary for him to separate from his wife.

A NEW INSIGHT REGARDING MOSHE'S PROPHECIES

Moshe Rabbenu received various types of prophecies. One type of prophecy contained a directive — a צווי from Hashem to teach a particular law to Bnai Yisrael. The second type of prophecy was an exclusively private revelation directed to Moshe Rabbenu himself. The Rambam defines this second type of prophecy as "נביא לעצמו", one to whom is revealed the mysteries and secrets of Torah, which are not to be disclosed to any other mortal. There were prophecies regarding how to lead Bnai Yisrael in their wanderings through the desert.

The first type of prophecy, teaching laws, are referred to as "דברות", instructions regarding the structure of a mitzva and how it is to be performed. This type of prophecy took place only during the day. This is the explanation of the words of the Mechilta: "והלא כל הדברות היו ביום" — "All *instruction* was given only during the day." The explanation for this is based on the fact that laws, משפטים, are only to be applied by the courts during the day. We learn this principle from the discussion in the Gemara *Sanhedrin 34a*, where it is stated that we know from the pasuk, "ביום הנחילו את בניו" that the laws of inheritance are negotiated by the Sanhedrin during the day. From here the Gemara derives the principle that *all laws* are administered only by day. Thus those prophecies which pertain to laws, those revelations which come under the category of "דברות", were revealed only during the day.

This is also the meaning behind the following statement in the "ספרא" (פרשת צו):

> אשר צוה ה' את משה בהר סיני ביום צוותו וגו' למדנו **לדברות** מדבר סיני אלא ביום. ומנין **לדברות** מצרים שלא נאמרו אלא ביום, שנאמר, ויהי היום דבר ה' אל משה בארץ מצרים. "ומנין **לדברות** אהל מועד" שלא נאמרו אלא ביום, תלמוד לומר: "במדבר סיני באהל מועד". מקיש **דברות** אהל מועד **לדברות** מדבר סיני. מה דברות מדבר סיני ביום אף דברות אהל מועד ביום.

Thus all the "דברות", the laws given to Moshe Rabbenu,

whether at Sinai, in Egypt or in the Tent of Meeting, אהל מועד, were given only during the day.

However, those matters which did not involve teaching laws to Bnai Yisrael were revealed to Moshe Rabbenu *even at night*. Consequently, all the above questions can be answered, for we find that when Moshe prophesied at night, this did not involve the teaching of laws.

This approach was anticipated by HaRav Chaim Paltiel, a disciple of Rav Meir of Rothenberg, in his classic sefer "פירוש התורה לר' חיים פלטיאל", which was printed from a manuscript in the year תשמ"א. There we find the following:

והקשה מ"ה [מורי הרבי] למה פירש משה מן האשה, והלא כל עליותיו שלו בהשכמה, ולא היתה שכינה מדברת עמו אלא ביום כדכתיב: ביום דבר ה' אל משה... ותירץ דוודאי לא דיבר עמו **במצוות** רק ביום, מיהו שאר דברים דיבר אפילו בלילה.

Therefore, when Rashi here asks how Hashem showed Moshe Rabbenu the moon during the day, he meant that since Torah law was only to be given by day, how could Hashem have spoken to Moshe at night and shown him the size of the moon which was to be sanctified, when this information was directly involved with halacha, which could only be revealed during the day?

VI

Is Rosh Chodesh one day or two?

As previously discussed, there are two methods of astronomical calculation. One is the calculation of the "מולד האמיתי" the precise moment of conjunction. And the other is called "מולד האמצעי", which is the moment of conjunction based on averaging the motion of the sun and the moon. This averaged month does not vary and its duration is: *29 days, 12 hours, 44 minutes, 793 chalakim.*

In *Chapter 8:3,* the Rambam writes:

> If a lunar month was exactly 28 and a half days long, the years would be divided evenly into full months (30 days) and months which were lacking a day (29 days), and there would be exactly 354 days to a lunar year. Thus, there would be six full months and six months which lacked a day. It is the units (חלקים) that exist in every month that exceed the half day, which ultimately adds up to hours and days and thus cause certain years to have more months which lack a day than months which are full, and other years which have more full months than months which lack a day.

THE RAMBAM'S EXPLANATION

The Rambam here continues to explain the phenomenon of whether Rosh Chodesh is one or two days.

> According to this reckoning, the 30th day is always established as Rosh Chodesh. [For a month consists of 29 days and 12 hours, and therefore the molad would be on the 30th day.]

If the previous month is lacking [has only 29 days], then the 30th day is Rosh Chodesh for the subsequent month. If, however, the previous month was full [had 30 days], then the incoming month will have *two days* of Rosh Chodesh. The 30th day will be Rosh Chodesh, since part of the day is actually Rosh Chodesh [as explained, every month consists of at least 29 days and 12 hours]. Nevertheless, it will be counted in the completion of the previous month, which was full. Thus the *31st* day was also designated as Rosh Chodesh, and from that day one counts the days of the coming month. This is the day established as Rosh Chodesh.

Thus, according to this calculation, there are some months that have only one day of Rosh Chodesh [the 30th day] and other months that have two days of Rosh Chodesh [the 30th and the 31st days of the month].

[הלכה ג]: אילו היה חדשה של לבנה תשעה ועשרים יום ומחצה בלבד, היו כל השנים חדש מלא וחדש חסר. ויהיו ימי שנת הלבנה שלש מאות וארבעה וחמשים, ששה חדשים חסרים וששה חדשים מלאים. אבל מפני החלקים שיש בכל חדש וחדש יותר על חצי היום, יתקבץ מהן שעות וימים, עד שיהיו מקצת השנים חדשים חסרים יותר על המלאים. ובמקצת השנים חדשים מלאים יותר על החסרים.

[הלכה ד]: יום שלשים לעולם עושין אותו ראש חדש בחשבון זה. אם היה החדש שעבר חסר יהיה יום שלשים ראש חדש הבא. ואם יהיה החדש שעבר מלא יהיה יום שלשים ראש חדש, הואיל **ומקצתו** ראש חדש, ויהיה תשלום החדש המלא שעבר, ויהיה יום **אחד ושלשים** ראש חדש הבא, וממנו הוא **המנין, והוא יום הקביעה**. ולפיכך עושין ראשי חדשים בחשבון זה, חדש אחד **יום אחד בלבד** וחדש אחד **שני ימים**.

Rosh Chodesh in the Era of Eyewitnesses

Thus we see that when the calendar month was "fixed" by means of calculation, there were one or two days of Rosh Chodesh.

The halachic question was raised regarding earlier times, when the months were determined by means of eyewitness reports of having seen the new moon. In those days, was there one day or two of Rosh Chodesh and how was this determined? The answer to this question is that there is a difference of opinion among the Rishonim regarding this issue.

THE OPINION THAT ROSH CHODESH WAS ONLY ONE DAY

At the end of the first chapter of Mesechtas Rosh Hashanah, the שלטי הגבורים clearly states that when the month was determined by eyewitnesses, there was always only one day of Rosh Chodesh.

> בזמן הזה, אנו נוהגים לעשות ראש חדש מלא שני ימים שמקדשין יום ל' ויום ל"א, ומתפללין בשניהן תפלת מוסף לפי שרוב פעמים המולד נולד ביום ל' אחר חצות ואי אפשר שתראה הלבנה בו ביום וראוי לקבוע בו. **ובימים הראשונים** לא היו עושין כן כמבואר בקונטרס הראיות בפ"ב של תענית.

RASHI'S VIEW

From Rashi's comments in *Mesechtas Baba Metzia 59b,* it is clear that he is of the opinion that only one day was observed even when a *full* month occurred. The Gemara relates an incident which demonstrates R' Eliezer's insistence that the halacha be decided according to his view, even though all the other Sages opposed it. As a result, he was excommunicated. Rabban Gamliel, the head of the Sanhedrin, authorized the excommunication of R' Eliezer. Then came the following episode.

Ima Shalom, the wife of R' Eliezer, was the sister of Rabban Gamliel. From that incident [in which Rabban Gamliel excommunicated R' Eliezer] onwards, she did not let R'Eliezer recite the Tachanun supplication [for she feared that if he recited it, her brother, Rabban Gamliel, would be harmed]. One day she thought that it was Rosh Chodesh, when the Tachanun supplication is not recited. However, she had confused a full month with a deficient one [She thought that the month just ending had 29 days, so that Rosh Chodesh would be fixed on the 30th day. Hence, she did not pay attention to her husband's prayers on that day, assuming that it was Rosh Chodesh and he would not say Tachanun. But in fact the month was a full month, so Rosh Chodesh fell on the 31st day. Thus R' Eliezer was able to say Tachanun unhindered on the 30th day.]

This is the explanation of the incident given here by Rashi. The question arises, if indeed the month was full [the previous month consisted of 30 days and Rosh Chodesh was on the 31st day] what does this matter? For even if the 31st day is designated as Rosh Chodesh, as we have explained, yet the 30th day would still be observed as Rosh Chodesh. Why, then, did R' Eliezer say Tachanun? The answer would appear to be that at the time of R' Eliezer, Rosh Chodesh day was still determined by eyewitnesses and only one day of Rosh Chodesh was observed in a full month. [See the commentary here of the מהרש"א, who describes this incident in a different way and concludes that according to his interpretation this does not prove the answer to our question.]

THE OPINION THAT ROSH CHODESH WAS TWO DAYS

The שבלי הלקט (סימן קסח) and the שו"ת תשב"ץ (חלק א, סימן קנג) were of the opinion that Rosh Chodesh was always observed for two days, even in the days when Rosh Chodesh was determined by eyewitnesses.

Their proof is based on the incident of Yonason planning to meet David in secret, as related in *The Book of Shmuel I: 27*.

> ויהי ממחרת החדש השני ויפקד מקום דוד, ויאמר שאול אל יהונתן בנו, מדוע לא בא בן ישי גם תמול גם היום אל הלחם.

> And it was on the morrow of the new moon, the second day [of Rosh Chodesh] that David's place was vacant, and Saul said to Yonason his son, "Why has not the son of Jesse come to the meal either yesterday or today?"

Yesterday was Rosh Chodesh, as indicated by the reading of the text here, and thus the next day is referred to as *the second day of Rosh Chodesh*. Thus we see clearly that even in the period of the Prophets, when the month was determined by eyewitnesses, they still celebrated *two* days of Rosh Chodesh.

Another Proof That Two Days Were Always Observed

The Gemara in *Ta'anis 29a* makes the following statement: "ראש חדש איקרי מועד" — "Rosh Chodesh is called a *moed* [a holiday]." This statement was based on an insight of Abbaye, who said:

> כדאמר אביי, תמוז דההיא שתא מלויי מלויה דכתיב, קרא עלי מועד לשבור בחורי.

> As Abbaye said: Tammuz of that year was declared a full month [of 30 days], as it is written, He had called upon me [Yerushalayim] an appointed time [moed] to shatter my young men.

Abbaye's statement refers to the spies who were sent to scout out the land of Yisrael *(Bamidbar 13:14)*. These spies were sent out on the 29th of Sivan, and they returned at the end of forty days. That year, Tammuz was determined by eye-witnesses, and all opinions concurred that two days of Rosh Chodesh were observed.

WHY TWO DAYS OF ROSH CHODESH?

Even if we were to maintain that when the new month was determined by the Sanhedrin, two days of Rosh Chodesh were observed, then the question would still arise, why was this necessary? There are two possible answers.

"מטעם ספק" — In the days when the month was determined by eye-witnesses, only those living in Yerushalayim would have known when Rosh Chodesh was declared by the Bais Din. Those who lived in the Disapora, however, would have to observe two days of Rosh Chodesh, since they were *in doubt* as to when Rosh Chodesh day actually occurred.

"מטעם תקנה" — The Mishna tells us in *Mesechtas Rosh Hashanah 30b*: "Originally, they accepted testimony all day [on the 30 th of Elul] concerning the new moon. It once transpired that the witnesses were delayed in coming, and the Levites went awry in the singing of the daily hymn. [i.e., they did not know whether to sing the weekday hymn or the hymn designated for Rosh Hashanah.] Consequently, the Sages instituted that the Bais Din should accept witnesses only until Mincha time. And if witnesses came after Mincha, they would observe that day [the 30th of Elul] and the following day [the 31st of Elul] as holy. In other words, when witnesses arrived after the Afternoon Sacrifice, the Korban Mincha, they would not be received and Rosh Hashanah would be deferred until the 31st. However, the Sages ordained that the rest of the 30th day would be observed as a yom tov, with work being prohibited.

For if this precaution was not taken, the people might fail to keep even the first part of the day holy in the following year.

This enactment of keeping two days seemed to apply only to Rosh Hashanah. Yet this enactment of not receiving witnesses after Mincha and thus observing two days also applied to every Rosh Chodesh day. Therefore, in those days when eyewitnesses determined the date of Rosh Chodesh, we also observed two days of Rosh Chodesh because of this particular enactment.

There is a disagreement of opinion among the Acharonim over whether the observance of two days is the result of "doubt" or of the Rabbinical "enactment".

THE OPINION OF THE "בנין אריאל"

The halacha states that if one fails to recite "יעלה ויבוא" on Rosh Chodesh, one must compensate for this by reciting the Amidah twice in the following prayer, once for the regular prayer and the second time, to make up for failing to say "יעלה ויבוא" in the previous Amidah. This practice raises the following question. If one failed to say "יעלה ויבוא" at Mincha on a day when Rosh Chodesh was only one day, can he make it up in the following Maariv evening prayer? The issue here is that at Maariv time it is no longer Rosh Chodesh and thus a recitation of "יעלה ויבוא" is not appropriate. The Rishonim express different opinions on this matter (see Chapter II for a discussion of the rationale behind their difference of opinion).

The Magen Avraham, in סימן קח, ס"ק ט"ו, maintains that this question only applies if Rosh Chodesh is one day. However, if we have a two-day Rosh Chodesh, then one could make up the prayer at night (for this would be the second day of Rosh Chodesh).

The Magen Avraham's decision is challenged in the sefer

"בנין אריאל" by HaRav Shaul of Amsterdam. The author there argues that even if Rosh Chodesh is two days, one should not offer a makeup prayer. The rationale behind this is that since we observe two days only because of the element of *doubt* as to whether Rosh Chodesh is really on the first or on the second day, therefore if we forgot to say "יעלה ויבוא" on the first day, and if the second day is Rosh Chodesh, the reader made no mistake, for today is not really Rosh Chodesh and thus a makeup prayer is not required. And if indeed *today* was really Rosh Chodesh and calls for a makeup prayer, then tomorrow (the 31st day of the month) is not Rosh Chodesh and so cannot be eligible to serve as a makeup prayer.

ובעיני דין זה תמוה דהאיך יאמר בלילה בתפלה השנית יעלה ויבוא, הלא תפלה זו באה בשביל תפלת המנחה של יום שעבר ששכח בה לומר יעלה ויבוא, ואם כן צריך לומר שהיום שעבר היה ראש חדש, ומשום הכי אותה תפלה ששכח לומר בה יעלה ויבוא היה כמאן דליתא. ואם כן האיך אפשר לומר יעלה ויבוא בתפלה זו, דליכא למימר יום שני כיון שיום ראשון היה ראש חדש, ואם יאמר יעלה ויבוא עכשיו, הרי הוא מחזיק את יום השני כראש חדש, ואז אין מקום לתפלה זו כל עיקר שהרי אינה באה אלא להשלים התפלה ששכח לומר בה יעלה ויבא ביום ראשון, וכיון שהוא רוצה לומר עכשיו יעלה ויבא לפי שראש חדש עכשיו הרי התפלל ביום ראשון כהוגן בלא יעלה ויבוא ושוב אין צריך להשלים תפלה זו...

The opinion of the צל"ח

The צל"ח, in his commentary on *Mesechtas Berachos 26b*, defends the decision of the Magen Avraham. The צל"ח contends that observing Rosh Chodesh for two days is not based on the consideration that we are in doubt as to which day is actually Rosh Chodesh. Rather it is because of the enactment of not accepting witnesses on the 30th day from Minchah and onwards, which applies to every Rosh Chodesh. This means that both the 30th and the 31st days are indeed Rosh Chodesh, and therefore the decision of the Magen Avraham is valid.

> ואני אומר שהתקנה שתיקנו שלא יהי מקבלים עדות החודש אלא עד המנחה...מפני שנתקלקלו הלוים היא לא על חדש תשרי לבד היתה כי אם על כל חדשי השנה שבכלם שייך תקלה זו שבודאי שבכל ראש חדש היה שיר ובפרט לדברי הרמב"ם בפ"ג מקידוש החדש שהתקלה היתה בקרבן מוסף, פשיטא ששייך בכל החדשים...

The insight of the "אור גדול"

The "אור גדול" מהגדול ממינסק (סימן נח) also agrees that we observe Rosh Chodesh for two days, not because of doubt but rather because of the fact that the 30th day is always Rosh Chodesh because the מולד always occurs on this day.

> גם בזמנם שהיו מקדשים על פי הראי' גם כן היו עושין יום ל' ראש חודש מפני חשבון המולד, וכמ"ש הראשונים הנ"ל, דאם לא כן מפני מה נשתנה בזמן הזה לעשות בכה"ג ב' ימים ראש חודש ולאוסרם בתרוייהו בתענית ובהספד, על כרחך נראה לכאורה עיקר כרבינו ישעי' וכרבינו שלמה, והשבלי הלקט, שכן הי' נהוג אף בזמן שהיו מקדשים על פי הראי'...

VII

The Bais Din Determines the New Month

Designating the new month is the exclusive right of the Bais

Din. We know this from the verse in *Vayikra 23:4* which states:

אלה מועדי ה' מקראי קדש אשר תקראו אתם.

These are the festivals of Hashem, holy convocations *which you shall declare.*

In *Mesechtas Rosh Hashanah 25a,* Rashi comments as follows:

אשר תקראו: בקריאת בית דין תלאו הכתוב.

When the verse states "which you shall declare", it indicates that the matter [of designating the day of Rosh Chodesh and the holy days] is totally dependent on the declaration of the Bais Din.

And so the שאילתות דרב אחאי גאון points out that based on this expression "תקראו" — "you shall declare them", we find that the determination of Rosh Chodesh and the leap year are dependent on the declaration of the Bais Din.

We find that the words "תקראו אותם" are written twice in *Parashas Emor (Vayikra 23:2 and 23:4),* and in verse 4 Rashi comments that the first verse speaks of adding a month to the year and the verse here speaks of sanctifying the moon:

אלה מועדי: למעלה מדבר בעבור שנה וכאן מדבר בקדוש החדש.

The שאילתות states, in שאילתא מט:

דמחייבין בית ישראל למיקבע ירחי ולקדושינהו ולתקוני מועדי ובבי דינא תליא מילתא למיקבעיה לירחא לחסוריה

ולעבוריה, דכתיב, אלא מועדי ה' אשר תקראו אתם מקראי קדש, מדקאמר "תקראו" למימרא דבידכו תליא מילתא.

And the Netziv, in his classic commentary "העמק שאלה" on the שאילתות, writes that even though the determination of the new moon is dependent on the molad, the appearance of the new moon and the determination of leap years are dependent on the calculation of the spring season according to the solar year, yet the Torah handed over to the Bais Din the jurisdiction to declare a new month and a leap year.

ר"ל אע"ג דקה"ח תלי' במולד הלבנה, ועיבור השנה תלי' בחשבון האביב לפי שנות החמה, מכל מקום נמסר לבית דין כידוע מדרשם בראש השנה כ"ה, תקראו אתם, אתם אפילו שוגגין אתם אפילו מזידין...

The opinion of the ריטב"א

The ריטב"א contends that if the Bais Din does not designate Rosh Chodesh day then the subsequent holy days can not be observed. He bases this contention on a statement in *Mesechtas Chullin 101b*, that "One year there was a purge against religious practice by the government and they did not allow Rosh Chodesh day to be declared by the Sages. Consequently, they sent word from Eretz Yisrael that the Day of Atonement of that year should be observed on Shabbos day". Thus, even though Shabbos day was not the correct date for Yom Kippur, it was transferred to Shabbos day, so that they would not forget to observe the day of Yom Kippur. From this we can see that if the Bais Din does not declare Rosh Chodesh day, then Yom Kippur, as well as the other holidays, cannot be observed as prescribed by the Torah.

ומפרש הריטב"א שם...דשעת גזירה היה שגזרו שלא

לעשות יום הכפורים ולא עשה באותה שנה יום הכפורים
בעשור וקבעוהו בשבת, ואף על פי שאינו בעשור, וכדי שלא
תשכח תורת יום הכפורים, והאויבים לא יכירו בו משום דכל
שבת לא עבדי מלאכה...

This prompts Tosafos to ask, how is it possible that Yom Kippur day was not observed, but was rather dispensed with, when we have a rule that if any coercion is exerted against us, even to change the color of our shoelaces, for religious purposes, we are commanded to forfeit our lives rather than capitulate. Therefore if they tried to nullify Yom Kippur day in order to persecute us, we should have observed Yom Kippur even if it meant that we would lose our lives.

The ריטב"א dismisses this question and answers that the declaration of Rosh Chodesh is a positive commandment, and the law reads that for the sake of preserving a positive commandment we do not have to forfeit our lives. This, then, explains why Yom Kippur was never declared in that year.

והקשו בתוספות, האיך אפשר שבטלו יום הכפורים בשעת
גזירה, הא בשעת גזירה אפי' אערקתא' דמסני' יהרג
ואל יעבור...ונראה לי [הריטב"א] דהא לא קשיא, דקידוש
חדשים דבית דין עשה הוא, ועל עשה יעבור ואל יהרג...
ואפשר דהכי גזרו אומות העולם לבית דין שלא **לקדשו**
דאין כאן יום הכפורים.

VIII

Sanctifying the day of Rosh Chodesh

After the witnesses were interrogated and subsequently accepted as valid, the Bais Din would declare the month sanctified

— "מקודש". The significance of this ceremony, and its purpose and function, is a matter of dispute among the Tana'aim in *Mesechtas Rosh Hashanah, 24a.*

> ראש בית דין אומר: מקודש, וכל העם עונין אחריו: מקודש מקודש. בין שנראה בזמנו בין שלא נראה בזמנו מקדשין אותו ר' אליעזר בר' צדוק אומר: אם לא נראה בזמנו אין מקדשין אותו שכבר קידושהו שמים.

The head of the Bais Din says: "It is sanctified." And all the people respond after him: "It is sanctified! It is sanctified!" Whether the new moon appeared at its expected time [on the 30th day] or whether it did not appear at its expected time, they sanctified it.

R' Eliezer ben Tzaddok says: "If it did not appear at its expected time, [on the 30th day] they do not sanctify, for it has already been sanctified by Heaven."

The Gemara then cites a Baraisa:

> תניא פלימו אומר: בזמנו אין מקדשין, שלא בזמנו מקדשין אותו. ר' אלעזר (בר' שמעון) אומר: בין כך ובין כך אין מקדשין אותו שנאמר "וקדשתם את שנת החמשים", שנים אתה מקדש ואי אתה מקדש חדשים.

It was taught in a Baraisa: Plimo says, if the moon was sighted at its appropriate time, they do not sanctify Rosh Chodesh, but if the moon was not seen at its appropriate time, they sanctify Rosh Chodesh.

We have here three different opinions:

R' Elazar, the son of Shimon, contends that we never sanctify the moon, either on the 30th or the 31st day of the month. Rather the mitzva of sanctifying only applies to the Jubilee year, יובל. And the Yerushalmi explains that when the Mishna cites the practice of the head of the Bais Din declaring "מקודש, מקודש", this does not mean "to sanctify" but rather "מקויים", that the Bais Din *confirms* and *designates* this day as Rosh Chodesh.

The opinion of the Tanna Kamma is that the Bais Din declared the month sanctified, whether the moon appeared on time, and thus the 30th day is designated as Rosh Chodesh, or whether the moon did not make its appearance by the 30th day and consequently, the month automatically began on the 31st day. In either case, the Torah declared, "מקראי קדש", that it is a mitzva to pronounce Rosh Chodesh day, whenever it occurs, as sanctified.

R'Elazar bar Tzadok is of the opinion that Rosh Chodesh was declared on the 30th day, since it is the Bais Din who declares this day as Rosh Chodesh. Therefore, they also sanctify the month. On the 31st day, however, they no longer have the jurisdiction to determine this day as Rosh Chodesh, for since a month can never be longer than 30 days, and in addition on the 31st day the "Heavenly Court" declares this day sanctified, thus the Bais Din cannot justifiably declare, "מקודש, מקודש" — "be sanctified!"

Based on what we have delineated above, it is not surprising to find the following question raised in the sefer "כלי חמדה" (מהרב מאיר דן פלאצקי, פרשת בא). Since the conclusion of the Gemara just cited is that the halacha follows the opinion of R'Elazar bar Tzadok, that if the Bais Din does not declare the 30th day sanctified, then the 31st day automatically becomes sanctified. Why, then, does the Ritba contend that if the Bais Din does not declare a day of Rosh Chodesh, all the subsequent holy days can not take place, since each of the holy days falls on a prescribed calendar date, and since we do not have the first day of the month, then we can not determine the tenth day (Yom Kippur) or the fifteenth day (Pesach).

והרי ההלכה כר"א בר' צדוק, בר"ה כד, א, דאם אין בית דין מקדשין אותו בזמנו הרי זה מעובר, ואם כן מאי נפקא מיניה בזה שלא קידשוהו בית דין את החודש, הא מכל מקום יום הכפור הוא בעשרה בתשרי רק דההחודש הוא מעובר ומדברי הריטב"א ז"ל נראה דאם אין הבי"ד מקדשין את החודש, אין כאן חודש תשרי כלל...וממילא אין כאן יום כפור, וזה תימא.

IX

WHAT IS MEANT BY "קידשוהו שמים"?

The Gemara in *Mesechtas Sanhedrin 10b* cites the opinion of R' Elazar, the son of R' Tzadok, that on the 31st day no sanctification is needed by the Bais Din, for it has already been sanctified in heaven.

We have several opinions as to when exactly the Heavenly Court sanctifies the new month.

RASHI'S OPINION

Rashi, in *Mesechtas Sanhedrin (ibid.)* writes as follows:

שכבר קדשוהו בשמים: בית דין שלמעלה מאתמול.

Anticipating that no court would sanctify the 30th day as Rosh Chodesh, the Heavenly Court sanctified the 31st day in advance on the 30th day.

THE OPINION OF TOSAFOS

Tosafos cites several opinions as to exactly when this Heavenly sanctification takes place:

יש מפרשים דבית דין של מעלה מקדשין אותו לעולם בשעת המולד.

Some explain that this sanctification takes place at the moment of conjunction (the time of the appearance of the molad).

Tosafos himself rejects this opinion, for if it is true, then this heavenly sanction should also be acceptable when Rosh Chodesh occurs on the 30th day. Therefore, Tosafos contends that if the Bais Din did not declare the 30th day as Rosh Chodesh, then the Heavenly Court does so *on the morning of the 31st*. According to this view, a verbal declaration of sanctification is always necessary. On the 30th day this is done by the Bais Din on earth, and on the 31st day, by the Heavenly Court.

ANSWERING THE QUESTION OF THE "כלי חמדה"

Based on what we have outlined here, we can now appreciate some of the answers given to solve the problem posed by the "כלי חמדה" of how the Ritba can say that if the Bais Din does not declare Rosh Chodesh, then there can be no Yomin Tovim, when we know that the month may be declared by the Heavenly Court. In fact, the "כלי חמדה" himself points out that the Bais Din on High would sanctify the month only if it is possible for a human Bais Din to be able to do so. However, if a human Bais Din can not sanctify the month, then a Heavenly court does not act.

R' Yaacov Moshe Charlap ("ונצדק הצדיק" בקנטרס ,ח"ג ,"בית זבול"
סימן מב, אות ב) maintains that automatically sanctifying the 31st day of the month can take place only in order to determine Rosh Chodesh day. However, determining a day of Yom Tov requires that a human Bais Din declare Rosh Chodesh, as the pasuk indicates:

אלה מועדי ה' אשר **תקראו אותם** מקראי קדש במועדם.

These are the holy days that *you* declare as holy convocations in their prescribed times.

דאע"פי שקביעת החדש נעשה מאיליו אין זה אלא לקביעיות החודש בלבד, אבל לענין קידוש המועדות דכתיב "אלה מועדי ה' אשר תקראו אותם מקראי קדש במועדם" לא סגי בלא שישראל יקדשינהו לזמנם פה למטה על פי בית דין ועד כאן לא קאמר ר' אלעזר בר' צדוק שלא בזמן אין מקדשין אותו אלא בשאר החדשים אבל בניסן בתשרי ודאי מקדשין משום המועדות, דלגבי המועדות לא סגי במה שכבר קדשוהו שמים...

HaRav Yaacov Betzalel Zolti, in his sefer "משנת יעבץ" (אור"ח סימן כה) offers the following answer. There are two laws which determine the designation of Rosh Chodesh day. One of these involves the determining and designating of Rosh Chodesh day, and the second involves sanctifying the day of Rosh Chodesh. This is accomplished by offering an additional (Mussaf) sacrifice on the altar and by singing a special hymn which is different from the usual psalm of the day (שיר של יום).

Thus the 31st day, although it was not sanctified by the Bais Din declaring "מקודש" was nevertheless given the *consent* of the Bais Din that this day be designated as Rosh Chodesh day.

This insight is based on the contention of the Ramban, cited in the Sefer HaMitzvos (מצוה קנג) that Kiddush HaChodesh, declaring the day of Rosh Chodesh sanctified, is only a *desired* mitzva but not a *decisive* one. On the other hand, the *consent of the Bais Din in designating* this day is itself decisive — מעכב.

ואני סובר שאין קידוש החודש מעכב ולא הצריכו חכמים לומר מקודש אלא שהוא מצוה או לפירסומי מילתא בעלמא, אבל מכיון שהסכימה דעת בית דין שיהי' החדש הזה מלא או חסר קורא אני בו אשר תקראו אותם, שהרי ר' אלעזר בר' צדוק אומר בין מלא בין חסר אין מקדשין אותו...ור' אלעזר בר' צדוק שהלכה כמותו אמר אם לא נראה בזמנו אין מקדשין אותו אלמא אין קדוש מעכב. וכן אמרו שמצוה לקדש על פי הראיה ואינה מעכב...ומה שאמרו (ב"ב קכ"א) מועדי ה' צריכין קדוש בית דין, זהו למצוה. אי נמי צריכים בית דין קאמר לחשוב בהן **ולהסכים** בהן אם מלאים אם חסרים...

X

The Opinions of the Meiri, Rabbenu Yona and the Chiddushei HaRan

Other Rishonim contend that the statement of "שכבר קדשוהו שמים" is to be understood in a different way. That no actual sanctification took place in the Heavenly Court, but since a month can not be more than 30 days, the 31st day automatically becomes Rosh Chodesh. Thus there is no need for even the consent of the Bais Din to designate this day as Rosh Chodesh. So writes the Rabbenu Yona *(ibid.):*

פי' כיון שלא בזמנו אינו תלוי בדעת בית דין ואינו צריך קדוש מפני **שממילא** הוא מקודש, **וקידש שמים** היא שאין החדש יכול לפחת עוד. אבל אם נראה ביום שלשים יכולים לקדשו מפני שהדבר תלוי בדעתם שאם יקדשו מקודש ואם לאו אינו מקודש בפרק אין מכירין, אשר תקראו אותם במועדם אפילו שוגגים ואפילו אנוסים, ואפילו מוטעין.

And the Ran writes:

שכבר קדשוהו שמים, כלומר, שאין צריכין לומר ביום ל"א
מקודש מקודש לקדש החודש השני, שממילא היא מקודש,
דלעולם אין לך חודש יותר משלשים יום...

And similarly, the Meiri states:

קדשוהו שמים: רצה לומר, שמאיליו הוא מתקדש ואין
צריך קדוש בי"ד וברור כדבריו.

Thus we must say that the Ritba disagrees with their interpretation of "קדשוהו שמים", that Rosh Chodesh day occurs automatically. Rather he holds the same opinion as does the Ramban, namely that even though no sanctification is required on the 31st day, since the day is automatically sanctified by Heaven, yet positive consent by the Bais Din is required. Thus, since in that particular year when the government prevented the Bais Din from sanctifying the new month, there was no Yom Tov.

THE CONSEQUENCES OF THESE DIFFERENT OPINIONS

There are definite practical differences here to be found among the opinions we have outlined above by the Ba'alei Tosafos and the "יש מפרשים". For example, the law states that if we forgot to recite "יעלה ויבוא" on Rosh Chodesh night, one is not required to repeat the Amidah prayer, for the Bais Din does not sanctify the new month at night. However, the Ba'alei Tosafos, in *Mesechtas Berachos 30b,* cite the opinion of the "יש מפרשים", that some maintain that only on the first night of Rosh Chodesh do we say that one need not repeat the Amidah prayer if one forgot to say "יעלה ויבוא". However, if there are two days of Rosh Chodesh, then on the second night one would have to repeat the Amidah prayer if he forgot to say "יעלה ויבוא". However, the Ba'alei Tosafos contend "ולא נראה לחלק" — there is no difference between whether one forgot on the first or second night of Rosh Chodesh; one need not repeat the Amidah prayer on either day.

Therefore, we might say that the opinions we have discussed here are dependent on the version cited in *Mesechtas Sanhedrin, 10b,* that the 31st day is sanctified in Heaven, "שכבר קידשוהו בשמים". The commentary "יש מפרשים", which contends that one need not repeat the Amidah if one forgot to recite "יעלה ויבוא" on the second night of Rosh Chodesh, supports this opinion by interpreting the statement in Sanhedrin to mean that the month was sanctified in heaven from the molad on the previous day. Consequently, on the night of the 31st, Rosh Chodesh was *already in effect* and therefore a repetition is certainly required. However, the Ba'alei Tosafos in Berachos, who maintain that no repetition is required, base this opinion on their interpretation of the version in Sanhedrin that the month is sanctified on the morning of the 31st. This means that the previous evening was not yet Rosh Chodesh, and therefore neglecting to recite "יעלה ויבוא", even on the second night of Rosh Chodesh, does not require a repetition of the Amidah.

Further discussion of this issue can be found in the "אור שמח" (הלכות תפלה, פרק י, הלכה יא), and in the sefer (סימן סב) "תורת רפאל".

XI

Which Takes Precedence: Eyewitnesses or Calculation?

We see that there are a number of methods for determining the new month. Which one are we to adopt and which takes precedence over the others? The answer to these questions involves a difference of opinion among the Rishonim, particularly between Rabbenu Saadia Gaon and the Rambam. These divergent opinions can be presented as follows.

Rabbenu Saadia Gaon and Rabbenu Chananel maintain that we are to determine the new month by calculation, חשבון.

עיקר מצות קביעת החדש על פי החשבון ולא על פי הראיה.

The Rambam's position is that both methods are rooted in a halacha given to Moshe Rabbenu at Sinai, הלכה למשה מסיני, which stipulates that when the Sanhedrin functioned to determine Kiddush HaChodesh, it based this determination on the account of eyewitnesses, קידוש על פי הראיה. However, now that the Sanhedrin no longer exists, and it is no longer possible to see the moon, we must determine new months based on calculations handed down from the time of Moshe Rabbenu.

Some Rishonim consider that it was only the determination of the new month *by eyewitnesses* that was a halacha from Moshe at Sinai, and in contrast, determining the new month by means of calculation, as we do it today, was introduced by Hillel Ha Nasi.

The opinion of Rabbenu Saadia Gaon, the רס"ג

Rabbenu Saadia's Gaon's opinion, that determination of our calendar was by means of calculation, is articulated in his responsa, and in particular his opinion is cited in the classic commentary of Rabbenu Bachya in *Parashas Bo*. There Rabbenu Chananel is said to maintain that Klal Yisrael adopted the method of חשבון, calculation, rather than eyewitnesses to determine the new month. He presents two proofs for this contention. How was it possible, he asks, to have determined the new month by means of eyewitnesses during the forty year period when Bnai Yisrael traveled in the desert, when the heavenly clouds and the pillar of fire covered the moon. From this fact we must conclude that Rosh Chodesh was determined by means of calculation.

In addition, in דברי הימים (יב, לג) we find described the uniqueness of the tribe of Yissachar

ומבני יששכר יודעי בינה לעתים לדעת מה יעשה ישראל.

From the sons of Yissachar, those with profound understanding of the times so they know what Yisrael should do...

The commentators (see both the רד״ק and the מצודות here) cite the interpretation of the Sages that this phrase refers to the tribe of Yissachar's special talent for astronomy. They were able to calculate the seasons and balance the lunar with the solar calendar, as well as being able to determine the precise moment of the molad for each month. These calculations were adopted by Klal Yisrael and they determined the date of Rosh Chodesh. Now, contends Rabbenu Chananel, if eyewitnesses are the ones who determined Rosh Chodesh, why was the tribe of Yissachar praised so highly for their expertise in calculation, when it was "קידוש על פי הראיה" that determined the month, and this process required no expertise?

To resolve this question, we must consider that from the time Bnai Yisrael left Egypt until the days of Antignous, Bnai Yisrael never determined the new month by means of eyewitnesses, rather everything was determined by calculation, על פי החשבון. However, Antignous had two rebellious students, צדוק וביתוס, who cast aspersions on the method of calculation, and therefore it became necessary to prove the validity of Antignous' calculations in order to show that the allegations of these two students were wrong. To accomplish this, Rabban Gamliel brought forth pictures of the moon and he asked eyewitnesses if they were comparable to the new moon they had seen. Yet despite this, the month was still determined essentially by calculation.

וכתב רבינו חננאל ז"ל קביעת החדשים אינה אלא על פי החשבון ולא על פי ראיית הלבנה והראיה. שכל ארבעים שנה שהיו ישראל במדבר היה הענן מכסה אותם יומם ועמוד האש לילה, ולא ראה בכולם שמש ביום ולא ירח בלילה...ומהיכן היו קובעין על פי ראיית הלבנה, אלא **ודאי עיקר המצוה בכתוב על פי חשבון**...

ומפורש תמצא בכתוב "ומבני יששכר יודעי בינה לעתים לדעת מה יעשה ישראל ראשיהם מאתים וכל אחיהם על פיהם", ואין לך דבר שצריך חכמה ובינה לקבוע עתים ומועדים כי אם החשבון שהוא סוד העיבור, אבל ראיית הלבנה דבר ידוע, כי כשהלבנה נראית הכל יודעין שהוא ראש חודש...אבל החשבון אינו אלא לחכמים מחשבין ומודיעין לישראל והם עושין על פיהן... כך היו נוהגים כל ישראל לקבוע חדשים על פי החשבון אלף ומאה שנים מימות משה רבינו ועד אנטיגנוס ראש גולה וראש סנהדרין, והיו בכלל תלמידיו שנים, והם צדוק וביתוס...

והתחילו לעורר בזה בקביעת הירח, ואמרו כי אין עיקר המצוה לקבוע חדשים על פי החשבון כי אם בראיית הלבנה והוא הדבר הצודק והמכוון, והוצרכו חכמי הדור להכחיש דבריהם ולהודיע להם בראיות גמורות, וכן אמרו זכרונם לברכה, כך אמר רבן גמליאל אל תחושו לראית הירח, החשבון הוא העיקר, כך מקובלני מבית אבי אבא שאין חדשה של לבנה פחותה מכ"ט יום ומחצה ותשצ"ג חלקים. והנה דברים הללו מוכיחין שלא היה רבן גמליאל סומך על ראיית הלבנה כי אם על פי החשבון...ומה שתמצא לרז"ל, דמות צורות לבנות היו לרבן גמליאל בעלייתו על הטבלא בכותל שבהן הי' מראה אתה הדייטות הכוונה בזה, כי רבן גמליאל עשה צורות הללו לבאר לתלמידי צדוק וביתוס ידיעתו במהלך הלבנה בכל חדש וחדש, וכי הוא יודע בכל חדש וחדש באיזה צורה תולד, אם בארוכה אם קצרה... נתבאר להן שאין העיקר אלא החשבון, ובטלו דברי החולקים, ואע"פ שהיו מקבלים העדים זכר לדבר, לא היו סמיכת בית דין כי אם על החשבון...

This opinion of Rabbenu Chananel can be traced to Raabenu Saadia Gaon (see "תורה שלמה" כרך יד, פרק ג, עמ' מא).

THE RAMBAM'S OPINION

The Rambam, in his commentary to the Mishna, *Rosh Hashanah 2:6* dismisses this contention of Rav Saadia Gaon:

ואני מתפלא על אדם [היינו רבינו סעדיה גאון] שמכחיש ומתוכח בדבר ברור ואומר שדת היהודים אינו בנוי על ראיית החדש אלא על החשבון בלבד...

The Rambam himself is of the opinion that when we have a functioning Sanhedrin, then Kiddush HaChodesh is established by means of eyewitnesses, "על פי הראייה". However, if the Sanhedrin is no longer functioning, then we apply the method of calculation, חשבון, to determine Rosh Chodesh. Thus the Rambam writes as follows in *Hilchos Kiddush HaChodesh 5:2*:

ודבר זה הלכה למשה מסיני הוא: שבזמן שיש סנהדרין קובעין על פי הראיה. ובזמן שאין שם סנהדרין קובעין על פי החשבון הזה שאנו מחשבין בו היום, ואין נזקקין לראיה.

The calendar based on the sighting of the crescent of the new moon continued throughout the period when the Bais HaMikdash stood, and for a considerable period thereafter. There came a time, however, when persistent oppression by Roman rulers prevented the Sanhedrin from being able to function, and consequently, in the days of Abaye and Rava, the fixed calendar of Hillel II was established. It is this calendar we follow to this day. The Rambam discourses on this in *Chapter 5, Halacha 3*, where he writes:

ומאימתי התחילו כל ישראל לחשב בחשבון זה? מסוף חכמי הגמרא, בעת שחרבה ארץ ישראל, ולא נשאר שם בית דין קבוע. אבל בימי חכמי המשנה, וכן בימי חכמי הגמרא עד ימי אביי ורבא על קביעת ארץ ישראל היו סומכין.

THE OPINION OF THE RAMBAN

The Ramban challenges the opinion of the Rambam by asking where is his source for saying that there exists a halacha of Moshe from Sinai — הלכה למשה מסיני — that when the Sanhedrin was functioning we determined the month by means of eyewitnesses and when there was no Sanhedrin, we apply the means of calculation? We do not find such a law mentioned anywhere in the Talmud, asserts the Ramban. He articulates this view in his commentary on the Sefer HaMitzvos of the Rambam, in מצות קנג:

נתקשה לו [הרמב"ם] עוד העניין ושם הדבר מסורת וקבלה והלכה למשה מסיני מה שלא נאמר בתלמוד ולא הוזכר בו בשום מקום...

The Ramban writes that it was Hillel the Nasi, the son of R' Yehudah the Nasi, who established all of the future months until the time when Moshiach will appear.

אבל מרפא הקושיא הגדול הזה הוא שרבי הלל הנשיא בנו של רבי יהודה הנשיא שתקן חשבון העבור, הוא קדש חדשים ועבר שנים הראויים להתעבר לפי מניינו עד שיבוא אליהו ונחזור לקדשנו על פי הראייה בב"ד בבית הגדול והקדוש...

XII

QUESTIONING THE POSITION OF RAV SAADIA GAON

The position of Rav Saadia Gaon raises many questions and leads to many proofs being offered in its support. For some of these questions and proofs, see the sefer "תורה שלמה" מהרב מנחם כשר (כרך יג, עמ' 45), and see also my sefer (עמ' עה-עח) "תפארת למשה". For the purposes of this discussion, however, we will focus on one of the most salient questions which is raised to refute the position of Rav Saadia Gaon.

We are told that during the forty-year journey of Bnai Yisrael in the desert, the calendar was determined by calculation, חשבון, rather than on eyewitnesses. (See "שו"ת זרע אברהם" מהרב אברהם לופטביר, סימן ו' אות כב.)

The Tosefta in *Mesechtas Rosh Hashanah (Chapter 1, Halacha 10)* tells us:

וכן אתה מוצא בעומר של מן, אם בא חדש בזמנו, מיד הוא כלה, ואם לאו, מתעכב הוא לג' ימים.

As the Torah states, the manna did not "rain down" on Shabbos day; therefore on Friday, erev Shabbos, a double portion was given, intended to last for two days, Friday and Shabbos. Therefore the Mishna here informs us that if Rosh Hashanah falls out on the 30th day of Elul, (since Elul is a month of only 29 days, חסר, and the 30th day is the first of Tishrei), then the manna would have lasted two days, that is, Erev Rosh Hashanah and the day of Yom Tov. This is similar to the situation on erev Shabbos, when Bnai Yisrael were provided with a double portion, since the manna did not come down on Shabbos.

However, if Rosh Hashanah were to fall on the 31st, which means that Rosh Hashanah was observed for two days, then the manna would last for *three* days. Thus, as Rav Saadia Gaon maintains, if during the forty years when Bnai Yisrael found themselves in the desert they determined the new moon by means of calculation, then why would they have determined two days of Rosh Hashanah? We must conclude that even while in the desert, the month was determined by eyewitnesses. This refutes the contention of the רס"ג.

HaRav Yechezkiel Abramsky, in his classic commentary to the Tosefta here dismisses this question and maintains that even though the months were determined by calculation, it was still possible to observe two days of Rosh Hashanah. This would occur, when the Bais Din itself debated whether the calculation required that the 30th day be observed as Rosh Hashanah. Their discussion lasted the entire 30th day and they did not come to a final decision as to when to declare Rosh Hashanah day. Consequently, Rosh Hashanah was determined to fall on the 31st day. Thus we can understand how two days were observed even when the month was determined by means of calculation.

ואולי יש לומר שאפילו בזמן שקובעין ר"ח על פי חשבון
משכחת לן במקרה ראש השנה שני ימים, כגון שנשאו ונתנו
כל יום השלשים על עצם החשבון אם לקבוע ראש חודש
היום או למחר, ומספק נהגו היום קדש, ואחרי כן באו לידי
הסכם בחשבונם לקבוע ראש חדש למחר, או שמצאו אחר
כך צורך לעבר את החדש... ונמצא ראש חדש שני ימים.

CHALLENGING THE RAMBAM'S POSITION

There are a number of issues to be considered before determining on what day Rosh Hashanah should occur. These considerations could bring about a postponement of Rosh Hashanah by one or even two days. These postponements are referred to as "דחיות". There are several applications of this concept of "דחיות"; however we will confine ourselves to a discussion of that application which relates to our present subject. This "דחיות" is called "לא אדו ראש", which means that Rosh Hashanah day can never fall on a Sunday (יום א), Wednesday (יום ד), or a Friday (יום ו). The reason for this postponement is that if Rosh Hashanah falls on a Sunday, then the festival of Hoshanah Rabbah, which is celebrated on the seventh day of Succos, will fall on Shabbos. The festival of Hoshanah Rabbah includes the beating of the willow twigs, ערבה. Since this custom was forbidden on Shabbos day, an enactment was instituted to ensure that Hoshanah Rabbah never falls on a Shabbos. This is what is meant by the saying "לא א(דו) ראש".

If Rosh Hashanah falls on a Wednesday (ד), then the tenth of Tishrei, Yom Kippur, would fall on a Friday. This would cause a great deal of inconvenience and would bring about unsanitary consequences. For now we would have two consecutive days, on which work is forbidden (Shabbos and Yom Kippur). This means that vegetables which were intended for food would decompose and so too would dead bodies remaining buried for this length of time — "משום ירקא ומתיא".

Thus it would seem that the "דחיות", including that involving "לא אדו ראש" only applies when the calendar was determined by calculation (see the "לחם משנה" פרק א, הלכה ח, מהלכות תמידים ומוספין).

When eyewitnesses determined Rosh Chodesh and Rosh Hashanah, these considerations did not apply. Consequently, we are left with the following question.

The Mishna in *Rosh Hashanah 1:3* tells us that on six specific months messengers were dispatched to inform the Jewish communities which day had been declared as Rosh Chodesh. One of these months was Elul — "על אלול מפני ראש השנה". Since the month of Elul always consisted of 29 days, when the people knew when Rosh Chodesh Elul was to occur, they would then know that 29 days later would be Rosh Hashanah, on the first of Tishrei.

The Mishna then tells us that messengers were dispatched in order to inform the people when the beginning of Tishrei would occur. Once they had this information, they would then know that Yom Kippur was ten days later and Succos was fifteen days later. This leads the Gemara to ask the obvious question: If messengers went out for Rosh Chodesh Elul and Elul was only 29 days, and thus the 30th day was Rosh Hashanah, why did they need to dispatch messengers for the month of Tishrei (in order to ensure that Yom Kippur and Succos would be celebrated at their prescribed times), when we already knew when Rosh Hashanah was by the testimony of the witnesses for the month of Elul?

The Gemara answers this question by saying that Elul is *usually* 29 days. However, if the need arises then there is a possibility for it to have 30 days and then Rosh Hashanah would occur on the 31st day. Therefore it was necessary to inform the people which day was Rosh Hashanah, whether the 30th or the 31st. And from then, ten and fifteen days were counted to ensure that Yom Kippur and Succos would be observed on their prescribed days.

This prompts Tosafos to ask: If we apply here the theory of "לא אדו ראש", then why do we need messengers to determine whether Elul was 29 or 30 days. For surely the Jews in golus had a method by which they could calculate when Rosh Hashanah day would occur. For example, if the 29th day of Elul would fall on a Shabbos, then everyone would realize that the 30th day can not be Rosh Hashanah, due to the consideration of "לא אדו ראש" — that Sunday can never be Rosh Hashanah. Therefore Rosh Hashanah would be on the 31st day, which was a Monday. And similarly, if the 29th day would fall on a Tuesday, once again, everyone would know that the 30th day, Wednesday, could not be Rosh Hashanah, and therefore it would be on the 31st day, which would be Thursday. Why, then, did they need messengers for the month of Tishrei in order to determine Rosh Hashanah day?

From this question of Tosafos we can understand that the

"לא אדו ראש" consideration was also in force when the month was determined by eyewitnesses — "קידוש על פי הראייה" — for here we speak of the time of the Mishna, when the determination of the new month by eyewitnesses was still in effect. Thus we see that the position of the Rambam here is refuted, for according to him, the consideration of "לא אדו ראש" only applied when the determination by calculation, חשבון, was in effect, and not when the determination was by means of eyewitnesses.

Defending the Rambam

An answer to this question is offered by both the "שו"ת תשב"ץ" (חלק א, סימן קלה) and by the "פני יהושע" *(ibid.)*, who point out that determining the month by eyewitnesses can be accomplished by means of two methods. The first method is by witnesses who actually saw the moon and then testify to that effect, and the second is when witnesses did not see the moon but were intimidated by the Bais Din to say that they did, על פי איום. This could have happened, for example, if the witnesses think they simply saw a flash in the sky or in the clouds, and the Bais Din convinces them that it was really the new moon that they saw.

The פני יהושע contends that if the witnesses testify that they *actually saw* the moon, we do not apply the law of "לא אדו ראש", for if they saw the moon on Sunday, then Sunday is Rosh Chodesh and Rosh Hashanah. However, if they only *testify by coercion*, then the Bais Din can apply this formula of "לא אדו ראש", based on the considerations they may have for postponing Rosh Hashanah.

Consequently, those who lived in the Diaspora would not know if the determination of the day of Rosh Hashanah was due to eyewitnesses who actually saw the moon or those supposed eyewitnesses, and thus Sunday could really be Rosh

Hashanah. Therefore it was necessary for messengers to inform the people exactly how Rosh Hashanah day had been determined, and it could not be determined simply by applying the consideration of "לא אדו ראש".

And thus if we do apply this consideration of "לא אדו ראש" in this period we can only do so if Rosh Chodesh has been determined by coercion, איום, of the eyewitnesses. But if the witnesses actually saw the moon we can not apply this consideration.

XIII

A SOURCE FOR THE RAMBAM'S POSITION

As we have discussed, the Ramban questions the contention of the Rambam that when the Sanhedrin was no longer in existence, we must determine the new moon by means of calculation. Where is the Rambam's source for this statement, asks the Ramban, for it is nowhere to be found in the Gemara. The Griz HaLevi, though, does provide a source for the Rambam. The Gemara in *Mesechtas Rosh Hashanah 20b* tells us the following:

אמר שמואל: יכילנא לתקוני לכולה גולה.

> Shmuel said: I am able to establish the proper date of Rosh Chodesh for the entire Disapora.

Shmuel claimed to be so expert in the field of astronomy associated with calculating the new moon that he could calculate the new month for the communities of the Disapora.

The Brisker Rav, R'Velvele, bases his explanation on the commentary of Rabbenu Chananel, who contends that since the

Sanhedrin at that time was no longer in existence, therefore the new month was determined by means of calculation. This is as the Rambam contends. Thus Shmuel was telling us that by means of calculation he was able to determine the months and create calendar months for the Jews who live in the Disapora until Moshiach will make his appearance and once again reinstate the Sanhedrin and the practice of eyewitnesses determining the new month.

והנראה לומר כדעת הרמב"ם דיסוד דבריו לקוחים הם מהסוגיא דר"ה כ, דאיתא שם, אמר שמואל יכילנא לתקוני לכולה גולה...והנה יעו"ש ברש"י שכתב 'יכילנא לתקוני בלא ראיית עדים כי בקי אני לתולדות הלבנה והילוכה וסדר המזלות' הרי דמפרש לדברי שמואל דקיימי בזמן שמקדשים על פי הראייה ועל זה הוא דקאמר כי הוא יכול לתקן גם בלי ראיית העדים. וזה לכאורה צ"ב, מאי נפקא מיניה בזה? והלא סוף סוף אין מקדשים אלא על פי עדים. וכמבואר בסוגי' שם, דנפקא מיניה מהחשבון רק לאחכושי סהדי ועוד מאי לישנא "דכולה גולה", דנקט שמואל במימרי'?

ויעו"ש בר"ח שכתב שם וז"ל "יכילנא לתקונה לכולה גולה, כלומר יש לי כח לחשוב חשבון השנים ולתקן איזה שנה צריכה עיבור וכן בחדשים איזה חדש צריך להתעבר עד ביאת הגואל וישוב בסנהדרין." נראה מדבריו דמפרש דהא דקאמר שמואל יכילנא לתקוני לכולה גולה, דרצה לומר בזה, דהשתא דאין סנהדרין **ואין הקידוש על פי הראייה רק בחשבון, וכמו שכתב הרמב"ם**, וזה החשבון יוכל לעשות בעצמו עד ביאת הגואל וישוב הסנהדרין, שאז יחזרו לקדש על פי הראייה, **והן והן דברי הרמב"ם**, דבזמן שיש בית דין קובעין על פי הראייה, ובזמן שאין בית דין קובעין על פי החשבון.

THE GRIZ HALEVI: NOT BY MERE CALCULATION ALONE

This Gemara quotes the remark that was made to Shmuel by אבא אבוה דרבי שמלאי:

ידע מר האי מילתא דתניא בסוד העיבור, נולד קודם חצות או נולד אחר חצות. אמר לי': לא. אמר ליה: מדהא לא ידע מר, איכא מילי אחרנייתא דלא ידע מר.

Does the master know the explanation of this matter that was taught in the Baraisa of the compilation entitled "the secret of intercalation"? There is a difference when the moon was in conjunction before midday or in conjunction after midday. Shmuel replied: No. He thereby said to Shmuel: Since the master does not know this statement, there may be also other things that the master does not know.

The point here is that there was a tradition, מסורה, that if the mean conjunction falls on or after midday, then Rosh Hashanah is postponed until the following day. This postponement is referred to as "דחיית י"ח" or "מולד זקן". What Shmuel was being told was that the calculations to determine a new month and a new year are not simply based on mathematical considerations, but also include a tradition and particular laws to be implemented when considering when and how to calculate the new month and year.

The Griz HaLevi concludes that when Hillel II introduced the fixed calendar it was based on these traditions and laws of how to calculate.

והביאור בזה, דאבא בר אבוה דר' שמלאי קאמר לשמואל, דגם בזמן שאין סנהדרין והכל נעשה על פי החשבון, מכל מקום אין זה חשבון פשוט של סדר תקופות ומזלות, רק יש בזה דינים ומסורת מהלכה למשה מסיני ואי אפשר לעשות זאת מעצמו על פי החשבון בלבד בלי מסורת וקבלה וזה מפורש כדברי הרמב"ם דאיכא הלכה מסוימת של קביעת על פי חשבון, וממילא דהחשבון יש לו דינים ומסורות מתי לקבוע ומתי לדחות ולעבר.

> אבל אי לא היה כלל דין מסוים מהלכה למשה מסיני של קביעת על פי חשבון, רק שר' הלל הנשיא בעצמו תקן את החשבון הזה, וקידש ועיבר על ידו, הרי לא שייך בזה מסורות כלל, והרי זה יסוד דברי אבא אבוה דר' שמלאי, דיש בחשבונו מילי אחרניתא דתליין במסורות ולא בחשבון בלבד...

The Chazon Ish, however, takes issue with this position and concludes that any manner of calculation, חשבון, suffices to determine the new month and the statement that calculation is a halacha which finds its source at Sinai simply means that the Sages were given sanction to determine the new month by calculation and they were not restricted by the input of eyewitnesses.

And so the Chazon Ish writes in his commentary to Mesechtas Orla, in סימן טז (see also the commentary of the Chazon Ish on the Rambam's Hilchos Kiddush HaChodesh and the sefer "אגן הסהר", פרק יט, עמ' רפ"ד-רפ"ו):

> ובעיקר החשבון שלנו שכתב הר"מ שהוא הלכה למשה מסיני, אין הכוונה שנמסרו פרטותיו בהלכה אלא שנמסר רשות לחכמים לעשות חשבון קבוע שעל פי זה יסודרו השנים ויתאימו שנות החמה ושנות הלבנה וע"פ זה קבע הלל וב"ד את חשבונו, אבל לא נמנע לקבוע חשבון אחר שגם על פיו יסודרו שנות החמה והלבנה, וכאמור שמואל ר"ה כ, ב, יכילנא לתקונו לכולה גולה, ואם החשבון הלל מקובל מסיני מה אנו צריכין לשמואל בזה.

Chapter Nine
Kiddush HaChodesh only in Eretz Yisrael

I

THE SOURCE FOR THIS HALACHA

The Gemara in *Sanhedrin 11b* cites two sources for this requirement that Kiddush HaChodesh must take place in Eretz Yisrael.

ת"ר: אין מעברין את השנים אלא ביהודה...אמר קרא "לשכנו תדרשו ובאת שמה" (דברים י"ב, ה'), כל דרישה שאתה דורש לא יהיו אלא בשכנו של מקום.

> The Rabbis taught: we intercalate a month into the year only in Judea...because the Scripture states "His dwelling place you shall seek and there shall you come."

The term used for 'seek', תדרשו, alludes to the idea of *investigation*. The thrust of the pasuk then, is *any matter which it is necessary to investigate*, should be investigated only at Hashem's dwelling place, i.e., in Judea.

Thus we see that the pasuk which serves to teach us that only in Eretz Yisrael is Kiddush HaChodesh to take place is the verse of: "לשכנו תדרשו ובאת שמה". However, the Gemara in Berachos (ס"ג) presents a different pasuk (ישעיה ב,ג):

משום שנאמר, כי מציון תצא תורה ודבר ה' מירושלים.

It is stated, "For from Zion shall go forth Torah, and the word of Hashem from Yerushalayim". The implication here is clearly that only from Zion, that is, from Eretz Yisrael, can the law of Kiddush HaChodesh be determined and declared.

Thus, according to the Gemara in Berachos, the source for requiring that the month must be determined in Eretz Yisrael is the verse of "כי מציון תצא תורה וגו'".

The obvious question, then, is why do we need two different verses? Why wasn't the Gemara in Berachos satisfied with the pasuk of "לשכנו תדרשו ובאת שמה", which is from the Torah itself and is cited in a Baraisa in Sanhedrin. Why then was it necessary to refer to another pasuk from נ"ך, the Prophets, as the source for this requirement?

THE POSITION OF THE מהרש"א

The מהרש"א in *Mesechtas Berachos,* א, ס"ג (ה'מעבר שנים פרש"י ד"ה) is of the opinion that these two pasukim allude to two different concepts. The pasuk of "לשכנו תדרשו ובאת שמה" rules out the גליל — the area of Eretz Yisrael known as the Galilee—from serving as the proper place for the ceremony of Kiddush HaChodesh; whereas the pasuk of "כי מציון תצא תורה" rules out the Diaspora, חוץ לארץ, and indeed all of the rest of Eretz Yisrael and requires that the Kiddush HaChodesh process be done only in Yerushalayim.

...כי מציון תצא תורה ודבר ה' מירושלים וגו' ומיניה ממעט כל ארץ ישראל אלא דוקא בירושלים. ומקרא ד"לשכנו תדרשו" לא ממעט אלא גליל כדאמרינן התם (בסנהדרין י"א, ב).

Thus we can conclude from the insight offered by the מהרש"א that if we merely utilize the pasuk of "לשכנו תדרשו ובאת שמה" only the Galilee is ruled out, however the entire geographical area that comprises Judea is valid for the declaration of Kiddush HaChodesh. And the חידושי הר"ן is of the same opinion. In fact, the חידושי הר"ן explains that the term "לשכנו" — "His dwelling place", takes on different meanings in relation to different laws. For example, when the Torah speaks of the laws of sacrifice, קרבנות, there the term "לשכנו" alludes to the Bais HaMikdash itself. However, when the Torah speaks of the place where the sacrifices may be eaten, there "לשכנו" alludes to Yerushalayim. And when we speak of the law that we are to intercalate a month into a year, "לשכנו" there alludes to Judea. And in relation to a "זקן ממרא" the rebellious elder, we say that "לשכנו" there refers to the "לשכת הגזית", the Chamber of Hewn Stone, situated within the Bais HaMikdash. Thus we see that the חידושי הר"ן is of the same opinion as the מהרש"א that "לשכנו תדרשו" alluded to Judea.

> ...והוי יודע, שלשון "שכנו" הוא לשון כולל כוונות חלוקות לפי העניין הנאמר עליו, כשהוא מדבר בקרבנות הוא **על בית המקדש בלבד** ופעמים על **ירושלים** כשהוא מדבר על אכילת קדשים קלים. ופעמים **על כל ארץ יהודה** כמו שאמרו כאן אין מעברין אלא ביהודה. ולקמן אמרינן גבי זקן ממרא, מלמד שהמקום גורם, והוא **לשכת הגזית דוקא.**

The צפנת פענח (פרק א' הלכה ח' מהל' קידוש החודש) also points to Rashi's comments in *Mesechtas Kiddushin*, ("ד"ה 'תבעי קידוש' ל"ז, ב', ד"ה) which indicate that all of Judea is qualified as a place from which to declare the month sanctified.

> ד"ה תבעי קידוש: בית דין ולא נהיג קידוש אלא ביהודה כדאמר בסנהדרין (דף י"א, ב') כל דרישות שאתה דורש יהא בשכנו של מקום.

However, from Rashi's comments here in *Mesechtas Sanhedrin*, it would seem that he explains the pasuk of "לשכנו תדרשו" to refer exclusively to Yerushalayim. Rashi writes as follows:

> אין מעברין את השנה אלא בבי"ד הקבוע ביהודה: **שכנו של מקום**: ירושלים והיא ביהודה.

This statement of Rashi's here prompts the יד הרמ"ה to ask, if Yerushalayim is required here, as Rashi contends, why didn't the Baraisa clearly spell out the word "ירושלים", rather that simply mentioning "יהודה". Therefore, contends the הרמ"ה, it must be the case that *all of Judea* is deemed appropriate for determining and declaring Rosh Chodesh.

ולא מסתבר, דאם כן "בירושלים" מיבעי ליה אלא מסתברא דאכולה ארץ יהודה קאי, דכולה ארץ יהודה שכנו של מקום מיקרי, מאחר דהוי בית המקדש בגוה, דהא כולה חדא נחלה היא וחד חלוקה הוא דהויא.

II

THE VIEW OF THE צל"ח

The צל"ח, in his classic commentary to *Mesechtas Berachos*, questions and rejects this contention of the מהרש"א that Kiddush HaChodesh can be determined only in Yerushalayim or in Judea. The צל"ח maintains that the issue of place (Yerushalayim or elsewhere) only pertains to עבור השנה, the intercalation of a leap year. Regarding Kiddush HaChodesh, however, all of Eretz Yisrael is valid for the Bais Din to convene and declare the new moon. Only the Diaspora was ruled out as not being a proper place in which to declare the new moon.

וכה כתב: "...ואמנם ראיתי כאן בדברי מהרש"א דבר שהוא פלא בעיני...ובאמת לא מצינו לומר שיאמרו 'אין מקדשין את החדש אלא בירושלים או ביהודה', ולא מצינו אלא כאן שהקפידו שעשה כן בחו"ל. אבל בעבור שנים שנינו בברייתא שם בסנהדרין שאין מעברין את השנה אלא ביהודה. וז"ל הרמב"ם פרק א' הלכה ח': אין מחשבין וקובעין חדשים ומעברין אלא בארץ ישראל שנאמר 'כי מציון...' ואם עבר וקבע, לא עשה כלום. הרי שמקרא ד' 'כי

מציון' לא מיעט אלא חו"ל אפילו דיעבד אינו מועיל וגם ממעט **קביעת חדשים ועבור שנים**."

ובפרק ד' הלכה י"ב כתב "**ואין מעברין את השנה** אלא בארץ יהודה שהשכינה בתוכה שנאמר 'לשכנו תדרשו'. ואם עברוה בגליל מעוברת'. הרי שאדרבא מ'לשכנו תדרשו' ממעט יותר דבעי לשכנו היינו מקום ששכינה שריא, ושם לא **הזכיר קביעת חדשים** כלל. ולפי הנראה, דעתו דקביעת חדשים מותר אפילו לכתחילה בכל ארץ ישראל אפילו גליל."

Explaining the Thinking of the צל"ח

Perhaps we could explain the difference between קידוש החודש and עבור השנה regarding the requirement of the proximity of ירושלים and the שכינה, based on the following insight of the "סדר משנה" מר' זאב וואלף מבאסקאוויץ. The Mishna in *Sanhedrin 2a* tells us that when determining a leap year, the matter was first deliberated by three members of the Sanhedrin. It was then discussed by five Sanhedrin judges, and the matter was finally concluded by deliberation among seven judges. It was necessary for the Nasi to be directly involved in the discussion or at least to concern himself with the final decision when it was reached. This process raises a number of questions.

Why is the Nasi's presence required here, when it is not called for in other cases? What is the source for the necessity of the Nasi's participation in this matter? The Gemara in *Sanhedrin 10b* gives two possible explanations of the significance of the numbers three, five, and seven. These numbers correspond to the Bircas Kohanim, the Priestly Blessing, which consist of three, five and seven words: "יברכך ה' וישמרך" (three words); "יאר ה' פניו אליך ויחנך" (five words); and "ישא ה' פניו אליך וישם לך שלום" (seven words).

"Three" corresponds to the "three keepers of the utensils"

mentioned in *Kings II, 25:18*. "Five" corresponds to the "five who saw the King's face" mentioned one verse later *(Kings II, 25:19)*. Finally, "Seven" corresponds to the "seven ministers of Persia and Media who saw the king's face", from the *Book of Esther, 1:15*.

The סדר משנה comments that two separate sources are given here for the required numbers three, five and seven, because one of them: "the five who saw the king's face", refers, according to the Ba'alei Tosafos, to the members of the Sanhedrin. Thus, in order to participate in the deliberations concerning the determining of a leap year, one had to be a member of the Great Sanhedrin. The second source, alluding to the number of words in the Priestly Blessing, refers to the Nasi, who had to be present during the deliberations in determining a leap year.

How is the Nasi referred to here? The Nasi stood in place of Moshe Rabbenu, and Moshe represented Hashem in the Sanhedrin; this is spelled out for us by the Rambam at the beginning of Hilchos Sanhedrin. If we then examine the three phrases of the Priestly Blessing, we can see that the second word of each phrase is the name of Hashem. Thus when the initial group of Sanhedrin judges consisted of three, the Nasi was seated between the other two; just as the name of Hashem "sits" between the other words of the Priestly Blessing in the first part of the three-word phrase. When the deliberating council was comprised of five or seven, the Nasi then sat second (from the end) paralleling the makeup of the five-part and seven-part phrases of the Priestly Blessing (where the second word was the name of Hashem). This signifies that the presence of the Nasi, who represented Hashem in the Sanhedrin, ensured that the Shechinah would rest on the Sanhedrin. Thus the ultimate purpose of the Nasi's participation in the decision-making process was to ensure that divine wisdom and guidance would prevail and righteous judgements would be rendered by the Great Court.

This shows us that the determination of a leap year called for divine assistance. And similarly, we can understand why the determination of a leap year must be carried out in the vicinity of Yerushalayim, which was the place where the Shechinah rested. However, the determination of a new month was based on the testimony of eyewitnesses or on calculation, which involved mathematical formulas, and therefore it did not call for the immediate presence of the Shechinah. And so the "לשכנו תדרשו", the need for the proximity to "His abode", was required for determining a leap year, עבור השנה, but not necessarily for sanctifying the new month, קידוש החודש. For that purpose, the Shechinah which was present *throughout Eretz Yisrael*, sufficed for the process of Kiddush HaChodesh. In contrast, the particular presence of the Shechinah *in Yerushalayim and in the Bais HaMikdash* is what was needed for determining a leap year, עבור השנה.

III

The Insight of the "דורות הראשונים"

HaRav Yitzchak Isaac HaLevi, in his sefer "דורות הראשונים" (חלק ב' פרק י"ז, "יהודה והגליל"), touches upon the issues discussed here and contends that indeed although גליל was acceptable as far as עבור השנה, declaring a leap year, yet in relation to קידוש החודש, establishing Rosh Chodesh, Judea was the choice of the Sanhedrin. He bases his view on that which is cited in the Yerushalmi Sanhedrin (פרק א' הלכה ב'):

> ר' אלעזר בשם ר' חנינא: מעשה בעשרים וארבע קריות של בית רבי שנכנסו לעבר שנה בלוד ונכנסה בהם עין רע ומתו כולם בפרק אחד. מאותה שעה עקרוה מיהודה וקבעוה בגליל. בעיון מיעקר אף הן סימנא. אמר לן ר' סימן, אין אנו מניחין ביהודה אפי' זכר?

R' Elazar related in the name of R' Chanina what had transpired in his days when they assembled to intercalate the calendar year in the city of Lod, which is situated in Judea. A large crowd assembled there and brought about "the evil eye" — עין הרע, which caused the death of those assembled. Thereafter it was decided to move from Judea to the Galilee.

However, the process of Kiddush HaChodesh was never attended by an especially large crowd and therefore it remained in Judea. Once an attempt was made to move the process of Kiddush HaChodesh from Judea. In response, Rabbi Simon bemoaned the fact that this would leave Judea without any symbol? And so he insisted that the Kiddush HaChodesh ceremony continue in Judea.

Thus we see that even though, according to halacha, it was possible for the Galilee to serve as a place for the declaration of Kiddush HaChodesh, an attempt was made to continue to carry out this process in Judea.

IV

WHERE IS KIDDUSH HACHODESH ALLUDED TO?

As mentioned earlier, it is from this pasuk of "כי מציון תצא תורה" that we derive the concept that it is mandatory for Kiddush HaChodesh to take place in Eretz Yisrael, and in Yerushalayim. The obvious question here is where in this pasuk is Kiddush HaChodesh alluded to? The "מפרש", in his commentary to the Rambam in *Hilchos Kiddush HaChodesh 1:8*, asks this question and suggests the answer that although it is true that the matter of Kiddush HaChodesh is not specifically spelled out here, yet this pasuk is all-encompassing and alludes to *all* the mitzvos of the Torah. And so we can say that Kiddush HaChodesh is also included.

וז"ל המפרש:
זה הפסוק בספר ישעיה וגם כמותו בתרי עשר...ואם
תאמר זה הפסוק אינו מורה על הגבלת קביעת חדשים
בלבד, אלא הוא כולל כל התורה כולה שנ' כי מציון תצא
תורה וכו'. והתשובה אף על פי שהפשט מורה על זה,
יועיל זה הפסוק לנו בזה הענין שהרי הוא מכלל התורה
והואיל והתורה כולה יצאה מירושלים גם זה הענין יוצא
מירושלים..

The צל"ח however, in Berachos סג,א rejects this view. And he points out that if Kiddush HaChodesh is included in the overall meaning of the pasuk of "כי מציון תצא תורה" then this would imply that *all* the laws of the Torah should emanate only from Yerushalayim, yet we know that each Bais Din, no matter where it is situated, can legally administer Torah law. Therefore the צל"ח offers his own interpretation of this pasuk. The halacha states that if an error was made in issuing a decision declared by a court, and subsequently that error was discovered, then it is incumbent on the Bais Din to retract its original decision and now rule according to the new circumstances. Moreover, in regard to Kiddush HaChodesh, the law reads "אתם אפילו שוגגין", if the decision handed down by Bais Din in relation to establishing the calendar month was mistaken, it nevertheless stands. Kiddush HaChodesh is the only Torah law which is not revoked after the original decision has been handed down, and thus, since this law was initially declared by the Bais Din of Yerushalayim we can understand and appreciate the impact of this verse. "כי מציון"— since this law came forth from Zion and Yerushalayim, therefore "תצא תורה"—its decision remains valid, even if the original decision was mistaken.

The author of the sefer "ישועה בישראל" also questions this rationale of the "מפרש" and offers his own view of what this verse means. He maintains that this pasuk of "כי מציון תצא תורה" speaks about the future messianic era. Even though in the future all the nations of the world will become familiar with the mitzvos of the Torah, yet the

"סוד העבור" — the secret of calculating the new moon — will still be withheld from them, and therefore they will be forced to travel to Yerushalayim to learn this "secret", for only from Zion will the Torah emanate: "כי מציון תצא תורה (קידוש החודש)". Thus he maintains that in this way Kiddush HaChodesh is alluded to in this pasuk.

V

THE SECOND APPROACH OF THE מהרש"א

The מהרש"א in *Mesechtas Berachos* offers a different solution as to why the Gemara in Berachos quoted the pasuk of "כי מציון תצא תורה" rather than the pasuk mentioned in *Mesechtas Sanhedrin* of "לשכנו תדרשו ובאת שמה". He contends that the pasuk of "לשכנו תדרשו" rules out the Diaspora as an acceptable place to perform the עבור השנה process, but this was true only during the period when the Bais HaMikdash was intact.

For the word "לשכנו" alludes to the presence of the Shechinah, which was present when the Bais HaMikdash stood. Thus, after the destruction of the Bais HaMikdash, this pasuk of "לשכנו" could no longer be utilized to rule out the Diaspora, and therefore the pasuk of "כי מציון תצא תורה" was applied in order to rule out the Diaspora. For Torah decisions regarding the calendar must emanate from Yerushalayim and from Zion.

THE INSIGHT OF HARAV BEZALEL HAKOHEN OF VILNA

In the preface to the sefer "תולדות חכמי ירושלים", written by הרב ארי' ליב פרומקין, the eminent Gaon HaRav Bezalel HaKohen, the Dayan of Vilna, explains most beautifully how the pasuk of "לשכנו" alludes to the period when the Bais HaMikdash stood and the pasuk of "כי מציון וגו'" refers to the period after the destruction of the Bais HaMikdash, as the מהרש"א contends.

The pasuk of "לשכנו תדרשו" concludes with the words "ובאת שמה" — "and you shall come there", alluding to the Three Pilgrimage Festivals, שלש רגלים, when Klal Yisrael were required to make the pilgrimage to Yerushalayim to the Bais HaMikdash. This pilgrimage took place when the festivals were determined by eyewitnesses, who would present their testimony to the Sanhedrin situated in the Bais HaMikdash. Consequently, we are aware that this pasuk alludes to the period when the Temple stood. However, the pasuk of "כי מציון תצא תורה" is preceded by the verse, "ציון שדה תחרש", that Zion shall be plowed up and will lie desolate. Yet despite this, "מציון תצא תורה", the law, including the determination of the calendar, shall come forth from Zion and from Yerushalaim. Thus we see that this pasuk of "כי מציון תצא תורה" alludes to the period *after* the Destruction.

...ד."לשכנו" קאי על עבור השנה...דדריש לה על עבור השנה מדכתיב בתרי' "ובאת שמה" והיינו רגלים בזמן הבית, שאז זמן ראיה שמחויבים לבוא למקדש...וקביעת הרגל תלוי בבית המקדש שבירושלים על פי חשבון העבור שלהם. וזה "תדרשו ובאת" שצריך לדרוש מבית דין מתי לבוא שמה... אך מקרא ד"כי מציון" נפקא לי' שפיר גם בזמן הזה...ואולי נפקא לי' משום דמקמא הכי כתיב "לכן ציון שדה תחרש", "והיה באחרית הימים". "כי מציון" ומדלא כתיב "אז מציון" לכן דרשו אפילו בזמן הזה "אשר ציון שדה תחרש", משום דקדושת התורה שבציון וירושלים אפי' בחורבנה גדולה מכל מקום שבעולם...

TWO POSSIBLE WAYS OF UNDERSTANDING "כי מציון"

There are two possible ways of understanding this pasuk of "כי מציון תצא תורה", as referring to the period after the destruction of the Bais HaMikdash. We could say that the pasuk which rules out the Diaspora as a place for carrying out the process of עבור השנה is the verse, "לשכנו תדרשו". However, the pasuk of "כי מציון" only teaches us that this pasuk of "לשכנו תדרשו" is to be *extended* to include the period even after the destruction of the Bais HaMikdash.

If we accept this approach we can answer the question posed by the מהרש"א in *Mesechtas Berachos*. Rashi comments on the question asked there, namely "How could R' Chanina have intercalated years and established months outside Eretz Yisrael?"

ותנן אין מעברין את השנה אלא ביהודה דכתיב לשכנו תדרשו.

Thus we see that Rashi bases the prohibition against intercalating years outside of Eretz Yisrael on the pasuk of "לשכנו תדרשו". And this prompts the מהרש"א to ask why Rashi did not rely on the pasuk of "כי מציון תצא תורה" cited in the Gemara of Berachos?

מי הכריחו לכך, דהא שמעתין מייתי לה מקרא אחרינא, כי מציון תצא תורה?

I do not know what forced Rashi to cite here the pasuk of "לשכנו תדרשו" when the Gemara at present cites the pasuk of "כי מציון תצא תורה".

The מהרש"א leaves this question unanswered; however, in light of the assertion that the pasuk of "כי מציון" extends the requirement of "לשכנו תדרשו" we could say that Rashi quoted the pasuk of "לשכנו תדרשו" rather than that of "כי מציון" because the former is actually the source for prohibiting intercalation of leap years in the Diaspora. Yet we might suggest that each pasuk is independent of the other and can be distinguished by historical period. For indeed "לשכנו תדרשו" applies to the period when the Bais HaMikdash stood and "כי מציון" to that period after its destruction. Thus the Gemara in Sanhedrin refers to the period when the Bais HaMikdash stood, cited the pasuk of "לשכנו תדרשו"; whereas the Gemara in Berachos speaks of the period after the Destruction, and thus cites the pasuk of "כי מציון וגו'".

In addressing the original question of the מהרש"א (i.e., why did Rashi cite the pasuk of "כי מציון" rather than that of "לשכנו תדרשו"), we could perhaps answer as follows. In the Gemara in *Sanhedrin 11b* not all accept the application of this pasuk of "לשכנו וגו'". Some commentators do not consider this pasuk as decisive in ruling out places other than Yerushalayim. Therefore, in the Gemara in Berachos, where the Rabbis questioned חנניא בן אחי ר' יהושע for calculating leap years outside of Eretz Yisrael, they confronted him with the pasuk of "כי מציון". For had they cited the pasuk of "לשכנו תדרשו", he might have replied that he differed with their interpretation that this pasuk rules out the Diaspora.

Rambam's position questioned

If we adopt the view that we need the pasuk of כי מציון, since the Bais HaMikdash is no longer intact, this would imply that the Shechinah, the Divine Presence, no longer dwells there. This, therefore, provokes the following question. The Rambam in *Hilchos Bais HaBechira,* פרק ו', הלכה ט"ז, states:

ולמה אני אומר שקדושת המקדש וירושלים קדשה לעתיד לבוא... לפי שקדושתן מפני שכינה ושכינה אינה בטלה.

> Why do I say that the original consecration sanctified the Bais HaMikdash and Yerushalayim for eternity... because the sanctity of the Bais HaMikdash stems from the Shechinah, and *the Shechinah can never be nullified.*

Thus we see that the Shechinah remains, even though the Bais HaMikdash remains desolate. Why, then, do we not still apply the pasuk of "לשכנו תדרשו"? We might suggest a possible answer based on insights we offered in our sefer (עמ' פט-צא) "תפארת למשה".

The above-mentioned statement of the Rambam that even after the destruction of the first Bais HaMikdash the Shechinah was still present in the בית מקדש seems to contradict what was just stated in the Gemara of *Yoma 21b*. There the Gemara enumerates five things that were present in the First Temple but were missing in the rebuilt Second Temple.

אלו חמשה דברים שהיו בין מקדש ראשון למקדש שני ואלו הן: ארון וכפורת וכרובים ואש ,ושכינה' ורוח הקודש ואורים ותומים.

These are the five things which the Second Temple was missing; the Ark, the Ark-cover, the cherubim, the fire from Heaven, the Divine Presence, the Holy Spirit of Prophecy and the Urim VeTumim.

This issue was already touched upon in various seforim (see "שו"ת יביע אומר" מהרב עובדי' יוסף נ"י, חלק ה', יור"ד, סימן כו, ובספר "טבור הארץ" מהרב ר' משה קלירס, עמ' ו'). All contend that we must make a distinction between when the Shechinah is "בגלוי" — in a revealed state, when it can be seen or sensed by all, and when it is merely *present*, not revealed, but rather hidden. Thus, when the Gemara in Yoma tells us that the Shechinah was missing, this was meant only in relation to the fact that it was no longer openly revealed, yet it was indeed still present, even though it could not easily be seen. This then is the meaning behind the prayer:

ותחזינה **עינינו**.. המחזיר שכינתו לציון

May our *eyes* behold... Who restores His Presence to Zion.

Although the Shechinah even today is present at the site where the Bais HaMikdash was built, we pray that we may merit to see it *with our own eyes*, openly revealed. Thus there is no real contradiction here in the Rambam's words. However, what still remains problematic is the fact that if indeed the Shechinah is always present, why do we reject the pasuk of "לשכנו תדרשו ובאת שמה"?

Defending the Rambam

The Rambam asserts that the Shechinah remained even after the destruction of the Bais HaMikdash. The full text of the Rambam in *Hilchos Bais HaBechirah*, (ו:ט) reads:

ולמה אני אומר במקדש וירושלים קדושה ראשונה קדשה לעתיד לבוא, ובקדושת שאר ארץ ישראל לענין שביעית ומעשרות וכיוצא בהן, לא קדשה לעתיד לבוא? לפי שקדושת המקדש וירושלים מפני השכינה, ושכינה אינה בטלה. והרי הוא אומר "והשמותי את מקדשיכם" ואמרו חכמים: אף על פי ששמומין בקדושתן הן עומדים. אבל חיוב הארץ בשביעית ובמעשרות אינו אלא מפני שהוא כבוש רבים, וכיון שנלקחה הארץ מידיהם בטל הכבוש ונפטרה מן התורה ממעשרות ומשביעית, שהרי אינה ארץ ישראל. וכיון שעלה עזרא וקדשה, לא קדשה בכבוש אלא בחזקה, שהחזיקו בה, ולפיכך כל מקום שהחזיקו בה עולי בבל ונתקדש בקדושת עזרא השנייה, הוא מקודש היום ואף על פי שנלקח הארץ ממנו...

Why do I say that the original consecration sanctified the Bais HaMikdash and Yerushalayim for eternity, while in regard to the consecration of the remainder of Eretz Yisrael, in the context of the sabbatical year, tithes, and other similar laws, the original consecration did not sanctify it for eternity?

Because the sanctity of the Bais HaMikdash and Yerushalayim emanates from the Shechinah, and the Shechina can never be nullified. Therefore it is said (in *Vayikra 26:31*) "Even though they have been devastated, their sanctity remains."

In contrast, the original obligation to keep the laws of the sabbatical years and tithes on produce from the earth originated from the fact that the land was conquered by a community, a צבור. Therefore, when the land was taken from their hands, their original conquest was nullified. According to Torah law, with their defeat the land was freed from the obligations of the sabbatical year and tithes because it was no longer considered to be Eretz Yisrael.

When Ezra returned to Eretz Yisrael and reconsecrated the land, it was not sanctified by conquest but rather through possession — חזקה. This means that every place that was repossessed by the exiles returning from Bavel when Ezra consecrated the land this second time is considered to be sacred to this day.

From this assertion of the Rambam, we see clearly that if the initial annexation was made by conquest, it can be nullified when others conquer the land. This holds true regarding the agricultural laws of Eretz Yisrael. However, concerning the sanctification of the Bais HaMikdash and Yerushalayim, which came about as a result of the Shechinah which rested there, that *initial consecration can never be nullified,* just as sanctification by means of possession—חזקה—can never be nullified. Thus, when we say, "שכינה אינה בטלה", this is not to be understood to mean that the Shechinah was never nullified, but rather that the *initial consecration* which came about as a result of the Shechinah resting there can never be nullified. In light of this interpretation, there is no contradiction here between the Gemara in *Yoma 21b* and the Rambam in Hilchos Bais HaBechirah.

VI

Exploring the Rambam's Position

In *Hilchos Kiddush HaChodesh 4:12,* the Rambam rules as follows:

ואין מעברין את השנה אלא בארץ יהודה, שהשכינה בתוכה, שנאמר, לשכנו תדרשו. ואם עברוהו בגליל מעוברת.

A leap year may be instituted only in the territory of Judea, for the resting place of the Divine Presence (the Shechinah) is there, as implied in the verse, 'You shall seek out His dwelling.' If a leap year is instituted in the Galilee, the year *remains* full.

We find the source for this halacha in the Gemara *Sanhedrin 11b,* where we read:

תנו רבנן: אין מעברין את השנים אלא ביהודה, ואם עיברוה בגליל **מעוברת.** העיד חנניה איש אונו: אם עיברוה בגליל **אינה מעוברת.** אמר ר' יהודה ברי' דרבי שמעון בן פזי, מאי טעמא דחנניה איש אונו, אמר קרא, לשכנו תדרשו ובאת שמה' "כל" דרישה שאתה דורש לא יהיו אלא בשכנו של מקום.

The Rabbis taught: A leap year is only instituted in Judea, and if instituted in the Galilee, it is effective. Chananiah of Ono testified: if a court sought to institute a leap year in the Galilee—it is *ineffective.* R' Yehudah, the son of R' Shimon ben Pazi said: What is the reasoning behind the ruling of Chananiah of Ono? Because the Torah says:

His dwelling-place shall you seek, and there you shall come.

From this it would appear that the Sages, who argue with Chananiah of Ono and do recognize the establishment of a leap year in the Galilee, do not apply here the verse of "לשכנו תדרשו", as Chananiah of Ono himself does. The Rambam rules according to the opinion of the Sages, which is that even though initially the process should take place in Judea, yet if it took place *after the fact* in the Galilee, it would nevertheless take effect there too. Why, then, does the Rambam quote the verse of "לשכנו תדרשו", when, as we have seen, the Sages reject this verse as being decisive for determining the issue?

In defence of the Rambam, we might suggest that that he had a different version of the text than we do. There are several opinions regarding what that text was.

The Netziv, in the name of his son-in-law, HaRav Raphael Shapira, explains that both the Sages and Chananiah of Ono apply here the verse of "לשכנו תדרשו", the words "מאי טעמא דחנניה איש אונו" should be removed and the text should simply read, "מאי טעמא". This is how the Sages and Chananiah of Ono base their views on this verse. However, whereas Chananiah of Ono insists that this verse is decisive in accepting only Judea as the place where Kiddush HaChodesh and the leap year are to be determined, the Sages are of the opinion that Judea is only initially designated, and the Galilee is also acceptable *after the fact*, מדיעבד. Thus the Rambam, who rules as the Sages do, quotes the verse of "לשכנו תדרשו".

Other commentators, however, maintain that the text which the Rambam relied on was that of the Tosefta in *Sanhedrin 2:6*:

אין מעברין את השנה אלא ביהודה, ואם עבר בגליל, הרי זה מעובר. **העיד** ר' חנניא איש אונו לפני רבן גמליאל, שאין מעברין את השנה אלא ביהודה, ואם עברוה בגליל שהיא מעוברת.

According to this text, R' Chananiah of Ono not only agrees with the Sages, he also acted to reinforce their opinion. Thus, we can see that every opinion, even that of the Sages, relies on the pasuk of "לשכנו תדרשו".

VII

CALCULATION IN THE DIASPORA

We have previously discussed the question posed by the Ba'alei Tosafos in *Sanhedrin 11b* (ד"ה אין מעברין) as to why the Gemara here specifically rules out the possibility of a leap year being determined in the Disapora, based on the verse, "לשכנו תדרשו"; whereas the Gemara in *Berachos 63b* rules out the Diaspora by applying a completely different verse, that of "כי מציון תצא תורה".

The Ritba, in his commentary to *Mesechtas Berachos* (ibid.) contends that the statement mentioned here, "שהיו מעברין בחוצה לארץ", that "there were those [including Rabbi Akiva] who *did* intercalate years *outside Eretz Yisrael*", is not to be taken literally. For we know, based on the verse cited in *Mesechtas Sanhedrin 11b* — "לשכנו תדרשו" — that to institute leap years outside the Land of Yisrael was certainly forbidden. However, what the Gemara meant here in Mesechtas Berachos was that there were those who *calculated* leap years outside the Land of Yisrael, even though the actual *implementation* of the leap year took place only in Eretz Yisrael. Consequently, even this attempt to calculate outside the Land of Yisrael was challenged and forbidden, based on the verse of "כי מציון תצא תורה". Thus, according to the Ritba, both the calculation and the implementation of leap years is strictly forbidden in the Disapora.

לאו דוקא מעברין בחוץ לארץ דהא אמרינן בסנהדרין דאין מעברין את השנה אלא בארץ, אבל **מחשבין** היו והעבור לא היה אלא בארץ, ואפילו על החשבון היו מקפידין, כדכתיב, כי מציון תצא תורה ודבר ה' מירושלים.

Based on this opinion of the Ritba, HaRav Moshe Hershler (cited in his commentary to the Ritba) answers the question touched upon by Tosafos as to why here in Mesechtas Sanhedrin the verse of "לשכנו תדרשו" is quoted, whereas Mesechtas Berachos relies on another verse — "כי מציון תצא תורה" — to prove the same point. The answer he suggests is that the Gemara in Sanhedrin focuses on the issue of implementation. Therefore the verse of "לשכנו תדרשו" is quoted.

On the other hand, the issue addressed in Mesechtas Berachos is that of calculation. Thus the verse of "כי מציון תצא תורה" is quoted to prove that even mere calculations must be made in Eretz Yisrael.

Given this interpretation, we might say that the Ba'alei Tosafos, who pose this question, reject this contention of the Ritba. The Gemara in *Berachos 26a* states:

ר' חייא בר זרנוקי ור"ש בן יהוצדק הוי קאזלי לעבר שנה בעסיא, פגע בהו ריש לקיש, איטפיל בהדייהו. אמר איזיל אחזי היכי עבדי עובדא. חזייה דההוא גברא דקא כריב [חריש רש"י] אמר להן כהן חריש? אמרו לו, יכול לומר, אגיסתן [שכיר רש"י] אני בתוכו.

Once during the sabbatical year, R' Chiya bar Zarnokei and R' Shimon bar Yehotzadok were travelling to a city in Asia to intercalate the year. Reish Lakish met them and joined them, saying: I will go along and see how they perform the procedure of intercalation. As they travelled, Reish Lakish saw a man plowing [in the sabbatical year] and he remarked to them, "This man is a kohen and he is plowing?" [a violation in the sabbatical year]. They said to him, "Why assume that he is transgressing?" He might excuse his actions by saying, I am only a hired worker for a non-Jew.

Tosafos here (ד"ה לעבר שנה בעסיא) asks, how did they intend to intercalate a leap year in Asia, when it is situated outside Eretz Yisrael? Tosafos then answers, What "לעבר" means is not to actually implement but rather to make the necessary calculations pertaining to a leap year. Proof of this is that since this incident took place during Shmittah (in the sabbatical year), and we know that leap years are not established in the seventh year. Thus it must be the case that they only went there to calculate. From this we may conclude that since Tosafos defends their action of going to Asia to calculate a leap year, it seems clear that mere calculation, חשבון, is permitted in the Diaspora. This means that Tosafos disagrees with the Ritba, and the question posed by Tosafos remains. Why are different sources given in *Mesechtas Sanhedrin* and *Mesechtas Berachos* to support the ruling that leap years can not be intercalated outside the Land of Yisrael?

THE RAMBAM'S POSITION

The Rambam here in *Hilchos Kiddush HaChodesh, Chapter One* states:

> אין **מחשבין** וקובעין חדשים ומעברין שנים אלא בארץ ישראל, שנאמר: כי מציון תצא תורה ודבר ה' מירושלים. ואם היה אדם גדול בחכמה, ונסמך בארץ ישראל, ויצא לחוץ לארץ, ולא הניח בארץ ישראל כמותו-הרי זה **מחשב** וקובע חדשים ומעביר שנים בחוצה לארץ, ואם נודע לו שנעשה בארץ ישראל אדם כמותו, ואין צריך לומר גדול ממנו ואם קבע ועבר לא עשה כלום.

The calculations and the establishment of months and leap years is carried out in Eretz Yisrael, as the verse points out; "For out of Zion will come the Law and the Word of Hashem from Jerusalem."

If a great sage who received semicha (ordination) in Eretz Yisrael left for the Diaspora without leaving a colleague of equal stature in Eretz Yisrael, he may make calculations to establish the monthly calendar and institute leap years in the Diaspora. If, however, it becomes known to him that a sage of his stature has arisen in Eretz Yisrael, and surely if a sage of greater stature remains in Eretz Yisrael, it is forbidden for him to establish and institute leap years in the Diaspora. If he transgresses and attempts to structure the calendar, his actions are of no consequence.

The (מצוה ד, אות א) "מנחת חינוך" concludes: If we examine the initial statement here of the Rambam, אין מחשבין, "we do not calculate except in Eretz Yisrael", this would appear to indicate that even *mere calculation* is forbidden outside Eretz Yisrael.

The following statement, which allows a "great sage" to make calculations in the Diaspora, once again indicates that if there is no "great sage" available, then making calculations is forbidden in the Diaspora. However, what becomes problematic is the concluding statement here —that if a great sage emerges in Eretz Yisrael, then it is forbidden to institute and intercalate leap years in the Diaspora, and if one did attempt to institute a leap year, *it* will not take effect. Thus only the key words "קובע" and "עיבור" are stated here, to indicate that "*it* is of no consequence." Yet there is no mention made that "the *calculations* are of no consequence." From this we can conclude that if the institution of the leap year is made ultimately in Eretz Yisrael, the *calculations* which were made in the Diaspora are indeed recognized.

However, the sefer "מנחת סולת" contends that if a great sage arises in Yisrael, then even the calculations made in the Diaspora are of no consequence. The reason that the Rambam did not point this out was that it is obvious that if a great sage were to arise in Eretz Yisrael, he need not rely on the calculations made in the Diaspora, but he would rely on his own calculations.

VIII

The law of "לא הניח כמותו"

The Rambam in *Hilchos Kiddush HaChodesh, Chapter One, Halacha 8,* based on the previously mentioned Gemara in *Berachos* סג,א, makes the following ruling:

אין מחשבין אלא בארץ ישראל שנאמר כי מציון תצא תורה. ואם הי' אדם גדול בחכמה, ונסמך בארץ ישראל ויצא לחוץ לארץ ולא הניח בארץ ישראל כמותו הרי זה מחשב וקובע חדשים ומעבר שנים בחוצה לארץ...

The calculation and establishment of months and leap years is carried out only in Eretz Yisrael, as the verse states, "For out of Zion will come the Law..." If a great sage who received semicha in Eretz Yisrael left for the Diaspora without leaving a colleague of equal stature in Eretz Yisrael, he may make calculations, establish the monthly calendar and institute leap years in the Diaspora...

The justification for this law is alluded to in the pasuk quoted, comments the "חסדי דוד". The pasuk reads, "From Zion will go forth the Law". This can be explained to mean that if the greatest sage of the generation (the Gadol HaDor) is in Eretz Yisrael, then Torah will emanate from there and the proclamation declaring a new month will "come forth from Yerushalayim". However, if the Torah does not come forth from Yerushalayim, i.e., if the Gadol

HaDor finds himself in the Diaspora, then the "Word of Hashem" will not come forth from Yerushalayim.

The opinion of the Pirkei d'Rebbe Eliezer

The view of the Pirkei d'Rebbe Eliezer is that if the scholars are to be found in the Diaspora and the "simple shepherds", i.e., the unlearned, are to be found in Eretz Yisrael, then we establish the leap year by the determination of the shepherds of Eretz Yisrael.

וז"ל הפרקי דר' אליעזר, פרק ח:

יצחק מסר [הסוד העיבור] ליעקב. ונכנס בסוד העיבור ועבר את השנה. יצא יעקב בחוץ לארץ וביקש לעבר את השנה בחוץ לארץ. אמר לו הקב"ה: "יעקב, אין לך רשות לעבר את השנה בחוץ לארץ, הרי יצחק אביך הוא יעבור את השנה בארץ, שנ' וירא ה' אל יעקב עוד בבוא מפדן ארם, ויברך אותו." ולמה "עוד" שפעם ראשונה נגלה עליו ומנעו מלעבר את השנה בחוץ לארץ, וכשבא לארץ, אמר לי' "קום עבר את השנה..." מכאן אמרו אפילו צדיקים וחכמים בחוצה לארץ ורועי צאן ובקר בארץ ישראל, אין מעברין את השנה אלא על ידי רועי צאן ובקר. אפילו נביאים בחוץ לארץ והדיוטים בארץ ישראל, אין מעברין את השנה אלא על ידי הדיוטים שבארץ. גלו לבבל היו מעברין את השנה על ידי הנשאר בארץ. לא נשאר אחד בארץ היו מעברין את השנה בבבל. עלה עזרא וכל הקהל עמו ורצה יחזקאל לעבר את השנה בבבל, אמר לו הקב"ה "יחזקאל, אין לך רשות לעבר את השנה בחוץ לארץ, הרי ישראל אחיכם, והם יעברו את השנה" שנ' (יחזקאל לו, י"ז) בן אדם בית ישראל יושבים על אדמתם, שלהן היא לעבר את השנה...

Thus we see that according to the Pirkei d'Rebbe Eliezer we are to restrict the process of declaring a new month to those who live in Eretz Yisrael, even if the greatest sage of the generation may live not there but in Bavel.

Reconciling the issues

In the "קובץ חדושים", printed at the end of the sefer (חלק א) "שיטה מקובצת על מסכת פסחים", a distinction is made between the period when the Bais HaMikdash was intact and after its destruction. Since R' Eliezer lived during the period of the Bais HaMikdash, it was mandatory that the determination of the new month be made in the Bais HaMikdash, the dwelling place of the Great Sanhedrin. The rationale for this requirement was that since the Shechinah was to be found there, it was the proper place to act upon this matter. Consequently, this ruled out the stipulation that "the greatest sage in Yisrael" could not act in these matters, were he to be found outside the Land of Yisrael. However, the episode recorded in Mesechtas Berachos, which depicted the sages acting to institute leap years, happened after the destruction of the Bais HaMikdash, and therefore, since the greatest sage in Yisrael was now to be found in the Diaspora, we thus apply the principle that "Torah came forth from Bavel", rather than from Yerushalayim.

The Chasam Sofer agrees

The Chasam Sofer suggests a similar insight, based on an incident he experienced as a child. He was introduced by his father to the Rav of Prague, the most eminent gaon of his generation, the Nodeh B'Yehudah. This great sage asked young Moshe Sofer the following question, which is reproduced in his sefer "צל"ח-פסחים" (מ,א). The Gemara in *Pesachim 47a*, tells us about the shewbread,

לחם הפנים, the twelve loaves of bread placed on the Table, שלחן, in the Bais HaMikdash. This bread remained there and stayed fresh from one Shabbos to the next. On the second Shabbos the loaves were eaten by the Kohanim and replaced with twelve new loaves. Thus the shewbread was eaten on the ninth, tenth or eleventh day after it was baked. It was baked on the previous Friday before Shabbos. In a normal week, if it was baked on a Friday and not eaten until the following Shabbos day, this meant that there was a delay of nine days after it was baked and before it was eaten. If, however, Yom Tov was on Erev Shabbos, then it was baked a day earlier, on Thursday, and it was not eaten until ten days later. If the two days of Rosh Hashanah fell on Thursday and Friday, then the לחם הפנים was baked on Wednesday, and this meant that it was eaten eleven days after it was baked, on the second Shabbos.

Rashi explains that we have two days of Rosh Hashanah if the witnesses who sighted the moon did not appear by Mincha time on the 30th day of Elul. In this case, the Rabbis declared the 30th day of Elul as Rosh Hashanah as well as the next day, the 31st. Thus we have two days of Rosh Hashanah even in Yerushalayim. Rashi concludes by saying that Rosh Hashanah was the only holiday that was celebrated for two days, for when the Bais HaMikdash stood, none of the other holidays were celebrated for two days.

ושני ימים טובים של ראש השנה נקט, דבזמן לחם הפנים,
לא היו שני ימים טובים של גליות.

The צל"ח asks, why did Rashi have to tell us that when we offered the shewbread, i.e., when the Bais HaMikdash stood, two days of yom tov were never celebrated, for even *after* the destruction of the Temple they never celebrated two days of yom tov in Yerushalayim?

The young Chasam Sofer answered the great sage as follows. In these days, a situation can arise in which a two-day celebration of yom tov in Yerushalayim can take place. For example, it might transpire that the greatest sage of the generation was at a certain time in the Diaspora, involved in declaring a new month, in keeping with the law of "לא הניח חכם כמותו".

Meanwhile, in the city of Yerushalayim, witnesses coming to inform the people when Rosh Chodesh was to occur were not able to arrive until after yom tov. In such a case, two days of yom tov would be celebrated in Yerushalayim as well. However, in the period when the shewbread was offered, i.e., when the Temple stood, this law of "לא הניח חכם כמותו" — that the greatest sage of the generation has the power to declare Rosh Chodesh even outside the Land of Yisrael—did not apply. This, then, is what Rashi meant to explain by saying that when the shewbread was offered at the time of the Bais HaMikdash there were never two days of yom tov. After the young man finished this explanation, the Nodeh B'Yehudah commended him for his brilliant insight.

ונהרינא כד הוינא טליא בעברי דרך ק"ק פראג, זכיתי לראות פני הגאון הצל"ח, ואמרתי לו במה שתמה בספרו על פי רש"י הנ"ל, הא בירושלים אפילו בזמן הזה ליכא ב' ימים טובים של גליות, ומאי איריי' בזמן לחם הפנים?

ואמרתי לו, מי לא אשכחן ליה כשרוב חכמי ישראל בחוץ לארץ, ולא הניח כמותם בארץ ישראל, שאז מעברין בחוץ לארץ...ואם יהיו רחוקים, על כרחך יעשו שם [בירושלים] שני ימים מספק, ויהי' גם בארץ ישראל ב' ימים טובים של גליות, והוי מצי התנא למינקט ב' ימים טובים של גליות סתם. אלא משום שאי אפשר זה בזמן לחם הפנים דאז לעולם בית דין הגדול שבירושלים סמוך למקדש. אבל בזמן הזה כבר הי' אפשר שיקרה כן...וישרו דברי בעיני הגאון ואמר 'קאלוס' [יישר כח]...

Thus we see that the principle of "שלא הניח כמותו" did not apply at the time when the Bais HaMikdash was intact. It was only after its destruction that we began to apply this law.

A SECOND DISTINCTION

Another distinction is made by my rebbe, HaRav Chaim Zimmerman, ז״ל, in his classic sefer (עמ' רמב) "אגן הסהר" between the period when the month was determined by eyewitnesses — קדוש על פי הראייה — and the time when the determination was by calculation חשבון האמצעי.

We know that anyone living in Eretz Yisrael could arrange the calendar, since the method of calculation did not require a genius to figure it out. As the Rambam writes in *Chapter 11:14,* "even a child could have made this calculation." The Pirkei d'Rebbe Eliezer speaks of such a period. Consequently, we do not apply the law of "לא הניח כמותו", that a sage in the Diaspora can determine this matter. However, the Rabbis who did act in this capacity in the Diaspora lived at a time when the determination of the new month by eyewitnesses was still in practice, and therefore the power to determine the new month was exclusively under the jurisdiction of those who lived in Eretz Yisrael.

However, the sefer (עניני עבור השנה, אות ג) עמק ברכה, which initially suggested this answer, ultimately dismissed this approach and questioned its validity.

The concluding statement of the Pirkei d'Rebbe Eliezer here is that even after the Babylonian exile the power to determine the calendar was under the jurisdiction of those who lived in Eretz Yisrael. However, one might ask why, since all the scholars had been exiled to Bavel. Shouldn't the determination have been placed in their hands? Thus we must conclude, contends the עמק הברכה, that the Pirkei de R' Eliezer is of the opinion that under no circumstances is the calendar to be determined *outside* Eretz Yisrael.

IX

THE QUESTION OF תוספות חדשים

The Mishna in *Mesechtas Yevamos 122a* relates the following incident:

> R' Akiva said: When I went down to Nehardah to fix the leap year I met Nechemia of Bais Deli and he said to me: I heard that only R' Yehudah ben Bava maintains that a woman can marry based on the testimony of one witness [who testified that her husband had died]. However, the Sages disagree with him. And I said to him: It is true. He then said to me: You know that due to the dangerous situation here it is impossible to travel to Eretz Yisrael, and therefore you should tell them in my name that I have a direct tradition from Rabban Gamliel the Elder, that we may allow a woman to remarry by the testimony of one witness. When I [R' Akiva] related this testimony to Rabban Gamilel [the Second] he rejoiced at my words and declared that we now have confirmation from R' Yehudah ben Bava.

Tosafos *(ibid.)* remarks here that even though declaring leap years was not done in the Diaspora, and Nehardah was located outside Eretz Yisrael, yet since, as the Gemara tells us in Mesechtas Berachos, R' Akiva declared leap years outside Eretz Yisrael, this was accepted because he left no one of equal stature behind in Eretz Yisrael (שלא הניח כמותו בא״י). This explains how he was able to declare leap years in the Diaspora.

This leads the תוספות חדשים *(ibid.)* to ask the following question. It would seem that this incident mentioned in *Mesechtas*

Yevamos regarding the encounter between R' Akiva and Nechemia of Bais Deli, and the incident mentioned in Mesechtas Berachos, where R' Akiva declared a leap year in the Diaspora, are one and the same. If this is so, then one might raise the following question. This incident regarding the testimony given by R' Akiva in the name of Nechemia Bais Deli is cited at the end of *Mesechtas Edyiot, Chapter 8, Mishna 5*. It is well known that these Mishnayos (עדיות) were taught on the day R' Eliezer ben Azaryia was appointed Nasi (president) of the Sanhedrin to replace Rabban Gamliel. And at that time Rabban Gamliel, R' Yehoshua, the teachers of R' Akiva, were still alive and were present at that session. Therefore how could R' Akiva have declared leap years in the Diaspora on the basis of the halachic principle that he left no one of equal stature behind him, when his teachers and R' Eliezer ben Azaryia were then living in Eretz Yisrael?

X

WHO WAS GREATER: R' AKIVA OR R' ELAZAR BEN AZARIA?

This assumption of the תוספות חדשים, that R' Elazar ben Azaria was greater than R' Akiva can be challenged. Indeed, it can be said that R' Akiva was the greatest Sage of his generation. This is borne out in a statement by Tosafos in *Mesechtas Kesuvos 105b* (ד"ה דחשיב). There he asserts that when several people are mentioned, it is not necessarily the case that the one mentioned first is more important than the others. He attempts to prove this theory by relating the following incident. Chazal tell us that there was once an issue raised that needed to be resolved. It was decided to present the issue to R' Dosa ben Horkenos. And so a delegation consisting of R' Yehoshua, R' Elazar ben Azaria and R' Akiva were sent to R' Dosa. Even though R' Elazar ben Azaria was ushered in first and seated before R' Akiva, this was done only out of consideration for the fact that R' Elazar's ancestry was far greater than that of R' Akiva's and because he was the Nasi of the Sanhedrin. However, R' Akiva was indeed the greater sage. Proof that he was recognized as such can be seen from the manner in which he was addressed by R' Dosa. For when R' Dosa was introduced to R' Akiva, he greeted him by saying: "Akiva ben Yosef, whose name resounds from one end of the world to the other." From this we can see that R' Akiva was recognized as being the greatest of his generation, for this was the implication of R' Dosa's greeting.

A second proof that he was considered greater than R' Elazar ben Azaria was the fact that when a replacement for Rabban Gamliel was being considered, the leading candidate for the position of Nasi was R' Akiva. It was only because of certain considerations that he was finally rejected and R' Elazar ben Azaria was selected instead. This shows us, however, that he was considered to be the greatest sage of his day. More details of this selection of a Nasi to succeed Rabban Gamliel are given in the Yerushalmi Berachos, פרק תפלת השחר, סוף הלכה א.

There we find that after R' Elazar ben Azaria was selected as Nasi, R' Akiva consoled himself by saying that R' Elazar ben Azaria was chosen because he was a direct descendant of Ezra the Scribe.

ר' עקיבא יושב ומצטער ואמר, לא שהוא בן תורה יותר ממני אלא שהוא בן גדולים יותר ממני. אשרי אדם שזכו לו אבותיו. אשרי אדם שיש לו יתד להיתלות בה, וכי מה היתה יתידתו של ראב"ע, שהיה דור עשירי לעזרא...

WHO IS GREATER IN TORAH OR IN ASTRONOMY?

Although R' Akiva was a student of both R' Eliezer and R' Yehoshua, in time he excelled in his studies to such an extent that he outdistanced even his own teachers. He became so proficient in the field of astronomy that he could calculate the calendar several years in advance. And so the sefer "מנחת סולת" suggests that the issue here is not who is greater in Torah knowledge, but rather who is greater in the field of astronomy. For it is this subject which is relevant here. This approach is shared by the "אור שמח" in הלכות קדוש החדש ד:טז, where we find the following:

> דרבינו כוון לתרץ בזה הך עובדא דר"ש בן יהוצדק דאזיל לעבר שנה באסיא...שהקשו דאיך הלך לעבר שנה באסיא דהוי חוצה לארץ, ואי משום דלא הניח כמותו בארץ, הלא ר' יוחנן הי' גדול מהם...אין זה כלום...ואם כי היה גדול בתורה מהם מכל מקום מקרי לא הניח כמותו בארץ ישראל.

And so the Yerushalmi in *Sanhedrin* (פ"א ה"ב) and in *Nedarim* (פ"ו ה"ח) present this concept and conclude that only one who towers over his contemporaries in the field of astronomy can be referred to as one who fulfills the law of "שלא הניח אדם כמותו".

XI
THE QUESTION OF THE "דורות הראשונים"

A similar question was asked by HaRav Yitzchak Isaac HaLevi in his classic sefer (חלק ב' פרק ה) "דורות הראשונים". The Gemara in *Berachos* סג recounts an incident in which R' Chananiah traveled to the Diaspora for the purpose of adjusting a leap year. The Gemara in *Mesechtas Succah 20b* tells of a similar incident.

> אמר ר' חנניא כשירדתי לגולה מצאתי זקן אחד ואמר לי מסככין בבוציא, וכשבאתי אצל ר' יהושע אחי אבא הודה לדבריו.

R' Chananiah said: When I went down to the Diaspora I came across an old man who said that a reed mat may be used as a Succah covering. And when I came before R' Yehoshua, my father's brother, he agreed with his words.

Rashi comments here: "When I went down to the Diaspora" alludes to the same incident in *Berachos* סג, where it is mentioned that "Chananiah went down to the Diaspora to arrange the interpolation of an extra month in the calendar."

The "דורות הראשונים" writes that he finds this comment of Rashi's difficult to understand, for surely these two incidents refer to two separate occasions. In Mesechtas Succah it clearly states that this incident occurred during the lifetime of R' Yehoshua, for Chananiah reported to R' Yehoshua what he had heard in the Diaspora. Therefore, if the incident in Mesechtas Berachos happened on the same occasion, how could he have acted to adjust the leap year in the Diaspora, when the greatest sage of that generation, R' Yehoshua, was still alive and in Eretz Yisrael? Thus we must conclude that the incident mentioned in Mesechtas Berachos was a separate incident which must have happened much later, at the time when the eminent sages of that generation had already died. For only then would Chananiah have dared to intercalate a leap year in the Diaspora.

ודברי רבינו [רש"י] נפלאו מאד, שהרי זה ודאי שהם שני מעשים בזמנים שונים, ורחוקים מאד. שהרי כאן במסכת סוכה מפורש שהי' זה בימי ר' יהושע ושגם כשחזר משם לארץ ישראל הי' עדיין ר' יהושע חי. אבל המעשה במסכת ברכות שם מבואר מתוכה שהלך לארץ ישראל אחרי תום כל הדור ההוא. ולא לבד אחרי ר' יהושע זקן הדור, כי אם גם אחרי מות הצעירים ממנו כר' עקיבא ור' ישמעאל, דהיינו הרבה אחרי ימי ביתר.

ולשון הגמ' בברכות...אמר [חנניא] להם, והלא ר' עקיבא בן יוסף היה מעבר שנים וקובע חדשים בחוץ לארץ. אף אני לא הנחתי כמותי בארץ ישראל...והם השיבו לו, גדיים שהנחת נעשו תיישים בעלי קרנים.

Thus it would appear that R' Yehoshua and R' Akiva and his generation were no longer alive. And therefore we must say that this undertaking of Chananiah in the Diaspora happened much later than the one recorded in *Mesechtas Succah*.

However, the sefer "אגן הסהר" comes to the defense of Rashi and points out that in light of the statements made in the Yerushalmi and in the Ohr Sameach, which we previously discussed, that both incidents happened at the same time, and even though R' Yehoshua and the elders of his generation were still alive, and they were certainly greater than Chananiah in their knowledge of Torah, yet in the field of astronomy Chananiah surpassed them all, and thus he was entitled to act in the matter of adjusting the leap year.

THE אבני נזר ADDRESSES THESE QUESTIONS

The אבני נזר, in his שו"ת (אור"ח ח"ב סימן שי"ד) reiterates the question of the תוספות חדשים and adds the insight that if Rabban Gamliel was still alive, then certainly R' Eliezer was also still alive, for he outlived Rabban Gamliel (see *Bava Metzia*, נט, א). R' Eliezer was the teacher of R' Akiva, and he was also the greatest sage of his generation. How, then, could R' Akiva act in the Diaspora in accordance with the law of "שלא הניח כמותו" — that there was no one greater than he in the Diaspora? The אבני נזר resolves this apparent contradiction by pointing out that it is well known that R' Eliezer was excommunicated, and thus he was no longer considered the greatest sage of his generation in laws determined by the Bais Din.

הדבר ברור שברכוהו לר' אליעזר, וכתב הרמב"ם שהמנודה
אין מזמנים עליו כיון שהבדילוהו מביניהם אי אפשר
שיצטרפוהו, והוא הדין שאין מצטרפין אותו לקידוש החודש
שהיא בשלשה מן התורה...

The אבני נזר adds here a wonderful insight regarding this law of "שלא הניח כמותו", which is that the greatest sage may act in the Diaspora. He asks the following question. If indeed the Torah requires that all matters pertaining to Kiddush HaChodesh and עבור השנים must be restricted to Eretz Yisrael, then how can the principle of "שלא הניח אדם כמותו" have any application in the Diaspora? He answers that the advantage of Eretz Yisrael over the Diaspora in matters related to adjusting the calendar is that Eretz Yisrael is a place which serves to unite all Jews, both those living in the Land of Yisrael and those who live in the Diaspora. Similarly, the greatest sage of the generation serves the same purpose – i.e., he unites Jews living all over the world, since they all look up to him. And therefore even in the Diaspora, he can act on behalf of all Jewry.

כי יש כאן שאלה כיון דמדאורייתא לא מהני חוץ לארץ, מה יועיל מה שלא הניח כמותו בארץ ישראל... אמנם נראה לי ברורין של דברים, כי מעלת ארץ ישראל על חוץ לארץ להשוכנים בה כתב מהר"ל...כי הארץ עושה להשוכנים עליה כאיש אחד, שמאחר שהיא מיוחדת לישראל הארץ מצרפתם להיות אחד... ועל כן הגדול מכל חכמי ישראל, וכל ארץ ישראל נמשכין אחרי הגדול שצריכים לתורתו, כמו שהי' באמת בר' עקיבא דכולה סתימאי אליבא דר"ע, הרי יש לו בעצמו מעלת הכלל ישראל והוא עדיף משוכן בא"י...

XII

WHAT IF THE GADOL HADOR IN ERETZ YISRAEL CANNOT ACT?

The מנחת חינוך in "מצוה ד' אות א" asks the following question. If the greatest sage — the גדול הדור — was in Eretz Yisrael, yet due to circumstances it was not possible to determine the new month or the leap year in Eretz Yisrael, would the other sages, even though they were not as great, be able to determine the month and the leap year in the Diaspora?

> והנה אם יש גדול הדור בארץ ישראל אך שאינו יכול לקבוע שם מחמת איזה אונס, אינו מבואר בר"ם אם יוכלו הקטנים מהם לקדש בחוץ לארץ, או עכ"פ [על כל פנים] השוים כמותם.

Initially, the "מנחת חינוך" seeks to bring proof from Tosafos in *Sanhedrin 11b* (ד"ה אין מעברין). There Tosafos cites a Yerushalmi that seems to explicitly state that if the Kiddush HaChodesh process can not take place in Eretz Yisrael, then it may be effected in the Diaspora, just as the prophets Yirmiyahu, Yechezkail, and Baruch ben Neriah calculated the year in the Diaspora, because at that time it could not be done in Eretz Yisrael. Thus we see, contends the "מנחת חינוך", that if circumstances warrant, the calendar can be determined in the Diaspora.

However, the sefer "מנחת סולת" dismisses this proof of the מנחת חינוך regarding the words of Tosafos here. For what Tosafos seems to be saying is that even though it is true that the greatest sage of the generation may act in the Diaspora, yet there is a condition attached, and that is, if it is possible for him to return to Eretz Yisrael and proclaim the new month or the leap year in Eretz Yisrael, then he must do so. He may only act in the Diaspora if circumstances prevent him from determining the month and the leap year in Eretz Yisrael.

> אך התוס' סברי דאם אפשר להגדול לנסוע לארץ לקבוע שם, מוכרח לעשות כן מכח "כי מציון תצא תורה"...אך באם לא אפשר לו לעשות כן מותר לו לעשות הכל בחוץ לארץ. לכן הוכיחו זה מירושלמי, דבא"י בא"י דהיינו הגדול הדור לא יכול לנסוע שמה יכול לעבר בחו"ל, כמו שעשה ירמי'... שלא יכלו לנסוע לארץ, לכן קבעו בח"ל...

Chapter Ten

The Role of Sanhedrin in Sanctifying the Month

I

Bais Din HaGadol or Semicha

There is a basic difference of opinion between the Rambam and the Ramban regarding who has jurisdiction in the matter of establishing the calendar year. The Rambam is of the opinion that only the Sanhedrin HaGadol or those who have semicha (ordination) and were granted permission to act in this matter, may establish the month or the leap year. The source for this requirement can be traced to the מכילתא בפרשת בא, which states:

> ר' יאשיה אומר: מנין שאין מעברין את השנה אלא בבית דין הגדול שבירושלים, שנאמר "ראשון הוא לכם וכו' דברו אל כל עדת ישראל."

The Ramban holds a different opinion, maintaining that all that is necessary is ordination (סמיכה). Any Bais Din whose members are ordained can establish the calendar. The proof he offers for this contention is from the pasuk which dictated the mitzva of Kiddush HaChodesh. This pasuk reads: "**החודש הזה לכם**" — "This month shall be *for you*". In other words, those who determine the calendar shall be *like you*, i.e., "**מומחים**", ordained. Had the Torah called for the Sanhedrin HaGadol to act here, then the verse would have read: "**החודש הזה לך**", similar to the pasuk from which we derive that indeed only the Sanhedrin HaGadol can act: "**הדבר הגדול יביאו אליך**" — "All great matters will be brought to *you*", and here the word "you" alludes to Moshe Rabbenu, who originally acted as judge and was later succeeded by the seventy-one elders.

Therefore, since the verse here states "לכם", it would seem that all that is required is that those referred to should be the same as Moshe and Aharon, in the sense that they have received semicha, ordination.

THE OPINION OF THE RAMBAM

The Rambam outlines his thinking here in the Sefer HaMitzvos, מצוה קנג, where he writes:

> המצוה קנג היא שצונו לקדש חדשים ולחשוב חדשים ושנים וזו היא מצות קדוש החדש. והוא אמרו ית' "החדש הזה לכם ראש חדשים" ובא הפירוש שעדות זו תהא מסורה לכם כלומר שמצוה זו אינה מסורה לכל איש ואיש כמו שבת בראשית שכל איש ימנה ששה ימים וישבות בשביעי, כשיראה כל איש ואיש גם כן הלבנה שיקבע היום ראש חדש או ימנה ענין תוריי ויקבע ראש חדש או יעיין אחור האביב וזולתו ממה שראוי להסתכל בו ויוסיף חדש, אבל מצוה זו לא יעשה אותה לעולם אלא **בית דין הגדול לבד ובארץ ישראל לבד**...

> ...in explication, they said *(Rosh Hashanah 22a)*: "This testimony [regarding the appearance of the moon] is relegated to you" [Sanhedrin]. That is, this mitzva is not relegated to each individual, as is the Shabbos of Creation, where each one counts six days and rests on the seventh, so that anyone who saw the moon could declare the new moon or compute the new moon through the Torah's [festival based] computation, or see that spring has come late and add a month. Rather, this mitzva is relegated for all time to the Great Sanhedrin, specifically and in Eretz Yisrael.

And the Rambam states in *Hilchos Kiddush HaChodesh 5:1*:

> כל מה שאמרנו מקביעות ראש חודש על הראיה ועבור השנה מפני הזמן או מפני הצורך אין עושין אותו אלא סנהדרין שבארץ ישראל, או בית דין הסמוכים בארץ ישראל שנתנו להן הסנהדרין רשות.

שכך נאמר למשה ואהרון: החודש הזה לכם ראש חדשים
ומפי השמועה למדו איש מאיש ממשה רבינו, שכך הוא
פירוש הדבר: עדות זו תהי' מסורה לכם וכל העומד אחריכם
במקומכם...

All the statements made previously [in Chapter Four] regarding the [prerogative to] sanctify Rosh Chodesh because of the sighting of the moon and to establish a leap year to reconcile the calendar or out of necessity, apply to the Sanhedrin in Eretz Yisrael. For it is they alone, or a court of judges who have been ordained (have semicha) that holds sessions in Eretz Yisrael and was granted authority by the Sanhedrin.

This concept is derived from the command given to Moshe and Aharon *[Exodus 12:2]:* "This month shall be for you the first of months." The Oral Tradition as passed down from teacher to student, from Moshe our teacher, explains that the verse is to be interpreted as follows: This testimony is entrusted to you and to those sages who will arise after you and who will function in your position [i.e., the Sages of the Sanhedrin]...

THE RAMBAN'S OBJECTIONS

The Ramban vehemently objects to this contention of the Rambam's, that a Sanhedrin is required to bring about the sanctification of the new moon. For if this were so, the Ramban points out, it is well known that forty years prior to the destruction of the Bais HaMikdash, the Sanhedrin went into exile (See *Mesechtas Avodah Zarah 8:b),* leaving the premises of the Bais HaMikdash. How, then, were they able to sanctify the new moon by means of eyewitnesses, a process which, according to the Rambam himself, lasted only until the days of Abaye and Rava [see the Rambam's *Hilchos Kiddush HaChodesh 5:3* which states: "וכן בימי חכמי הגמרא עד ימי אביי ורבא על קביעת ארץ ישראל היו סומכין".].

So writes the Ramban in his gloss on *Sefer HaMitzvos, Mitzva 153*:

...והתימא מן הרב כי הוא אומר שהמצוה הזאת לא יעשו אותה לעולם אלא בי"ד הגדול ובא"י ולפיכך בטלה אצלינו היום בהעדר הב"ד הגדול...והנה דבר ברור הוא וידוע הוא שבית דין הגדול בטל מארץ ישראל ואפילו קודם החרבן...כמו שאמרו בפ"ק מעבודה זרה [ח', ב', וראה בשבת ט"ו, ב'] ארבעים שנה עד שלא חרב הבית גלתה הסנהדרין וישבה לה בחנות, למאי הלכתא, לומר שלא דנו דיני נפשות, כיון דחזי דנפישי להו רוצחים אמרו מוטב נגלה ממקום למקום, דכתיב 'ועשית על פי הדבר אשר יגידו לך **מן המקום ההוא** אשר יבחר ה'' [דברים י"ז, י'], מלמד שהמקום גורם כלומר שכל זמן שסנהדרי גדולה במקומם בלשכת הגזית סנהדרי קטנה נוהגת בכל מקום אפילו בחוצה לארץ, ודנין דיני נפשות בכל מקום, אבל משגלתה סנהדרי גדולה מן המקום ההוא בטלו דיני נפשות מכל ישראל.

ואפילו ביציאתם משם לטייל מעט ולחזור בטל כוחן ורשותן מהם עד שיהיו במקומן...מלמד **שהמקום גורם**, וכל שכן לאחר החורבן...

ואם כן לא היו יכולין לקדש ע"פ הראיה מזמן הארבעים שנה קודם החורבן. וידוע הוא בכמה מקומות בגמרא שהיו עושין כך עד זמן קרוב לסתימת התלמוד, ובין בראיה ובין בחשבון בזמן הרע הזה שאין בארץ ישראל סנהדרין ולא בית דין סמוכין כלל, ואין בחו"ל בית דין שנסמך בארץ, לא יועיל חשבוננו שום תועלת בשום פנים **כפי דברי הרב**, שכבר נעדר מארץ ישראל בית דין שנסמך בארץ...

Thus, according to the Ramban, if the Great Sanhedrin is not situated in the Chamber of Hewn Stone, it no longer retains the status of the Sanhedrin HaGadol. How, then, could the Rambam account for the obvious fact that Kiddush HaChodesh lasted long after the destruction of the Bais HaMikdash?

DEFENDING THE RAMBAM

Once the Sanhedrin left the confines of the לשכת הגזית, they lost their authority to function as the highest judicial authority — בית דין הגדול. How, then, did they determine the matter of Kiddush HaChodesh, if, as the Rambam contends, the Sanhedrin was required to sit in its designated place? The classic commentaries to the Sefer HaMitzvos, the מגילת אסתר and the לב שמח answer this question by suggesting that only in relation to certain issues is the Sanhedrin required to be situated in its designated place "סנהדרין הגדול במקומם"— in the Bais HaMikdash, בלשכת הגזית. This condition would apply, for example, in cases involving murder. However, the Sanhedrin was also recognized outside the confines of the Bais HaMikdash and was able to function as the Great Sanhedrin of Klal Yisrael in many matters, including the sanctification of the month, Kiddush HaChodesh. Proof of this, points out the "לב שמח", is that if the Sanhedrin had completely lost the ability to function as a סנהדרין של ע"א, why would they have left there in the first place? So writes the לב שמח:

> לכאורה הוא טענה זו חזקה מאד. וכד מעייניו שפיר לאו מילתא היא...דמאותה שעה [שגלתה מהבית] נמי בטלו כל הדינין התלויין בבי"ד... נלע"ד שאין התחייבות הזה צודק. כי דברים כפשוטן גלתה סנהדרין...שלא דנו התלויין בהם משמע. ומה זו שאלה [ששואל הגמ' במסכת ע"ז] למאי הלכתא? ומה זו תשובה שלא דנו דיני נפשות? אבל זה מורה **דאדרבה משום שראו דעדיין מילתא דסנהדרין בדוכתא**

קיימא לכמה מילי, שאלו [הגמ'] למאי הילכתא...ותירצו היינו [רק] לדיני נפשות...והמובן ממנו הוא דלשאר מילי **לא בטלה**, ולכך ודאי היו מקדשין בראיה עד זמן אביי.

Proof that the Sanhedrin continued to function [with full authority] is that everyone recognized the "בי"ד של ע"א ביבנה", the Sanhedrin of seventy-one in the city of Yavne, which carried with it all the authority of a בית דין של ע"א [except in those cases that were specifically restricted to the Sanhedrin in its original location, referred to as "מקום הנבחר"]. Therefore, when it came to sanctifying the new month, Kiddush HaChodesh, this Bais Din qualified as having the proper authority to act on those matters of adjusting the months, the leap year and the calendar.

CLARIFYING THIS RATIONALE

We have attempted to explain this phenomenon elsewhere (see *The Commentators' Gift of Torah*, pp. 270-272). There we pointed out that the Great Sanhedrin, סנהדרין הגדול, served the following functions: It was the supreme judicial body of Klal Yisrael and it functioned in a purely judicial capacity, and it acted as the representative of Klal Yisrael in matters that require the sanction of the community.

A classic example of this second feature is the declaration of Kiddush HaChodesh. The Sanhedrin acted on behalf of Klal Yisrael, who actually has the power to declare new months, yet as the Mechilta points out, they relinquished this right in favor of the Sanhedrin, and it was then that the Sanhedrin acted on their behalf. Thus what is essential here is a Sanhedrin which can function as the representative of the community of Klal Yisrael. All the Higher Courts, even after the Destruction of the Bais HaMikdash, functioned as the representative of Klal Yisrael, and therefore they can act on their behalf as long as those courts remained intact [until the time of Abaye and Rava]. However, had the matter of Kiddush HaChodesh required the Sanhedrin to act as a judicial body rather than as a representative of the congregation of Yisrael, we would have had a problem. Thus, we can conclude [see *The Commentators' Gift of Torah, ibid.*] that in relation to Kiddush HaChodesh, the role of the Sanhedrin was simply to act as a representative body. [See Part III for an explanation of this concept by HaRav Yosef Dov Soloveitchik and the [עמ' מ"ז-ס"ד] from "קובץ חידושי תורה" (אסופות מאמרים מאת הגרי"ד)].

II

OTHER OBJECTIONS CITED BY THE RAMBAN

The Ramban has yet another objection to this contention of the Rambam's, that Kiddush HaChodesh and inserting a leap year require a בית דין הגדול and the full participation of all the members of the Sanhedrin. The Ramban, on the other hand, presents a number of sources that clearly indicate that all that is required here is the participation of three judges. He cites the following opinions.

The first Mishna in *Mesechtas Sanhedrin* states:

> עבור החדש בשלשה. עבור השנה בשלשה.

> The intercalation of a day into the month [creating a month of 30 days] is done by a court of three. The intercalation of a month into the year is done by a court of three.

From this we see that all that is called for are three judges, not the whole of the Sanhedrin. The Mishna in *Mesechtas Rosh Hashana 25b* states:

ראוהו **שלשה** והן בית דין, יעמדו השנים ויושיבו מחבריהם אצל היחיד... ויאמרו מקודש מקודש...

> If only three people saw the new moon and they are members of the Great Court, two of them should stand ready to testify and should seat two other sages from among their colleagues beside the single judge... and they should then proclaim, "It is sanctified, it is sanctified."

The Gemara in *Sanhedrin 26a* cites the following incident:

רבי חייא בר זרנוקי ור' שמעון בן יהוצדק הוי אזלי לעבר שנה בעסיא פגע להו ריש לקיש...

> Once, during the seventh year, R' Chiya bar Zarnoki and R' Shimon ben Yehotzadak were traveling to Asia to intercalate the year. Reish Lakish met them and joined them...

The Ramban points out that none of these sages were members of the Sanhedrin. Thus we see again that those who have the authority to intercalate a leap year are not required to be members of the Sanhedrin, but they *must be ordained*.

In the Yerushalmi Sanhedrin פ"א ה"א we are told that a vote was taken regarding whether or not to intercalate the year. The vote began with R' Yochanan, who was the "smallest" among those seated. Thus again we see that membership in the Sanhedrin is not required, for R' Yochanan was never a member of the Sanhedrin.

The "מגילת אסתר" dismisses these proofs

The "מגילת אסתר" defends the Rambam, despite these citations, by pointing out that all that was required here were three judges. However, they must be members of the Sanhedrin. The Rambam never meant to imply that Kiddush HaChodesh calls for the Great Sanhedrin to act in this matter, i.e., that all its members must participate, but rather all they had to do was to empower three of their colleagues to take part in the process of determining the new month.

אמנם הרמב"ן לא הבין דעתו, שאין רצונו שיצטרכו כל הסנהדרין גדולה כדי לקדש או לעבר, רק שעל פי שלשה מהם תעשה זאת המצוה, וזהו פירוש המשנה שהביא הרמב"ן מריש סנהדרין שאומר קדוש החדש ועבור השנה בשלשה ר"ל [רוצה לומר] שלשה מסנהדרי גדולה...

And as for the proofs for those who participated in the process of establishing the leap year, who were not members of the Sanhedrin, the answer would be that these sages "left no one of their own stature in Eretz Yisrael" — "ולא הניח בארץ ישראל כמותו" — and just as R' Akiva was able to declare a leap year in the Diaspora based on this halacha, so too were they allowed to act here based on the same concept.

...נראה לי, שאין מכאן טענה עליו, לפי שאלו החכמים לא הניחו כמותם בארץ ובזה הדבר היה מעבר ר' עקיבא.. וכן חנניא בסוף הרואה..

The Ramban's view: three סמוכים suffice

As we have pointed out, the Ramban maintains that all that is required in order to declare a new month and a leap year is that the process be carried out by three individuals who have received ordination, סמיכה. One can advance proof that membership in the Sanhedrin is not required, for if this had been the case, the pasuk would have stated: "החודש הזה לך" — "The matter of Rosh Chodesh is designated to *you*, Moshe." As we know, when we refer to Moshe, we mean the Great Sanhedrin, for Moshe Rabbenu alone was considered to have had the authority equivalent to the full seventy-one member Sanhedrin, "משה במקום ע״א עומד". And so, when Moshe acted upon an issue, it was as if seventy-one judges participated in his decision. The Ramban therefore contends that since the plural form was used here: "לכם" — "to *you*", which included Aharon HaKohen, this alluded to "those who are like you", i.e., מומחה, which refers to those who had been ordained.

ואל תשתומם בזה ממאמרם (סנהדרין יא, ב) "משה במקום ע״א קאי..." שצווי הכתוב "לכם" אינו אלא למומחים, כיוצא בכם, שאילו הי׳ מסור לסנהדרי גדולה בלבד, היה אומר החודש הזה **לך**. כמו שאמרו (שם טז) "אין דנין כהן גדול אלא בב״ד של ע״א" דכתיב "את הדבר הגדול יביאו **אליך**" ומשה במקום שבעים ואחד קאי, ולא היה לאהרון זכר בקדוש החודש. אלא מפני שאומר "לכם" הכניס אהרון בכלל, להורות שצריך שנים דומים לשניהם בהמחאה, ותוספת השלישי ידוע מדין אין בית דין שקול, וחזר הדבר לכל שלשה מומחין...

Defending the Rambam

The "מגילת אסתר" once again comes to the Rambam's defense by pointing out that had the Torah indeed written: "החודש הזה לך", we would have been given the impression that not only do we need seventy-one elders of the Sanhedrin to act in this matter, but indeed *all* of them must participate and not merely designate three of its members.

ומה שהביא עוד, כי ממה שאמר הכתוב "החודש הזה
לכם", ולא "לך" משמע שאין צריך ב"ד הגדול אלא מומחים
כמוהו. ונראה לי, כי ממה שלא כתב "לך" הוא לפי שהיה
במשמע שיצטרך הבית דין הגדול **כולו** בזאת המצוה, לכן
כתב "לכם" לומר שדי במומחים כמותם, אבל צריך שיהיו
מב"ד הגדול, דומיא דמשה. ומה שהזכיר אהרן שמא היה
לרמוז שבזמן שאין ב"ד הגדול שדי במומחין...

[See how the view of the Rambam is reconciled by the
פרשת בא in מהרי"ל דיסקין על התורה.]

III

THE SEMICHAH CONTROVERSY

It is well known that in the year 1538 an attempt was made by HaRav Yaacov Berav, מהר"י בירב, to reinstate the ordination (סמיכה) process. This would have meant that those empowered with semichah would have been able to judge monetary cases which involved fines, punish a guilty party with lashes, etc. and declare the new month and a leap year. What prompted this venture was the following halachah: Anyone who was liable to kares (כרת) and who was flogged *by the court* instead, is freed from this Divine punishment, as it is said, "and your brother will be dishonored before your eyes" *(Dvarim 25:3)*. Once he has been flogged, he is like 'your brother'; i.e., he is now exempt from punishment *(Makos 3:15)*.

This was the period when the Marranos, who had converted to Christianity out of fear but continued to practice their religion in secret, now openly returned to Judaism. However, they were plagued with guilt for having practiced Christianity and therefore felt they deserved the punishment of kares, as prescribed for one who practices idolatry. They believed that the only way to "cleanse" themselves was to receive lashes from a Bais Din. This was the reason Rav Yaacov Berav attempted to convene a proper Bais Din, which would then be empowered to administer lashes according to Torah law. He attempted to do this by invoking a law stated by the Rambam in *Hilchos Sanhedrin 4:11*:

> נראין לי הדברים שאם הסכימו כל החחכמים שבארץ ישראל למנות דיינים ולסמוך אותם הרי אלו סמוכים ויש להם לדון-דיני קנסות, ויש להם לסמוך לאחרים...

> It would appear to me: should all the Rabbis living in Eretz Yisrael appoint judges and *ordain* them, then this declaration of semicha would be official. These newly-ordained Rabbis would then have the power to judge cases of fines and also to ordain others.

Rav Yaacov Berav ordained Rav Yosef Karo (author of the Shulchan Aruch), Rav Moshe Torani (known as the MaBit), Rav Moshe Galante and Rav Moshe Cordovero.

Immediately after completing the ordination ceremony, Rav Yaacov Berav sent a dignified emissary to Yerushalayim with a letter personally conferring Semicha on the Rav of Yerushalayim, Rav Levi Ibn Chaviv, the RalBach. The רלב"ח not only refused the ordination but objected to this attempt to reinstate the process of conferring Semicha by pointing out the far-reaching ramifications of such a bold act. (For a detailed study of this whole controversy, see the sefer "תולדות חכמי ירושלים", חלק א, מאת הרב ארי ליב פרומקין.)

Here we will deal only with what relates directly to our subject matter, as recorded in the classic "קונטרס הסמיכה", included in the sefer "שו"ת הרלב"ח".

The Objection of the RalBach

One of the main objections of the רלב"ח against the attempt to reinstate the process of ordination was related to the issue of adjusting the calendar. As we have pointed out, the Ramban believed that all that was needed to establish the new month was "סמוכים", the authorization of one who has been ordained. Thus, if ordination was to be re-established, this would mean that the present Bais Din, made up of those who had received ordination, would have to reinstitute the process of determining the month by means of eyewitnesses — "קדוש על פי הראייה".

This would mean that it would no longer be possible to determine the month according to the fixed calendar of Hillel II. And this would lead to there being a blatant discrepancy between these two systems. For Rosh Chodesh would no longer fall on the same day as that designated by the fixed calendar. Consequently, if the halacha followed the opinion of those who argue with the Rambam, that we cannot renew the Semicha process, then Rosh Chodesh would have to remain as it had been set down by the fixed calendar of Hillel II. Thus we would have here a conflict as to when to establish Rosh Chodesh. The RalBach writes as follows:

"ועתה יראו רבני צפת כמה הכניסו עצמם בין שני הרים גדולים, הרמב"ם והרמב"ן ז"ל...כי אפילו במינוי שלשה סמוכים לבד יש חשש קלקול המועדות, וזה שאולי השלשה היא קיימת כסברת הרמב"ם שלא כדברי הרמב"ן [שלפי שיטת הרמב"ן אי אפשר בסמיכה בזמן הזה עד שיבוא המורה צדק]. ולא ידענו עם זה אם קדוש החודש צריך סנהדרין ונשיא כדברי הרמב"ם ולדעתו קביעות המועדים הם כפי העיבור שבידינו, או אינם צריכים סנהדרין ונשיא, כי אם שלשה סמוכים כדברי הרמב"ן ויהיו קביעותם על פי הראייה..."

Rav Yaacov Berav's Response

Rav Yaacov Berav countered this objection by pointing out that since the calender fixed by Hillel has been accepted, therefore the halacha that an inferior Bais Din cannot annul a law established by a greater Bais Din would apply, and thus no problem in this regard would be encountered.

מפני שראיתי לאחד מן התלמידים שטעה בזה. ואמר שאם היינו יכולים לסמוך היינו יכולים לעבר שנים ולקבוע המועדות...ועתה נשאר לנו לבאר אם הם סמוכים שנעשו בזמן הזה אם יכולים לקדש חדשים ולקבוע מועדות על פי הראייה. ונאמר שפשיטא ופשיטא שאין להם יכולת לבטל מה שעשה ר' הלל ובית דינו, דהא קי"ל בכל דבר שבמנין צריך מנין אחר להתירו ולא ימצא מנין אחר עד יבוא מורה צדק. ותיקן החדשים והמועדות שתיקן ר' הלל ובית דינו היה בשנת ד' אלפים ששים לבריאת עולם...

The Ralbach Answers Rav Berav

The רלב"ח dismisses this contention of Rav Berav by attempting to prove that the halacha that a lesser Bais Din cannot nullify a decision of a greater Bais Din does not apply here. For the matter of determining the new month is based on a halacha given to Moshe Rabbenu at Sinai — הלכה למשה מסיני — namely, that when there is no Bais Din, the new month is determined by means of calculation. However, when there is a Bais Din, the month is determined by that Bais Din through the testimony of eyewitnesses. Thus, if we were to reinstitute the process of ordination, the new month would automatically be determined by eyewitnesses and there would be no question of nullifying a decision by a greater Bais Din.

גם הטענה האחרת שכתב לפנים לזה מטעם שהחשבון

העיבור נתקן על ידי הלל ואין שום בית דין רשאי לבטל בית דין חבירו אלא אם כן גדול ממנו בחכמה ובמנין וזה לא נמצא עד ימות המשיח, גם זאת הטעגה **אינה כלל** של דעת הרמב״ם שתלה הדבר בהלכה למשה מסיני הלל לא תיקן **אלא לזמן** דליכא סנהדרין ואי הוו הדרי סנהדרין לדוכתייהו אף על גב דלא ליהוי בית דינייהו גדול בחכמה מבית דינו של הלל היינו מחויבין לקדש על פי הראייה...

IV

THE RAMBAM'S VIEW IN SEFER HAMITZVOS

The Rambam in Sefer HaMitzvos, מצוה קנג, after he states his position that only the Great Sanhedrin can act to determine the new month, makes the following observation:

> Therefore, this mitzva regarding the declaration of a new moon does not obtain for us today, because of the absence of a Great Sanhedrin, just as the Offerings do not obtain today because of the absence of the Bais HaMikdash....Know that this reckoning which we employ today, by which we determine new moons and festivals, is permitted only in Eretz Yisrael. And it is only in difficult straits and in the absence of Sages from Eretz Yisrael that *a Bais Din which has been ordained in Eretz Yisrael* is permitted to intercalate years and determine new moons outside the Land of Yisrael, as R' Akiva did...

And there is a great foundation here of the faith which is known and felt only by those of probing intellect, namely our present-day reckoning outside Eretz Yisrael by the calendar which has come down to us, by which we declare one day to be the new moon and another day a festival. By no means whatsoever do we make it a festival because of our reckoning, but only because the Bais Din in Eretz Yisrael has determined that day to be a festival or a new moon, whether their declaration is the result of calculation or of observation [by eyewitnesses], as we have received it in the Kabbalah [received tradition] *(Rosh Hashanah 25a).* 'The festivals of Hashem, you shall call them' *(Vayikra 23:2).* 'I have no other festivals but these.' That is, these which the Bais Din declare to be festivals, even if they do so under duress, even if they are mistaken...The only reason we do the reckoning today is to know the day determined by those in Eretz Yisrael; for it is in this manner that they determine it today, not through observation. And it is on their determination that we rely, not on our reckoning...

I shall add some explanation. If we were to assume, for example, the absence of the Sages of Eretz Yisrael from Eretz Yisrael, God forbid that this should occur, for He had already assured us that the remnant of the people will not be utterly destroyed and uprooted. And if we were to assume that no Bais Din were to be found there, or that there would not be found outside the land a Bais Din ordained in Eretz Yisrael, this reckoning of ours would not avail us at all. For outside of Eretz Yisrael we are not to intercalate years and determine new moons except under those conditions we have mentioned, as we explained *(Isaiah 20:3),* "For from Zion shall go forth Torah and the Word of Hashem from Yerushalayim."

...ודע שחשבון זה שנמנה אותו היום ונדע בו ראשי חדשים והמועדים אי אפשר לעשותו, אלא בארץ ישראל לבד ובעת הצורך ובהעדר החכמים מארץ ישראל אז אפשר לב"ד הסמוך לארץ ישראל שיעבר השנים ויקבע חדשים בחוצה לארץ כמו שעשה ר' עקיבא...

ובכאן שרש גדול משרשי האמונה לא ידעוהו ולא יתבוננן במקומו אלא מי שדעתו עמוקה וזה שהיותנו היום בחוצה לארץ מונים במלאכה העבור שבידינו ואומרים שזה היום ר"ח וזה היום יו"ט, לא מפני חשבוננו נקבענו יו"ט בשום פנים אבל מפני שב"ד הגדול שבארץ ישראל כבר קבעוהו

זה היום ר"ח או יו"ט ומפני אמרם שזה היום ר"ח או
יו"ט יהי' ר"ח או יו"ט בין שהיתה פעולתם זאת בחשבון או
בראיה כמו שבא בפירוש אשר תקראו אותם אין לי אלא
מועדות אלו כלומר שיאמרו הם שהם מועדות אפילו אנוסין
אפילו מוטעין אפילו שוגגין כמו שבאה הקבלה ואנחנו
אמנם נחשב היום שקבעו הם ר"ל בני ארץ ישראל בו ר"ח
כי במלאכה הזאת בעצמה מונין וקובעין לא בראיה ועל
קביעותם נסמך לא על חשבוננו אבל חשבוננו הוא לגלויי
מלתא בעלמא...

ואני אוסיף לו באור, אלו הנחנו דרך משל שבני ארץ ישראל
יעדרו מארץ ישראל חלילה לא-ל מעשות זאת, כי הוא
הבטיח שלא ימחה אותת האומה מכל וכל ולא יהי' שם ב"ד
ולא יהי' בחוצה לארץ ב"ד שנסמך בארץ הנה חשבוננו
זה לא יועילנו כלום בשום פנים לפי שאין לנו לחשב חדשים
ולעבר שנים בחוצה לארץ אלא בתנאים הנזכרים כמו
שביארנו כי מציון תצא תורה...

Rav Yaacov Berav's explanation

Rav Yaacov Berav attempts to answer the following questions raised by the Ramban: The Sanhedrin is required to determine the new month. How then, could they have determined the new month in the days of Abaye and Rava, when the institition of the Sanhedrin was no longer in existence? Furthermore, how do we determine new moons and holidays today, when we no longer have a Sanhedrin.

Rav Yaacov Berav answers these questions by citing the view of the Rambam in Hilchos Sanhedrin, that since it is possible for all those living in Eretz Yisrael to reach a consensus, they have the right to reinstate the process of ordination, even if it is only for the purpose of adjusting the calendar month. Proof of this contention is that the Rambam, in Sefer HaMitzvos, speaks of the promise that there will *always* be Jews living in Eretz Yisrael.

He does not speak here of a *Bais Din*, but rather of *Bnai Yisrael*, which means that even if an actual Bais Din does not exist, the *community of Yisrael* has the authority and the power to appoint a Bais Din. Thus we can justifiably assume that Bnai Yisrael does indeed concur that the present leaders of the community in Yisrael should be "ordained" for this purpose alone—that is, to determine the new moons and the festivals.

לכן אני אומר לתקן זה הקושי הגדול [של הרמב"ן] שהרב הולך לשיטתו שהוא סובר שאם נתקבצו כל חכמי ארץ ישראל יכולין לסמוך מי שירצו. ועתה כשקובעין ואומרים יום פלוני הוא ראשי חדשים או יום פלוני הוא מועד הוי לי' כאילו מסכימים כלם שחכמיהם יהיו סמוכים לעניין קדה"ח וקביעות המועדים. שיכולים הם לסמוך סמוך א' לקצת דברים ולקצת דברים לא יהי' סמוך. ובודאי שבעניין כזה אין שום חולק בכל א"י ולא בחכמים ולא בהמון העם שלא יסכימו שיהיו חכמיהם סמוכין לזה העניין.

ואם תדקדק בלשון שכתב הרב בס' המצות שלו...משם מתבאר לך שמה שכתב "שהוא הבטיח שלא ימחה אות האומה מהכל וכו' נראה מה שכתבתי ולמה לן להזכיר "בני ארץ ישראל" לא הוי ליה להזכיר אלא הב"ד והחכמים. אלא ודאי הכוונה הוא שאף על פי שלא יהי' שם ב"ד בפירוש אנן סהדי מן הסתם שכל החכמים וכל ישראל מסכימים שיהי' הראשי' מהם סמוכין לעניין קביעות החדשים, ואף על פי שלא יפרשו ובזה יתורצו כל הקושיות שעשה הרמב"ן על הרב ז"ל.

The Ralbach answers the Ramban

The רלב"ח also addresses the question posed by the Ramban of how the Rambam manages to justify the implementation of a calendar after we no longer have the required Sanhedrin. He suggests two possible approaches: The Rambam recognizes the

Ramban's contention that it was Hillel II who established a fixed calendar for Klal Yisrael. And when the Rambam says: "מפני שבית הגדול שבא"י כבר קבעו זה היום", that "the Bais Din HaGadol already set today's date as Rosh Chodesh", his emphasis on the "בי"ד הגדול" and "כבר" — "already", alludes to the enactment of Hillel II. For Hillel was the head of the Sanhedrin and he "already" fixed the calendar. This answers the Ramban's question. However, the Ramban seems to have asked his question in the first place because he appears to have had a different version of the text, for even though the "בית דין הגדול" was mentioned, the word "כבר", "already", did not appear. This leads him to question how the Rambam justified the instituting of a fixed calendar.

A second approach offered by the Rambam is that we have two systems of adjusting the calendar. They are the following: The first system introduces complicated mathematical formulas that can only be calculated by the Bais Din HaGadol by means of a tradition handed down by Moshe at Sinai.

The second system applies a fixed formula. As the Rambam himself writes, even a child can understand how to apply this formula. In the first case, we need a Great Sanhedrin, however in the second, all we need is that this formula should be applied in Eretz Yisrael. This answers the Ramban's questions.

והנני בא לישב כל זה ואומר כי בקביעות החדשים ועבור השנים ע"י החשבון שבידינו היום או אי זה חשבון אחר יש בו ב' דברים. האחד המצאת החכמה ההיא וחדוש כלליה ועיקריה וסדורם. הב' **ההשתמשות** אחר כך באותם השרשים והכללים והקביעה בכל שנה ושנה על ידם ולומר שהשנה הזאת היא פשוטה או מעוברת...והנה שום אחד מאלו הב' דברים אין אנו יכולים לעשות בח"ל, אם הדבר הא' שהוא המצאת החכמה וחדוש כל אותם הכללים הוא מבואר ואפילו בא"י אין כח לעשותו ולחדשו אם לא יהי' מקובל בידם הלכה למשה מסיני או ע"י בי"ד הגדול. אם הדבר הב' אף על גב דהוא חושבנא דעלמא ואין בו חכמה ומזה הטעם יכולים לעשותו בארץ אפילו אותם שאינם סמוכים, מכל מקום בחוצה לארץ אין יכולים לעשותו מטעם

דקרא "כי מציון תצא תורה." אף על פי שהם [ר"ל בי"ד
הגדול] לא קבעו אותו אלא שחדשו לנו דרכים לקבוע אותו...
הרי הוא כאלו קבעו אותו כיון שע"י שחדשו הם החכמה
ההיא יכולים בני א"י אף על פי שלא יהיו סמוכים לקבוע
חדשים ומועדות בכל שנה ושנה...

THE ACHARONIM AND THE QUESTIONS OF THE RAMBAN

Various Acharonim address the questions raised by the Ramban. His two major questions are the following: How does the Ramban justify the implementation of the halachic calendar after the Destruction of the Bais HaMikdash, when there no longer existed a Sanhedrin HaGadol? How do we have a calendar today without the Sanhedrin HaGadol?

The Acharonim basically give the same answers as does the מהר"י בירב, Rav Yaacov Berav.

THE INSIGHT OF THE "שו"ת נפש חיה"

HaRav Elazar Vachs, the author of the responsa "שו"ת נפש חיה" (סימן א), addresses the question of how the calendar was implemented after the Destruction of the Bais HaMikdash. The answer he gives is that the House of the Nasi, the president of the Great Sanhedrin, lasted until after the time of Hillel II, and the Nasi had the authority to act on this matter of adjusting the calendar. His authority was recognized not only by Klal Yisrael but was accepted at that time by all Jewry all over the world.

והנה אף שבטלו הסנהדרין, עדיין היה ראשי הגולה
ונשיאים אשר יש בהם כח על כל ישראל וגזירתם נתפשטה

> על כולם וכל ישראל נכרכים אחריהם עדיין הי' יכולים
> לקדש חדשים ולעבר שנים. ובזה ייתישב תמיהת הרמב"ן
> על הרמב"ם דלשיטתו דרך בית דין הגדול יכולים לקדש
> ולעבר והוא הביא בעצמו דחכמי המשנה והתלמוד נהגו
> לקדש על פי הראייה. ולפי הנ"ל ניחא דכל זמן שהיו נשיאים
> עד ר' הלל הנשיא והי' בכחם על כל ישראל עדיין היו
> יכולים לקדש ולעבר, וכן מי שיצא בחו"ל ולא הניח כמותו
> בארץ דהי' יכול לקדש הוא גם כן מההיא טעמא דכל
> ישראל נמשכו אחריו...

V

JUSTIFYING THE LEGALITY OF OUR CALENDAR

Today, how can we legally justify our ability to proclaim the new month, since we no longer have a Great Sanhedrin in existence nor have our present-day sages received ordination, סמיכה? These two requirements were crucial to the Rambam (who insisted on the presence of the סנהדרין הגדול) and the Ramban (who required מוסמכים). A possible answer might be that since Hillel II established a fixed calendar, this set forth the times of the new months from his day until the time of the Moshiach. Alternatively, it is the present-day Jews living in Eretz Yisrael who today declare Rosh Chodesh.

Yet these attempts to solve the problem raise a number of further questions. If indeed Hillel set up a calendar that declared the day of Rosh Chodesh until the times of Moshiach, why does the halacha insist that if one forgets to recite the "יעלה ויבוא" prayer at night, then he need not repeat the Amidah prayer, since Rosh Chodesh will only be proclaimed the next morning? This is puzzling, for if Hillel already designated all the forthcoming days of Rosh Chodesh, then the night of Rosh Chodesh has automatically already been declared as well. This question was raised by the "שו"ת אבני נזר" in אור"ח סימן ש"י, where we find:

דהנה קשה לי לשיטת הרמב"ן דעל חשבון הלל אנו
סומכים, שקידש כל החדשים ועיבר כל השנים עד שישוב
הסמיכה לישראל, הא אמרינן בסוף פרק תפלת השחר,
דף ל,ב, והלכה רווחה בישראל, שכח לומר יעלה ויבוא
ערבית אין מחזירין אותו, שאין מקדשין החודש בלילה, ואם
כן כיון שקדש הלל כל החדשים, הרי **כבר נתקדש החדש
מימי הלל**...

If Hillel II in his day already sanctified the months, why do we still require a ישוב, a settlement of Jews in Eretz Yisrael, to declare the new moon, when Kiddush HaChodesh has already been accomplished for the present and the forseeable future (until the time of Moshiah)? How are we to understand the dynamics of what Hillel accomplished in sanctifying Rosh Chodesh?

The answer to the question of the אבני נזר is that Hillel only sanctified the period which is appropriate to declare as Rosh Chodesh, that is, the daytime. The nighttime, however, was never considered as a possible time for declaring Rosh Chodesh. Thus we can conclude that only the daytime is to be seen as Rosh Chodesh, never the nighttime.

ומכל מקום בענין דוקא שיבא אחר כך זמן הראוי לקדש חל
למפרע, אבל בלילה שעדיין לא בא זמן הראוי לקדש, עוד
לא חל קידוש הלל למפרע, כמו בנכנסים שנפלו לו כשהוא
גוסס, שכיון שעכשיו אינו ראוי להקנא לא חל למפרע, רק
בראש חודש כשהגיע השחר ראוי לקדש...

Answering the Second Question

To answer our second question, if Hillel II already sanctified all the forthcoming months, why is there still the need for a settlement of Jews in Eretz Yisrael?

There are a number of ways to explain Hillel's thinking here. The מהר"י בירב, HaRav Yaacov Berav, contends that since there is the potential to offer ordination by a consensus of opinion by the present-day Jews in Eretz Yisrael, this explains the need for a congregation of Jews living in Eretz Yisrael. For they are the ones who have the power to appoint those who can act to sanctify the new month by initiating the process of Kiddush HaChodesh. According to the רלב"ח, all that is needed to determine the day of Rosh Chodesh is to apply a simple mathematical formula. However, the ability to apply this simple calculation depends on the halachic requirement that there be a community of Jews living at that time in Eretz Yisrael.

According to מהרי"ל דיסקין (see הגאון מהרי"ל דיסקין על התורה פרשת בא), Hillel II designated the month on the condition that the Jews who live in Eretz Yisrael agree to that particular determination of Rosh Chodesh. This proves the importance of having a Jewish presence in Eretz Yisrael which will give its consent to the calculations made by Hillel II.

> עיקר תקנת המועדות שלנו מתקנת ר' הלל הנשיא ובית דינו ור' הלל בעצמו שתיקן חשבונו תיקן באופן שיסכימו לזה יושבי ארץ ישראל בדורות הבאים אחריו ומכיון שיושבי ארץ ישראל מסכימים לתקנותיו נעשים הם כשלוחי ר' הלל ובית דינו המסכימים לקדש ולעבר בזמנו, וכמו שמקבלים גרים בחו"ל, ובהסכמת יושבי ארץ ישראל יקום החשבון של ר' הלל לאיתנו, כמו שקבע בעצמו בזמנו. ואחרי אשר בררנו כי תקנת ר' הלל תלו' בהסכמת יושבי ארץ ישראל אם כן מובן שאין חשבונו מועיל אלא כשיש ישראל בארץ ישראל, ואם ח"ו יעדרו מארץ ישראל אזי יתבטל החשבון של ר' הלל...

We previously explained the approach of HaRav Yosef Dov Soloveitchik, that the Sanhedrin acts as the representative body of Klal Yisrael. The determination of Rosh Chodesh is the prerogative of Klal Yisrael, and when the Sanhedrin was in existence, Klal Yisrael waived that right and transferred their jurisdiction in this matter to the Sanhedrin, which then acted on their behalf. Consequently, after this institution was abolished, the responsibility for Kiddush HaChodesh reverted back to Klal Yisrael. Thus it is the Jews who now live in Eretz Yisrael who have the authority to determine Rosh Chodesh. They do so, not by means of a formal representative body, but by observing the designated day as Rosh Chodesh, reciting all the requisite prayers and following all the particular laws and customs of this day. HaRav Yosef Dov Soloveitchik articulates this in his sefer, "שעורים לזכר אבא מורי ז"ל" (חלק א, עמ' ק"ל), where he writes as follows:

ואילו בזמן הזה אין בית דין קבוע, כי אם כל ישראל קובעים. ממילא, אין כאן פעולה מסויימת שניתן לציינה כקובעת, דבר זה יצוייר רק כשישנה סמכות מיוחדת לבית דין הגדול או לבית דין שנתמנה על פיו לצורך קידוש...

ברם בזמן הזה שאין בית דין הגדול קיים והקביעת עברה לרשות כל ישראל, אין **מעשה** קביעה אפשרי כלל, כי מי הוא שיאמר מקודש מקודש. עכשיו, כנסת ישראל כולה מקדשת, ללא פעולה מוגדרת, את החדשים והמועדים על ידי ניהוגם. על ידי זה שאנו מסכימים לחשבון שנקבע על ידי רבותינו **ונוהגים על ידו**, עושים מועדות וראשי חדשים בהתאם לו — **נקבעים המה הזמנים על ידי קביעות של ניהוג**...

Thus, once again, we see the need for the Yishuv of Eretz Yisrael, a community of Jews living in the Land of Yisrael. For it is they who designate Rosh Chodesh by the way they conduct themselves on this day and accept all its particular observances.

In this way we can answer our third question of how we are to understand the innovation of Hillel II in establishing the calendar. For even though some might maintain that ideally the new month should be determined by the potential Bais Din of those sages of Yisrael who are eligible today to receive ordination, סמיכה, yet, as we have explained, in actual practice it is rather the community of Jews residing in Eretz Yisrael who bring about the new month, by their acceptance of the calendar which was established by Hillel II, and more specifically, by their conduct on this day, e.g., when they recite Half-Hallel and Ya'aleh V'Yavoh in the Amidah prayer and thus show us by their actions that today is Rosh Chodesh.

VI

THE INSIGHT OF THE "אוצר התפלות"

The following questions are raised by the בעל אוצר התפלות. Why do we bless and declare the new month on the Shabbos *before* Rosh Chodesh, rather than on Rosh Chodesh itself? The Gemara in *Sanhedrin 13b* gives credit and recognition to R' Yehudah ben Bava for salvaging the laws regarding fines, for he ordained Rabbis who could then rule on these matters, even though this cost him his life. The בעל אוצר התפלות questions this. R' Yehudah ben Bava lived before the time of Hillel II. Why, then, did they not show *him* their appreciation for preserving the institution of Kiddush HaChodesh, which, according to the opinion of the Ramban, requires ordination, סמיכה?

The בעל אוצר התפלות concludes that even without ordination, Klal Yisrael has the power to declare Rosh Chodesh. Consequently, Rav Amram Gaon declared the new month on Rosh Chodesh day itself.

והנה מנהג כל תפוצות כל ישראל להכריז ר"ח בשבת שלפניו...אבל בסידור רב עמרם גאון מסודרת הכרזת ראש חודש ביום ר"ח עצמו...

אבל רב עמרם גאון סובר כר' יאשיה במכילתא... דברו
אל כל עדת בני ישראל, ופירש הרמב"ן שהי' להם [הבית
דין הגדול] רשות מכל ישראל...ומצינו למידין שהמצוה
הזאת מוטלת על כל עדת ישראל וב"ד סמוכין שליחותייהו
עבדינן...א"כ כל זמן שיש בי"ד בעולם יש מצוה על הקהל
לעשותם שלוחים לקדש בשבילם את החדשים. אבל בזמן
הזה שאין בית דין כלל **חזרה** המצוה לחמשלח מכח שלוחיו,
וכשעומדים כל ישראל ביום ראש חודש ואומרים בצבור
"היום ר"ח פלוני" זהו קדוש החודש גמור...

יש להביא ראיה לדברינו ממה שאמרנו במסכת סנהדרין
יג, ב, "ברם זכור אותו האיש לטוב, ור' יהודה בן בבא שמו,
שאילמלא הוא נשתכחו דיני קנסות מישראל" והדבר פלא,
הלא ריב"ב הי' כמה דורות לפני הלל הנשיא האחרון
חמתקן העבור לדעת ר' אברהם בר חייא הנשיא, והרמב"ן,
ואמאי לא אמר מר, שאילמלא הוא בטלו המועדים על ידי
ביטול הסמיכה, שהרי אם לא הסמיך את חמשה הזקנים
לא הגיעה הסמיכה להלל, וביטול המועדים יותר נכבד
מביטול דיני קנסות אלא ודאי שלצורך המועדים אין
הסמיכה נחוצה כל כך, שאפשר לקדש חדשים על ידי כל
ישראל כמו שעשה רב עמרם גאון ז"ל...

Reinforcing the approach of the אוצר התפלות

We might suggest that what is stated in the Sefer HaMitzvos of the Rambam, *Mitzva 153,* is the source for the approach of the אוצר התפלות. In this mitzva the Rambam points out that the mitzva of Kiddush HaChodesh was never placed in the hands of the individual but rather it was under the jurisdiction of the Bais Din and it must be performed only in Eretz Yisrael. One might wonder why the Rambam had to add this statement that only in Eretz Yisrael is the ceremony of Kiddush HaChodesh allowed to take place. For the question at hand was not one regarding place, but rather it focused exclusively on who had the authority to declare the day of Rosh Chodesh—whether the individual or the Bais Din? The Rambam concludes that it is the Bais Din alone which has the right to declare Rosh Chodesh. Why, then, was it necessary to add here the requirement of Eretz Yisrael to this mitzva?

We might suggest that the Rambam added this requirement of Eretz Yisrael here in order to define the role and function of the Bais Din in this matter. For the purpose of emphasizing Eretz Yisrael here is to underline the fact that it is the community of Klal Yisrael that was empowered to act to establish this mitzva. Consequently, we can understand that if the Bais Din *does act* here, this is only in their capacity as the representative of Klal Yisrael. Thus Eretz Yisrael was mentioned here to emphasize that it is not the individual that acts here, but rather the צבור, the community of Yisrael.

Thus we can now appreciate why the Rambam added the assurance "that there will always be Jews in Eretz Yisrael". In addition, the מהר"י בירב asks why the Rambam mentioned this fact. He should have said that "there would always be a *Bais Din* in Eretz Yisrael". But in light of our previous discussion, we can understand that it is not the Bais Din that is crucial, but rather the *community of Jews* who live in Eretz Yisrael. Therefore, it was necessary for the Rambam to assure us that there would always be a Jewish presence in Eretz Yisrael.

Chapter Eleven
The Rosh Chodesh Witnesses

I

THREE CATEGORIES OF WITNESSES

In relation to the mitzva of Kiddush HaChodesh, there are three categories of possible witnesses. The first category is עידי הראיה — eyewitnesses, who sighted the new moon and came to the Bais Din to testify to that effect. The second category is עידי הכרה — character witnesses. If the Bais Din in Yerushalayim did not know the eyewitnesses, the local Bais Din where the eyewitnesses came from would send competent witnesses to verify the trustworthiness of the eyewitnesses. The third category is עידי הודעה — witnesses sent as messengers by the Bais Din to inform the people when Rosh Chodesh day was declared.

There are a number of practical halachic differences entailed by each of these three categories of witnesses. These differences include whether the witnesses were justified in desecrating the Shabbos in order to fulfill their particular mission, and how many witnesses were required.

EXPLAINING THE ORDER OF MISHNAYOS ROSH HASHANAH

The classic commentator to the Mishna, the "מלאכת שלמה", raises the following question. The first Mishna that deals with Kiddush HaChodesh is the mishna of (א:ג) "על ששה חדשים השלוחים יוצאים" — "For six months messengers go forth."

Would it not have been more appropriate to cite this Mishna *after* the Mishna cited in *Chapter 2:2:* "בראשונה היו משיאין משואות" — "Originally they informed the people, by means of lighting torches, which day Rosh Chodesh would occur."

ונלע"ד דבדין הוא דברישא היה לו למיתני בראשונה היו
משיאין משואות משקלקלו הכותים התקינו שיהיו שלוחים
יוצאין, ובתר הכי למיתני על ששה חדשים. אלא איידי דתני
ד' ראשי שנים בד' פרקים, תנא נמי על ששה חדשים...
והדר תני באידך פירקא בראשונה היו משיאין משואות...

This question can be framed in two different ways. Initially, the method used to inform the people was by lighting torches, and only afterwards was the practice of sending messengers introduced. Therefore, would it not have been more appropriate to first mention the mishna describing how torches were lit and only then to mention the mishna which deals with sending messengers?

Would it not have been more logical to first tell us *how* the people were to be informed (by the lighting of torches) and only then to inform us *when* this should be done — "על ששה חדשים".

The answer given by the "מלאכת שלמה" is that since the previous two mishnayos here in Mesechtas Rosh Hashana list various calendar dates and detail what exactly occurred on these dates, it follows that this mishna concerning Kiddush HaChodesh should also list the names of the months when messengers were dispatched to inform the people about the day of Rosh Chodesh.

Although the question raised here by the "מלאכת שלמה" is a valid question, yet an even more obvious question can be asked. As we have previously pointed out, there are three categories of witnesses: eyewitnesses, character witnesses, and messengers sent out to inform Klal Yisrael when will be Rosh Chodesh.

Consequently, we might have expected the first mishna regarding Rosh Chodesh to deal with the laws of eyewitnesses; and then to go on to discuss the matter of character witnesses, and only then to address the issue of how and when to inform the people about Rosh Chodesh— "על ששה חדשים השלוחים יוצאין".

To resolve this discrepancy we might suggest the following. The reason why the mishna which deals with the sending out of messengers was placed here was for a more important reason than just because it followed the same formulation as the previous two mishnayos. Rather this mishna serves as an introduction to the whole subject of the mitzva of Kiddush HaChodesh and its relevance to Mesechtas Rosh Hashanah. For the six months, "ששה חדשים" were the months in which there were holidays, and all of them are totally dependent on when Rosh Chodesh day occurs. Thus the Tanna (Rebbe) first mentioned this mishna in order to point out the importance of the mitzva and the process of sanctifying the new month. Therefore we can see that this mishna serves as an introduction to the mesechta and thus, even though the issue of messengers seems out of sequence, what is more important here is the consideration that the whole matter of Kiddush HaChodesh is being introduced, and that takes precedence over the matter of sequence.

In light of this, we can now appreciate the comments of Rashi on the words of the next mishna *(1:4)*. There we find the following: "על שני חדשים מחללין את השבת" — "For two months the witnesses may desecrate the Shabbos."

Rashi comments: "עדים **שראו** את החדש" — "The witnesses we speak of are those *eyewitnesses who saw the moon.*"

We might further suggest that beyond the mishna's halachic implications of eyewitnesses being allowed to desecrate the Shabbos that Rashi explains for us, he also alludes to the fact that the subject matter of Kiddush HaChodesh commences here with the laws of eyewitnesses. Thus the proper sequence of Kiddush HaChodesh is being followed. In this mishna and in the subsequent misnayos of the first chapter of Rosh Hashanah, the issue concerns eyewitnesses. The beginning of Chapter Two describes character witnesses, and this is followed by the mishna of "בראשונה היו משיאין משואות" how we are to inform the people when Rosh Chodesh will occur.

EYEWITNESSES

Eyewitnesses are permitted to desecrate the Shabbos in order to inform the Bais Din that they have sighted the moon, so that Rosh Chodesh day will be declared at its proper time. According to Rashi, the mishna in *Rosh Hashanah 21b* delineates this for us:

על שני חדשים מחללין את השבת, על ניסן ועל תשרי, שבהם שלוחין יוצאין לסוריה ובהן מתקנין את המועדות. וכשהיה בית המקדש קיים מחללין אף על כולם מפני תקנת הקרבן...

> For two months the witnesses may desecrate the Shabbos; Nissan and Tishrei, for in these months the messengers go forth to Syria, and in them they fix the holy days. And when the Bais HaMikdash stood, they desecrated the Shabbos even for all the months, because of the determination of the Sacrifice.

Rashi, in his comentary on the statement, "Shabbos may be desecrated", writes that this alludes to "the witnesses who saw the new moon." These *eyewitnesses* may desecrate the Shabbos in order to come forth and testify to the sighting of the new moon. However, there is a difference regarding which months these eyewitnesses were allowed to desecrate the Shabbos. When the Bais HaMikdash was in existence, they could desecrate the Shabbos for the sake of *all* the months of the calendar year. After the Temple was destroyed, however, Shabbos could be desecrated only for the months of Nissan and Tishrei.

Thus we must understand why only these two months could be desecrated and not the other months of the year, and what was the reason that these two months could be desecrated.

The Rishonim present the sources

There is a difference of opinion among the Rishonim regarding the source that allows the eyewitnesses to desecrate the Shabbos. Some maintain that Shabbos may be desecrated in order to fulfill the mitzva of sanctifying the month by means of eyewitnesses — "קדוש על פי הראיה". And so the Rashba, in ר"ה כא, ב states clearly: "דעיקר חילול משום קריאתן על פי ראיה".

And for the reason why this is so only for the months of Nissan and Tishrei, the Meiri explains that since the mitzva of Kiddush HaChodesh was written in the Torah in conjunction with Rosh Chodesh Nissan ("החודש הזה לכם") this indicates that Rosh Chodesh of Nissan should be declared sanctified, even if this means that Shabbos day has to be desecrated. Tishrei is also included here, because of its similarity to Nissan, for it too determines on which day the forthcoming holidays (Yom Kippur, Sukkos, etc.) will occur. Therefore in order to ensure that they fall on their proper dates, the Shabbos may be desecrated. Thus the Meiri writes as follows:

מפני שמצות הקידוש נאמרה בניסן בפרט, ר"ל "כזה ראה וקדש". ואנו משוים לו תשרי שהוא שוה לו בתקון המועדות, שכל תקוני המועדות ביום פסול ויום כשר תלוים בקבוע ניסן ותשרי...

Rashi and Tosafos maintain that since Rosh Chodesh is called a festival, "מועד", we find that whenever the Torah refers to the word "מועד", the Shabbos can be superceded for the sake of the particular mitzva, even if this means that the Shabbos must be desecrated. For example, the daily sacrifice is offered on Shabbos, since the word "במועדו" was written here. This then allows the slaughtering of animals on Shabbos, even though this would involve a violation of the Shabbos. So here too we see that Shabbos can be desecrated for the sake of this mitzva.

Rabbenu Chananel *(ibid.)* points out that since an additional offering, קרבן מוסף, is to be brought on this day of Rosh Chodesh, just as on Shabbos, the Korban Mussaf supercedes Shabbos; so too we allow the Shabbos day to be desecrated by the eyewitnesses in order that the Korban Mussaf of Rosh Chodesh should be offered on this day.

> יסוד העיבור שהיה מסור לבי"ד להקריב מוסף ר"ח על הראייה וכיון שמוסף ר"ח קרב אפי' בשבת לפיכך **הותרה** שבת גבי עדי החדש לבוא מחוץ לתחום ולהעיד כדי להקריב מוסף החדש בזמנו בכל חדשי שנה.

> וזה בזמן שהיה בית המקדש קיים, אבל עתה אין מחללין אלא על ניסן ועל תשרי בלבד שצריכים לקרוא המועדים שכתוב בהם במועדם...

This explanation of Rabbenu Chananel seems difficult to understand; for we might ask, if we do not declare Rosh Chodesh on Shabbos day (because Shabbos would have to be desecrated) then there would be no need for a Korban Mussaf on this day. Why, then, desecrate the Shabbos? Why not wait until Sunday to declare Rosh Chodesh and then offer the Korban Mussaf? And furthermore, since the Korban Mussaf is always offered on Shabbos, we have no alternative but to slaughter an animal on the Shabbos for this purpose. However, on Rosh Chodesh there is an alternative. We can wait until Sunday, which can be also legitimately declared as Rosh Chodesh. This question was anticipated in the sefer of HaRav Aharon Kohen ("בית אהרן-על המועדים, ח"א, סימן ה), where we find the following:

> אבל באמת טעמו של הר"ח צריך ביאור דאיך ידחה קריאת הזמן של ראש חודש את השבת כדי שיקריב את הקרבן בזמנו, הא מה שצריך החדש להיות בזמנו אינו מחמת זמן הקרבן אלא הוא דין בקביעות זמן ר"ח עצמו, ואחר שנקבע הזמן של ר"ח, דין המועד של ר"ח הוא המחייב את הקרבן, ואם יאחרו קביעות החדש אז יהי' איחרו רק בגורם חיוב הקרבן, ולא בדין חיוב קרבן עצמו...

HaRav Aharon Kohen answers this question by saying that perhaps, since in relation to the Korban Mussaf the Torah uses the following language: "זאת עולת חדש בחדשו" — "This is the elevation offering of the month upon its *renewal*." This is to be understood as the Torah's desire that the Korban Mussaf of Rosh Chodesh be offered on the actual "day of renewal", not on the next day, even though that day is also called Rosh Chodesh. This means that Shabbos can be desecrated by the eyewitnesses in order to ensure that the Korban Mussaf will be offered on its proper day — "the day of its renewal".

ואפשר דכתיב "זאת עולת חדש בחדשו" אם כן יש דין בקרבן ר"ח שיהי' בזמן **התחדשות החדש**. ועיין בת"א שתרגם "דא עולת ריש ירחא באתחדתותי"...

REFUTING RAV SAADIA GAON

If eyewitnesses may desecrate the Shabbos for any of the reasons cited here, then one might question the contention of Rav Saadia Gaon (see our previous discussion on how the month is determined) that the main method of determining a month is by חשבון, calculation. Why, then is it necessary for the eyewitnesses to desecrate the Shabbos, for hasn't the month already been determined by the application of a mathematical formula to determine the exact day of the month? This question was raised by the מהר"י ב"ר ברוך, and he suggests that since the Korban Mussaf took precedence over the Shabbos, this allowed the eyewitnesses to come even on Shabbos and this enabled the Korban to be brought at its proper time, even though the actual determination was accomplished by applying mathematical calculations.

הבאתי שיטת הר"ח...וכיון שמוסף ר"ח קרב אפילו בשבת לפיכך הותרה שבת גבי עדי החדש לבוא מחוץ לתחום, ולהעיד כדי להקריב מוסף החדש בזמנו...

The sefer "אגן הסהר", on the other hand, contends that although a month can be *determined* in any manner, there is however a separate mitzva to *sanctify* the month by means of eyewitnesses, "על פי עידי הראייה". And therefore, even if the month was determined by calculation, "על פי החשבון", as Rav Saadia Gaon maintains, yet even he agrees that eyewitnesses may desecrate the Shabbos in order to *sanctify* the month.

> וזה פשוט דמצוה דקדוש החדשים ע"פ ראיה לא נאמרה
> דוקא בחלות הקביעיות אלא אף אם הקביעיות קבועה כבר
> וקימה נאמרה המצות עשה לקדש על פי ראיה, אף שאינו
> פועל שום דבר בחלות הקביעיות כמבואר בהדיא בגמרא
> שאף אם אדר הסמוך לניסן לעולם חסר...בכל זאת איכא
> מצוה לקדש ע"פ הראייה, ומחללין שבת עליה...

II

Time allotted for travel on Shabbos

The Rambam in *Hilchos Kiddush HaChodesh 3:1* tells us:

> עדים שראו את החודש: אם היה ביניהם ובין מקום שיש
> בו בית דין מהלך לילה ויום או פחות הולכין ומעידין. ואם
> היה ביניהם יתר על כן לא ילכו. שאין עדותן אחר יום
> שלשים מועלת, שכבר נתעבר החדש.

When witnesses see the moon and there is a journey of a night and a day or less between them and the place where the court holds its sessions, they should undertake the journey and testify. If the distance between them is greater, they should not undertake the journey. For the testimony they shall deliver after the thirtieth day will be of no consequence since the month will already have been made full.

The Acharonim here point out that the journey cannot be a complete night and a day but must be slightly less, because otherwise they would not arrive in time for their testimony to be of any value, since the Bais Din would not have time to declare Rosh Chodesh before it was too late — at night. (See here the following seforim: "ספר הזכרונות" להג' ר' צדוק הכהן, עמ' 44, "בחדושי רש"ש", ר"ה, כב, א, (ד"ה שעל מהלך וכו', "ערוך השלחן העתיד", הל' קדוש החודש, סימן צא, אות א).

ונראה דראו הלבנה בתחלת ליל ל' אבל ראוה בתחלת יום
ל', צריך שיהי' רק מהלך יום.

The sefer "לחם שמים" מהג' היעב"ץ, in ד"ה שעל מהלך ר"ה פרק א משנה ט (ראה שם פרק ג משנה א אות ב) contends that when the mishna says "a night and a day" it makes no distinction even if the sighting took place during the day. And if one were to ask of what value is the testimony in such a case, the answer would be that the Korban Mussaf can not be offered on a day which is really not Rosh Chodesh (the 30th day).

שעל מהלך לילה ויום, וא"ת [ואם תאמר] למה יחללו שבת
אף בכדי מהלך זה, מה תועיל עדותן לכשיבואו אחר כלות
יום שלשים שכבר נתעבר החדש, יש לומר, דמהני לענין
הקרבן של יום שלשים וא', שלא יקריבו בו מוסף של ר"ח,
ובכה"ג [ובכי האי גונה] שעדיין לא נתפרסם כלל קביעות
ר"ח, ויש בו ג"כ תיקון הקרבן.

THE QUESTION OF THE YERUSHALMI

A most interesting question is raised here in the Yerushalmi (at the end of Chapter One) as to how we allow the desecration of the Shabbos "for a night and a day"? The desecration of Shabbos commences on Friday night, whereas the declaration of Rosh Chodesh by the testimony of eyewitnesses takes place only on

Shabbos day. This means that we are to view the Friday night journey to Yerushalayim as a preparation for a mitzva, מכשירין, for Rosh Chodesh can not be declared on Friday night. The halacha stipulates that a preparatory mitzva does not supercede the Shabbos.

The Yerushalmi offers two possible answers. Since it is impossible to sanctify the Shabbos day without travelling on Friday night, consequently, both Friday night and Shabbos day are to be viewed as "one day". Alternatively, since Shabbos day will subsequently be declared as Rosh Chodesh, then Friday night will also be declared retroactively as Rosh Chodesh. Thus both the night and the day are equal in relation to the desecration of the Shabbos — "למפרע הוא קודש". And so the Yerushalmi asks:

דבר שהוא דוחה שבת ביום, מכשירין מהו שידחו את השבת בלילה?

ופי' הקרבן עדה שם: מיבעיא ליה דבר שקבוע לו זמן ונאמר בו במועדו אם מותר להתיר מכשירו בליל שבת לצורך מחר, ובמכשירין שאי אפשר לעשותן מערב שבת איירי.

והירושלמי שואל: התיב ר' יעקב בר סוסי והתיניין שעל מהלך לילה ויום מחללין את השבת ויוצאין לעדות החודש.

פי', יוצאין בלילה להעיד על עדות החדש ביום, דלילה אין מקדשין את החדש, הרי שבלילה מחללין לדבר שהוא יום.

ועונה על זה הירושלמי: אמר להון: מכיון שהוא צורך לילה, ולילה צריך ליום כמו שכולו יום.

פי', שביום לבד בלי הלילה אי אפשר להם להגיע למקום הוועד. הרי הלילה גם כן זמנו ומצטרף ליום. כן פירש הקרבן עדה שם.

תשובה אחרת בירושלמי שם: מר יודא בי רבי בון, ולא למפרע הוא קודש, מכיון שהוא קודש למפרע, הוא יום הוא לילה.

ופי' הפני משה שם: שהרי העדים שראו את החדש בתחילת
הלילה של שלשים הן שבאים לפני בית דין שיקדשוהו
למחר ביום, ואם יקדשו למחר, וכי לא למפרע הוא קדוש
משעה שראו אותה. אם כן, הוא יום הוא לילה, דהכל
אחד הוא, ולפיכך מחללין השבת גם בלילה שלפניו, לבוא
להעיד ולקדשו.

III

Desecrating the Shabbos to Provide Eyewitnesses

The Gemara in *Rosh Hashanah 19b* explores the issue of whether an additional month—the second month of Adar—added to a leap year is to have 29 or 30 days. To resolve this issue, the Gemara points to the mishna which states that "two months are to be desecrated for the sake of establishing Rosh Chodesh in its proper time, and these are the months of Nissan and Tishrei." The Gemara explains the rationale for this in the following way. One might understand why the month of Adar that comes before Nissan is always deficient (will have only 29 days). Then we desecrate the Shabbos, for there is a mitzva to sanctify Rosh Chodesh through the sighting of the moon, and if the eyewitnesses do not come at the proper time, then the court will be forced to sanctify the new moon without witnesses.

However, if one were to say that this month is sometimes full (30 days) and sometimes deficient (29 days), why should we desecrate the Shabbos? To prevent this, let us simply make Adar a full month (30 days) and sanctify Rosh Chodesh tomorrow, in order to avoid desecrating the Shabbos. Let the court institute in the present case that the witnesses should not desecrate the Shabbos, but rather they should wait to come and testify until the 31st, which will be a Sunday. The court will then sanctify the month (the 31st day) based on the testimony given on Sunday.

However, the Gemara dismisses this proof:

> If the thirtieth day fell on a Shabbos, indeed we would do this. We would make Adar a full month and thus would not desecrate the Shabbos. But here, what are we dealing with— when the 31st fell on the Shabbos. In such a case, witnesses *must* desecrate the Shabbos, because it is a mitzva to sanctify the month upon the sighting of the new moon (i.e., the moon was not sighted on Thursday night, which was the beginning of the 30th day of the month. Since the court could not sanctify the month on Friday, the 30th, they would have to sanctify it on Shabbos, even if no sighting was made, because a month is never longer than thirty days. The Mishna therefore rules that witnesses who saw the moon on Friday night *should* desecrate the Shabbos and come, so that the court could base its sanctification of the moon the next day on their testimony.)

THE QUESTION OF THE טורי אבן

The טורי אבן points out that in this matter of eyewitnesses, we do try to avoid desecrating the Shabbos whenever possible. However, even if we seek to avoid desecrating the Shabbos (by not allowing the witnesses who saw the moon on the 30th to appear on Shabbos, but rather to wait until Sunday), nothing is gained, for those who live a two-day journey from the Bais Din and saw the moon on Friday night *would have to* travel on Shabbos in order to sanctify Rosh Chodesh on Sunday. On the other hand, those who live a day's journey away from the Bais Din would *not* be allowed to travel on Shabbos because they could come instead on Sunday. Yet if they saw the new moon on Friday night, they would have to travel on Shabbos in order to come on Sunday and fulfill their obligation to sanctify even the 31st day. This means that in the end Shabbos will be desecrated by those who have to travel for two days.

The טורי אבן resolves this question by citing the Yerushalmi which stipulates that Shabbos can only be desecrated if the time period which has been desecrated (i.e., Friday night) is also the same period which is subsequently to be designated as Rosh Chodesh. In the present case, those who must travel for two days in order to reach their destination in time will not be allowed to desecrate the Shabbos, since the Shabbos day will not subsequently become Rosh Chodesh, but rather Rosh Chodesh will be on Sunday.

Yet we might still ask, isn't there another opinion in the Yerushalmi which allows for the desecration of Shabbos if we have no alternative but to travel on Shabboas in order to testify to the sighting of the new moon and consequently to sanctify Shabbos as Rosh Chodesh, "דיום צריך לילה". This means that Shabbos can indeed be desecrated by those who live two days' journey from the Bais Din. (This question is touched upon in the sefer "מכתבי תורה" מהרב מרדכי קאלינא, מכתב סג').

Answering the טורי אבן

We might suggest some possible answers to this question of the טורי אבן. According to the Yerushalmi, we allow the desecration of the Shabbos only if there is no other alternative. But here it appears as if we do have an alternative, and this should prevent the desecration of the Shabbos. The Bais Din could decree that those who live two day's away from Yerushalayim should not come at all, for we have the testimony on Sunday of those who live only one day's journey from the Bais Din. With this solution, we can avert the desecration of the Shabbos altogether.

However, we might dismiss this possibility, for the Bais Din would never prevent witnesses from coming, for it is possible that those who live a day away from the Bais Din did not in fact see the moon, but rather it was spotted only by those who live a distance of two days. Thus our question remains.

TRAVELLING MORE THAN 24 HOURS ON THE SHABBOS

The Rambam, in his commentary on the Mishna in *Rosh Hashanah 3:1*, writes that even though the sun has set, the night does not begin until the appearance of the stars, and therefore it is possible to sanctify the new moon during this time.

> וממה שאתה צריך לדעת כי הירח כשנראה בזמנו והוא יום כט ערבית, ונשאר מן היום כדי שיאמרו "מקודש" קודם שיראו הכוכבים כי זה מותר אע"פ שהעריב השמש, כי הלילה אצלינו אינו אלא משעת צאת הכוכבים...וזכרתי לך שלא תחשוב כי קידוש החודש לא יהי' לעולם אלא יום שלשים, כי אפשר שיהי' קודם יום שלשים.

And similarly, the Rambam states in *Hilchos Kiddush HaChodesh 3:9*:

> If the Bais Din themselves see the new moon at the conclusion of the 29th day, before a star has emerged on the night of the 30th day, the court may declare, "It has been sanctified, it has been sanctified," for it is still day...

However, even though the Bais Din sanctifies the month on the 29th, this does not mean that the 29th day is Rosh Chodesh, for, as we have said, a month cannot consist of less than 29 days.

Therefore, what the Rambam means here is that when the Bais Din declares, "It is sanctified", they are referring to the 30th day.

If so, then the following question arises. Since it is possible to sight the moon on the 29th day, then the possibility exists that witnesses saw the moon on the 29th day before nightfall. Therefore they must travel in order to testify before the Bais Din and consequently they may have to travel more than a night and a day before reaching their destination. This leads the רש"ש to ask the following question in ר"ה, כב,א:

וכתב התוי"ט בשם הרמב"ם בחבורו "שאם הי' ביניהם יותר לא ילכו"...וק"ל שאם יראו ביום השבת יום כט למה לא ילכו ביום השבת בכדי שיבואו ליום א בעוד יום ויקדשו אותו שהוא יום ל'...

The רש"ש answers that according to the above cited Yerushalmi, desecrating the Shabbos is only allowed if Shabbos day itself will also be Rosh Chodesh. However, here the desecration of Shabbos will take place just before the Shabbos day comes to an end; whereas Rosh Chodesh will not be declared until the next day, Sunday. Thus we do not allow the Shabbos to be desecrated for the sake of the next day.

Yet one may still ask, according to the other answer suggested in the Yerushalmi ("ליום צריך לילה") that since it would be impossible to arrive on time without travelling on Friday night, we therefore allow the witnesses to desecrate the Shabbos in order that they come and sanctify the month on Shabbos day. Once again, we may raise the question that if they did not travel on the 29th day, which was also Shabbos day, how would they be able to sanctify the 30th day? It would not be possible, and therefore the witnesses are allowed to travel on Shabbos day, even if this means that they will be traveling more than "a night and a day".

Thus we are left with two salient questions. Sometimes it is necessary for the witnesses to travel for more than a night and a day. Why, then, does the law allow one to travel only for a night and a day? And consequently, we may desecrate the Shabbos day even for a distance that is greater than a night and a day. How is this allowed?

TWO POSSIBLE SOLUTIONS

We might suggest two possible answers to these questions. Indeed it is possible for witnesses to travel more than a night and a day. However, when the Rambam restricted travel, we are not to take this statement literally of a night and a day, "לילה ויום", according to the Shulchan Aruch, which reminds us that the Bais Din needs enough time to receive the witnesses and to declare Rosh Chodesh sanctified. Therefore "a night and a day", לאו דוקא, is not an exact measurement of time but represents rather "a little less" than a night and a day. Similarly, we might take "a little more" than a night and a day, which might include the 29th day and the night and day of the 30th.

We might apply here the rationale of the "תרועת המלך" (סימן מו בסוף אות ד) who offers an answer to the question raised by the טורי אבן as to why we do not allow the eyewitnesses to travel two days in order to give their testimony, "קדוש על פי הראייה", so that the 31st day should be established by virtue of eyewitnesses who saw the moon on the 30th day.

To this the "תרועת המלך" answers that this is not an issue, since how is it possible to sanctify the 31st day with eyewitnesses who saw the new moon on the 30th day? Certainly this would not be acceptable. However, if one were to testify on the 29th day that the 30th day is Rosh Chodesh, then this would be acceptable. For even though the 29th day cannnot be declared to be Rosh Chodesh, the eyewitnesses and the Bais Din can establish the

30th day as Rosh Chodesh, as a result of having accepted the testimony of the eyewitnesses on the 29th day. Therefore, it may be acceptable to travel even more than a night and a day even on Shabbos day.

IV

Can character witnesses desecrate the Shabbos

The Rambam in *Hilchos Kiddush HaChodesh 3:3* writes:

כשם שמחללין העדים שראו את החדש את השבת, כך מחללין עמהן העדים שמזכין אותן בבית דין, אם לא היו בית דין מכירין את הרואין.

Just as the witnesses who see the new moon should violate [Shabbos] to testify, so too, the witnesses who substantiate the credibility of the eyewitnesses should violate the Shabbos to accompany them, if the court is not familiar with the eyewitnesses.

The need for character witnesses is described in the first mishna in the second chapter of *Mesechtas Rosh Hashanah*.

בראשונה היו מקבלין עדות החדש מכל אדם, משקלקלו המינין, התקינו שלא יהו מקבלין אלא מן-המכירין.

Originally, they accepted testimony about the new moon from anyone, but after the heretics caused harm, a law was enacted that testimony could be accepted by the Bais Din only from known people.

The "מינין", referred to here are "Boethusians" — "בייתוסים", a group of heretics who tried to make Shavuos, the fiftieth day of the Omer, fall on a Sunday. One year they attempted to deceive the Bais Din when the 30th of Adar was a Shabbos and the new moon had not yet been sighted. They then hired witnesses to testify that they had seen it, thus making the Shabbos day Rosh Chodesh Nissan. As a result, the 16th of Nissan, when the Omer is brought, would fall on a Sunday and consequently so would Shavuos. This planned deception was discovered and thus the Sages introduced the ruling that eyewitnesses had to be verified by character witnesses.

One might ask, if the eyewitnesses had to prove their credibility, why not have the local Bais Din where the eyewitnesses lived send along with them letters of recommendation testifying to the reliability of these eyewitnesses? Indeed, the next mishna describes why they abolished the system of using lit torches to inform the Jews in the Diaspora when Rosh Chodesh was to be declared. The mishna tells us that it was because of the כותים, who sought to mislead the Jews of the Diaspora by lighting torches of their own. Therefore messengers were substituted for the earlier practice of lighting bonfires, משואות.

The Meiri here points out that the messengers had to take with them a letter from the Bais Din. From this we see that letters were acceptable to attest to the honesty of the eyewitnesses. Why, then, was there also a need for character witnesses?

If we examine the sequence of the first two mishnayos in Chapter Two, we learn of two attempts that were made to disturb the process of declaring Rosh Chodesh. In the first mishna we read of the attempt of the בייתוסים, and in the second mishna, the efforts of the כותים. The בייתוסים hired false witnesses to mislead the Bais Din, whereas the כותים sought to confuse the people by lighting torches on a day which was not intended to be declared as Rosh Chodesh by the Bais Din. In light of this description, we can now understand why in the second instance letters were acceptable, but not in the first. For the first mishna is concerned with eyewitnesses whose credibility had to be verified, and thus it was appropriate for the local Bais Din to send letters of introduction along with the witnesses testifiying to their reliability. And because there were a great number of local courts all over Eretz Yisrael, the Bais Din in Yerushalayim could not possibly recognize all of their signatures, and thus there was the danger of forgery. Therefore, only reliable witnesses, who were either known personally by the members of the Bais Din HaGadol in Yerushalayim or who were recognized in some way as honest people, had to be sent to ascertain the reliability of the eyewitnesses. However, in the incident described here regarding the כותים, which concerns informing the people when Rosh Chodesh will be, the Bais Din sent out letters and the signatures were difficult to forge. And therefore these letters were seen as sufficient evidence to verify the reliability of the messengers (שלוחי בי"ד) sent to announce Rosh Chodesh day.

Trying to Fool the Bais Din

Fear that the Bais Din would be fooled by false witnesses does not seem justified according to the halacha. This leads the טורי אבן to ask the following question. There is a rule that every Jew is assumed to be trustworthy as a kosher witness. How, then, can a single false witness disprove this principle?

משום שוטה אחד נוציא את הכל מחזקת כשרות.

> Because of one fool, should we assume that all who appear before the Bais Din are liars?

In addition, the Chasam Sofer asks the following. The בייתוסים only intended to fool the Sages in the month of Nissan, in order to gain their objective of having the holiday of Shavuos fall on a Sunday. Why, then, was it necessary to require character witnesses throughout the year?

A possible answer is that initially we introduced character witnesses because of the deception of the בייתוסים in the month of Nissan. However, the Sages extended their need for character witnesses because of the deception of the כותיים. What is difficult to understand here, however, is that even though the כותיים denied the Oral Law, they nevertheless observed the mitzvos of the Written Torah. How then could they justify hiring false witnesses to desecrate the Shabbos and thus require the Bais Din to send character witnesses? The Chasam Sofer answers that although in the days of the Mishna the כותיים were initially observant of the mitzvos of the Written Torah, however gradually they totally deviated from the ways of the Torah and thus were even prepared to send false witnesses on Shabbos day, since they no longer seriously observed the mitzvos.

The sefer "משנת בנימין מהרב בנימין רבינוביץ" answers both the question of the טורי אבן and that of the Chasam Sofer by pointing out that the witnesses who desecrated the Shabbos came from around the vicinity of Yerushalayim, of which the majority of the inhabitants were כותיים. Thus there was no longer a question of just "one fool" trying to deceive the Bais Din, and therefore it was crucial that the status of the witnesses had to be verified.

דיש לומר דסביב מקום בי"ד הגדול מהלך לילה ויום היו הבייתוסין מרובים מכשרים, ואם כן אזלינן בתר רובא ומדאורייתא פסול לקבל מאין מכירין כיון דרוב הדרים במשך מקום הנ"ל הם פסולים ולא אזלינן בתר רובא דעלמא שהם כשרים כיון דאותן הרחוקים יותר ממהלך יום ולילה אין ראויים להעיד עדות החדש.

DESECRATING THE SHABBOS EVEN WHEN IN DOUBT

The Rambam in *Hilchos Kiddush HaChodesh 3:3* states:

ואפילו הי' זה שמודיע אותן לבית דין עד אחד הרי זה הולך
עמהם ומחלל מספק, שמא ימצא אחר ויצטרף עמו.

Even if only a single individual can testify regarding the witnesses, he should accompany them and violate the Shabbos because of the possibility that they might encounter an individual who can testify together with him.

The source for this halacha is the Gemara in *Rosh Hashanah* 22b which records an incident in which R' Nehorai travelled to Usha with the eyewitnesses to verify their credibility in the hope of finding another person there who would be able to testify together with him.

ור' נוהראי הלך להצטרף עם עד אחר...ומהו דתימא דלא
ידע אי משכח לי' מספיקא לא מחללין שבת, קמ"ל.

The "מפרש", the commentator on the Rambam's *Hilchos Kiddush HaChodesh* asks the following question. The law states that if a baby boy is born late Friday afternoon after sunset, but before actual nightfall, he should not be circumcised on the following Shabbos. For there is a doubt as to whether the baby was born on Friday or on Shabbos. From this halacha we see that if there is a doubt, ספק, we do not desecrate the Shabbos. Why then is a single character witness permitted to desecrate the Shabbos when there is doubt whether he will find a second character witness along the way?

The "לחם משנה" here answers: Circumcision can be performed at a later date, whereas the sanctification of the new moon cannot be postponed.

דשאני קדה"ח דתלוי בי' תקנת המועדות ועל שום ספק
מחללין משא"כ מילה שיכול לעשותה ביום אחר, ופשוט
הוא.

Yet others question this answer here, for even though it is true that circumcision can take place on another day, the possibility of performing the mitzva of "bris mila on the eighth day" will be lost. Other commentators therefore suggest that whereas circumcision is the obligation of an individual, Kiddush HaChodesh is a communal responsibility.

Another answer suggested is that travelling to Yerushalayim always involves the certainty of violating the Shabbos laws with only a *possibility* that the mitzva will be performed. For there is always the chance that the testimony of the eyewitnesses will be rejected by the Bais Din. Even so, we allow eyewitnesses to violate the Shabbos, even though a doubt exists, and thus here too we are justified in allowing a single witness to desecrate the Shabbos even though there is a chance that he might not find a second witness.

V

Messengers sent to proclaim Rosh Chodesh

The Rambam in *Hilchos Kiddush HaChodesh 3:8* states:

בראשונה, כשהיו בית דין מקדשין את החדש, היו משיאין משואות בראשי ההרים, כדי שידעו הרחוקים. משקלקלו הכותים, שהיו משיאין משואות כדי להטעות את העם, התקינו שהיו שלוחים יוצאים ומודיעין לרבים...

> Originally, when the court would sanctify the new moon, they would light bonfires on the mountain tops to notify the people in distant places. When the Samaritans began to conduct themselves in a debased manner and would light bonfires at the wrong times to confuse the people, the Sages introduced the practice of having messengers journey to notify the people...

Neither the Mishna nor the Gemara here states when this new innovation of sending messengers instead of lighting bonfires was introduced as a method of informing the people when it would be Rosh Chodesh. However, the *Talmud Yerushalmi* in *Rosh Hashanah, Chapter 2, Halacha 1,* states:

מי ביטל את המשואות? רבי ביטל את המשואות...

Who nullified the bonfires? Rebbe (R' Yehuda Ha Nasi) nullified the system of using torches.

This answer of the Yerushalmi led to the following question being asked. Isn't this view contradicted by the Mishna in 1:3: "על ששה חדשים שלוחין יוצאין", which mentions that messengers were sent forth even during the time of the Holy Temple, which had been destroyed long before Rebbe was born.

This question was raised both by HaRav Zev Wolf Rabinowitz in his sefer (ר"ה, פ"ב, ה"א) "שערי תורת ארץ-ישראל", and by HaRav Yitzchak Isaac HaLevi, in his classic work "דורות הראשונים" (חלק ראשון, כרך רביעי, עמוד 321). Both of these seforim suggest that it was not Rebbe who nullified the practice of lighting bonfires, but rather it was Rabban Gamliel.

והנה אי אפשר שרבי, דהיינו ר' יהודה הנשיא ביטל את המשואות, כי הרי מפורש במשנה ג, פרק א, שהשלוחין כבר היו יוצאין כשהיו בית המקדש קיים...ואם כן יש להסיק: או שבירושלמי חסרה המלה "גמליאל" לאחר רבי וצריך להיות "רבן גמליאל בטל". או כי הירושלמי מביא ברייתא עתיקה מימי רבן גמליאל הזקן, וכי גם הוא נקרא בזמנו סתם רבי כשם שבדורות הבאים נקראה הנשיא של הדור סתם רבי.

This answer was offered before the Meiri's commentary on Mesechtas Rosh Hashanah was printed. The sefer of the Meiri not only poses the question but offers a profound answer in the name of the ראב"ד (and subsequently the sefer "כתוב שם" the commentary of the ראב"ד to Mesechtas Rosh Hashanah was printed and it presented the answer given by the Meiri in the name of the Rava'ad). See also my sefer תפארת למשה" בעניין משיאין משואות, עמודים רכה-רלא, for an extensive treatment of this subject.

וראוי לשאול בזמן שבית המקדש היה קיים האיך היו שלוחים יוצאין, והלא במשואות היו מודיעין, שאף לאחר החורבן היו נוהגים בזה, כמו שאמרנו בתלמוד המערב "ר' בטל את המשואות", ור' לאחר חורבן היה. אלא שגדולי המפרשים [ה"ה הראב"ד] פירשו שלא היו המשואות נעשין תחלה אלא כנגד בבל. אבל סוריא ושאר מחוזות הרחוקים שבצדדים אין מקום להודעה על פי המשואות והיו שלוחים יוצאים להם לעולם והוא שנאמר במשנה שאחר זו "שבהם יוצאין לסוריא" כמו שיתבאר.

The Meiri quotes the ראב"ד who explains that torches were used only to notify the Jews of Babylonia as to the proper day of Rosh Chodesh, whereas Jews living in Syria and other places were *always* notified by messengers, even before Rebbe's ruling. Thus the Mishna 1:3 ("על ששה חדשים השלוחין את יוצאין") is referring to the messengers sent to Syria, while our Mishna speaks of Babylonia, where messengers were not sent until Rebbe abolished the use of torches. Consequently, we can appreciate the following Mishna 1:4: "For two months, the witnesses may desecrate the Shabbos, in Nissan and in Tishrei, for in these months the messengers go forth to *Syria*." Syria is mentioned because it was here that the messengers were sent even during the period when the Temple stood. Torches were lit at "other places" to inform the people who lived elsewhere.

The reason torches were used only in Bavel and not in Syria is simply because it was only in Babylonia that the torches could be seen, since Eretz Yisrael was situated higher than the land of Babylonia and thus they could see the flares from the higher mountain tops of Eretz Yisrael. Syria, however, is on the same level as the land of Yisrael, and therefore lighting torches would not succeed in making the inhabitants aware that the day of Rosh Chodesh was being signalled from afar. Another reason suggested was that there were areas where Jews did not live and therefore they could not light torches from those mountains, for the local government would not allow this. And so in Babylonia itself they lit torches only as far as the city of Pumpedisa. And even though Jews lived beyond there, they could not be reached by torches for the reasons outlined above, and therefore messengers had to be sent to inform them when Rosh Chodesh would be.

The following Mishna would seem to lend support to the view that the torches were abolished not by Rebbe but by Rabban Gamliel. The Mishna *2:4* states:

> ומאין היו משיאין משואות? מהר המשחה לסרטבא, ומסרטבא לגרופינא, ומגרופינא לחורן ומחורן לבית בלטין, ומבית בלטין לא זזו משם, אלא מוליך ומביא ומעלה עד שהיה רואה כל הגולה לפניו כמדורת האש.

> And from where did they light the torches? From the Mount of Olives to Sarteva, from Sarteva to Grofina, from Grofina to Chavaran, from Chavaran to Biltin. From Biltin they did not move but the one who signalled would wave the torch back and forth, up and down, until he saw the Diaspora before him as a mass of fire.

According to the view cited in the Yerushalmi—that **Rebbe** was the one who abolished the torch system which was in use until his time—this Mishna is difficult to understand. For **Rosh Chodesh** was declared by the Sanhedrin and after the Destruction of the Temple the Sanhedrin was forced to move from place to place until, at the time of R' Yehuda Ha Nasi, it was located in Bais Shearim, then in Tzippori, and finally in Tiberias, all in the

Galilee. Therefore it would be impossible for a Bais Din in Galilee, in the far north, to arrange for torches to be lit in Yerushalayim. This means that the description here of the arrangement of the lighting of torches is difficult to understand, unless we say that it was Rabban Gamliel the Elder, who lived at the time when the Temple flourished and the Sanhedrin was situated in Yerushalayim, who was the one who annulled the system of lighting torches.

We might suggest that there is no proof from this Mishna of the contention that it was Rabban Gamliel who abolished the system of lighting torches to announce the new month. The Yerushalmi tells us that it was Rebbe who completely abolished the practice of torches, though not the route that the torches followed. That route along which the torches were originally lit perhaps was abolished after the Sanhedrin left Yerushalayim and consequently they would no longer light from הר משחה, the Mount of Olives. Yet there were options to light from other mountains. It is not a strict law, הלכה למשה מסיני, to light torches only from certain mountains. The names of the mountains mentioned in the mishna were simply the ones used initially for lighting torches, and we know that later on other mountains were also used.

Proof of this contention that "other mountains" were acceptable for the torch lighting ceremony comes from the Gemara's statement in *Rosh Hashanah 23b:* "It was taught in the following Baraisa, R' Shimon ben Elazar says, torches were lit also on the mountains of Charim, Chayar, Geder and its companions."

Some believe that these mountains named by R' Shimon ben Elazar were situated between those points mentioned by the mishna, and accordingly, the listing of our mishna is not exhaustive, but rather R' Shimon ben Elazar supplements that list with other points which were part of the relay system which the mishna did not find it necessary to mention.

Others say that these points were situated on the other side of Eretz Yisrael. The reason for this was that two different sections of Eretz Yisrael stretch out towards Bavel and torches were lit in a system of relays along both routes.

תנא ר' שמעון בן אלעזר אומר: אף חרים, וכייר, וגדר, וחברותי. איכא דאמרי: ביני וביני הוו קיימי. איכא דאמרי: להך גיסא דארץ ישראל הוו קיימי. מר חשיב דהאי גיסא, ומי חשיב דהאי גיסא.

Thus we see that there were several relay routes along the way to Babylonia. And they all had the same objective, which was to reach Babylonia. Thus we might say that in the days of Rebbe and even before, the relay route did not begin at the Mount of Olives, and yet there were other routes to fulfill the requirement of informing the Jews of Babylonia when Rosh Chodesh would be. This situation existed until the days of Rebbe, when he eliminated this system of lighting torches. This means that even though the route outlined in the Mishna 2:4 had already been abolished before the lifetime of Rebbe, yet the system of lighting torches to proclaim Rosh Chodesh was still in existence.

WHY DIDN'T THE TORCH-LIGHTING SYSTEM PRECEDE THE SENDING OF MESSENGERS

Based on the Meiri's insight, we have seen that both the lighting of torches and the sending of messengers were ways to inform the people when Rosh Chodesh would be. But whereas messengers were dispatched to Syria, torches were lit in the direction of Babylonia. This leads us to address the question raised in the sefer (ר"ה כב,ב) "שפתי חכמים לש"ס".

We can see from the sequence in the mishna that torches were first lit and only after this system was abolished were messengers sent. But shouldn't this sequence of events have been reversed? Why didn't this mishna (2:2), which discusses the lighting of torches: "בראשונה היו משיאין משואות", have preceded the mishna (1:3) which deals with the sending of messengers: "על ששה חדשים היו השלוחין יוצאין".

However, in light of the Meiri here, who explains that messengers were always sent to Syria, we see that this first mishna (1:3) refers to those messengers who were despatched to Syria, especially since this is followed directly (1:4) by the mishna which tells us that they were sent to Syria in the months of Nissan and Tishrei. And since the system of lighting torches did not precede the sending of messengers, but came later, the Tanna rightly waited to introduce this concept until a later mishna (2:3,4).

VI

SHABBOS MUST NOT BE DESECRATED

Although eyewitnesses may desecrate the Shabbos day in order to come to the Bais Din to testify, messengers who are sent to inform the people may not themselves desecrate the Shabbos. This law is laid out for us in *Mesechtas Rosh Hashanah 21b:*

תנו רבנן: מנין שמחללין עליהן את השבת, תלמוד לומר, אלה מועדי ה' אשר תקראו אותם במועדם. יכול כשם שמחללין עד שיתקדשו, כך מחללין עד שיתקיימו, תלמוד לומר, אשר תקראו אותם, על קריאתם אתה מחלל, ואי אתה מחלל על קיומן.

The Rabbis taught in a Baraisa: from where do we know that the witnesses may desecrate the Shabbos to testify with regard to the new month? Scripture states *(Vayikra 23:4):* "These are the festivals of Hashem, that you are to designate in their appropriate time."

It might be thought that just as the witnesses may desecrate the Shabbos so that the festivals might be sanctified at their appropriate time, so too the messengers may desecrate the Shabbos so that the festivals might be kept at their designated time. Yet Scripture states, 'You are to *designate*.' This implies that you may desecrate the Shabbos only with regard to the *designation of the festivals*, but you may not desecrate the Shabbos in order to ensure that the festivals *be kept in their proper time*.

The "ערוך השלחן העתיד" (in סימן צב אות ב) makes the point that even though a decree set down by the Torah need not be explained rationally, yet there is nevertheless a logical reason here why this is so. For in regard to designating when the festivals will occur, this is an important matter which affects *all* of Klal Yisrael. Therefore Shabbos may be desecrated. However, we are not justified in desecrating the Shabbos for a matter which concerns only a small segment of Klal Yisrael. Therefore, for their sake we do not desecrate the Shabbos, since they have the option of observing the holidays for two days, just like those who live in the Diaspora, whom the messengers will never reach in time.

ואע"ג דגזירת הכתוב אין צריך טעם, מכל מקום גם טעם ברור יש בזה. דבשלמה לבא לבית דין הגדול שיקדשו החדש שכלל ישראל תלוים בקביעות הבי"ד שפיר מחללין, אבל לחלל על קיומן זהו רק בשביל מקצת מישראל, למה נחלל שבת עליהם, יעשו ב ימים מספק כמו הרחוקים לגמרי שהשלוחים לא יגיעו אליהם כלל, ומאי אולמא דהני מהני.

However, the Acharonim raise an important question. Why is it necessary to prove by a verse in the Torah that the desecration of the Shabbos is *not allowed* under these circumstances, when there is no corresponding verse in the Torah which can be cited to prove that the desecration of the Shabbos is *allowed* under certain circumstances? The fact that there is no such verse gives us a clear indication that Shabbos cannot be desecrated for this purpose. In answer to this question, one can point out that informing the people is included in the overall mitzva of Kiddush HaChodesh. This is the position of the Rambam, who writes as follows in *Hilchos Kiddush HaChodesh 1:7*:

> מצות עשה מן התורה על בית דין, שיחשבו וידעו אם יראה הירח או לא יראה... **וישלחו ויודיעו** שאר העם באי זה יום הוא ראש חדש, כדי שידעו באי זה יום הן המועדות, שנאמר, אשר תקראו אותם מקראי קדש. ונאמר, ושמרת את החקה הזאת למועדה.

> It is s positive commandment of the Torah for the court to calculate and determine whether or not the moon will be sighted....And to send forth messengers to inform the remainder of the people on which day Rosh Chodesh was observed, so that they will know the day on which to celebrate the festivals, as implied in the verse that "you will pronounce as days of holy convocation." And it is implied by the verse in *Exodus 13:10*, "and you shall observe this stature in its appointed season."

Thus, since 'informing the people' is also dictated by the Torah, this, like the eyewitnesses, can be a justification for desecrating the Shabbos. We are told that only in regard to *designating* Rosh Chodesh are we allowed to desecrate the Shabbos, but not for the sake of informing the people of this day that is being designated.

NO DIFFERENCE BETWEEN NISSAN, TISHREI AND ANY OTHER MONTH

Based on what we have discussed, it would appear that Shabbos is *never* to be desecrated, even if it is in Nissan or Tishrei.

And this seems indicative of the fact that the Rambam cites the law and does not mention any loophole in it. However, the Rambam, in his commentary to the mishna in Mesechtas Rosh Hashanah, does indeed make this distinction between Nissan and Tishrei. He writes as follows:

ואותן שלוחין יוצאין בשבת ומחללין את השבת על ניסן ועל תשרי לבד כדאמרינן על ב׳ חדשים מחללין את השבת שבהם שלוחין יוצאין מפני שכל המועדות תלוים בהם, ושאר החדשים אין שלוחים יוצאין בהן לקיימן.

This raises another question. All the commentators ask, where is the source for the Rambam's statement here, after the Gemara rules out this desecration of the Shabbos for the purpose of the messengers announcing the day to be designated as Rosh Chodesh?

The position of the gaonim is also that the Shabbos, which may be desecrated by the eyewitnesses, can also be desecrated by the messengers, since Shabbos has already been desecrated for the sake of Kiddush HaChodesh. And as regards the verse which does not allow for desecration, this is to be understood as referring to the actual day of designating Rosh Chodesh. Yet Shabbos may be desecrated even for the purpose of *announcing* the new moon. However, on any other day the messengers may not desecrate the Shabbos. For example, if Rosh Chodesh was designated on a Wednesday and the messengers went out to announce the new month, they cannot desecrate the Shabbos, since it is not the day on which Rosh Chodesh was proclaimed.

דשלוחין נמי מחללין שבת, אך אותה שבת שהעדים מחללין...וטעם דמילתא, דלהכי הסמיך "מועדי", "למקראי קדש", לומר דבעת הקריאה, דהיינו בעת קדוש החדש מחללין והא דקאמר על קריאתן אתה מחלל, הכי פי׳ בעת קריאת אתה מחלל גם בשביל קיום מועדי ה׳, ואי אתה מחלל על קיומן בלבד בלא עת קריאתו... (הערות הרב מרדכי זק"ש לפי׳ המשניות לרמב"ם, עמ׳ פג.)

One Witness is Enough

The Rambam in *Hilchos Kiddush HaChodesh 3:14* states:

אין השלוחין צריכין להיות שנים, אלא אפילו אחד נאמן. ולא שליח בלבד, אלא אפילו תגר משאר העם, שבא כדרכו ואמר: אני שמעתי מפי בית דין שקדשו את החדש ביום פלוני נאמן, ומתקנין את המועדות על פיו. שדבר זה דבר העשוי להגלות, ועד אחד כשר נאמן עליו.

> There is no need for there to be two messengers. Even a single individual's testimony can be believed. Moreover, this does not apply to messengers alone. Even if a travelling merchant of no particular distinction passes through on his journey and says, "I heard from the court that it sanctified the new moon on such and such a date," his statement can be believed, and the celebration of the festivals is arranged accordingly. The rationale is that this is a matter that will eventually be revealed. Therefore, the testimony of a single acceptable witness is sufficient.

The source for this decision is based on that which is cited in *Mesechtas Rosh Hashanah 22b,* where we are told:

כי אתא עולא אמר: **קדשוה** לירחא במערבא. אמר רב כהנא לא מיבעיא עולא דגברא רבה הוא דמהימן, אלא אפילו איניש דעלמא נמי מהימן. מאי טעמא, כל מילתא דעבידא לאגלויי לא משקרי בה איניש. תניא נמי הכי: בא אחד מסוף העולם ואמר קדשו בית דין מהימן.

> When Ulla came to Babylonia from Eretz Yisrael, he reported: "They have *sanctified* the new moon in Eretz Yisrael." Rav Kahana said: "Needless to

say, Ulla, who is a great man, is believed, when he reports when the Bais Din has sanctified the new moon. But even an ordinary person is also believed when he bears such testimony. What is the reason that a single witness is believed? His credibility is based on the principle that people do not lie about any matter that is likely to be revealed in time (i.e., it will eventually become public knowledge which day the Bais Din actually declared to be Rosh Chodesh). Therefore, the witnesses would not lie about this matter, since his lie would inevitably be revealed."

The טורי אבן, in his commentary here, touches upon two issues. Why does the Gemara have to resort to this principle to explain why a single witness is believed? Why not believe him simply on the basis of the principle that "one witness is believed in matters of ritual law" — "עד אחד נאמן באיסורין"?

From what is said here: "Ulla reported: they have sanctified the new moon", we know that this alludes to a month that is deficient (a month which has only 29 days). For a full month (a month of 30 days) does not require sanctification. We may thus conclude that his testimony would not be believed regarding a full month. What is the difference between a deficient and a full month that makes us say that a single witness is believed only in regard to a month that is deficient?

To answer the first question, the טו"א contends that we do not apply the principle of "עד אחד נאמן באיסורין" in this case, for we are dealing here with a very serious matter—the implementation of the holidays. Thus were it not for the fact that 'the matter will be ultimately revealed", we would not rely on the testimony of a single witness and consequently, he would not be believed.

As for the second question regarding a deficient month, the answer might be that since the name of the month about which the single witness testified is not specified, it therefore appears that in any of the twelve months of the year a single witness can be believed. This impression must be qualified, for regarding the month of Elul we are told (see *Rosh Hashanah 19b* and *Mesechtas Beitza 6a*) that since the days of Ezra Elul has always been deficient (29 days) and therefore a single witness would not be believed. For a single witness can not be believed if he testifies against the status quo or against a majority (רוב או חזקה). Thus Ulla is believed only if he testified in a month (including Elul) which was deficient. Had he said, however, that Elul was a full month, he would not have been believed, despite the principle that "the matter will ultimately be revealed".

The טו"א does not agree with the opinion of the Rambam in *Hilchos Kiddush HaChodesh 3:11*, that when messengers were despatched for "six months of the year", including the month of Elul, one messenger was sufficient.

However, we see from the "שאילתות דרב אחאי גאון" that he disagrees with the טורי אבן here. The שאילתות raises this very question as to whether a single witness is believed in regard to a full month, even if it is the month of Elul.

ברם צריך חד כי אתי ואמר מליוה לירחא וקדשוה קמי
מי סמיכנן עליה.

The (לנצי"ב) "עמק שאלה" explains here why the question relates to a full month (Elul) and not to a deficient month, for if the issue related only to a deficient month, we would not need to apply here the principle that "the matter will be ultimately revealed" — "עבידא דגלוי" for we could simply apply the rationale of "עד אחד נאמן באיסורין" to resolve the issue. Thus here we speak of a full month, which seems to contradict the fact that most of the time the month of Elul has only twenty-nine days and is therefore almost always deficient. This means that a single witness would not be believed. However, because of the consideration that the matter will be ultimately revealed, "עבידא דגלויי", he is nevertheless believed. Thus we see that the "שאילתות" contradicts the view expressed by the טורי אבן here.

THE MESSENGERS SENT OTHER MESSENGERS

The Rambam's statement that "even a single witness is believed" must be qualified. This does not mean that only one messenger was sent out. For how would it be possible for a single witness to inform so many cities, towns and villages where Jews lived throughout the Diaspora? And furthermore, there was not much time to travel to all these places. For there were only ten days available. In Nissan, when Pesach was on the fifteenth of the month, there were only twelve days left to travel, for we have to subtract the two Shabboses, and in the month of Tishrei we subtract Rosh Hashanah and Yom Kippur, for these were days when the messengers did not travel. Thus only ten days were left during which they could travel. Chazal tell us: "גזרת ניסן אטו תשרי". Even those who lived only twelve days away from Yerushalayim would still have to observe two days of Pesach. For if they were to observe one day, they would do the same in Tishrei, even though the messengers had not yet arrived. Thus we see that a single messenger could not possibly make the entire Diaspora aware of the exact day of Rosh Chodesh.

In light of this problem, HaRav Michael Tuketinsky suggests that what actually happened was that the Bais Din sent two messengers, and when they arrived in a city, a number of other messengers awaited them, and they then fanned out across the Diaspora.

אבל כיצד ידעו כל אלפי המקומות, העירות והכפרים
והמושבות שבכל פינות ומרכזי הארץ (אחרי ביטול המשואות)
שקדשו בית דין את החודש?

ואולי שלחו בי"ד רק שני שלוחים, למשל, אחד לצפון ואחד לדרום (או גם שני שלוחים למזרח ולמערב) ובכל עיר ועיר שהשליח עבר נשלחו משם שלוחים לרוח מזרח ומערב. לפי זה יתכן שאין שלוחי ירושלים הלכו לקצוות הארץ מהלך עשרה ימים...אלא שבכל עיר שבאו לשם נשלחו ממנה שלוחים אחרים לכל צדדי. (ספר ארץ ישראל, מהנ"ל, עמ' לא, הערה א.)

VII

THE "SIX MONTHS" WHEN MESSENGERS WERE SENT FORTH

The Mishna in *Rosh Hashanah 18a* tells us that:

על ששה חדשים השלוחים יוצאין:
על ניסן מפני הפסח;
על אב מפני התענית;
על אלול מפני ראש השנה;
על תשרי מפני תקנת המועדות;
על כסלו מפני חנוכה;
ועל אדר מפני הפורים.
וכשהיה בית המקדש קיים, יוצאין **אף** על אייר מפני פסח קטן.

In six specific months messengers were sent forth to inform the people which day was declared the first of the month.

On Nissan on account of Pesach;
On Av on account of the Fast of Tisha B'Av;
On Elul on account of Rosh Hashanah;
On Tishrei on account of the festivals of Yom Kippur and Succos;
On Kislev on account of Chanukah;
On Adar on account of Purim;

And when the Bais HaMikdash was still standing they went forth on Iyar as well, on account of Pesach Sheni.

According to this text, it would seem that when the Bais HaMikdash no longer existed, messengers went forth for the sake of the six months spelled out here in the Mishna. However, before the Destruction they went out for *seven* months, since the reading here is: "when the Temple stood they went out *also* on Iyar.".

According to the טורי אבן, however, there were always only six months. When the Bais HaMikdash stood they went out in "אייר" and not in "אב" (for at the time of the Temple, Tisha B'Av was not observed). After the Destruction, they no longer went out for Pesach Sheni (in Iyar) but they went out for Tisha B'Av (in Av).

From the Rambam we conclude that indeed there could have been a possibility that the messengers went forth seven times each year. For he writes as follows in 3:9:

על ששה חדשים היו שלוחין יוצאין...ובזמן המקדש קיים יוצאין אף על אייר מפני פסח קטן.

And when the Temple stood they *also* went out for Pesach Katan.

The Rambam here follows his position as set forth in his commentary to the Mishna here. There he contends that the Fast of Av was observed even during the period of the Second Temple. However, the טו"א maintains that the Fast of Av was not observed during this time. (For further discussion of this issue, see footnote 70 in my sefer "תפארת למשה" על הלכות קדוש החדש, עמ' ר"ו.)

VIII

Kislev on account of Chanukah

To the question raised by the Yerushalmi as to why we do not observe Chanukah for nine days (because of the issue of "ספיקא דיומא", doubt as to which day was really Rosh Chodesh, the places where the messengers did not reach in time would observe the festival for two days), the Avudraham answers that since Chanukah is a holiday of only Rabbinic origin, we are not stringent about its observance. But this seems to be challenged by the Mishna, which tells us that messengers were sent forth to inform the people of the exact day of Rosh Chodesh Kislev. Once they were aware of this information, they would be certain to celebrate Chanukah on its appropriate day, the 25th of Kislev. Thus it would seem that it was only those who were still in doubt as to the exact day of Rosh Chodesh who would have to celebrate two days of Chanukah. For if even those who did not know observed only one day (which would mean a total of eight days), then what would be the purpose of sending messengers? This would seem to contradict the contention of the Avudraham that Kislev was never observed for nine days.

This question was anticipated in the sefer "שקל הקודש" (מהרב שי"ח בן הג' השטייפלר באור ההלכה, עמ' לג מדפי הספר). There we find the answer given that even those who remained in doubt as to the exact day of Rosh Chodesh Kislev still observed one day, the 25th of Kislev. Yet messengers were sent, for if it is possible to alleviate doubt, we are obligated to do so.

דאע"ג דמספק לא עשו אלא יום א' מ"מ שולחין שלוחין,
דכל היכא דאפשר לברר מברינן...

HaRav Chaim Kanievsky, *shlita*, answers this question by referring to the well-known answer of the "דבר אברהם" (סימן לד) to the question of why we do not make "two countings" of the sefira each day since we celebrate "two days of Pesach". Thus perhaps the second day of Pesach is really the first day, and thus the counting should begin the day after the second day of Pesach? The concept of "counting" means that one must have a clear perception of what day one is counting, for if one counts two days in the hope that one of them is the right day, this invalidates the counting of the days of Sefirah. So here, too, since Chanukah must be celebrated on the 25th of Kislev, and subsequently we are to add a candle each night to indicate the eight days of the miracle (and that today is the second day, etc. of that miracle), we cannot therefore make "two first days" of Chanukah, for then the exact count would not be clearly indicated.

על דרך שכתב בספר "דבר אברהם" סימן לד, לתרץ קושיית הרז"ה סוף פסחים למה אין סופרים ב' ספירות, דב' ספירות אין זה ספירה כלל, דספירה צריך שידע איזה יום היום ואם יאמר כל יום את כל הספירות מספק לא יצא כלום, כיון שאינו יודע איזה יום היום ע"ש.

ולפי זה דבחנוכה דעיקרו הדלקה הנרות ומוסף והולך, לא שייך להדליק ב' הדלקות, דא"כ אין כאן מספר כלל ולא נודע איזה יום הוא. וכיון שחז"ל תקנו שיהיו מהדרין ומוסיפין כל יום אע"ג דמדינא יוצא בנר אחד כל יום מ"מ כיון שרצו שיהו גם מהדרין, לא רצו לתקן ב' ימים בחו"ל מספק דאם כן בטל המספר לגמרי...

The unique position of the "מנחת חינוך"

The "מנחת חינוך" in מצוה ש"א contends that it is only today that we observe eight days of Chanukah rather than nine. The reason for this is based on our fixed calendar, which ensures that we no longer have doubts about when the 25th of Kislev will be. However, in earlier times, when this doubt did exist, two days were designated for each festival, including Chanukah.

In the sefer "ברכת כהן", מהרב שמואל דוייטש (עמ' ר"נ), the author questions this position of the "מנחת חינוך", by pointing out that we see clearly from the Gemara in ערכין, י, א that even during the time when Rosh Chodesh was determined by eyewitnesses, Chanukah was observed only for eight days.

> דאמר רבי יוחנן משום רבי שמעון בן יהוצדק: שמונה עשר
> ימים שהיחיד גומר בהן את ההלל, שמונת ימי החג, ושמונה
> ימי חנוכה, ויום טוב הראשון של פסח, ויום טוב הראשון
> של עצרת. ובגולה עשרים ואחד: תשעה ימי החג ושמונה
> ימי חנוכה, ושני ימים טובים של פסח, ושני ימים טובים
> של עצרת.

> Rav Yochanan said in the name of R' Shimon ben Yehotzadek: eighteen days of the year even an individual who prays privately must recite the entire Hallel. These days are: the eight days of Succos, the *eight days of Chanukah*, the first day of Pesach and the day of Shavuos. And in the Diaspora, the entire Hallel is recited for 21 days of the year, and those days are: the nine days of Succos [i.e., seven days of Succos and two days of Shemeni Atzeres], the *eight days of Chanukah,* the two days of Pesach and the two days of Shavuos.

The author this Baraisa was R' Shimon ben Yehotzadek, who lived in the era when Rosh Chodesh was determined by the testimony of eyewitnesses, as indicated in *Mesechtas Sanhedrin 26a*, where we find the following description:

> Once during the Shmittah year, Rav Chiya bar Zarnokei and Rav Shimon ben Yehotzadek were travelling in Asia to intercalate the year...

This Rav Shimon ben Yehotzadek was a grandson of the R' Shimon ben Yehotzadek mentioned here in Mesechtas ערכין. For the issue referred to in *Mesechtas Sanhedrin* involved Rav Yochanan himself; whereas here, in Mesechtas ערכין, Rav Yochanan cited a law in the name of R' Shimon ben Yehotzadek, and this proved that he lived in the period when Rosh Chodesh was determined by eyewitnesses.

Thus, since the Baraisa of R' Shimon ben Yehotzadek explicitly states that "during the eight days of Chanukah all of Hallel is recited", this proves that even when the new month was determined by eyewitnesses Chanukah was still only eight days and not nine. This refutes the theory of the "מנחת חינוך" and of the other commentators who hold a similar opinion.

We might attempt to explain the rationale behind this clear indication that Chanukah was celebrated for only eight days in the Diaspora by pointing out that the Jews who lived in communities outside the land of Yisrael were informed when Rosh Chodesh would begin and thus when the festivals were to be celebrated. This was accomplished by the witnesses appearing before the Sanhedrin in Yerushalayim and giving their testimony that they had seen the new moon. This was accepted by the Bais Din, whose judges declared, "מקודש, מקודש" — "this day has been sanctified as Rosh Chodesh". Immediately afterwards, messengers were despatched to the Diaspora.

These messengers would then travel all week, except for Shabbos and Yom Tov. This means that in the month of Tishrei they travelled a total of ten days before Succos. Thus, they did not reach far into the Diaspora, and therefore, most of the Disapora communities kept two days of Yom Tov and therefore recited Hallel for *nine days* on Succos and on Shemeni Atzeres. Consequently, it was proper for the Baraisa to state that "in the Diaspora Hallel was recited for nine days of Succos."

However, in relation to Chanukah, the messengers travelled

until the 25th of Kislev. Although then, too, they did not travel all 24-25 days, since they could not travel on Shabbos, yet they managed to reach most but not all of the Diaspora communities. Thus, we could say that three-quarters of the Diaspora communities were aware by the 25th of Kislev when Rosh Chodesh was to be celebrated, and therefore they knew exactly when the 25th of Kislev would be. Thus there was no need for them to celebrate a ninth day of Chanukah because there was no element of doubt involved, "ספיקא דיומא". Yet the remaining communities, which the messengers were unable to reach, *would have to* celebrate an extra day. This is the contention of the "מנחת חינוך".

Since most of the Diaspora celebrated only eight days, had the Tanna stated that "in the Diaspora Chanukah is observed for nine days", this would be misleading, for, as we have explained, most of the Diaspora celebrated for only eight days. This is why the Tanna was able to state that "in the Diaspora eight days of Chanukah were observed", even though there were places where *nine* days were observed.

Thus the Gemara in ערכין cannot be used as a question directed against the "מנחת חינוך" as explained here [see *The Commentators' Al HaNissim — Chanukah*, pp. 270-273.]

IX

INELIGIBLE WITNESSES DISQUALIFY ELIGIBLE WITNESSES

The Mishna in *Mesechtas Makkos 5b*, states the following rule that applies to witnesses:

"על פי שנים או שלשה עדים יומת המת" (דברים יז,ו) אם מתקיימת העדות בשנים למה פרט הכתוב בשלשה, להקיש שלשה לשנים... ומה שנים נמצא אחד מהן קרוב או פסול

עדותן בטלה, אף שלשה נמצא אחד מהן קרוב או פסול עדותן בטלה...

"By the testimony of two or three witnesses shall the one who is to die be put to death" *(Devarim 17:6)*. Now if the testimony may be established by two, why did the Torah specify 'by three'? It is to compare three to two...Just as with two, if one of them is found to have been a relative or is disqualified to serve as a witness, their testimony is null and void; so too with three, if one of them is found to be a relative or a disqualified witness, their testimony is null and void...

This law applies, according to various Rishonim and Acharonim, only under the following conditions: If all the witnesses all saw together that which transpired; however, if the disqualified witness did not see this together with the others, he does not disqualify them. If all the witnesses here intended to testify to what they saw, but if not, then once again there is no disqualification here. And finally, if others contend that the disqualified witness disqualifies the other witnesses only if they all appeared together and testified together. And so the Aruch HaShulchan writes, in סימן לו:

(א) ודוקא כשראו כולם המעשה כאחד אבל אם הקרוב או הפסול לא ראו ביחד עם הכשרים עדותן קיימת (ש"ך).

(ב) במה דברים אמורים שבטלה עדותן, כשנתכוונו כולם להעיד אבל לא נתכוונו כולם להעיד תתקיים העדות בכשרים.

(ד) יש מגדולי הראשונים שכתבו...אין פוסלים...אלא אם כן העידו גם יחד בבית דין והגידו יחד...

Based on the second principle listed above (אות ב'), the "מנחת חינוך" asked a question which he boasted "made the rounds of the yeshiva's study halls."

The Mishna in *Rosh Hashanah 22a* recounts the following incident:

> אמר רבי יוסי: מעשה בטוביה הרופא שראה את החדש בירושלים הוא ובנו ועבדו משוחרר, וקבלו הכהנים אותו ואת בנו ופסלו את עבדו. וכשבאו לפני בית דין, קבלו אותו ואת עבדו ופסלו את בנו.

> Rabbi Yossi said: It once happened that Tuvia the doctor saw the new moon together with his son and a freed slave. The Kohanim accepted his testimony and that of his son, but disqualified the testimony of his former slave. But when they came before the Bais Din, they accepted him and his slave and disqualified his son.

And in this manner the "מנחת חינוך" asked: The halacha states that a disqualified witness disqualifies those who testify with him, and if the Kohanim disqualified the slave, how could the Bais Din have accepted Tuvia and his son. For wouldn't they too have been disqualified on account of the fact that they joined together with the (disqualified) slave? And if you were to say that they become disqualified only if they testify together, didn't they all appear before the Bais Din of the Kohanim? And therefore shouldn't we apply this law that a disqualified witness disqualifies all the other witnesses? However, in our time, when we have in our possession the newly printed manuscripts of the Rishonim, we find that this question was anticipated by them. (See here the Meiri in כב,א, Tosafos קיג,ב ד"ה ב"ק, רי"ד and the "ספר המכריע" סימן כה.) The "מנחת חינוך" concludes by saying:

> וב"ה, נתפרסם הקושיה הזאת בין הלומדים...

Resolving the Question of the "מנחת חינוך"

The sefer "בני ציון" מהרב בן-ציון מיטאווסקי offers the solution that we only apply this principle when the purpose of the witnesses is to clarify the situation for us, for example, in a case where "they say that Reuven borrowed money from Shimon". However, in relation to the laws of Kiddush HaChodesh, the Bais Din is already aware, by means of calculation, that a new moon now exists. Yet the Torah required that in addition, this fact must be attested to by witnesses. Therefore, we do not apply here the principle of a disqualified witness disqualifying the other witnesses.

> דגבי עדות קדה"ח לא נפסלים העדים מחמת זה שנמצא א' קרוב או פסול. דבשלמא גבי כל עדיות ענין עדותן הוא שהעדים **מבררים את הדבר** לפני בית דין, כגון בהלואה, שניהם מבררים דבר אחד שראובן לוה משמעון, ושפיר העדים מצורפין מחמת זה שהרי שניהם מעידים דבר אחד.
>
> אבל בעדות החדש הרי עצם הדבר שמעידין עליו (שכבר נתחדשה הלבנה) הלא ידוע לבי"ד על פי החשבון, רק שגזירת הכתוב הוא שיהיו עדים שראו את חידוש הלבנה. ונמצא שכל אחד מהעדים אינו מעיד **לברר** לפנינו שהי' חידוש הלבנה, אלא מעיד על עצמו **שהוא** ראה את הלבנה בחידושה, והשני מעיד גם כן על עצמו.. ואין עדותן **לברר** לפנינו שהי' לבנה בלילה זה...

The Insight of the "קהלת יעקב"

The "קהלת יעקב" reconciles this question here of the "מנחת חינוך" (see the sefer "שושנים לדוד" להרב דוד פארדא in his commentary on this Mishna) by maintaining that indeed it seems puzzling why the Bais Din of the Kohanim acted here to sanctify the new month?

For this matter of Kiddush HaChodesh is solely under the jurisdiction of the Bais Din HaGadol, the Sanhedrin, and has nothing to do with the Bais Din of the Kohanim.

The answer here must be that the Bais Din of the Kohanim acted only to screen the witnesses, and their decision would be passed on to the Sanhedrin, who would make the ultimate determination regarding the matter of Kiddush HaChodesh based on the reliability of the witnesses. Thus we can understand why they felt that a slave, even one who had been freed, would not be acceptable as a valid witness; whereas a relative (the son of Tuvia) could be accepted as a reliable witness. However, this group of witnesses never testified before the Bais Din of the Kohanim. And therefore we are not dealing with the problem of a disqualified witness disqualifying other witnesses, for this is not the context at all.

והדבר באמת תמוה לאיזו ענין יעידו טוביה ושאר עדים לפני הכהנים בזמן שאין שום תועלת בעדות זו, שהרי קדה"ח מסור לב"ד הגדול... ולזאת נלענ"ד דלא העידו כלל בפני הכהנים רק הכהנים היו בגדר מורי הוראה. ושאלו את הכהנים "תורה", אם יתקבל עדותן. והשיבו הכהנים כדעתם...וכל זה הי' דרך הוראה דין ולא קבלת עדות ממש...

Chapter Twelve
The Unique Laws of Kiddush HaChodesh

I

THE LAW OF "אתם"

The Mishna in *Mesechtas Rosh Hashanah 24b-25a* records the following two incidents:

מעשה שבאו שנים ואמרו "ראינוהו שחרית במזרח וערבית במערב.". אמר רבי יוחנן בן נורי "עדי שקר הם.". כשבאו ליבנה קבלן רבן גמליאל.

It happened that two witnesses came and said: "We saw the new moon in the morning in the east and that evening in the west." R' Yochanan ben Nuri said: "They are false witnesses" [i.e., they claimed to have seen the old moon in the morning and the new moon in the evening, and since there is always a 24-hour period between the disappearance of the old moon and the appearance of the new moon, it is obvious that they are liars.] But when the witnesses came to Yavneh, Rabban Gamliel accepted them as valid witnesses.

ועוד באו שנים ואמרו: "ראינוהו בזמנו" ובליל עבורו לא נראה. וקבלן רבן גמליאל. אמר רבי דוסא בן הרכינס: "עדי שקר הן. האיך מעידים על האשה שילדה, ולמחר כרסה בין שיניה?" אמר לו רבי יהושע: "רואה אני את דבריך."

On another occasion, two witnesses came and said: "We saw the moon in its time." [i.e., on the 30th day]. But on the following night the moon was not visible and Rabban Gamliel accepted them as valid witnesses and established the 30th day as Rosh Chodesh [Tishrei].

But R' Dosa ben Horkynos said: "They are false

witnesses. How can they testify about a woman that she gave birth, yet on the morrow we see she is still pregnant." [i.e., the fact that the new moon was invisible in the evening is the greatest proof that they did not see the moon earlier that day. For the moon becomes more visible as it moves away from the sun and grows progressively larger].

R' Yehoshua said to R' Dosa: "I see the correctness of your words [i.e., I agree that they are surely false witnesses]..."

The Mishna then continues:

שלח לו רבן גמליאל: "גוזרני עליך שתבא אצלי במקלך ובמעותיך ביום הכפורים שחל להיות בחשבונך". הלך ומצאו רבי עקיבא מיצר. אמר לו: "יש לי ללמוד שכל מה שעשה רבן גמליאל עשוי, שנאמר 'אלה מועדי ה' מקראי קדש אשר תקראו אתם' — בין בזמנן בין שלא בזמנן, אין לי מועדות אלא אלו."

Rabban Gamliel sent a message to him [R' Yehoshua]: "I decree upon you that you come to me with your staff and your money on the day Yom Kippur will fall according to your reckoning."

R' Akiva went and found him [R' Yehoshua] troubled so he said to him: "I can elucidate that whatever Rabban Gamliel did is validly done, for it says *(Va'yikra 23:4)*, 'These are the holidays of Hashem, holy convocations that you shall declare them' — whether declared in their correct time or not in their correct time, I [Hashem] have no other than these [i.e., 'You' here in this pasuk indicates that the matter is dependent solely on the declaration of Bais Din]..."

The Mishna continues:

> He [R' Yehoshua] came to R' Dosa ben Horkynos, who said to him: "If we come to reconsider the decisions of Rabban Gamliel's bais din, then we must reconsider the decisions of every bais din that arose from the days of Moshe until now; as it says *(Shemos 24:9):* 'There went up Moshe and Aaron, Nadiv and Avihu, and seventy of the elders of Israel.' Why are the names of the elders not expressly mentioned? Only to teach us that every three people who arose as a bais din for Israel are considered like the bais din of Moshe..."

The Gemara here, *25a,* further explains what R' Akiva said here in the Mishna:

> הלך ר' עקיבא ומצאו לר' יהושע כשהוא מיצר. אמר לו: "רבי, תרשיני לומר לפניך דבר אחד שלמדתני... הרי הוא אומר 'אתם, אתם, אתם' שלש פעמים. 'אתם' אפילו שוגגין 'אתם' אפילו מזידין 'אתם' אפילו מוטעין..."

> ...and R' Akiva said to R' Yehoshua: "Indeed it states in Scripture with regard to designating the festivals, three times, 'אתם, אתם, אתם' — 'you, you, you' [The phrase, 'These are the festivals that you shall declare' appears three times in the passage concerning the festivals *(Va'yikra 23: 2,4,27)* and in each occurrence the word אתם is spelled defectively, rather than 'אותם' with a 'ו' and therefore expounded as if it were vowelized 'אתם' — 'you']. These three occurrences indicate: The festivals that you, Bais Din, declare [through your designation of Rosh Chodesh] are valid even if you choose the wrong date of Rosh Chodesh in error (שוגגין), deliberately (מזידין), or were misled (מוטעין)..."

These two incidents as recorded here in the Mishna provoke the following questions, and indeed we need to clarify what happened here and to examine the impact of the application of this law of "אתם".

In regard to the first incident recorded, that of רבי יוחנן בן נורי and רבן גמליאל, where the witnesses saw the "old moon" and "new moon" on the same day, which prompted רבי יוחנן בן נורי to say "עדי שקר הן" — "they are false witnesses" two questions can be asked.

Rabban Gamliel was situated in Yavneh and it was there that the witnesses eventually came. Why, then, did they initially appear before ר' יוחנן בן נורי? Furthermore, the sefer "שפתי חכמים" suggests that the witnesses feared that they would not be recognized by the Bais Din in Yavneh; therefore they sought verification from ר' יוחנן בן נורי.

...מאחר שרבן גמליאל נשיא הי' ומושבו ביבנה הי' ואם כן למה באו בתחילה להעיד לפני ר' יוחנן בן נורי? ויש לומר לפי שהיה ספק בידם אי מכירין רבן גמליאל ובית דינו אותן, ובאו לפני בי"ד שבעיירם, היינו ר' יוחנן בן נורי ובית דינו להעיד עליהן לפני בית דינו של נשיא...

This answer seems difficult to comprehend, for if they sought a letter of introduction, they certainly did not get it from ר' יוחנן בן נורי, for indeed he considered them to be "false witnesses". And being that they feared not being recognized by Rabban Gamliel, why did they proceed to appear before him?

Why is it that only in the second incident involving ר' דוסא, רבן גמליאל and ר' יהושע do we apply the ruling of "אתם" and not here in this first incident of רבן גמליאל and ר' יוחנן בן נורי? For surely there too the new month was, according to ר' יוחנן בן נורי, designated by virtue of the testimony of false witnesses?

Concerning the second incident recorded here involving ר' דוסא, רבן גמליאל and רבי יהושע, we could ask the following questions.

Why did רבן גמליאל censure only ר' יהושע and not ר' דוסא? For after all, he also disagreed with רבן גמליאל. The דורות הראשונים (ח"א, כרך חמישי פרק כו) who also addresses this question, writes that the "חוקרים" — "Bible critics and scholars", as they always do, maliciously maligned the Sages and write that "R' Dosa was a rich man, and therefore Rabban Gamliel "turned the other cheek"; whereas R' Yehoshua was a poor man, therefore he let out his anger at him."

"והחוקרים האחרונים בסגנונם בכל מקום כתבו גם בזה, כי לר' דוסא העשיר נשא רבן גמליאל פנים ורק על ר' יהושע העני שפך כל חמתו."

I have always taught my students that these "critics" of our Torah and Chazal are not merely "apikorsim", heretics, but more so, "עמי הארץ" really very shallow. In addition they are not ethically honest. Although some of them possessed a vast amount of knowledge, they did not "understand" (and indeed they did not want to know) the material at hand. The "דורות הראשונים" shows that their approach and their criticism has no merit here and we shall also answer them. We would not even bother to cite their words, but I want to bring to the attention of the reader their "חוצפה", audacity in daring to suspect a Tanna, the Nasi of Yisrael, of such actions and of how they falsely evaluate our saintly sages.

After רבי עקיבא justified the decision of רבן גמליאל, why did ר' דוסא have to also appease ר' יהושע? The reason for mentioning these two incidents in the same Mishna, even though, as we pointed out, only the second incident involves the principle of "אתם", is that the common denominator here is that both cases involve false witnesses, "עדי שקר". However, we will endeavor to show there is another reason why both cases were mentioned together.

Answering the above questions

In examining these two recorded incidents, we can detect a vast difference between them. In the first incident involving ר' יוחנן בן נורי, he initially pronounced these two witnesses false witnesses, and thereby we could not declare Rosh Chodesh by virtue of their testimony. They then proceeded to appear before Rabban Gamliel, who believed that they were not to be viewed as false witnesses, and thus he declared Rosh Chodesh day. Since Kiddush HaChodesh can be enacted by "three judges" acting on behalf of the Sanhedrin HaGadol, R' Yochanan ben Nuri acted here in this capacity and ruled that we should not accept these "false witnesses" and act upon their testimony. Yet, רבן גמליאל the Nasi, who has the "last word" in this matter, ruled differently and declared that their testimony was valid. Viewed from this perspective, we can answer our two previous questions.

R' Yochanan's role in this matter was as a member of the Bais Din authorized to sanctify the month. This was the reason why the witnesses appeared before him. And although he invalidated and disregarded their testimony, yet they endeavored to appear before רבן גמליאל, the Nasi, who, as we pointed out, had the "last word" in this matter. Rabban Gamliel did not have to apply the principle of "אתם", for he felt they were honest witnesses and thus he declared the month sanctified. In the second incident, only after Rabban Gamliel accepted the witnesses, did ר' יהושע and ר' דוסא protest and they called for a recall of the decision of רבן גמליאל, to which ר' עקיבא pointed out that after a decision has been delivered, even if it was wrong, we must follow that decision, based on the principle of "אתם". In the first incident, the objection only occurred before the decision and not afterwards.

As to the questions raised in regard to the second incident cited here involving רבן גמליאל and ר' יהושע, ר' דוסא, why was only ר' יהושע censured and not ר' דוסא? Furthermore, why did

ר' יהושע need further assurance after ר' עקיבא justified the decision of רבן גמליאל?

We might suggest that one question here answers the other. R' Dosa, after he initially disagreed with Rabban Gamliel, later retracted his opinion and accepted the Nasi's original decision. This approach is borne out by the fact that after ר' יהושע received the consoling words of ר' עקיבא, R' Dosa then addressed R' Yehoshua and offered a different reason in order to appease R' Yehoshua. That is, R' Dosa maintains, that indeed we need not apply here the ruling of "אתם" but rather, if the Nasi already issued a decision, that decision is binding and all objections have to be dropped. Proof of this approach is from the fact that if we were to uphold all dissenting views, then we would have to investigate all the rulings of Bais Din from the time of Moshe Rabbenu and challenge them all. Thus, we see that not only did ר' דוסא seek to reassure ר' יהושע with another halachic justification, but he also challenged ר' יהושע to retract his opposing opinion, just as R' Dosa did. Therefore, Rabban Gamliel had no reason to censure R' Dosa. However, it seems that R' Yehoshua insisted on upholding his objection, and that is why Rabban Gamliel acted as he did.

THERE IS AN "ORDER" TO THE MISHNA

Why place these two incidents in the same Mishna, since the principle here of "אתם" only applies to the second incident? Why not cite these two incidents in two separate Mishnayos?

Before we attempt to answer this problem we would cite here the question raised by the "דורות הראשונים" *(ibid. pg. 306)* who asks: The sequence of the משניות in Chapter Two seems to be out of order.

In Mishna 6 we are taught:

כיצד בודקין את העדים? זוג שבא ראשון, בודקין אותו ראשון, ומכניסין את הגדול שבהן ואומרים לו: אמר, כיצד ראית את הלבנה. ואחר כך מכניסין את השני ובודקין אותו. אם נמצאו דבריהם מכונים, עדותן קיימת

How do we interrogate the witnesses? The pair that arrives first is interrogated first... how did you see the moon?... If their words are found to coincide, their testimony is valid.

Mishna 7 reads:

ראש בית דין אומר: "מקודש." וכל העם עונים אחריו "מקודש מקודש"...

The head of the Bais Din says: "It is sanctified;" And all the people respond after him: "It is sanctified, it is sanctified"...

Mishna 8 reads:

דמות צורות לבנות היו לו לרבן גמליאל בטבלא ובכתל בעליתו שבהן מראה את ההדיוטות ואומר: הכזה ראית או כזה.

Rabban Gamliel had moon-shaped forms on a tablet on the wall of his upper chamber which he would show the witnesses, and say: "Did you see the moon like this or like that?"

This sequence begs the following question. Since in Mishna 7, Bais Din has already accepted the testimony of the witnesses after they had been interrogated and thereby declared the month "מקודש", why now go back and teach in Mishna 8 the manner of how Rabban Gamliel interrogated the witnesses? Indeed it would have been more in sequence to mention Mishna 8 before Mishna 7. Shouldn't we have first been told how Rabban Gamliel interrogated the witnesses and then how Bais Din subsequently sanctified the month?

We might ask yet another question regarding the sequence of the משניות here in *Mesechtas Rosh Hashanah.* As previously mentioned, we have here three categories of witnesses: "עדי ראיה" — eyewitnesses who sighted the moon, "עדי הכרה" — character witnesses, and "שלוחי בית דין" — messengers sent out to inform the people. From Mishna 5 in the first chapter until the end of the first chapter we are told of the role of the eyewitnesses. (In Mishna 3-4 we have elsewhere explained their place in the sequence of this Mesechta.) The first Mishna in Chapter Two speaks about the role of the character witnesses. Mishna 2,3,4 of Chapter II, speaks of the procedure of lighting torches to "inform" the people of the exact day of Rosh Chodesh. Thus, until here we follow the sequence of the three categories of witnesses as outlined above. What becomes problematic is the next Mishna, Mishna 6 in Chapter 2.

חצר גדולה היתה בירושלים... ולשם כל העדים מתכנסים, ובית דין בודקין אותם שם...

> There was a large courtyard in Jerusalem... and there all the witnesses [the eyewitnesses] gathered and Bais Din interrogated them there...

Here the Mishna speaks of the interrogation of the eyewitnesses, thereby, one could ask the following. Wouldn't it have been more in place to cite this Mishna in Chapter I, where the issue of eye-witnesses is discussed? Why is it cited here, after we have already concluded with the declaration of the Bais Din "מקודש" — "the month is sanctified?" Why do we now revert to the matter of how we interrogated the witnesses? And this question relates to the subsequent mishnayos as well, since all of them center around the issue of how witnesses were interrogated. Why now and here, after we already proclaimed the month sanctified in Mishna 6?

To answer all of the above questions we would point to what we previously mentioned in Chapter Eight. Rosh Chodesh is determined by witnesses, and by Bais Din; the latter plays a major role in designating the day of Rosh Chodesh. Thus the following sequence emerges: Chapter One — eyewitnesses, Chapter Two — Mishna 1 character witnesses, Chapter Two — Mishna 2,3,4 informing the public, Chapter Two — Mishna 5 and 6. We revert to the role of the Bais Din. The stress here is not on interrogating the eyewitnesses but rather on the role of the Bais Din.

Mishna 7, which deals with the Bais Din, which "declared it sanctified", also touches upon the role of the Bais Din. However Mishna 8 now introduces the role of the Nasi. Indeed based on the insight of R' Chayim Brisker (see "הגר"ח החדש", מסכת ר"ה, "פרדס" תש"ד) that the two answers ר' יהושע received here relate to two different issues.

ר"ע pointed out that a mistake made by Bais Din does not nullify the decision of Bais Din. R' Dosa pointed out that even without the participation of Bais Din, the Nasi has full jurisdiction to designate the new month. So again, these mishnayos focus on the role of the Nasi.

In light of this insight, we can answer all of our previous questions. We can understand the relevance of these two incidents mentioned here, for both speak of the role of the Nasi. We can also answer the question of "דורות הראשונים" of why Mishna 7 regarding the maps of Rabban Gamliel was not mentioned prior to Mishna 6, after Bais Din had already declared the month sanctified. For in light of the above, we can now see that in Mishna 7 we begin with the role of the Nasi and continue with this theme until the end of Chapter Two.

II

WHEN TO APPLY THE LAW OF "אתם"

In the phrase of "אלה מועדי ה' אשר תקראו אתם" — "These are the festivals of Hashem that you shall call them", the word "אתם" appears three times in the passage concerning declaring the festivals. In each occurrence, the word "אתם" is spelled defectively (rather than "אותם" with a "ו") and is therefore expounded as if it were vowelized "אַתֶּם" — "you". These three occurrences indicate the following possibilities: "אתם אפילו שוגגין" — even if Bais Din erroneously chose the wrong date for Rosh Chodesh, "אתם אפילו מזידין" — even if Bais Din knowingly declared Rosh Chodesh on the wrong date deliberately, "אתם אפילו מוטעין" — even if Bais Din were misled into choosing the wrong date for Rosh Chodesh.

Yet in the Tosefta Rosh Hashanah 2:10 it states:

בית דין שקדשו את החודש בזמנו ונמצא עדים זוממים, הרי זה מקודש. קדשוהו בלילה אינו מקודש. קדשוהו אנוסים שוגגין מזידין ומוטעין, הרי זה מקודש.

> If Rosh Chodesh was sanctified in its proper time, however the witnesses were subsequently disqualified, Rosh Chodesh remains sanctified. If Bais Din sanctified it at night, it is thereby not sanctified. If they sanctified it by being forced to sanctify it, or they even deliberately chose the wrong date or were misled, the month is still sanctified.

Here in the Tosefta, "אנוסין" — "by force" is added. The רמב"ם states in *Hilchos Kiddush HaChodesh* 2:10:

בית דין שקדשו את החודש בין שוגגין, בין מוטעין, בין אנוסים הרי זה מקודש...

Once the court sanctifies the new month, it remains sanctified regardless, whether they erred unwittingly, they were led astray by false witnesses, or they were forced to sanctify it...

The Rambam here mentions "אנוסים", as mentioned in the Tosefta, however, he omitted "מזידין" — "deliberately", even though it is mentioned in both the Gemara and the Tosefta. It seems that the Rambam chooses here the reading as cited in the Sifra *(Parashas Emor)* and the Mechilta of the Rashbi. The חסדי דוד in his commentary on the Tosefta here raises the following questions.

The pasuk outlines only three times "אתם", yet here we include four cases. How are we to account for this discrepancy? Why did the Rambam delete מזידין, when it is mentioned in the Gemara and the Tosefta?

The חסדי דוד thereby offers the insight that "מזידין" is not to be viewed as if the Bais Din deliberately chose the wrong date, even though they knew that the new moon had not yet appeared, but rather they felt compelled to declare Rosh Chodesh due to dire circumstances "משום מתיא או משום ירקא" in order that Shabbos day and Yom Kippur not follow each other, thereby prohibiting the burial of the dead and causing vegetables to "spoil." Thus "מזידין" here is meant to be understood as being "compelled," thereby the Rambam wisely cited "אנוסים" (compelled) here instead of "מזידין", for by substituting "אנוסים" for "מזידין", he includes the example of being physically coerced by gentiles to declare Rosh Chodesh. Consequently, "אנוסים" here includes both "מזידין" and "אנוסים".

The "חזון יחזקאל" (by HaRav Yechezkel Abramsky) explains "מזידין" as follows. Usually we associate the word "מזידין", with doing something mischievous and wrong. If one is a "מזיד" he must have done something malicious. But Bais Din can not be accused of doing something malicious, and therefore "מזידין" here must be understood as doing something "intentionally". The law reads that if one kills someone by accident (בשוגג), the punishment of 'Galus', being exiled to the cities of refuge (ערי מקלט) is applied. Consequently, if a doctor, in the process of treating a "patient", killed him, or a teacher in disciplining a student struck the student and the student died, these acts are not to be viewed as "במזיד"—having been done maliciously, but rather they are to be understood that although they "knew" what they were doing, they meant no harm. Similarly, in relation to Kiddush HaChodesh, "מזידין" Bais Din "knows" that there are no witnesses, yet they intentionally proceed to act in declaring Rosh Chodesh.

...סתם "מזיד" הוא שעושה בצדיה דבר שלא כהוגן וזה לא שייך בבית דין המקדש את החדש, ואולי מפני זה לא העתיקו הרמב"ם בהל' קדה"ח סוף פרק ב...

...מושג הלשון הכא "מזידין" "מתכונים"... שמתכונים לקדש את החדש - בידעם שאין כאן עדות שנראה המולד הלבנה הרי זה מקודש...

All agree to the application of "אתם"

At the beginning of Chapter Two, Mishna Two, we are taught that due to the attempts of the Cutheans to deceive Bais Din they enacted a law that torches would no longer be lit as a means of informing the people of the exact day of Rosh Chodesh, but rather messengers would be sent. The reason the Cutheans sought to deceive Bais Din was that the 30th of Adar fell on a Shabbos day and the moon had not yet been sighted. Therefore false witnesses were hired by the Cutheans to testify that they had seen the "new moon", thereby making Shabbos day Rosh Chodesh Nissan. As a result, the 16th of Nissan would fall on a Sunday, and consequently so would Shavuos, which would have meant that it should always be according to the Cutheans.

This led Tosafos to raise the following question. Had they been successful in their attempt to establish Rosh Chodesh a day earlier, wouldn't that have meant that Pesach would have occurred on the wrong day. So what did they gain? [although Shavuos would have been celebrated on the "right" day according to them, yet Pesach would not have been celebrated on its correct calendar date, and thus the Pesach sacrifice would not have been properly brought].

Tosafos answers that Pesach would not have been designated on the wrong day based on the law of אתם אפילו מזידין, which stipulates that Rosh Chodesh declared even in error is deemed to be Rosh Chodesh.

...ואם תאמר ומה מרויחים והלא מתקלקלים לענין פסח. ויש לומר דלא חשיבי קלקול משום דדרשי אתם אפילו מזידין.

This answer of Tosafos appears to raise a problem. These heretics did not recognize or accept the validity of the Oral Law. How, then could they rely on the rule of "אתם", which is a product of Rabbinic exegesis — the Oral Law? The "דורות הראשונים" (part 11, page 418 - 422) concludes that contrary to the opinion that these heretics (כותים) adhered to the Written Law but disregarded the Oral Law, the truth is that they did not believe even in the Written Law. They only "put on a show" that they believed in the Written Law. Thus, if Pesach was on the wrong day, this meant nothing to them. (see the *Artscroll Mishnayos Rosh Hashanah*, pp. 36-38.)

In truth, however, this question here was already touched upon in the sefer "בני בנימין" (by האדר"ת אבי רבינוביץ בנימין הרב) who contends that although the Cutheans rejected the interpretations of the Rabbis and the application of the Oral Law, yet they agreed to the "simple" reading of the pasuk, "That you shall declare", which indicates that Bais Din has the last word. This means that if Bais Din had, even erroneously, declared Shabbos as Rosh Chodesh, it would have been legal, and Pesach would have been celebrated on its proper date.

III

"אתם" SAID ONLY "בזמנו"

Although Bais Din has the "last word" in designating Rosh Chodesh day, yet there are still restrictions on their authority. It is only when they declare Rosh Chodesh on a day which is fitting to be Rosh Chodesh, that we apply the law of "אתם", but this does not apply on a day which in itself is not fit to be Rosh Chodesh. However, there is a difference of opinion as to exactly what constitutes a day that is to be viewed as "fitting to be Rosh Chodesh" — "בזמנו" what is a proper day to apply the law of "אתם". Their views are based on their interpretation of the following Tosefta, R.H. 2:1.

קדשו החדש בזמנו ונמצאו זוממים, הרי זה מקודש.

> If Rosh Chodesh was sanctified in its proper time, yet the witnesses were subsequently disqualified, Rosh Chodesh remains sanctified.

The addition of the word "בזמנו" here prompts us to ask why the תוספתא stresses "בזמנו" — "in its time", which would seem to indicate that if not in its time, [i.e., at any other time] we would not apply the law of "אתם". Thus the question is what exactly do we mean by "בזמנו"?

HaRav Yechezkel Abramsky, in his commentary here to the Tosefta, maintains, based on the position of the Rambam in *(Hilchos Kiddush HaChodesh 2:9)* that if the witnesses saw the new moon at the end of the 29th day, Bais Din can by virtue of these witnesses sanctify then and there, the next day, the 30th, as Rosh Chodesh. This means that if immediately before sunset, Bais Din became aware that they had erred (or had been fooled), then their proclamation becomes null and void. This is so because they declared Rosh Chodesh day on a day (the 29th) which in itself cannot be Rosh Chodesh. Therefore we do not here apply the law of "אתם". It is only on the 30th and the 31st that it is viewed as, "בזמנו" and only then do we apply the law of בזמנו.

This approach is expanded by the "זכר יצחק" (R' Itzele Poniviser), who maintains that if Bais Din proclaims Rosh Chodesh not in accordance with the law, i.e., not on it proper day(s), then their proclamation has no merit and does not take effect. However, if they declare Rosh Chodesh at its "proper" time, then that declaration takes effect not only for Rosh Chodesh day, but for the subsequent days of the month.

> דכל שעברו שלא כדין שחל רק על פי דבורם, לא מהני כח דבורם כי אם בעת שיש על מה לחול, מה שאין כן היכא שמעברין כדין, שאז מהני אפילו על מה שעתיד להיות. ולפי זה גם בקידוש החדש כן.

The (סימן לט) "תרועת המלך", explaining why this is so, maintains that "שלא בזמנו" days which are not "fit" to be Rosh Chodesh can not become Rosh Chodesh by being declared so by Bais Din. The pasuk reads: "במועדו" — that they [Bais Din] declared it in "its proper time". This teaches us that the "מועד" — "holiday", is legally declared so only if this is done on its proper day "במועדו".

We now seem to view "בזמנו" as alluding to the 30th and the 31st days. However, according to the (מהרבי ר' יהונתן מפרג) "ערות דבש" and the (מהרב יעקב עמדין) "לחם שמים", "בזמנו" alludes only to the 30th day. Yet if Bais Din mistakenly declared the 31st day as Rosh Chodesh, we do not apply the law of "אתם" and a retraction of their declaration must be issued. This position is based on the question raised here, namely, how do we reconcile the law of "קדוש למפרע" [which means if witnesses subsequently appear after Bais Din had declared the 31st day as Rosh Chodesh and testify that they saw the moon "בזמנו" on the 30th day, Bais Din must retract and declare day 30 as Rosh Chodesh] with the law of "אתם", since if Bais Din declared Rosh Chodesh it is binding and can never be nullified. The answer to this is that since day 31 does not call for "sanctification" (the saying of "מקודש, מקודש") but is only designated as Rosh Chodesh, then subsequent witnesses can call for a retraction. However, day 30, which does call for "sanctification", can never be retracted, based on the law of "אתם".

Thus we see that "אתם" applies only to day 30 and not to day 31. However the sefer "אגן הסהר" points out that according to the "לחם משנה" and the "מרכבת המשנה", the law of "אתם" does apply even to day 31. This is based on the comments of the "לחם משנה" to the statement of the Rambam that if eyewitnesses had to travel more than a day and night before they would arrive before Bais Din, they should not come, since Bais Din would have already been declared on the 31st day as Rosh Chodesh.

We can conclude that even if they do come, their testimony would be of no avail, since we apply the law of אתם even to day 31. Summing up, there are those who rule that only day 29 is ruled out from אתם, however we do apply this law of אתם on days 30 and 31. Others, however, contend that אתם is only applied to the 30th day.

IV

The law of "אתם" in determining a leap year

As previously pointed out, Bais Din has the jurisdiction to declare Rosh Chodesh and leap years, and so the question is raised: Can the Bais Din declare a leap year even if it erred, based on the law of "אתם"? The צל"ח, in his chiddushim to *Mesechtas Berachos 63A,* contends that only in regard to Rosh Chodesh do we apply the law of "אתם"; however, in relation to declaring "leap years", we do not apply this law of "אתם". He presents the following three proofs to reinforce his position:

The Gemara in Sanhedrin lists a number of instances for which we would not declare a leap year. The law reads, if they did declare a leap year based on these considerations אינה מעוברת, the year is not declared as a leap year. Yet if we apply the law of "אתם" here, even though Bais Din should not have declared a leap year due to these considerations, even so, couldn't we say that their declaration should have been decisive and a leap year legally declared? Therefore, we must say that the law of "אתם" does not apply to leap years עבור השנה.

The Rambam only cites the law of "אתם" when he discusses the issue of *Kiddush HaChodesh (Chapter II)*. However, in Chapter IV, where he outlines the laws of declaring a leap year, he makes no mention of the application of the law of "אתם".

Again we have proof that the law of "אתם" does not apply to "עבור השנה". There is a discussion of the incident in which חזקיהו המלך declared a leap year after Rosh Chodesh Nissan was already declared and hence the appropriate time to declare a leap year (Adar I) had elapsed. חזקיהו המלך felt a sense of remorse for having done this, and thus the question is asked by Tosafos. Why did חזקיהו feel that he was guilty of wrongly for having declared a leap year? Why did he not apply the law of "אתם" that legalizes a mistaken designation? Tosafos answers that "אתם" only "affects day 30 and day 31 of a month", which would seem to indicate that only in matters affecting Rosh Chodesh do we apply the law of "אתם", and not in matters related to "leap years".

DISMISSING THESE PROOFS — מנ"ח

The מנ"ח (מצוה ד) and the נצי"ב (בהעמק שאלה) both cite the

תורת כהנים that states explicitly that we do in fact apply the law of
"אתם" to leap years — עבור השנה.

> לא היתה השנה צריכה להתעבר ועיברוה אנוסים או
> שוגגים או מוטעים, מנין שהיא מעוברת, ת"ל אשר תקראו
> אתם, אתם אפילו שוגגים, אתם אפילו מוטעין, אתם אפילו
> אנוסין, אם קראתם אתם מועד, ואם לאו אין מועד.

Thus we see how we can apply the law of אתם to עבור השנה. This position is also indicated in *Midrash Rabbah, Parashas Bo*. And as for the proofs presented by the צל"ח , they can readily be dismissed. Regarding the proof that if Bais Din declares a leap year based on "incidental matters" for which we should never declare a leap year, and thus the year is not declared a leap year, we can say that "אתם" is not applied in such a case. This proof can be dismissed as well, since even the Sages did not wish to declare a leap year, due to these considerations, and this also means that they ruled out the possibility of applying the law here of "אתם". For we can see that in such a case we are not justified in declaring a leap year.

And as for the fact that the Rambam did not cite this law of "אתם" when he discussed the laws of leap years, to this we might reply that he relied on the fact that the Sages are entitled to make decisions based on the consideration that they have the "last word" in regard to declaring a leap year. For example, the law reads that Bais Din cannot declare a leap year before Rosh Hashanah and if they do so, their declaration is invalid. This law is only a Rabbinic enactment, and yet we see that it is decisive, thus proving that the Sages retain jurisdiction in declaring a leap year. Consequently, they also retain the right of applying "אתם".

As for the proof from Tosafos that only in relation to day 30 and 31 do we apply "אתם" this can also be dismissed. For what Tosafos meant here was to point out that אתם can only be applied in its "proper" time, and the "proper time" here both in relation to Rosh Chodesh and to a leap year is on a day which is "fit to be declared Rosh Chodesh".

Thus in relation to Rosh Chodesh, days 30 and 31 are the proper days of Rosh Chodesh, and we apply to them the law of "אתם". However, after Rosh Chodesh Nissan has beeen declared, we cannot apply אתם to leap years, for the appropriate day has already elapsed — being that today is already Nissan. However if the issue is not "day 30", but rather another "mistake" was made, we would apply אתם even to the laws pertaining to leap years.

Defending the צל"ח

The "אגן הסהר" defends the position of the צל"ח by offering a novel interpretation of the above תורת כהנים. One has to wonder if, for example, Rosh Chodesh was designated on the 31st of the month and subsequently witnesses appeared to testify that they saw the moon on the 30th. If the 30th was declared to be Rosh Chodesh Nissan, then if Bais Din declared a leap year on the 30th (of Adar), before the witnesses appeared, and then they retroactively designate day 30 as Rosh Chodesh Nissan, their declaration of a leap year is now nullified. Or perhaps, just as the Rosh Chodesh sacrifices offered on day 31 are still acceptable, except that we now begin counting the calendar month from day 30, so too is the declaration of a leap year on day 30 still acceptable.

From this we see that the תורת כהנים does not touch upon the issue of whether אתם is applied to leap years, but rather the issue here is whether אתם is applied to Rosh Chodesh, and this has a direct affect on the determination of a leap year. We see this from the example cited, in which we retroactively designated day 30 as Rosh Chodesh Nissan. Yet, despite this, since "אתם" affects Rosh Chodesh, this would mean that day 31 is Rosh Chodesh as far as the offering of the Mussaf sacrifice is concerned. And we also apply אתם in relation to עבור השנה, leap years, and we might say that since a leap year was declared on day 30, then it this is the proper time to declare a leap year and the decision remains valid. However, we still do not apply "אתם" directly to the laws of leap years. The צל"ח is right, we cannot do so.

THE YERUSHALMI AND TOSEFTA DISPUTE THIS MATTER

The Rambam in *Hilchos Kiddush HaChodesh 4:10* states:

...ובעיבור השנה מתחילין מן הצד, ולקידוש החדש מתחילין מן הגדול.

...concerning the institution of a leap year, the opinion of the lesser judges should be offered first. Concerning the sanctification of a new month, we begin with the head of the court.

The source of this decision of the Rambam is the ירושלמי ר"ה, פרק ב הלכה ה':

בשם ר' יוחנן, לקידוש החדש מתחילין מן הגדול, לעבור השנה מתחילין צן הצד.

However, in the *Tosefta 27:2* it is clearly stated that even in regard to establishing leap years we begin from the head of the court.

...בקידוש החדש ובעיבור השנה, בדיני ממונות מתחילין מן הגדול. מפני מה בדיני נפשות מתחילין מן הצד? שלא יהא סמוך על דברי רבו.

Thus we have to understand what is the basic difference between the ירושלמי and the תוספתא, and what is the difference between עבור השנה and קידוש החדש. Regarding קידוש החדש, everybody agrees that we begin from 'the head of the court'. It is only in relation to leap years that we have a difference of opinion as to where to start.

The answer here is based on the rationale given as to why in matters of life and death, דיני נפשות, we begin with the lesser judges seated at the side of the table. For we are afraid that if we begin with the head of the court, then after hearing his view, the rest of the court would either refrain from offering an opinion, for by doing so they might transgress the infraction of not contradicting the head of the court, "לא תענה על הרב", or simply "follow the leader", i.e., vote as he did and thus we would not have the required opinions of 23 judges, but rather only "one" opinion.

This means that if both קדוש החדש and עיבור השנה begin with the head of the court, as the Tosefta contends, this would indicate we are not concerned with the opinions of the lesser judges, for even if they were to vote out of fear like the head judge did, yet the decision reached would be legally binding, based on the law of "אתם". However the ירושלמי and the Rambam contend that in regard to קדוש החודש we do start from "the head", for only in the matter of קדוש החדש do we apply the law of "אתם" whereas in the matter of leap years, עיבור השנה, we must start "from the side", for we do not apply the law of "אתם" in to עבור השנה.

Thus we can conclude that the Rambam holds the opinion that "אתם" does not apply to עיבור השנה, as the צל"ח points to the fact that the Rambam did not cite this הלכה of "אתם" when he speaks of עיבור השנה, thus proving that "אתם" is not applied to "leap years."

V

"אתם" ONLY RELATES TO BAIS DIN OF ERETZ YISROEL

The Gemara in *Rosh Hashanah 21a* records the following incident:

לוי איקלע לבבל בחדסר בתשרי אמר: בסים תבשילא דבבלאי ביומא רבה דמערבא. אמרי ליה: אסהיד. אמר להו: לא שמעתי מפי בי"ד מקודש.

Levi visited Babylonia on the 11th of Tishrei. He said to them: "The dish of the Babylonians is sweet on the day of Yom Kippur of the West." (i.e., Levi was remarking that what the Babylonians observed as the 11th of Tishrei was the day that those who reside in Eretz Yisrael were observing as Yom Kippur, because the Bais Din there had made the month of Elul "full" – that is, consisting of 31 days).

The Babylonians said (to Levi): "Testify that the Bais Din in Yerushalayim had made the month full, and we will accept the Yom Kippur fast upon ourselves and henceforth refrain from eating."

Levi said to them: "I did not personally hear from Bais Din the proclamation of 'sanctified' — 'מקודש'."

[The law reads that messengers do not go out to announce the month of Tishrei until they hear the Bais Din declare that the month has been sanctified. Thus, Levi could not testify that Tishrei was sanctified ten days earlier, because he did not hear Bais Din proclaim Tishrei sanctified].

Tosafos here raises the question of how did Levi travel on the day he regarded as Yom Kippur day. Tosafos offers two possibilities: "מתוך התחום בא", or that he arrived on the day the Babylonians observed as Yom Kippur late in the afternoon, which was according to him Erev Yom Kippur in Eretz Yisrael.

Tosafos then proceeds to ask:

והאיך יניחם לאכול ויש כאן ודאי איסור כרת מדאורייתא?

How did Levi let them eat on the day that was Yom Kippur and thereby desecrate Yom Kippur day?

To which Tosafos answers:

וי"ל... אתם אפילו שוגגין...

Based on the principle that a Yom Tov is declared solely by Bais Din, even in the instance that they erred in declaring the wrong day as Rosh Chodesh.

Thus it would seem that this law of "אתם" applies even to the Bais Din in the Diaspora. This means that the Babylonians had apparently relied on the fact that Elul is usually deficient (29 days) and thereby they declared Rosh Chodesh Tishrei 30 days after Rosh Chodesh Elul. Consequently, the Babylonians, having declared the 30th day as Rosh Chodesh, then celebrated the Yom Kippur fast on what they reckoned was the tenth of Tishrei, and on the 11th they ate. This erroneous declaration by the Babylonians of the 30th of Elul as Rosh Chodesh was legal, based on the principle of "אתם". This approach is offered by a number of leading ראשונים.

רשב"א: ואולי נאמר, דכיון שכבר קבעו בני בבל יום ל' ועליו סמכו והתענו ביום עשירי שלהן, אין להם לחזור ולהתענות ביום אחר כיון שאין כאן עד ששמע כשנתקדש שם יום שלשים ואחד, ויש להם לסמוך על מה שכתב התורה, אתם אפילו מוטעים, אתם אפילו שוגגים.

ומיהו אילו לוי ששמע או שידע מפי מי שראה שנתקדש החודש ביום שלשים וא', אע"פ שהם כבר קדשו יום ל', כיון דבני בבל בתר בי"ד שבארץ ישראל גררי טעותם אינו עומד וחייבים להתענות ביום עשירי לבני ארץ ישראל.

The ר"ן and the ריטב"א here also adopt this approach of the

רשב"א. Thus we see that "אתם" even applies to the Bais Din in the Disaspora.

THE טורי אבן QUESTIONS THESE VIEWS

The טורי אבן here questions this theory of the ראשונים that a Bais Din in the Diaspora can also declare Rosh Chodesh, and their declaration is recognized even if it is based on an erroneous decision. If so, asks the טורי אבן, this would mean that every one can declare Yom Tov, and then we would have a situation in which everyone can make Yom Tov on his own, and this would divide Klal Yisrael.

...ואני תמה מאד על זה. וכי אפשר לומר שכל אחד יעשה המועדות כפי דעתו ויהי לאלה מועד ובכרת על אכילת יוה"כ וחמץ בפסח ולאלה יום חול? וכן לענין שאר המועדות נמצא ישראל נעשים אגודות אגודות וניתנת תורה כל אחד ואחד בידו ח"ו לומר כן.

וההיא אשר תקראו בין בזמנם ובין שלא בזמנן אין לך מועדות אלא אלו היינו שמחוייבים כל ישראל לשמור יום המועד כפי קביעת בי"ד אע"פ שקבע ע"פ טעות אבל אם איזה מדינה או עיר עשו קביעות לעצמם שלא בקביעות בי"ד שבא"י הם ודאי אינו כלום.

THE INSIGHT OF THE "יסוד עולם"

The sefer "יסוד עולם" לרבינו יצחק בן יוסף הישראלי תלמיד הרא"ש ז"ל (פרק ה מאמר ד) provides us with an answer to the question raised here by the "טורי אבן". We must address the problem of those places which the messengers, dispatched by Bais Din in

Yerushalayim, could not reach in time, either because they were so far away, or because there were ongoing wars in those regions. How did they celebrate Rosh Hashanah and Yom Kippur?

The "יסוד עולם" answers that the הלכה למשה מסיני, the tradition handed down from Sinai, tells us that although we are to designate a new month by means of eyewitnesses, those who lived in distant lands were to determine the new moon by mathematical calculation. They would calculate the "מולד האמיתי" to determine when the actual moment of conjunction took place, and based on this they would declare Rosh Chodesh. They were in no way to take into consideration the testimony of eyewitnesses who sighted the "new moon." Rather they had no other choice but to determine the new month by means of "חשבון", calculation. However, if they became aware that the Bais Din in Yerushalayim had declared Rosh Chodesh - Rosh Hashanah, on a particular day, other then that day on which they had determined Rosh Chodesh, then they would have to defer their designation to that of the Bais Din of Yerushalayim. However, as long as they did not become aware of when the determination had been made in Eretz Yisrael, it was the Bais Din of the Diaspora that determined the new month for them, even if they erred in their determination.

...ושאר הגולה שלא היו השלוחים מגיעים אליהם, הן מפני ריחוק מקומם, או מפני מלחמות שהיו לשם בזמן ההוא, לא היו נזקקין לרא' כלל ולא רשאין להזקק לה, מפני שדין זה לא ניתן אלא לבי"ד הסמוך בא"י, כמו שנ' כי מציון תצא תורה... אלא על פי חשבון המולד היו בני המקומות האלו קובעין ר"ה ויה"כ ושאר המועדים...

THE ריטב"א DISAGREES WITH TOSAFOS

According to the ריטב"א the law of "אתם" does not apply to the Bais Din of the Diaspora. Rather a special compensation is made for the Jews of the Diaspora so that they can determine the months by means of calculation, just as we now determine months, in the way that Hillel II calculated all the months until the coming of Moshiach.

>אבל יש מפרשים...ויש להם לסמוך על מה שאמרה תורה
> אתם אפילו מוטעין כו' ואינו נכון בעיני... שאין קביעתם
> קביעות לומר אתם אפילו שוגגין...

The above mentioned "יסוד עולם" offers yet another possibility, which is that the Bais Din of Yerushalayim can determine Rosh Chodesh on behalf of the Jews in the Diaspora, and that day can be a different day than that of Eretz Yisrael. For example, it can precede it by a day, as in the instance of Levi in *Rosh Hashanah 21A*.

VI

THE DIFFERENCE BETWEEN לא תסור AND אתם

The question that troubles us is that if indeed Bais Din erred and then became aware of their mistake, how can we say that "אתם" 'smooths things over' and we are to celebrate Rosh Chodesh and the subsequent holidays based on an error? The Rambam and the Ramban offer two answers to this question.

In *Hilchos Kiddush HaChodesh 2:10,* the Rambam writes:

> בית דין שקדשו את החדש בין שוגגין, בין מוטעין, בין
> אנוסין, הרי זה מקודש. וחייבין הכל לתקן המועדות על
> היום שקדשו בו.

> אף על פי שזה יודע שטעו — חייב לסמוך עליהם, שאין
> הדבר מסור אלא להם. ומי שצוה לשמור המועדות הוא צוה
> לסמוך עליהם, שנאמר: אשר תקראו אתם וגומר.

Once the Bais Din sanctifies the new month, it remains sanctified regardless of whether they erred unwittingly, they were led astray by false witnesses, or they were forced to sanctify it. We are required to calculate the dates of the festivals based on the day that they sanctified as the beginning of the new month.

Even if a person knows that the Bais Din erred, he is obligated to rely on them, for the matter is entrusted to them alone. The One who commanded us to observe the festivals is the One who commanded us to rely on them, as implied by (Vayikra 23:2) 'Which you will proclaim as days of convocation.'

Thus, according to the Rambam, Bais Din has the authority and the ability to convert a regular weekday to a holy festival day, when it pronounces that day as מקודש — sanctified. And once they have proclaimed it, we are obligated to observe that day as such.

THE OPINION OF THE רמב"ן

The רמב"ן, in his commentary to the Torah (פרשת שופטים יז:יא) and his commentary to the Sefer HaMitzvos of the Rambam (שורש א), justifies Bais Din's error based on the pasuk of "לא תסור". And so he writes:

> על פי התורה אשר יורוך ועל המשפט אשר יאמרו לך תעשה, לא תסור מן הדבר אשר יגידו לך ימין ושמאל אפילו אומרים לך על שמאל שהוא ימין ועל ימין שהוא שמאל...

You shall not depart from the word which they shall tell you, either to the right or to the left. Even if the judge of the Great Sanhedrin tells you of the right, that it is the left, or the left that it is the right, you must obey him. Even if you think in your heart that they are mistaken,... you are not to say, "How can I permit myself to eat this red forbidden fat, or execute this innocent man." Instead you are to say, "The Lord Who enjoined the commandments commanded that I perform all of His commandments in accordance with all that they... teach me to do. He gave me the Torah as taught by them, even if they were to err. Such was the case of Rav Yehoshua and Rabban Gamliel...

Thus, according to the Ramban we are to listen to Bais Din even if they erred, and the source for this is the pasuk of "לא תסור" — "You are not to deviate from their words" cited in *Devarim 17:11.*

QUESTIONING THE RAMBAN

The following question arises here. According to the Ramban, we are to follow Bais Din even if it erred based on the pasuk of "לא תסור" if this is so, then why the need here of "אתם"? This question is addressed by the חמדת ישראל (בקונטרס "נר מצוה" אות לב) by הרב מאיר דן ז"ל, who answers by pointing out that the commandment of "לא תסור" applies to a ruling issued by the entire Bais Din HaGadol, סנהדרין הגדול. However, according to the Ramban the Bais Din which is authorized to act in the matter of Kiddush HaChodesh need not to be the Bais Din HaGadol, only one empowered by "semicha", thereby we certainly do need "אתם" to tell us that we must follow their ruling even if they erred. And even according to the Rambam, who contends that we need the participation of the סנהדרין הגדול, yet not all of the members, only three will suffice. Thus, once again we are in need of the pasuk of "אתם", for as we have said, "לא תסור" only applies to a ruling that was issued by the entire Sanhedrin.

Another solution is offered here by the sefer "מראה החדש" (סימן טז) that a mistake by Bais Din is overlooked only if it was a point of law that they erred in; however, if they erred in a "מציאות" then we disregard their decision. In relation to Kiddush HaChodesh, even such an error does not invalidate the decision already issued.

Another difference between these two concepts is that in regard to "לא תסור" it is true we must abide by the erroneous decision of Bais Din, as long as Bais Din themselves are not aware of their mistake. However if Bais Din becomes aware of their wrong rulings, it is incumbent that they retract their decision and issue a new decision. However in regard to "אתם", even if Bais Din becomes aware of its mistake, they need not retract their decision. So contends the sefer "מראה החדש".

However the "אגן הסהר" maintains that "אתם" only relates to the "עבר", the "past". What was *already done* is legal and accepted. For example if Bais Din declared Rosh Chodesh on day 30, and thereby offered the Mussaf sacrifice on that day, even though they subsequently became aware of their mistake, yet we say that which was already done is viewed as having been according to the law. However, regarding the future, Bais Din itself has to retract. Thus the calendar, the exact number of days this month, begins from day 31.

VII

SANCTIFYING THE MONTH RETROACTIVELY

The Rambam in *Hilchos Kiddush HaChodesh 3:15-16* states:

בית דין שישבו כל יום שלשים ולא באו עדים, והשכימו
בנשף ועברו את החדש... ואחר ארבעה או חמישה ימים באו
עדים רחוקים והעידו שראו את החדש בזמנו, שהוא ליל
שלשים, ואפילו באו בסוף החודש. מאיימין עליהם איום
גדול, ומטריפים אותם בשאלות, ומטריחין עליהן בבדיקות,
ומדקדקין בעדות, ומשתדלין בית דין שלא יקדשו חדש זה,
הואיל ויצא שמו מעובר ואם עמדו העדים בעדותן, ונמצאת
מכונת, והרי העדים אנשים ידועים ונבונים ונחקרה העדות
כראוי, מקדשין אותו, וחוזרין ומונין לאותו החדש מיום
שלשים, הואיל ונראה הירח בלילו.

When Bais Din held a session throughout the entire 30th day but witnesses did not arrive, the judges arose early in the morning and made the month full... and after four or five days witnesses came from distant places and testified that they had sighted the moon at the appropriate time, the 30th night. Indeed the same law applies if the witnesses came at the end of the month.

We unnerve them in a very intimidating manner, and we seek to disorient them with queries. We cross examine them very thoroughly and are extremely precise regarding their testimony. For the court endeavors not to sanctify this month, since it has already been declared full.

If the witnesses remain steadfast in their testimony, if it [their testimony] is compatible, if the witnesses are men whose character is well known and they are men of understanding, and if their testimony was scrutinized in a proper way, then the moon is sanctified retroactively. We recalculate the dates of the month beginning from the 30th day, since the moon was sighted on the appropriate night.

Thus we see that the opinion of the Rambam is that we can retroactively reset Rosh Chodesh day קדוש למפרע. However, many of the ראשונים as well as the אחרונים disagree with this opinion of the Rambam and cite proofs to disprove the theory held here by the Rambam regarding the law of קדוש למפרע.

THE OBJECTIONS OF THE ריטב״א AND רשב״א

The ריטב״א here brings proof from the *Mishna 3:1* that contradicts the theory of the Rambam and points to an apparent contradiction in the Rambam itself. The *Mishna R.H. 3:1* states:

> ראוהו בית דין וכל ישראל, נחקרו העדים, ולא הספיקו לומר: ״מקודש״ עד שחשכה - הרי זה מעובר.

> If Bais Din and all Yisrael saw the moon, the witnesses were interrogated, but they, the Bais Din, did not manage to say "It is sanctified" before it grew dark - it, the month, is full (31 days).

Asks the ריטב״א, according to the Rambam's opinion that we may sanctify the month retroactively, why should we declare a full month here? Why not let the witnesses reappear on the next day and then sanctify the 30th retroactively?" Furthermore, the Rambam himself writes *(3:1)*:

> When witnesses see the new moon and there is a journey of a night and a day... they should undertake the journey and testify. If the distance between them is greater, they should not undertake the journey, for the testimony that they will deliver *will be of no consequence*, since the month already would have been made full.

The question here is obvious: why would their testimony be of no consequence if, as the Rambam contends, we are allowed to sanctify the moon retroactively?

The רשב״א asks even more pointedly: If, as the Rambam contends, witnesses come after the 30th, we retroactively sanctify the 30th and do not leave it as a full month. Most certainly, if witnesses *already* came and testified to the fact that the moon was sighted on the 30th, we should not attempt to declare a full month.

> והשתא אם לא באו העדים כלל ביום שלשים ובאו אחר כך
> חוזרין ומקדשין ומונין מיום שלשים, ק״ו [קל וחומר] לבאו
> כבר העדים והעידו שראוה בזמנו שאין לעשות את החדש
> מעובר וימנו מיום שלשים כפי מה שהעידו העדים או ראו
> בי״ד וכל ישראל.

The טורי אבן also raises the same objections.

Defending the Rambam

A number of answers are offered to defend the Rambam from the above mentioned questions. The "מנחת חינוך" offers the answer by contending that when the Mishna states "הרי זה מעובר", that the month is declared full, this is not to be understood to mean that on the morrow, the next day, we declare the month full, but rather immediately on the forthcoming *night* of the 31st, the month is seen as a "full" month. However, if Bais Din decides to do so, it can retroactively sanctify the 30th the next morning.

> אם כן כוונת המשנה "הרי זה מעובר" היינו תיכף בליל
> ל״א, החודש מעובר ואין לו דין מקודש ביום שלשים, והוי
> ל' כמו שלא באו עדים היום כלל... וביום מחר תלוי ברצון
> הבי״ד, אם רוצים מקבלין עוד הפעם העדים ומקדשים יום

אתמול, ואם רוצים מעברין כשאר חדשים כמבואר בר"מ [3:17] שאם יראו שהחדש צריך לי' מעובר, מניחין אותו מעובר.

הגרי"ז הלוי THE OPINION OF THE

The הגרי"ז הלוי contends that our Mishna states that the month is left as full, that is, if Bais Din feels that there is a need to declare a full month. This is so, because Bais Din never legally declared the 30th as Rosh Chodesh. Therefore, they *may* declare the 31st as Rosh Chodesh. However, if Bais Din did declare Rosh Chodesh in time, although it also felt there was a need to declare a "full month", they would not be allowed to do so, as the Rambam himself writes in *3:17,* that we can declare a full month *only* if we do so before the witnesses appear, but if we already have witnesses, we are not to declare a "full" month:

...ומש"ה מפרש הרמב"ם דהמשנה קיימה באופן שיש צורך לב"ד לעבר, וע"ז הוא דתנן דאם לא הספיקו לומר מקודש עד שחשיכה הרי זה מעובר, וממילא דיכולין ב"ד להניח אותו מעובר כמו בבאו עדים אח"כ דמעברין את החדש לצורך... אבל אם היו מספיקין לומר מקודש קודם שחשיכה אז היה הדין דמקדשין אותו ואין מעברין, דבזמן שנראה הירח בזמנו ובאו עדים אין מעברין את החדש לצורך וכמבואר ברמב"ם [3:17]...

"נתיבות חיים" THE INSIGHT OF THE

The sefer "נתיבות חיים" מהרב חיים יצחק קארב (ח"ב סימן ח') offers the following insight. There is a law that applies to the law of קדשים, sacrifices, that something that was "fit" to be accepted as a sacrifice, then became legally rejected, even if it again becomes fit — it is not to be accepted, "נראה ונדחה שוב אינו נראה". However, something which was initially rejected but then became fit to be offered as a sacrifice — it is accepted, "דיחוי מעיקרא חוזר ונראה". This principle applies also to mitzvos and thus to our situation here regarding Kiddush HaChodesh. If witnesses did appear on the 30th but for some reason their testimony was not applied to declaring the new month. For example, if it became dark before Bais Din could declare "מקודש", then their testimony now is rejected נראה ונדחה שוב אינו נראה. However if they never appeared as witnesses on day 30, but only afterwards did they make their appearance, then we accept their testimony "הרי זה דיחוי מעיקרא" and retroactively sanctify the 30th day.

דהנה מצינו גבי קדשים דדבר שהי' ראוי למזבח ונדחה ממנה, שוב אינה חוזר ונראה, אבל דבר שנדחה מעיקרא הוא חוזר ונראה, ולא הוי דיחוי: וכן מצינו דיחוי גבי מצות. ולפי זה י"ל, דגבי קדה"ח נמי כן הוא, שאם הי' נראה לקידוש ביום שלשים כגון שבאו העדים ביום השלשים ונמשך הדבר אצל הבי"ד, ולא קידשו אותו עד שחשיכה, זה נקרא נראה ונדחה, ושוב אינו חוזר ונראה משום הכי גבי ראוהו בית דין וכל ישראל ולא הספיקו לומר מקודש עד שחשיכה. הרי זה מעובר משום דכיון שהי' נראה לקידוש ביום השלשים ונדחה שוב אינו חוזר ונראה. אבל הרמב"ם איירי שלא באו עדים כל יום שלשים, אם כן הוי זה דיחוי מעיקרא ולא הוי דיחוי, ומשום הכי אם באו אחר כך יכול לקדש את יום השלשים למפרע.

THE ANSWER OF THE "תרועת המלך"

The "תרועת המלך" (סימן סג אות ד) offers the following solution to the problems raised here. One must draw a distinction as to whether the witnesses wish to testify on the 31st [that they saw the moon on the night of the 30th] or afterwards. The law reads that if witnesses failed to appear on the 30th, then Bais Din declares day 31 as Rosh Chodesh. Day 31 thus becomes Rosh Chodesh, and we have no further doubts that this day is Rosh Chodesh. So much so is this day Rosh Chodesh that we may offer the Rosh Chodesh Mussaf sacrifice even though it is Shabbos day. And if witnesses were to arrive on day 31 and wish to testify that yesterday was Rosh Chodesh, this would mean no Korban Mussaf would be offered this day (day 31) and on this Rosh Chodesh in general. Thereby we reject their testimony and do not allow them to testify, in order to preserve this day as Rosh Chodesh. However, on the next day we may receive them and retroactively declare day 30 as Rosh Chodesh, and count the calendar days from day 30. Thus the Mishna 3:1 that declares day 31 as Rosh Chodesh, cannot, by virtue of the prior testimony of the witnesses that they saw the moon on the 30th, force Bais Din to retroactively sanctify day 30. However, if they appear four or five days later, we do accept their testimony and are מקדש למפרע.

The מנחת חינוך (מצוה ד אות ב) offers a similar approach in answering the question asked by the צל"ח regarding this position of the Rambam that we may retroactively sanctify day 30. The Mishna in *Rosh Hashanah 30b* reads:

> בראשונה היו מקבלין עדות החדש כל היום. פעם אחת נשתהו העדים מלבוא, ונתקלקלו הלוים בשיר, התקינו שלא יהו מקבלין אלא עד המנחה, ואם באו עדים מן המנחה ולמעלה - נוהגין אותו קדש ולמחר קדש...

> Originally they accepted testimony regarding the new moon all day. Once the witnesses were delayed in arriving and the Levi'im blundered in the daily hymn. So they ordained that they, Bais Din, accept testimony only until the time of Mincha, and if witnesses came from Mincha time onward - that day should be kept holy and also the next day should be kept holy.

The צל״ח here asks, if according to the Rambam we may be מקדש למפרע, retroactively sanctify day 30, then if here the Bais Din did not yet declare Rosh Chodesh from Mincha on and yet on day 31 we did not retroactively sanctify day 30, certainly if Bais Din already declared 31 as Rosh Chodesh, how can we later retroactively reverse this decision and declare day 30 as Rosh Chodesh?

...והרי בפירוש אמרו שהתקינו שלא יהיו מקבלין אלא עד המנחה ואם באו מן המנחה ולמעלה שיהי' אותו קודש ולמחר קודש, ולכאורה ק״ו הדברים, ומה כאן שעדיין לא עשו מעשה לעבר החדש שהרי באו עדים ביום ל' קודם הלילה, אפילו הכי מעברין אותו לכתחילה ואין מקבלין ק״ו היכי שכבר נעשה מעשה ועיברוהו איך יקבלו אחר כך עדים לבטל מעשיהם למפרע שעיברו החדש....

To which the מנ״ח answers that if we did indeed accept the witnesses after Mincha and on day 31 we retroactively sanctify day 30, we would thereby no longer be able to offer the sacrifices of Rosh Hashanah day. Thus, in order to preserve the Rosh Hashanah service, we do not at this time retroactively sanctify the month, but rather we wait until after Rosh Hashanah to do so.

"Four or Five Days" is to be understood literally

When the Rambam introduces the theory of קידוש למפרע he states:

ואחר ארבעה או חמשה ימים באו עדים...

...and after four or five days witnesses appear...

This raises the following question. Why did the Ramam here

spell out that "four or five" days later "witnesses appeared, why couldn't he have simply stated, 'and if later witnesses appear, even at the end of the month' why did he give here the example of four or five days? The sefer (סימן טו, עמ' 27) "מראה החדש" points out to us that the Rambam was very meticulous in spelling out "four or five days", for in light of the above מנחת חינוך that we do not accept witnesses if it would mean that by accepting them and retroactively sanctifying day 30 we would thereby no longer be able to offer the sacrifices of Rosh Chodesh - Rosh Hashanah, we do not accept them. Thus "these days" when we do not accept them add up to "four" days, as follows. If the witnesses saw the moon late in the day of the 29th or if they saw the moon on day 30, but on these two sightings they did not appear until day 31, we do not accept their testimony. Thus we see that there are "three days" that we do not apply the law of קידוש למפרע and only on day "four" do we apply "קידוש למפרע".

Another explanation of why "four or five days" were explicitly cited is explained at the end of the sefer "שלום יהודה" (להרב אליעזר פלצינסקי), based on what is stated in the Gemara Pesachim 10,B, that one is to begin to expound on the laws of Yom Tov Pesach two weeks prior to Pesach. The source for this halacha is the fact that the parasha of the laws of Pesach was given on Rosh Chodesh Nissan, as the pasuk says *(Shemos 12:1-2)* that Hashem spoke to Moshe on Rosh Chodesh, telling him of the laws of both Kiddush HaChodesh and Pesach. This leads Tosafos to ask: How do you know that Hashem spoke to Moshe on Rosh Chodesh? Perhaps He spoke to him "on the 4th or 5th" of the month. Thus, we can conclude that if Moshe was told not to initiate the mitzva of Kiddush HaChodesh until the fourth or fifth day of the month, this indicates, that he sanctified the month retroactively on day four. And this explains why the Rambam was particular to cite "four or five days", for it is from this source of 'four or five days later' that we arrive at the law of "קידוש למפרע".

VIII

PRESERVING THE RITUALS OF ROSH HASHANAH

Based on the above insight, we could answer the quite puzzling question touched upon by the commentators. Chapter three, beginning with Mishna Two deals with the subject of blowing the Shofar on Rosh Hashanah. The first Mishna here in Chapter Three is a continuation of the laws of Kiddush HaChodesh. Therefore one could ask, why was this Mishna not included in the previous chapter, and what relevance does the law mentioned here have to do with the laws of Yom Tov?

We have endeavored to show that there is a logical sequence in the Mishnayos of this Mesechtah of Rosh Hashanah. In Chapter One from Mishna III we touch upon the matter of Kiddush HaChodesh. Mishna III is a general introduction to the mitzva of Kiddush HaChodesh and discusses its importance and its place in Mesechtas Rosh Hashanah. All of the major holidays are dependent on when we declare Rosh Chodesh, and therefore we spell out the holidays and their dependence on knowing when Rosh Chodesh begins. The rest of Chapter One deals with the role of eyewitnesses. Chapter Two discusses character witnesses and the methods of how to inform the people when Rosh Chodesh was declared. The last Mishnayos are concerned with the roles of the Bais Din and the Nasi.

Chapter Four touches upon the matter of Kiddush HaChodesh. But in light of our previous discussion here, we can see that it is mainly concerned with preserving the celebration of the day of Rosh Chodesh - Rosh Hashanah. We do not apply here the law of קידוש למפרע, retroactively sanctifying the month, and in doing this we thereby preserve the rituals of Rosh Hashanah. Thus we can see how crucial is this first Mishna in Chapter Four to the main theme of Chapter Four—Rosh Hashanah and its mitzvos.

לזכרון עולם בהיכל ה'
לעילוי נפש

מרת שיינדל מרים בת יחיאל יוסף, ע"ה

In Memory of

Jean Erdfrucht

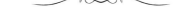

Dedicated by

Rabbi & Mrs. Shmuel Jablon

and Family

In Honor of our Esteemed

Grandfather

ר' אלעזר הכהן, כהן, נ"י

May Hashem bless you with long life

and good health.

Your Loving Grandchildren,

Marc & Debbi Geller and Family

לזכרון עולם בהיכל ה'
לעילוי נפש

ר' אפרים צבי ב"ר יצחק מאיר, ע"ה
מרת דבורה בת ר' יוסף מאניס, ע"ה

~~~

הונצח ע"י
הרב יוסף מאיר ושולמית רימל, נ"י

לזכרון עולם בהיכל ה'
לעילוי נפש

הרב ירוחם פישל גולדפדר, ע"ה

~~~

הונצח ע"י בנו
ר' אברהם צבי גולדפדר, נ"י